Editor
DIANA SCHUTZ

Designer
CARY GRAZZINI

Publisher
MIKE RICHARDSON

This volume collects issues 53-60
of the Dark Horse comic book series *Usagi Yojimbo Volume Three*.

Visit the Usagi Dojo web site
www.usagiyojimbo.com

Published by
Dark Horse Books
A division of Dark Horse Comics, Inc.
10956 SE Main Street
Milwaukie, Oregon 97222

First edition: September 2003
ISBN 1-56971-973-X

Limited hardcover edition: September 2003
ISBN 1-56971-974-8

1 3 5 7 9 10 8 6 4 2
Printed in Canada

USAGI YOJIMBO

— DUEL AT KITANOJI —

Created, Written, and Illustrated by

STAN SAKAI

With a cartoon appreciation by

JACK DAVIS

DARK HORSE BOOKS™

Usagi Yojimbo

A Cartoon Appreciation by Jack Davis

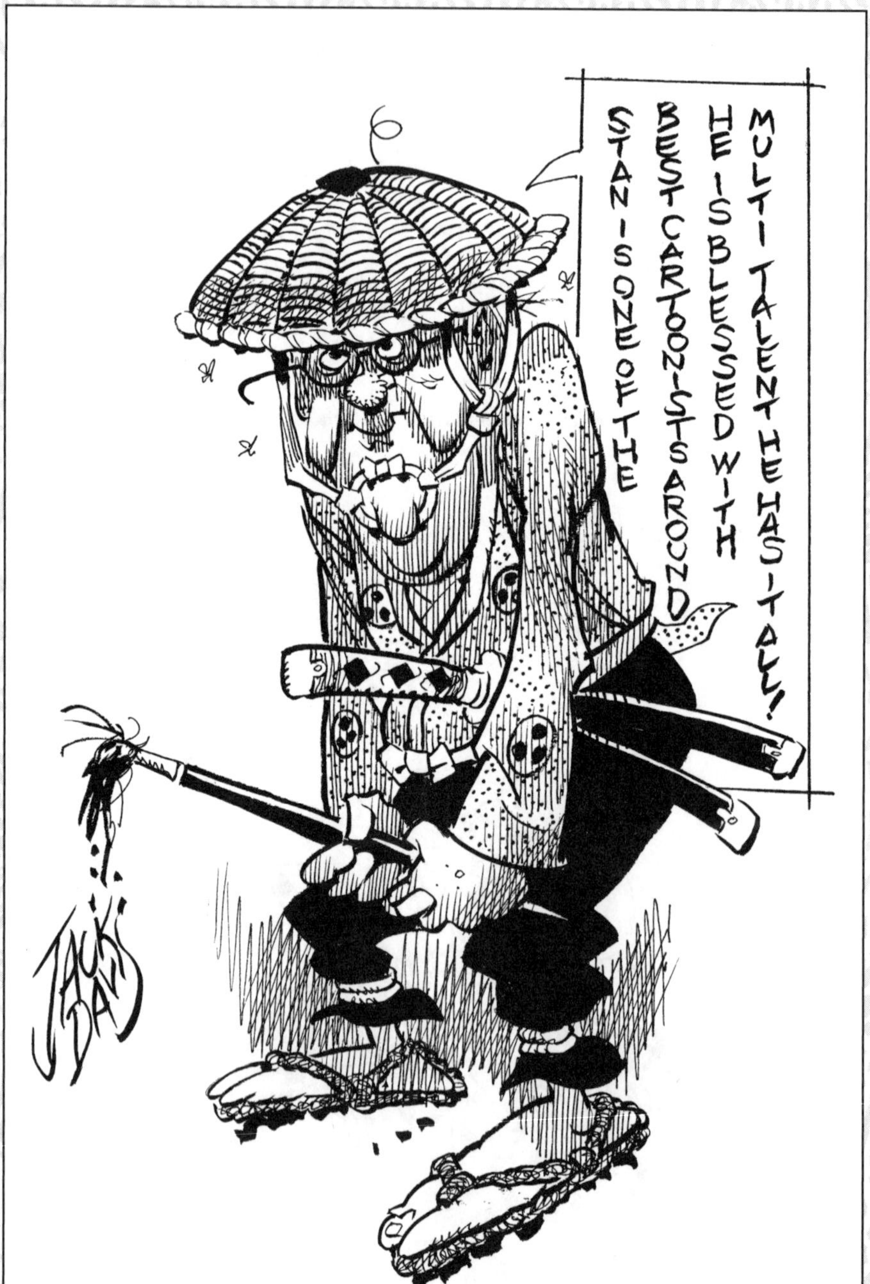
STAN IS ONE OF THE
BEST CARTOONISTS AROUND
HE IS BLESSED WITH
MULTI TALENT HE HAS IT ALL!
JACK DAVIS

Contents

For our good friends,
Kerry, Karon, Joshua, and Laura French.

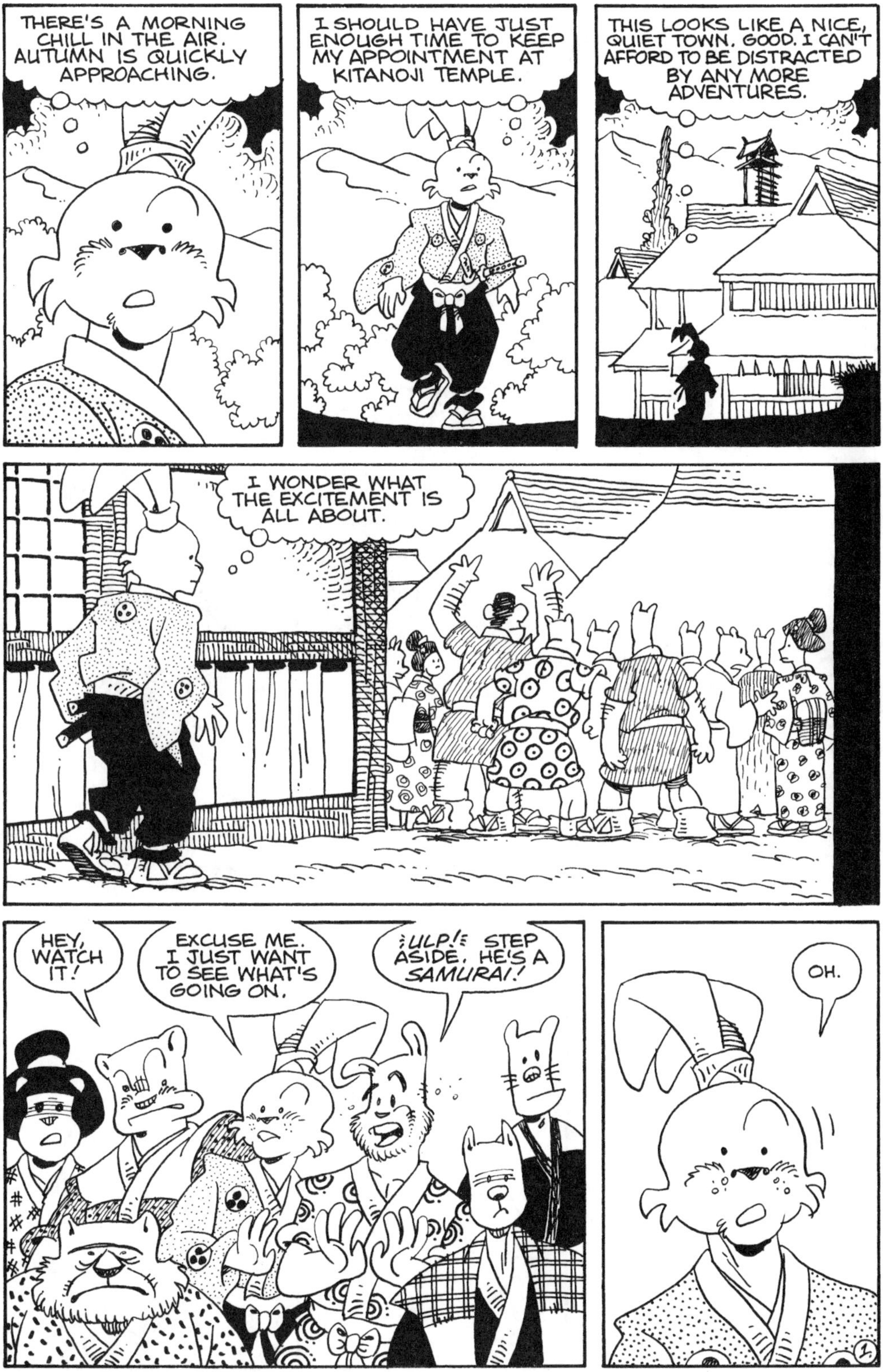
THERE'S A MORNING CHILL IN THE AIR. AUTUMN IS QUICKLY APPROACHING.
I SHOULD HAVE JUST ENOUGH TIME TO KEEP MY APPOINTMENT AT KITANOJI TEMPLE.
THIS LOOKS LIKE A NICE, QUIET TOWN. GOOD. I CAN'T AFFORD TO BE DISTRACTED BY ANY MORE ADVENTURES.
I WONDER WHAT THE EXCITEMENT IS ALL ABOUT.
HEY, WATCH IT!
EXCUSE ME. I JUST WANT TO SEE WHAT'S GOING ON.
ULP! STEP ASIDE. HE'S A SAMURAI!
OH.

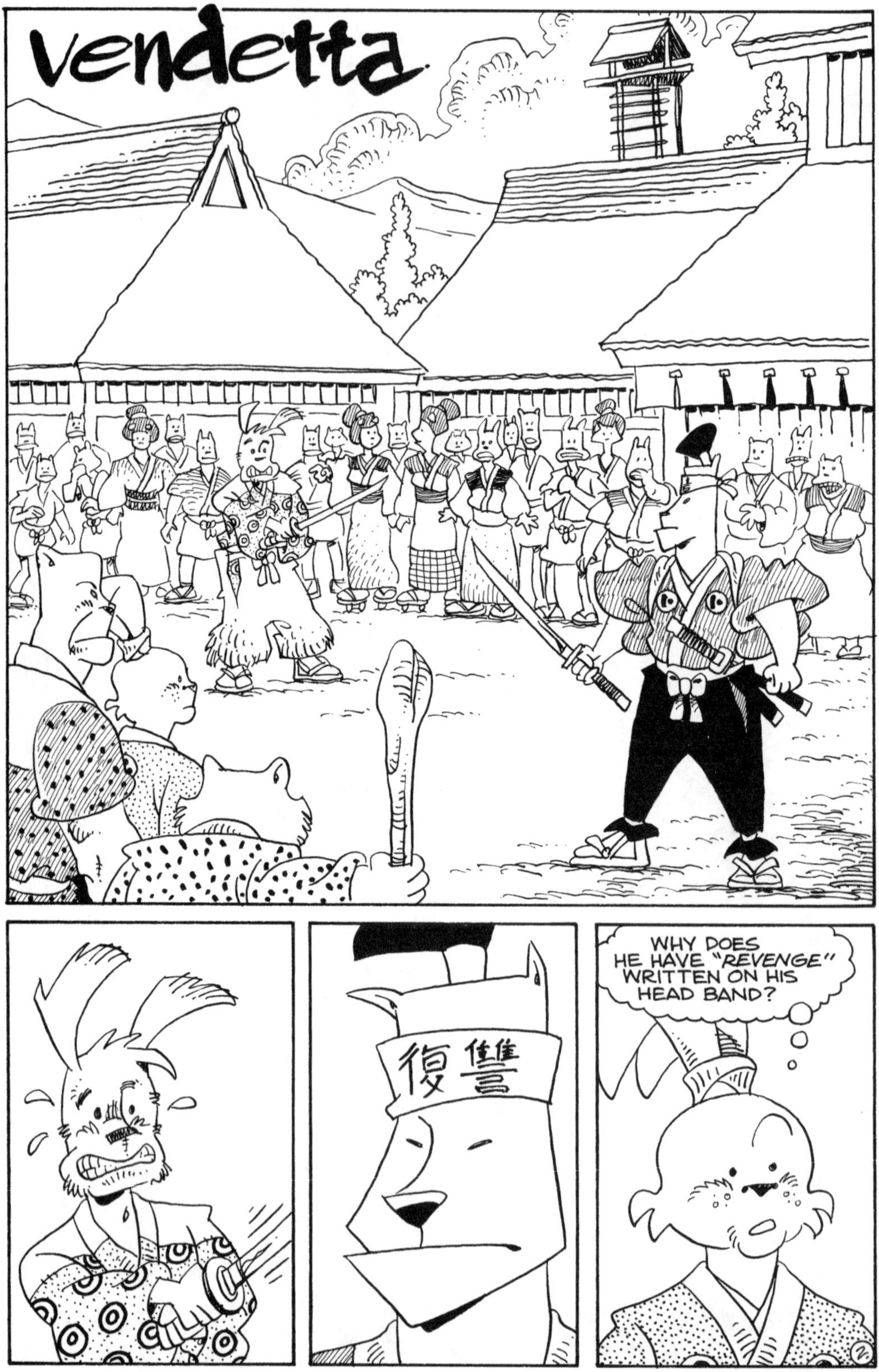
vendetta
復讐
WHY DOES HE HAVE "REVENGE" WRITTEN ON HIS HEAD BAND?

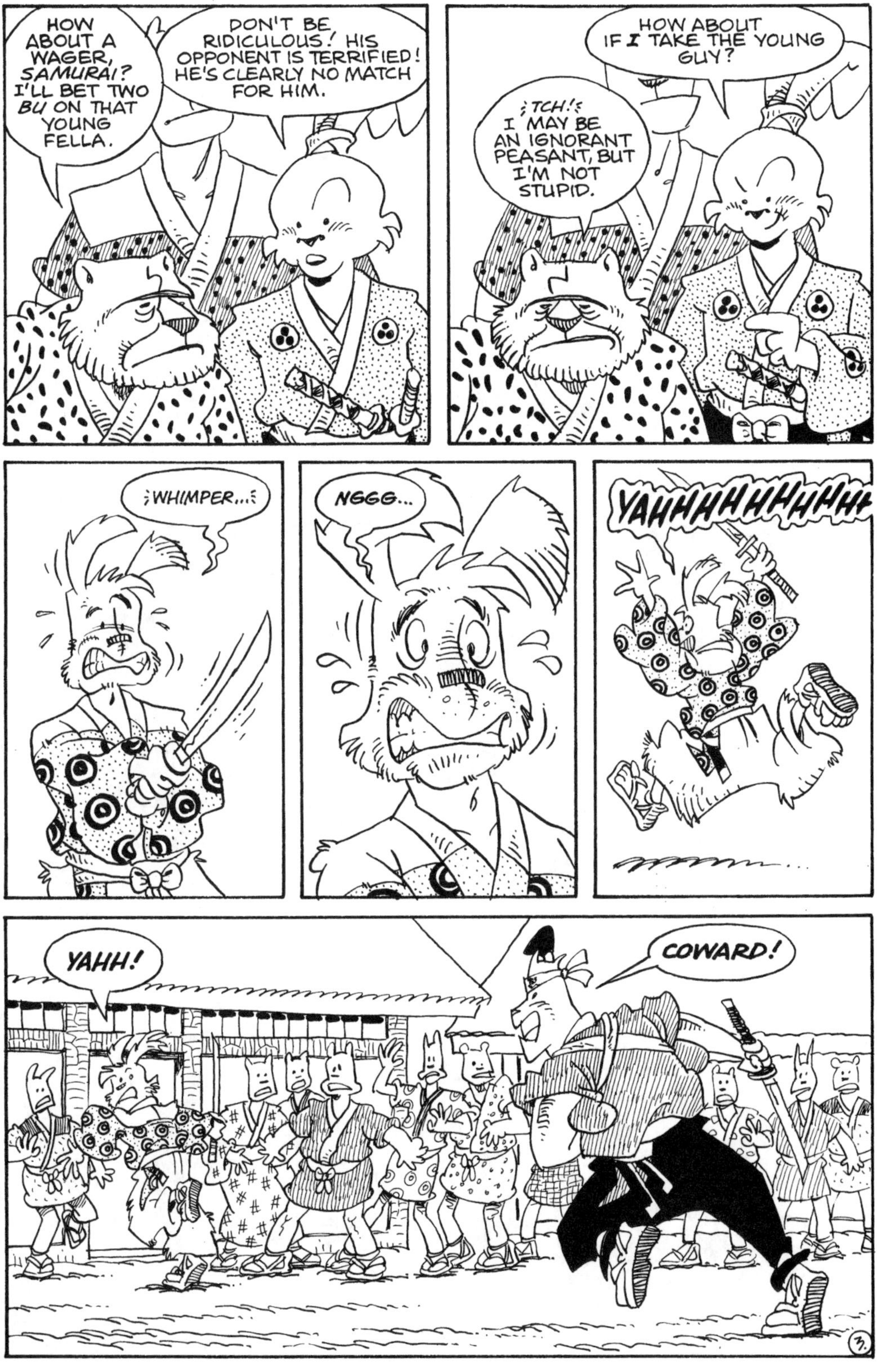
HOW ABOUT A WAGER, SAMURAI? I'LL BET TWO BU ON THAT YOUNG FELLA.
DON'T BE RIDICULOUS! HIS OPPONENT IS TERRIFIED! HE'S CLEARLY NO MATCH FOR HIM.
HOW ABOUT IF I TAKE THE YOUNG GUY?
TCH! I MAY BE AN IGNORANT PEASANT, BUT I'M NOT STUPID.
WHIMPER...
NGGG...
YAHHHHHHHHHH
YAHH!
COWARD!
3.

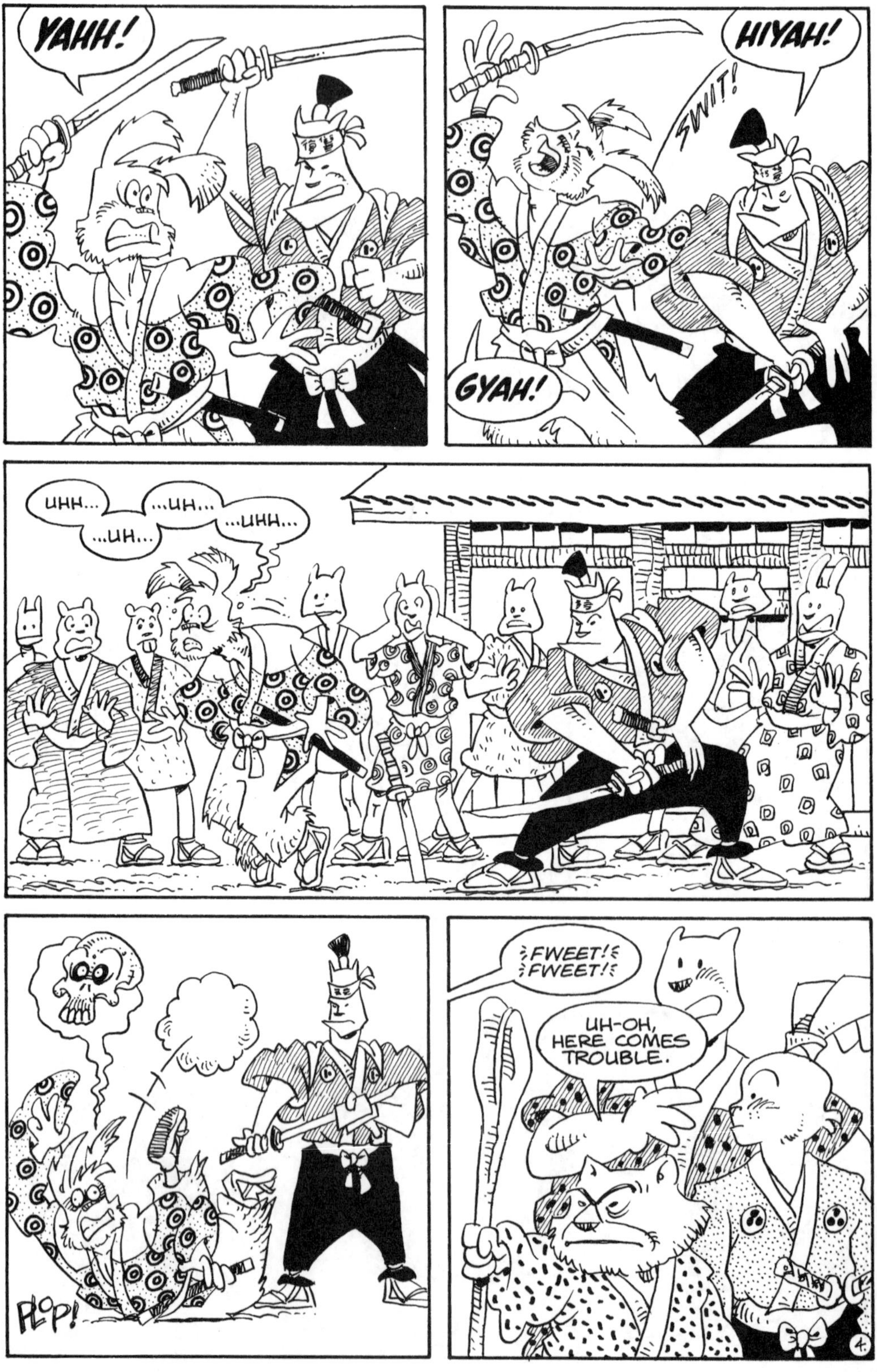
YAHH!
HIYAH!
SWIT!
GYAH!
UHH...
...UH...
...UH...
...UHH...
PLOP!
FWEET! FWEET!
UH-OH, HERE COMES TROUBLE.
4.

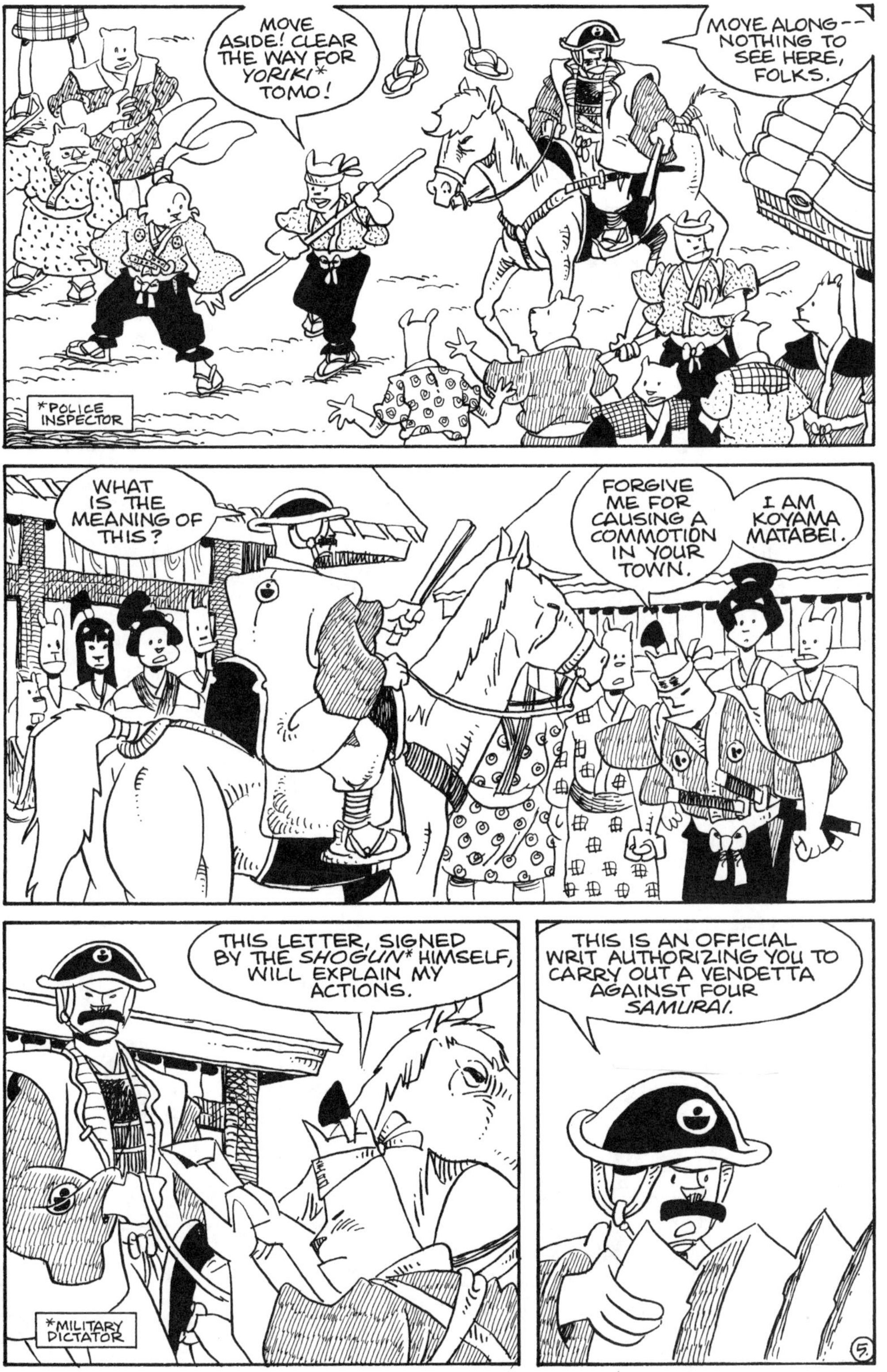
MOVE ASIDE! CLEAR THE WAY FOR YORIKI* TOMO!
MOVE ALONG-- NOTHING TO SEE HERE, FOLKS.
*POLICE INSPECTOR
WHAT IS THE MEANING OF THIS?
FORGIVE ME FOR CAUSING A COMMOTION IN YOUR TOWN.
I AM KOYAMA MATABEI.
THIS LETTER, SIGNED BY THE SHOGUN* HIMSELF, WILL EXPLAIN MY ACTIONS.
*MILITARY DICTATOR
THIS IS AN OFFICIAL WRIT AUTHORIZING YOU TO CARRY OUT A VENDETTA AGAINST FOUR SAMURAI.
5.

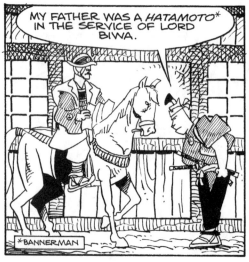

MY FATHER WAS A *HATAMOTO** IN THE SERVICE OF LORD BIWA.

*BANNERMAN

ONE NIGHT, FOUR *SAMURAI*, THEIR COURAGE BOLSTERED BY DRINK, ATTACKED AND KILLED MY FATHER.

THEY MANAGED TO ESCAPE LORD BIWA'S JURISDICTION, BUT WITNESSES WERE ABLE TO NAME THE MURDERERS.

I PETITIONED THE LORD *SHOGUN* AND RECEIVED THE RIGHT TO AVENGE MY FATHER'S KILLING.

MY VENDETTA WILL BE OVER WHEN I PLACE THEIR HEADS ON MY FATHER'S TOMB.

I HAVE BEEN HUNTING THEM FOR ALMOST A YEAR. THIS IS THE FIRST OF THEM TO DIE.

EVERYTHING SEEMS TO BE IN ORDER.

6.

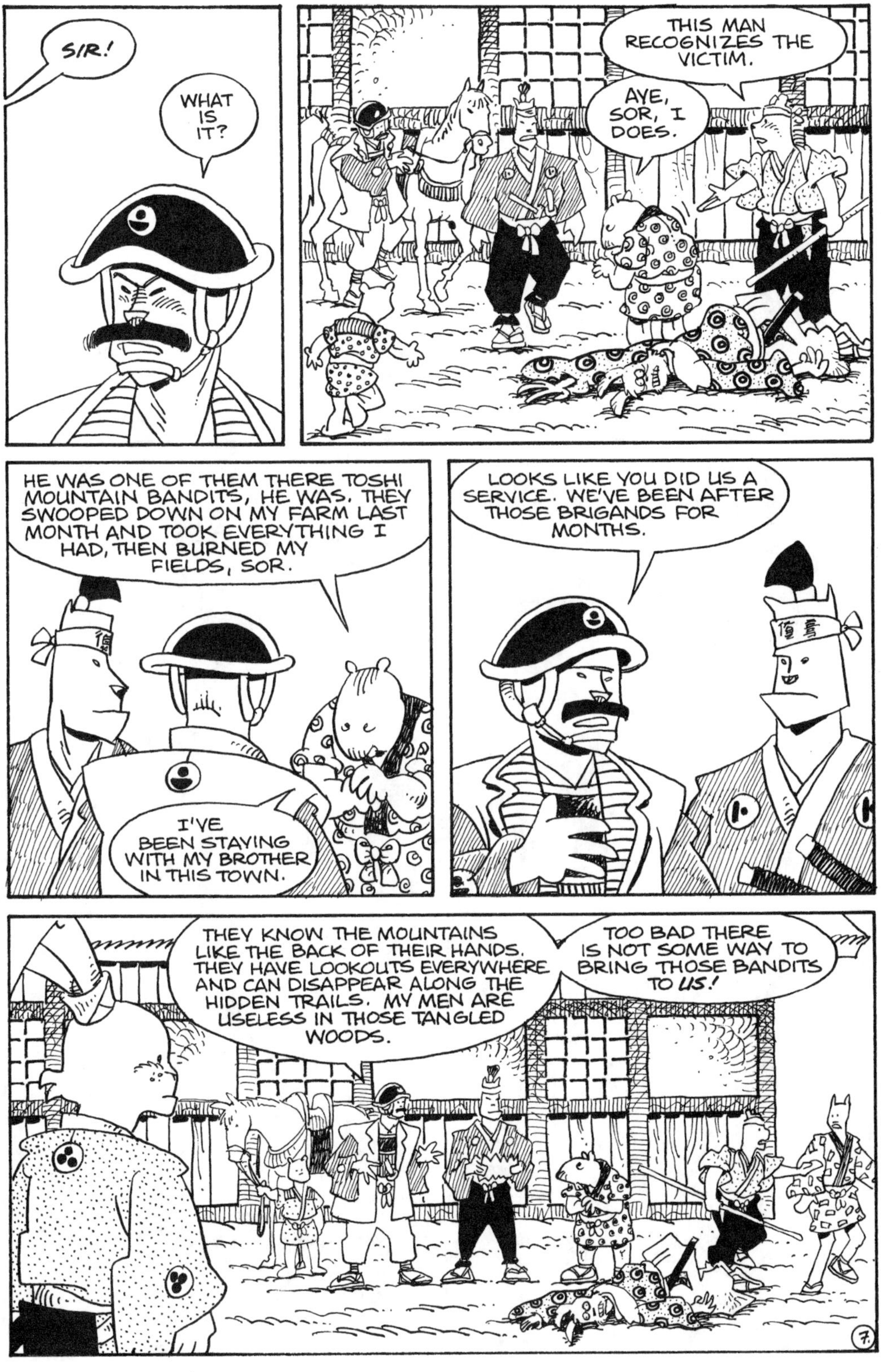

SIR!
WHAT IS IT?
THIS MAN RECOGNIZES THE VICTIM.
AYE, SOR, I DOES.
HE WAS ONE OF THEM THERE TOSHI MOUNTAIN BANDITS, HE WAS. THEY SWOOPED DOWN ON MY FARM LAST MONTH AND TOOK EVERYTHING I HAD, THEN BURNED MY FIELDS, SOR.
I'VE BEEN STAYING WITH MY BROTHER IN THIS TOWN.
LOOKS LIKE YOU DID US A SERVICE. WE'VE BEEN AFTER THOSE BRIGANDS FOR MONTHS.
THEY KNOW THE MOUNTAINS LIKE THE BACK OF THEIR HANDS. THEY HAVE LOOKOUTS EVERYWHERE AND CAN DISAPPEAR ALONG THE HIDDEN TRAILS. MY MEN ARE USELESS IN THOSE TANGLED WOODS.
TOO BAD THERE IS NOT SOME WAY TO BRING THOSE BANDITS TO *US*!
7

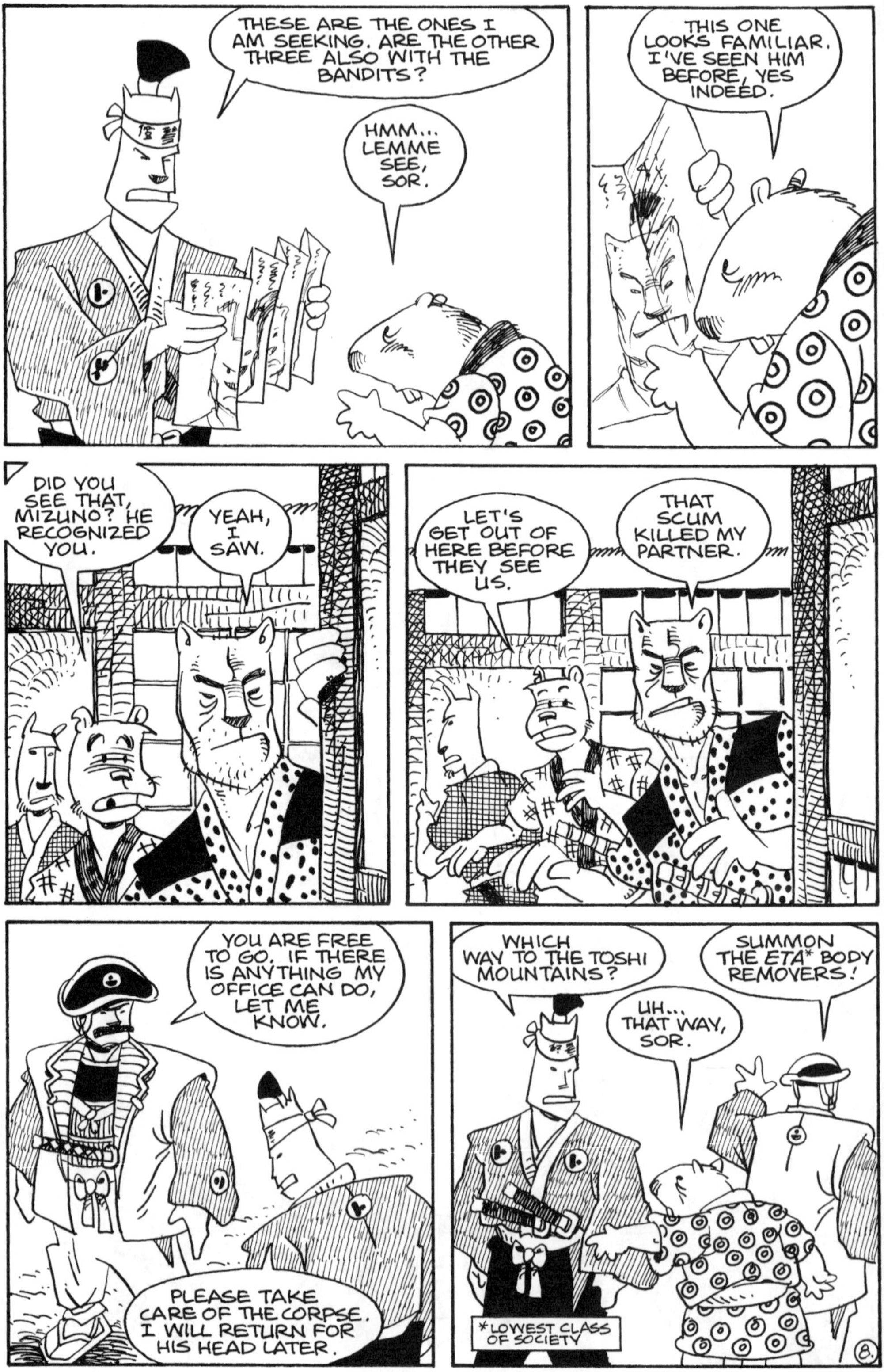
THESE ARE THE ONES I AM SEEKING. ARE THE OTHER THREE ALSO WITH THE BANDITS?
HMM... LEMME SEE, SOR.
THIS ONE LOOKS FAMILIAR. I'VE SEEN HIM BEFORE, YES INDEED.
DID YOU SEE THAT, MIZUNO? HE RECOGNIZED YOU.
YEAH, I SAW.
LET'S GET OUT OF HERE BEFORE THEY SEE US.
THAT SCUM KILLED MY PARTNER.
YOU ARE FREE TO GO. IF THERE IS ANYTHING MY OFFICE CAN DO, LET ME KNOW.
PLEASE TAKE CARE OF THE CORPSE. I WILL RETURN FOR HIS HEAD LATER.
WHICH WAY TO THE TOSHI MOUNTAINS?
UH... THAT WAY, SOR.
SUMMON THE ETA* BODY REMOVERS!
*LOWEST CLASS OF SOCIETY
8.

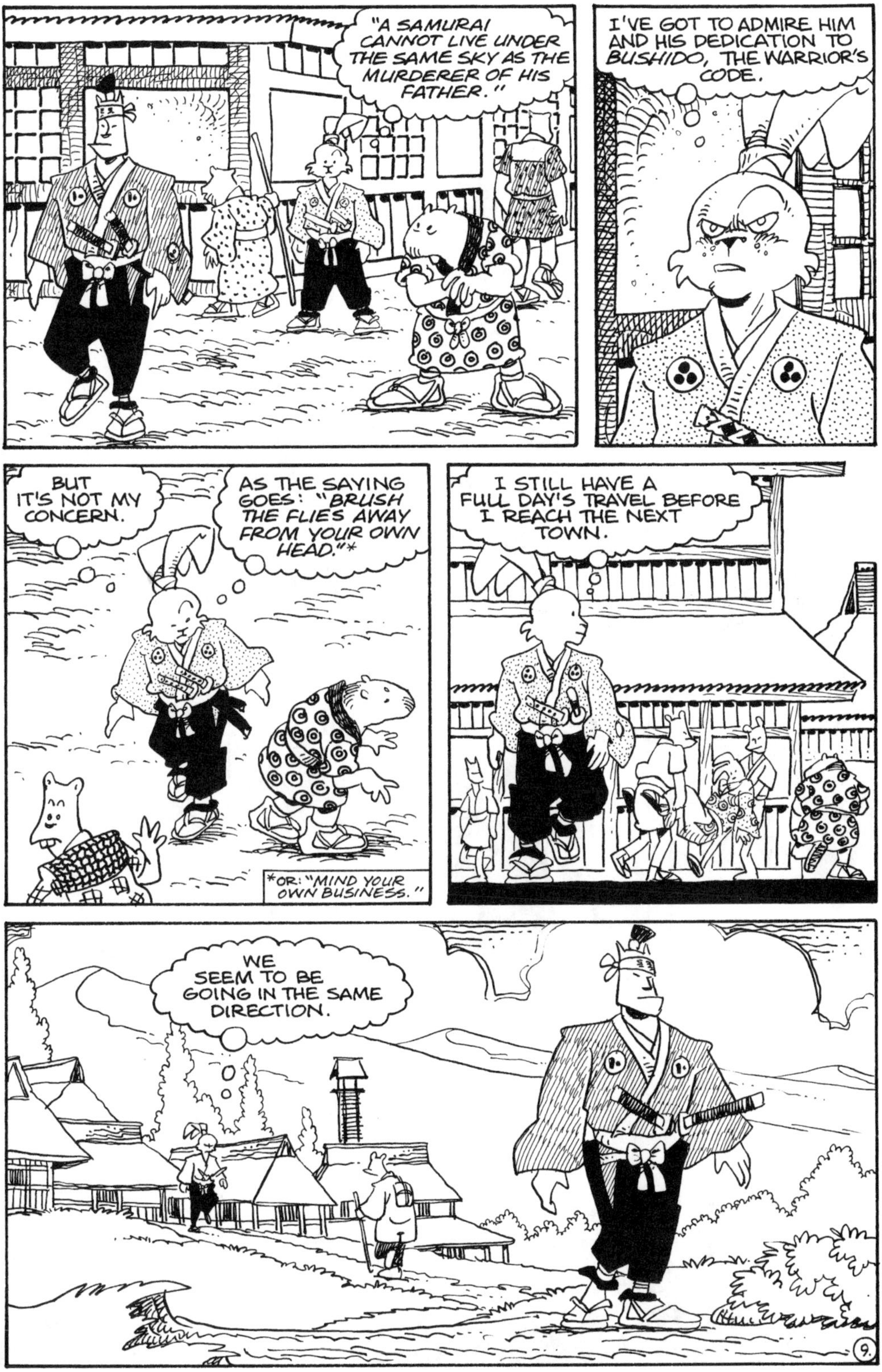
"A SAMURAI CANNOT LIVE UNDER THE SAME SKY AS THE MURDERER OF HIS FATHER."
I'VE GOT TO ADMIRE HIM AND HIS DEDICATION TO BUSHIDO, THE WARRIOR'S CODE.
BUT IT'S NOT MY CONCERN.
AS THE SAYING GOES: "BRUSH THE FLIES AWAY FROM YOUR OWN HEAD."*
*OR: "MIND YOUR OWN BUSINESS."
I STILL HAVE A FULL DAY'S TRAVEL BEFORE I REACH THE NEXT TOWN.
WE SEEM TO BE GOING IN THE SAME DIRECTION.
9.

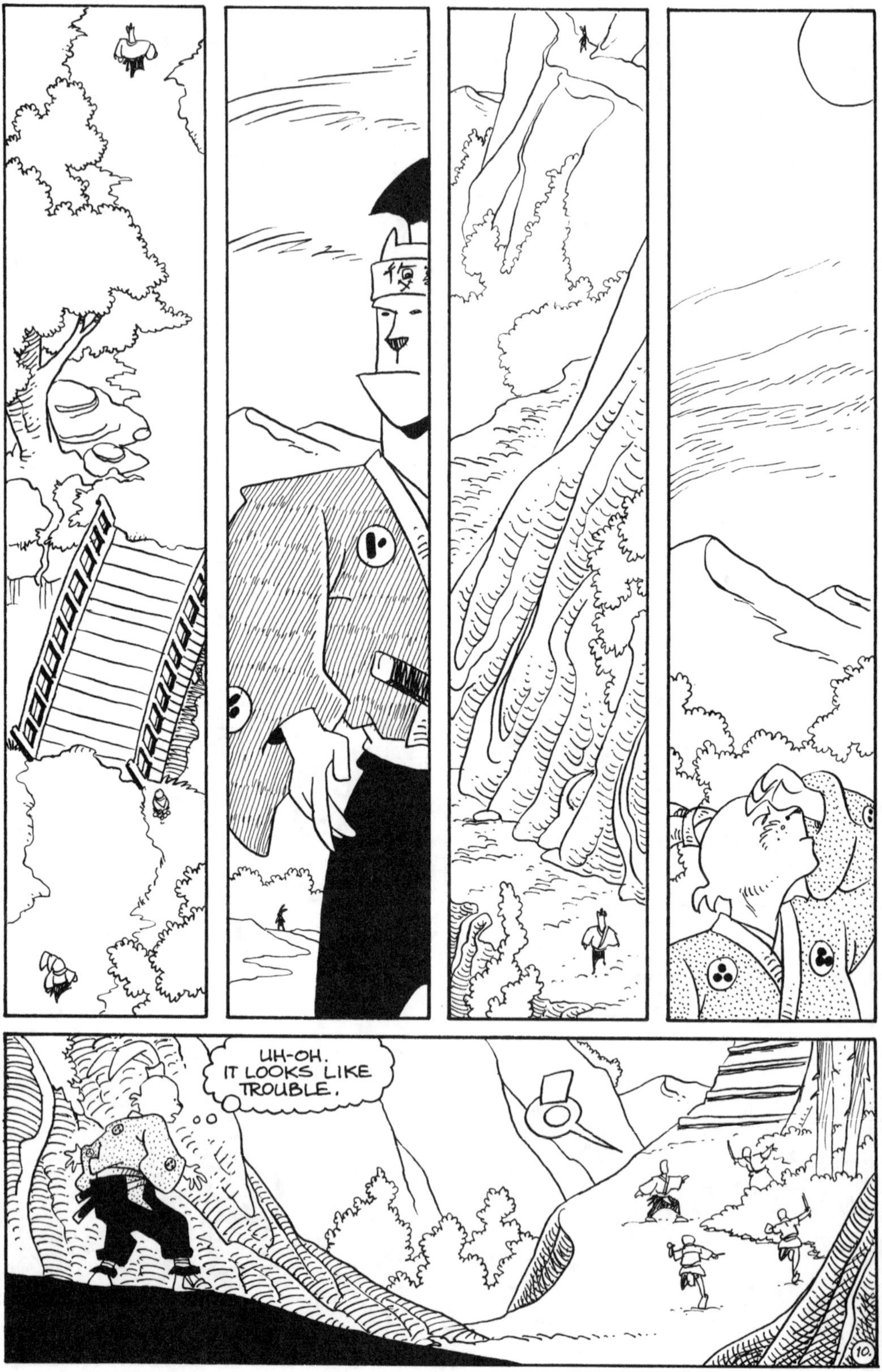
UH-OH. IT LOOKS LIKE TROUBLE.
10.

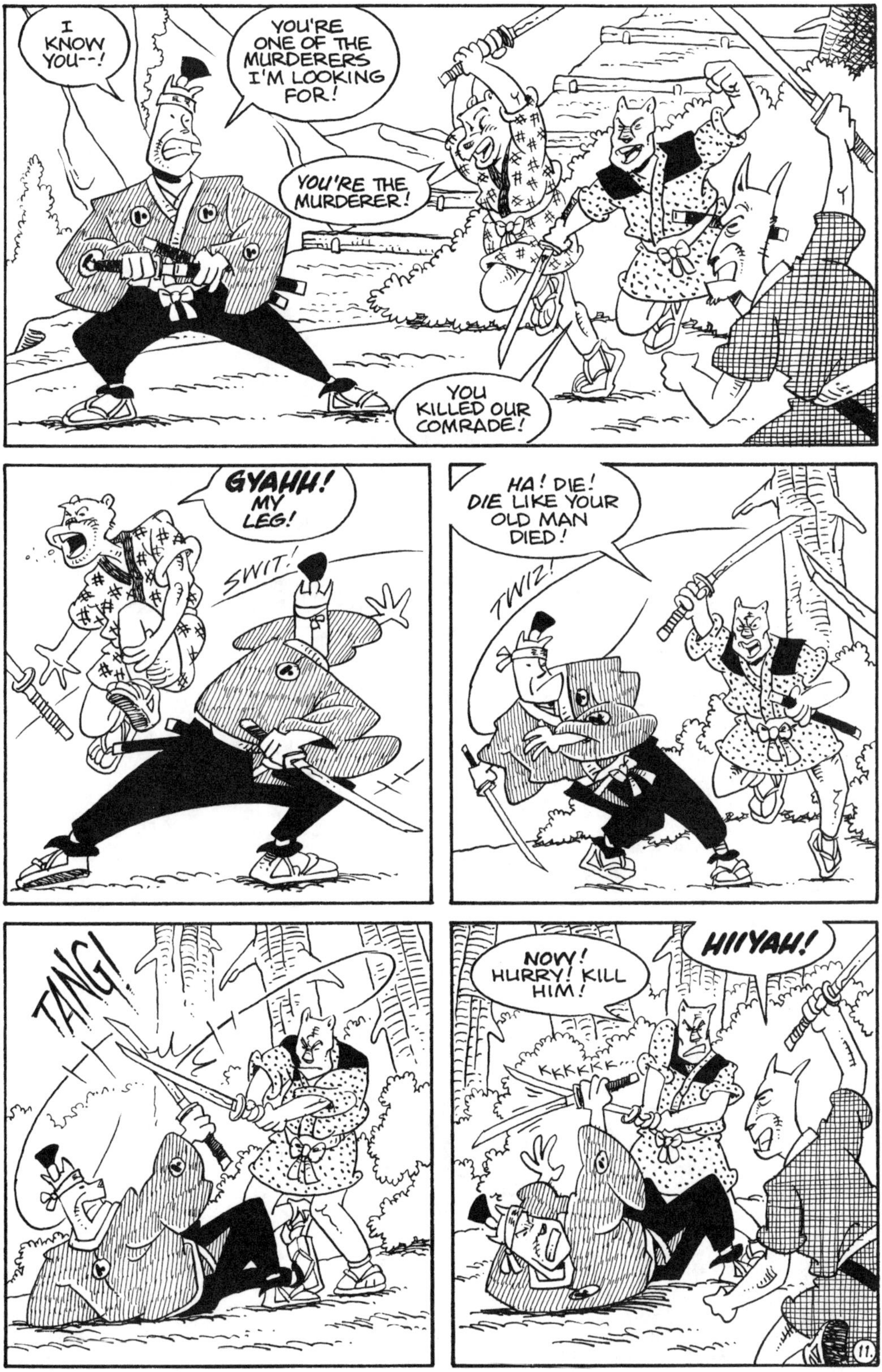
I KNOW YOU--!
YOU'RE ONE OF THE MURDERERS I'M LOOKING FOR!
YOU'RE THE MURDERER!
YOU KILLED OUR COMRADE!
GYAHH! MY LEG!
SWIT!
HA! DIE! DIE LIKE YOUR OLD MAN DIED!
TWIZ!
TANG!
NOW! HURRY! KILL HIM!
HIIYAH!
KKKKKK...
11.

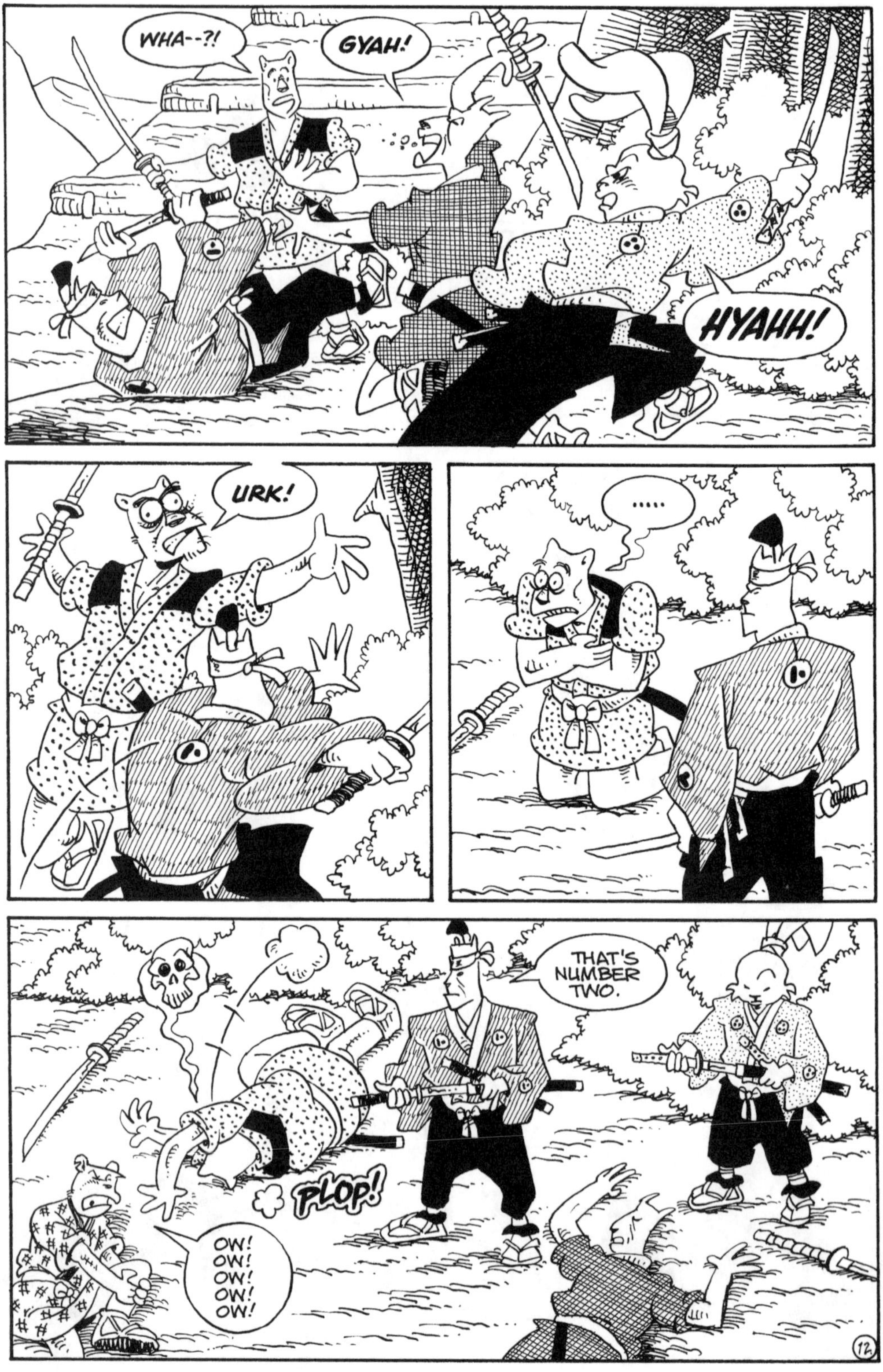
WHA--?!
GYAH!
HYAHH!
URK!
.....
THAT'S NUMBER TWO.
PLOP!
OW! OW! OW! OW! OW!
12

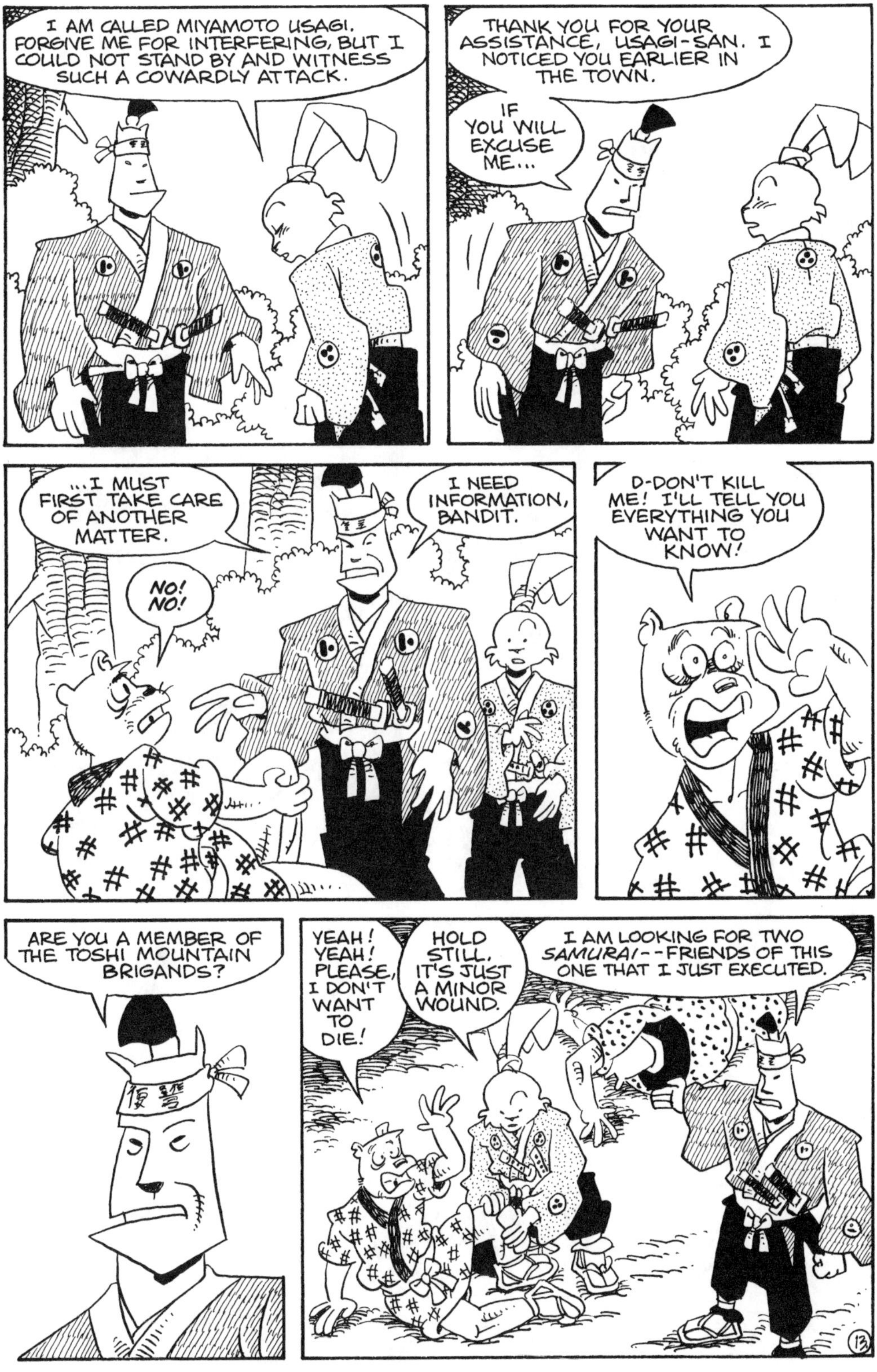
I AM CALLED MIYAMOTO USAGI. FORGIVE ME FOR INTERFERING, BUT I COULD NOT STAND BY AND WITNESS SUCH A COWARDLY ATTACK.
THANK YOU FOR YOUR ASSISTANCE, USAGI-SAN. I NOTICED YOU EARLIER IN THE TOWN.
IF YOU WILL EXCUSE ME...
...I MUST FIRST TAKE CARE OF ANOTHER MATTER.
NO! NO!
I NEED INFORMATION, BANDIT.
D-DON'T KILL ME! I'LL TELL YOU EVERYTHING YOU WANT TO KNOW!
ARE YOU A MEMBER OF THE TOSHI MOUNTAIN BRIGANDS?
YEAH! YEAH! PLEASE, I DON'T WANT TO DIE!
HOLD STILL. IT'S JUST A MINOR WOUND.
I AM LOOKING FOR TWO *SAMURAI*--FRIENDS OF THIS ONE THAT I JUST EXECUTED.
13

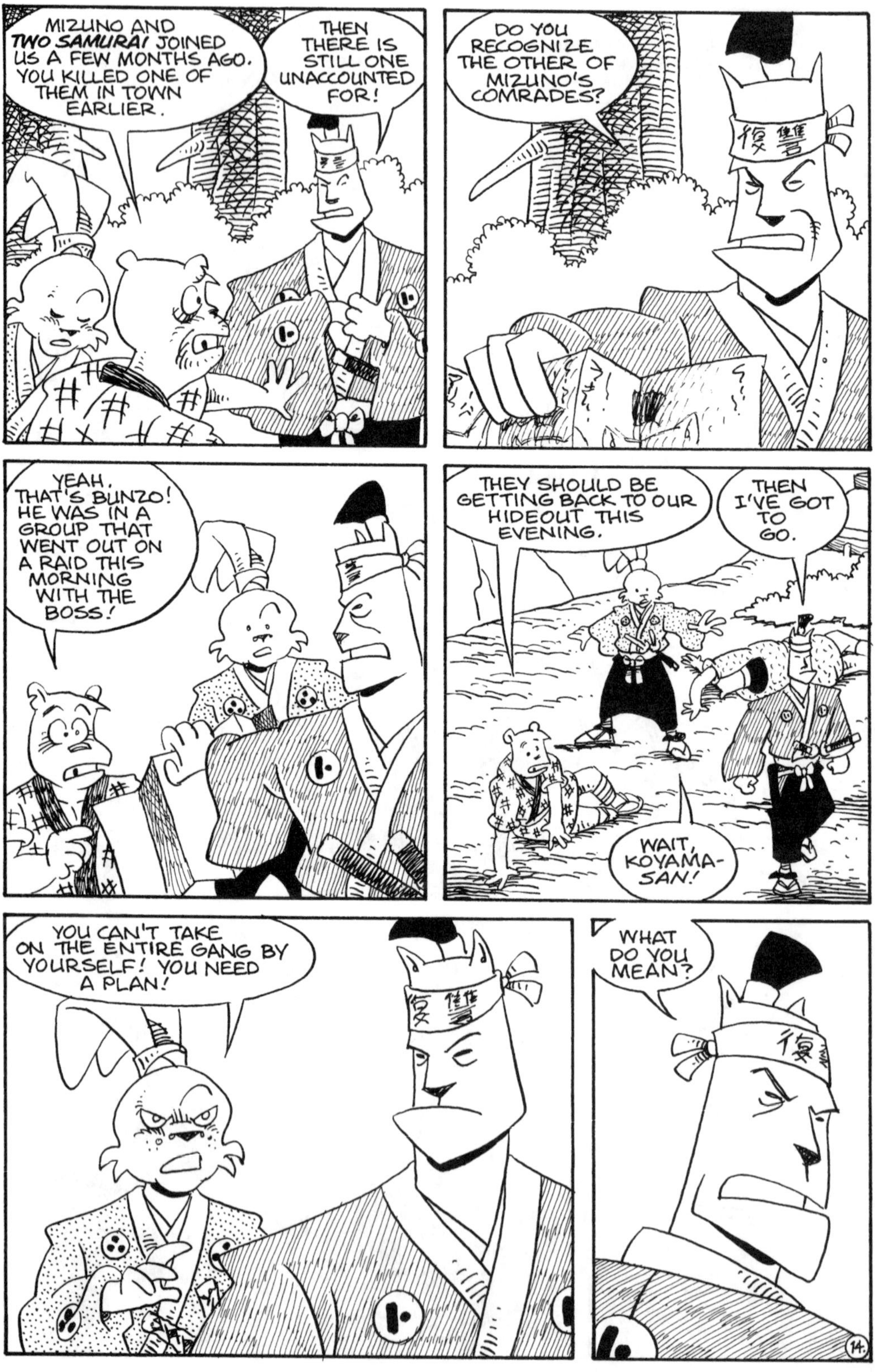
MIZUNO AND TWO SAMURAI JOINED US A FEW MONTHS AGO. YOU KILLED ONE OF THEM IN TOWN EARLIER.
THEN THERE IS STILL ONE UNACCOUNTED FOR!
DO YOU RECOGNIZE THE OTHER OF MIZUNO'S COMRADES?
YEAH, THAT'S BUNZO! HE WAS IN A GROUP THAT WENT OUT ON A RAID THIS MORNING WITH THE BOSS!
THEY SHOULD BE GETTING BACK TO OUR HIDEOUT THIS EVENING.
THEN I'VE GOT TO GO.
WAIT, KOYAMA-SAN!
YOU CAN'T TAKE ON THE ENTIRE GANG BY YOURSELF! YOU NEED A PLAN!
WHAT DO YOU MEAN?
14.

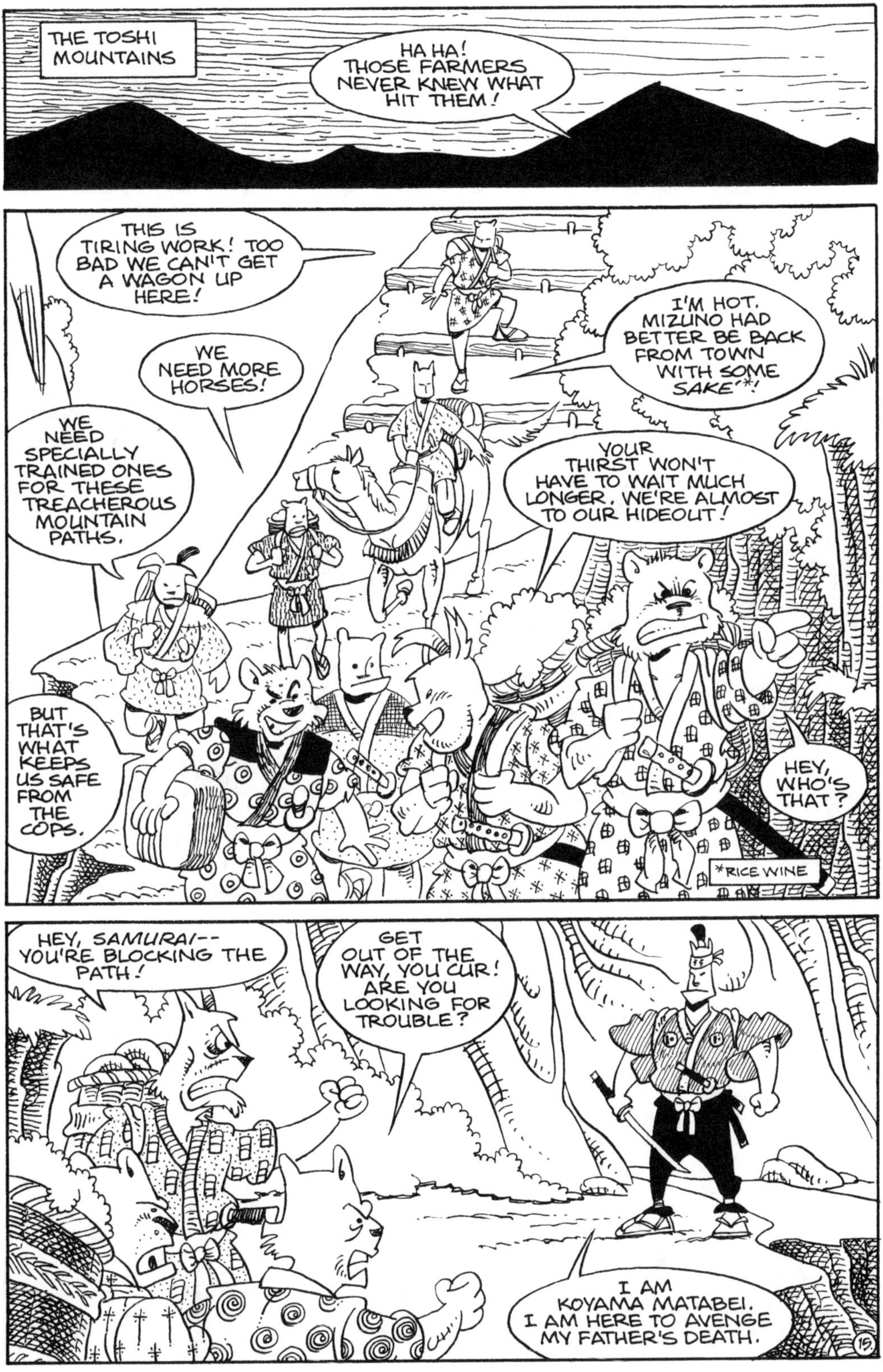
THE TOSHI MOUNTAINS
HA HA! THOSE FARMERS NEVER KNEW WHAT HIT THEM!
THIS IS TIRING WORK! TOO BAD WE CAN'T GET A WAGON UP HERE!
WE NEED MORE HORSES!
WE NEED SPECIALLY TRAINED ONES FOR THESE TREACHEROUS MOUNTAIN PATHS.
BUT THAT'S WHAT KEEPS US SAFE FROM THE COPS.
I'M HOT. MIZUNO HAD BETTER BE BACK FROM TOWN WITH SOME SAKE*!
YOUR THIRST WON'T HAVE TO WAIT MUCH LONGER. WE'RE ALMOST TO OUR HIDEOUT!
HEY, WHO'S THAT?
*RICE WINE
HEY, SAMURAI-- YOU'RE BLOCKING THE PATH!
GET OUT OF THE WAY, YOU CUR! ARE YOU LOOKING FOR TROUBLE?
I AM KOYAMA MATABEI. I AM HERE TO AVENGE MY FATHER'S DEATH.
15

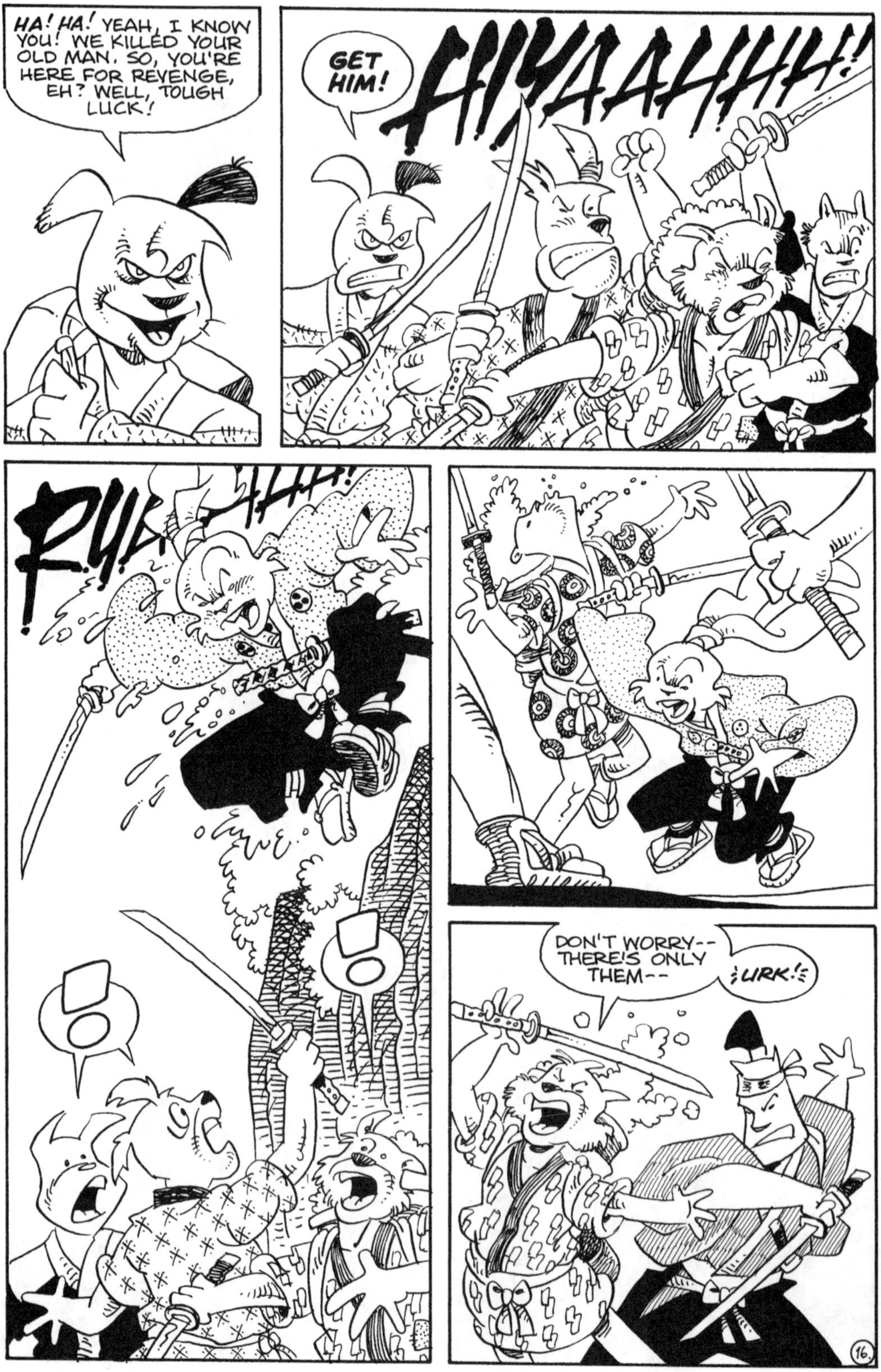
HA! HA! YEAH, I KNOW YOU! WE KILLED YOUR OLD MAN. SO, YOU'RE HERE FOR REVENGE, EH? WELL, TOUGH LUCK!
GET HIM!
HIYAAHHH!
DON'T WORRY-- THERE'S ONLY THEM--
URK!
16.

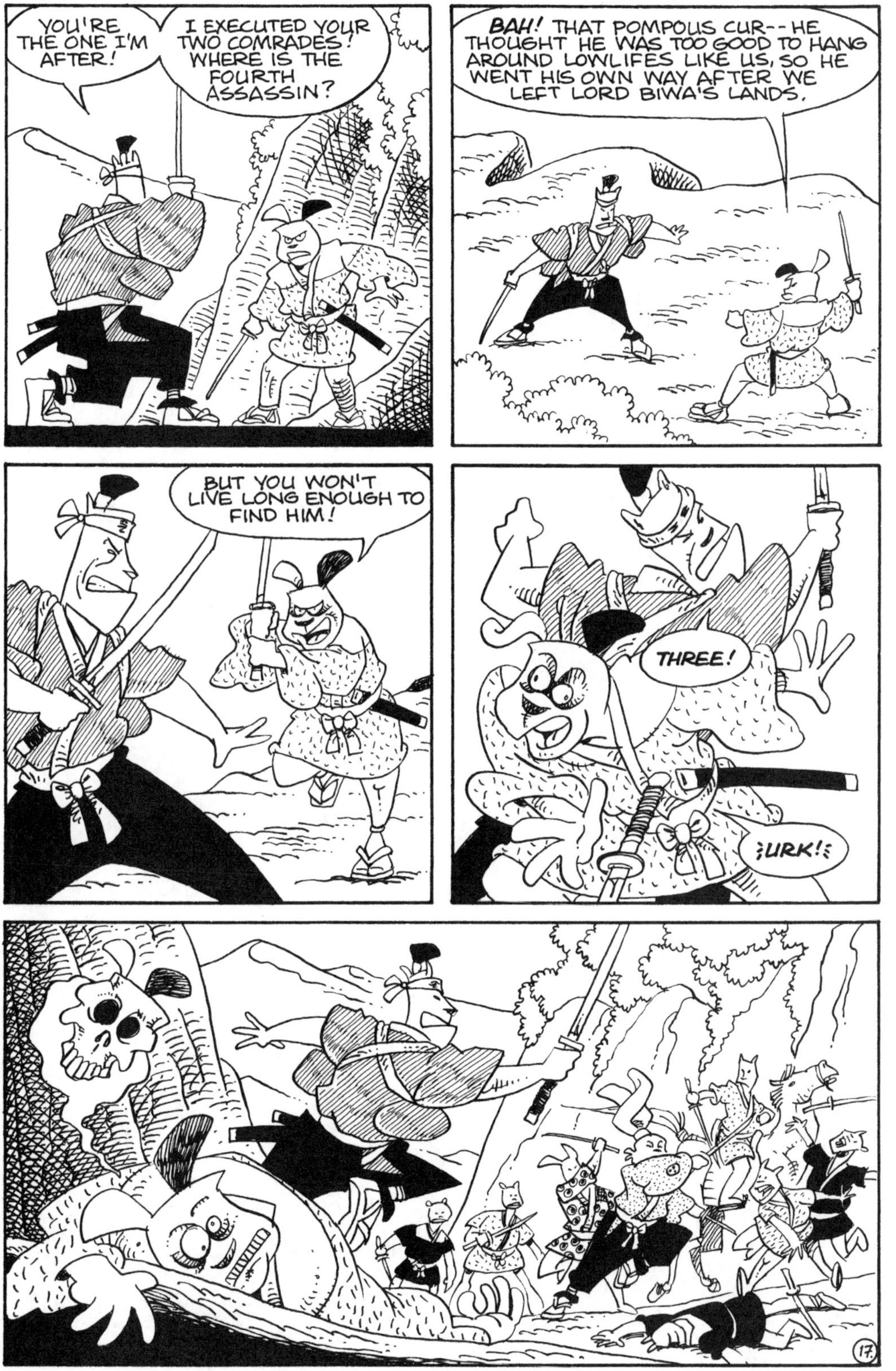
YOU'RE THE ONE I'M AFTER!
I EXECUTED YOUR TWO COMRADES! WHERE IS THE FOURTH ASSASSIN?
BAH! THAT POMPOUS CUR-- HE THOUGHT HE WAS TOO GOOD TO HANG AROUND LOWLIFES LIKE US, SO HE WENT HIS OWN WAY AFTER WE LEFT LORD BIWA'S LANDS.
BUT YOU WON'T LIVE LONG ENOUGH TO FIND HIM!
THREE!
URK!
17.

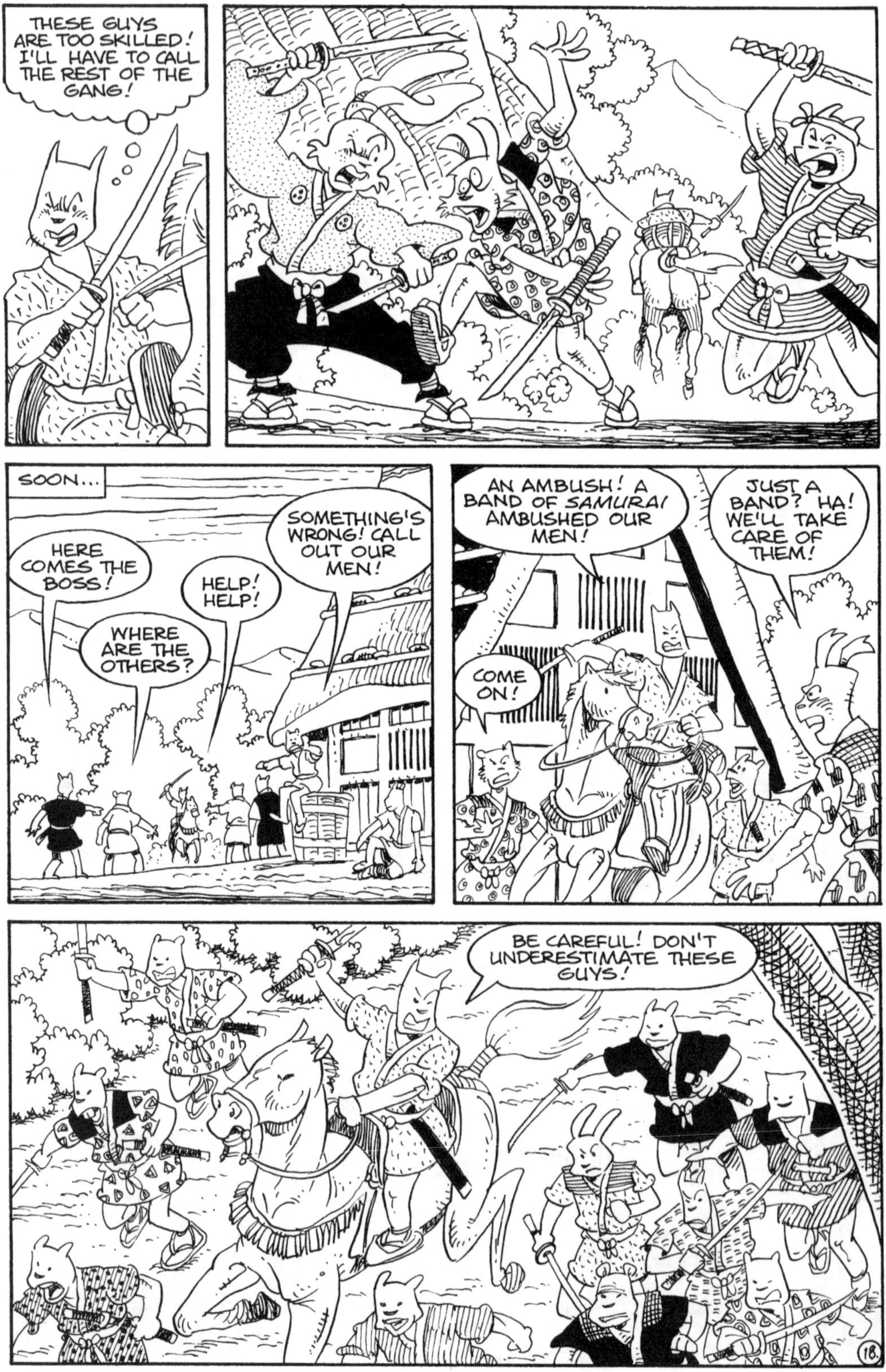
THESE GUYS ARE TOO SKILLED! I'LL HAVE TO CALL THE REST OF THE GANG!
SOON...
HERE COMES THE BOSS!
WHERE ARE THE OTHERS?
HELP! HELP!
SOMETHING'S WRONG! CALL OUT OUR MEN!
AN AMBUSH! A BAND OF SAMURAI AMBUSHED OUR MEN!
JUST A BAND? HA! WE'LL TAKE CARE OF THEM!
COME ON!
BE CAREFUL! DON'T UNDERESTIMATE THESE GUYS!
18.

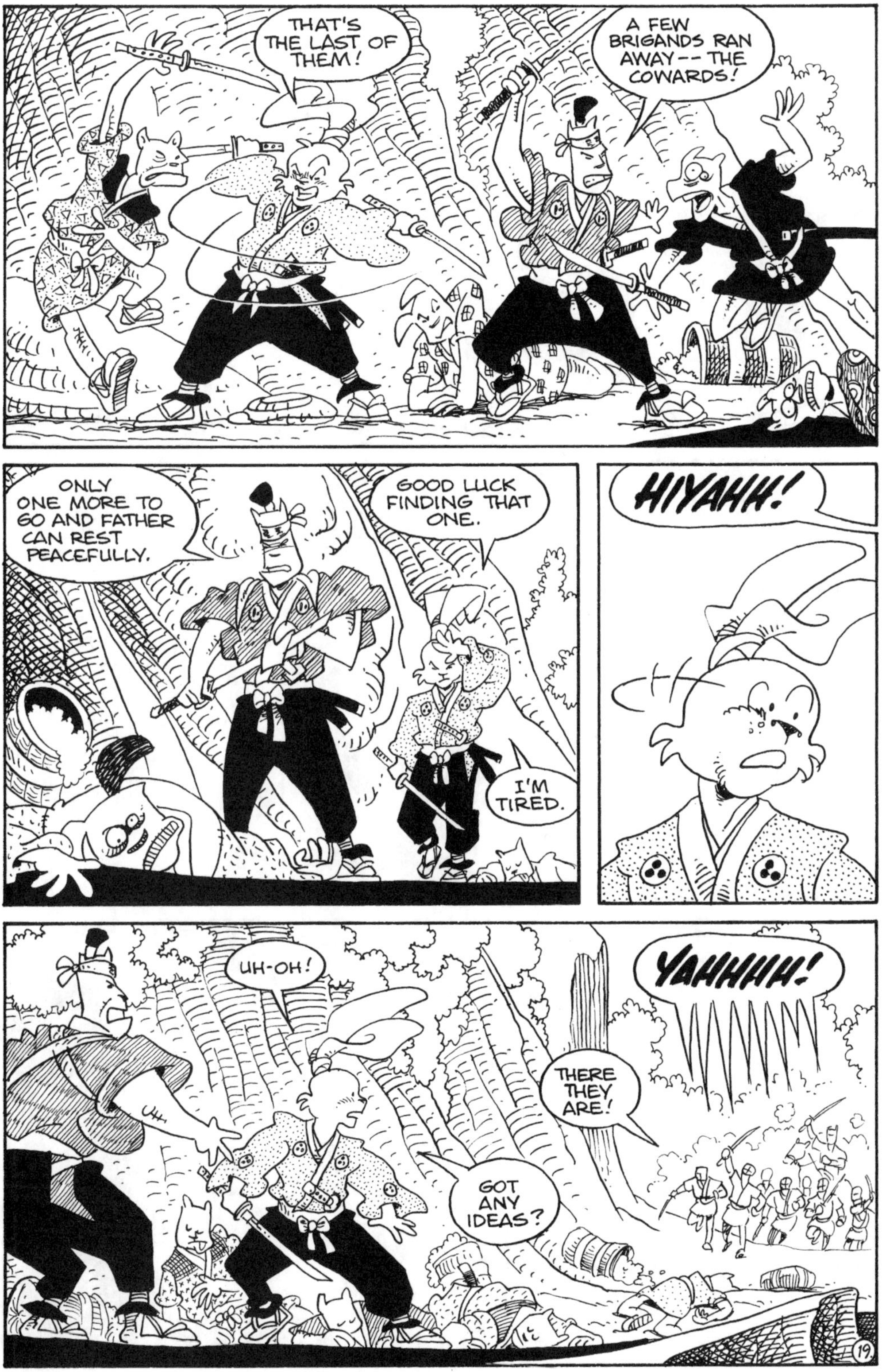
THAT'S THE LAST OF THEM!
A FEW BRIGANDS RAN AWAY-- THE COWARDS!
ONLY ONE MORE TO GO AND FATHER CAN REST PEACEFULLY.
GOOD LUCK FINDING THAT ONE.
I'M TIRED.
HIYAHH!
UH-OH!
YAHHHH!
THERE THEY ARE!
GOT ANY IDEAS?
19.

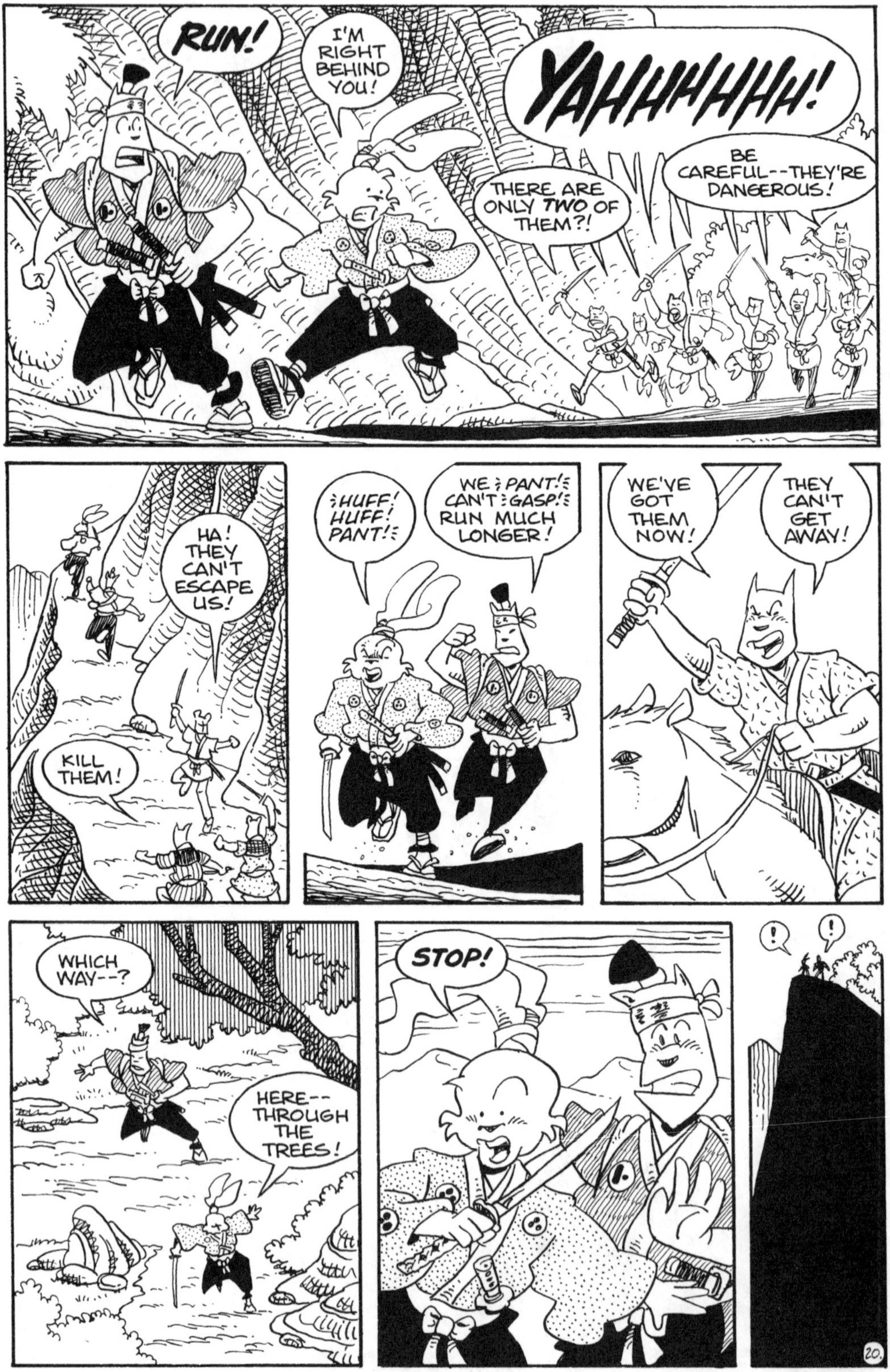
RUN!
I'M RIGHT BEHIND YOU!
YAHHHHHHH!
THERE ARE ONLY TWO OF THEM?!
BE CAREFUL--THEY'RE DANGEROUS!
HA! THEY CAN'T ESCAPE US!
KILL THEM!
HUFF! HUFF! PANT!
WE PANT! CAN'T GASP! RUN MUCH LONGER!
WE'VE GOT THEM NOW!
THEY CAN'T GET AWAY!
WHICH WAY--?
HERE--THROUGH THE TREES!
STOP!
!
!
20.

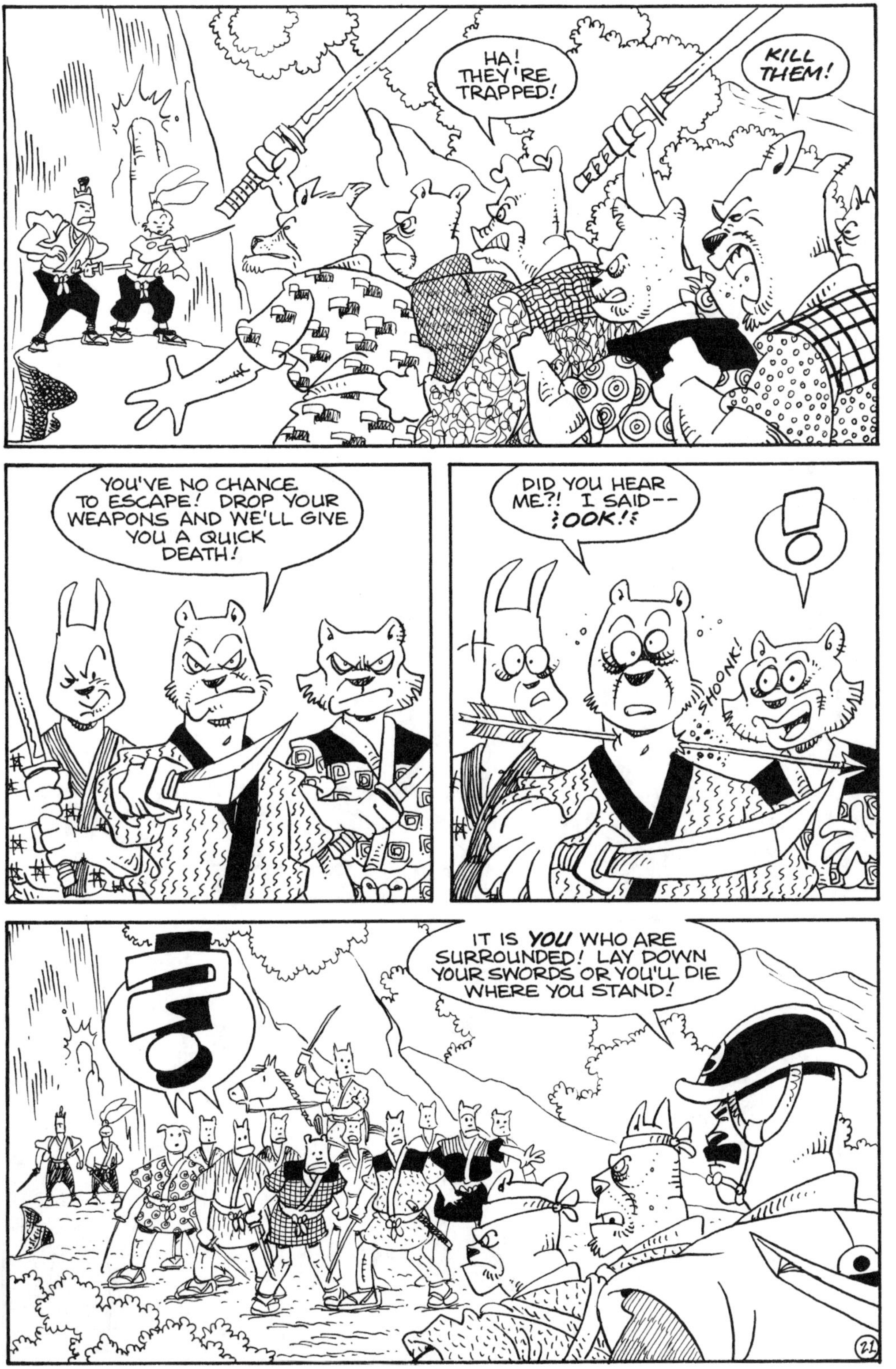
HA! THEY'RE TRAPPED!
KILL THEM!
YOU'VE NO CHANCE TO ESCAPE! DROP YOUR WEAPONS AND WE'LL GIVE YOU A QUICK DEATH!
DID YOU HEAR ME?! I SAID-- OOK!
!
SHOONK!
?
IT IS YOU WHO ARE SURROUNDED! LAY DOWN YOUR SWORDS OR YOU'LL DIE WHERE YOU STAND!
21

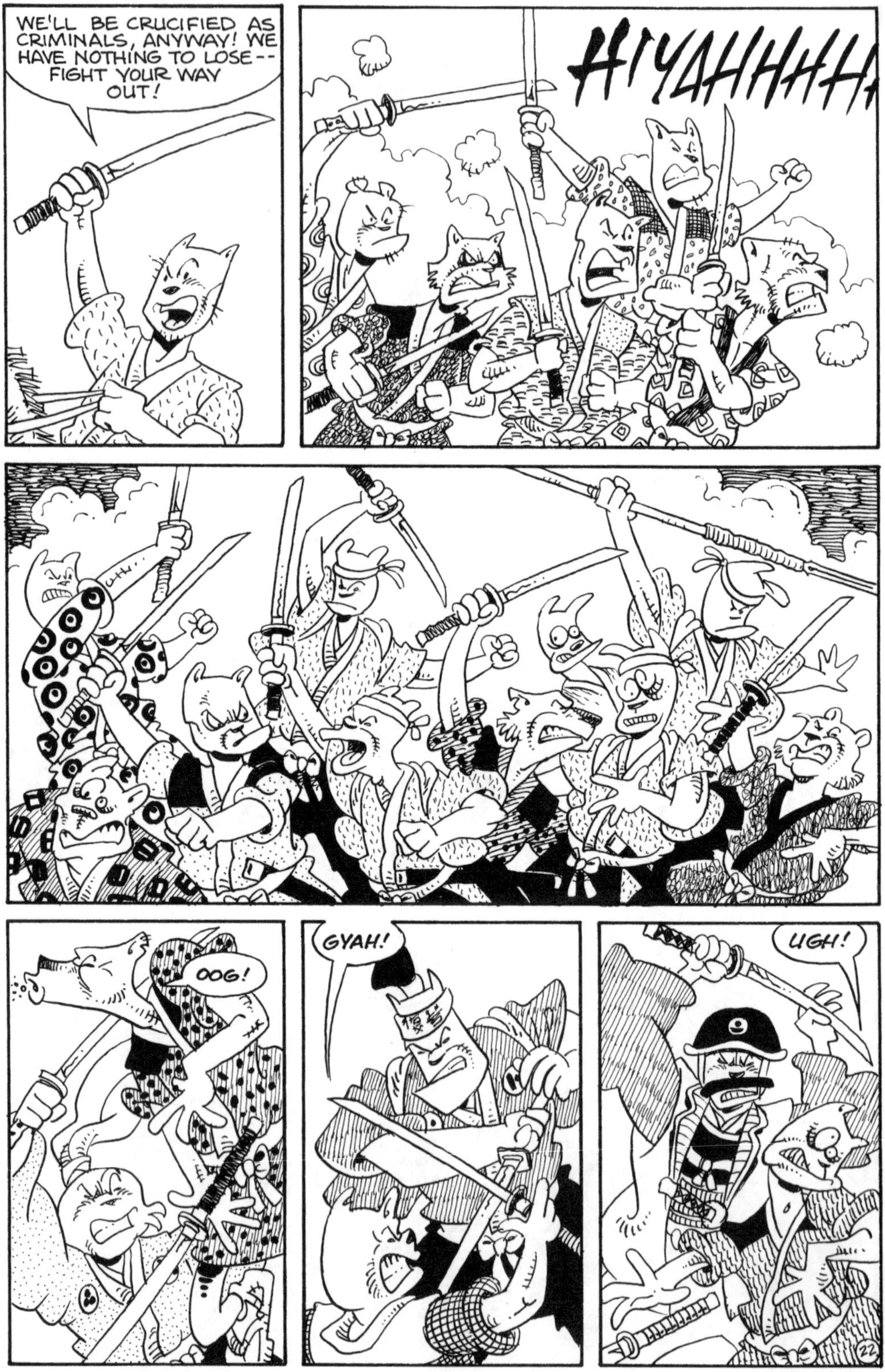
WE'LL BE CRUCIFIED AS CRIMINALS, ANYWAY! WE HAVE NOTHING TO LOSE-- FIGHT YOUR WAY OUT!
HIYAHHHHA
OOG!
GYAH!
UGH!
22

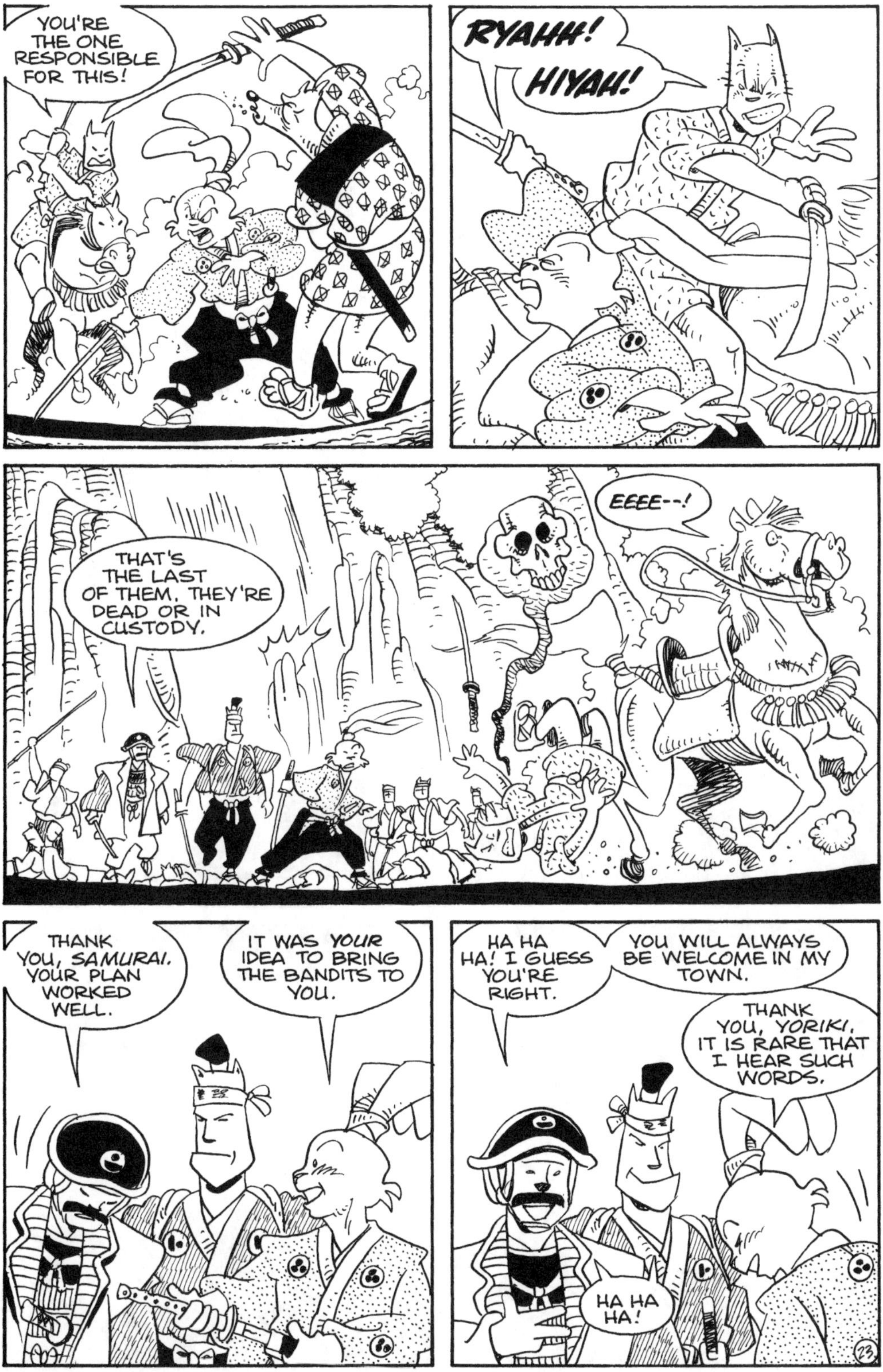
YOU'RE THE ONE RESPONSIBLE FOR THIS!
RYAHH!
HIYAH!
THAT'S THE LAST OF THEM. THEY'RE DEAD OR IN CUSTODY.
EEEE--!
THANK YOU, *SAMURAI*. YOUR PLAN WORKED WELL.
IT WAS *YOUR* IDEA TO BRING THE BANDITS TO YOU.
HA HA HA! I GUESS YOU'RE RIGHT.
YOU WILL ALWAYS BE WELCOME IN MY TOWN.
THANK YOU, *YORIKI*. IT IS RARE THAT I HEAR SUCH WORDS.
HA HA HA!
23

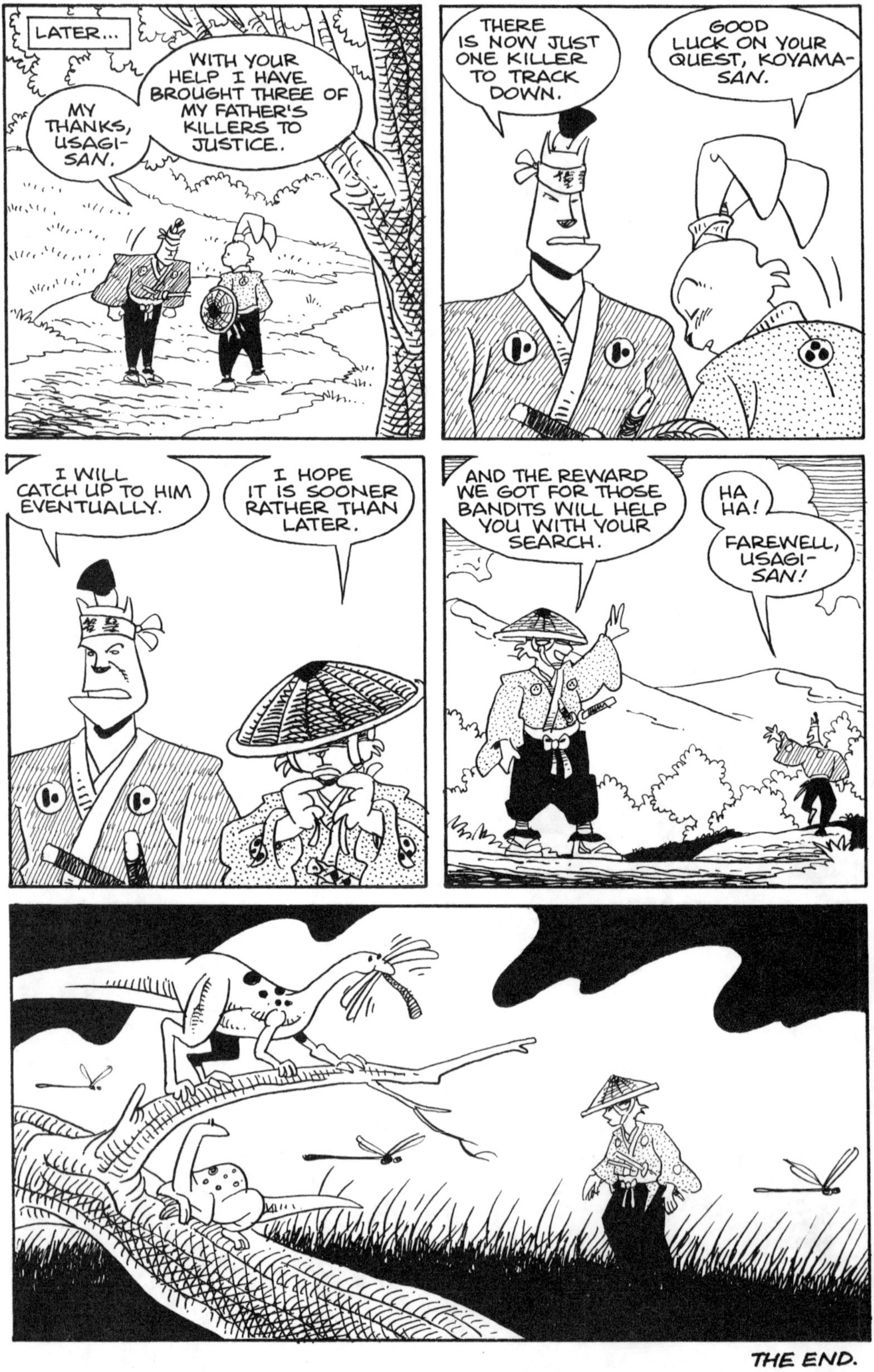
LATER...
MY THANKS, USAGI-SAN.
WITH YOUR HELP I HAVE BROUGHT THREE OF MY FATHER'S KILLERS TO JUSTICE.
THERE IS NOW JUST ONE KILLER TO TRACK DOWN.
GOOD LUCK ON YOUR QUEST, KOYAMA-SAN.
I WILL CATCH UP TO HIM EVENTUALLY.
I HOPE IT IS SOONER RATHER THAN LATER.
AND THE REWARD WE GOT FOR THOSE BANDITS WILL HELP YOU WITH YOUR SEARCH.
HA HA!
FAREWELL, USAGI-SAN!

THE END.

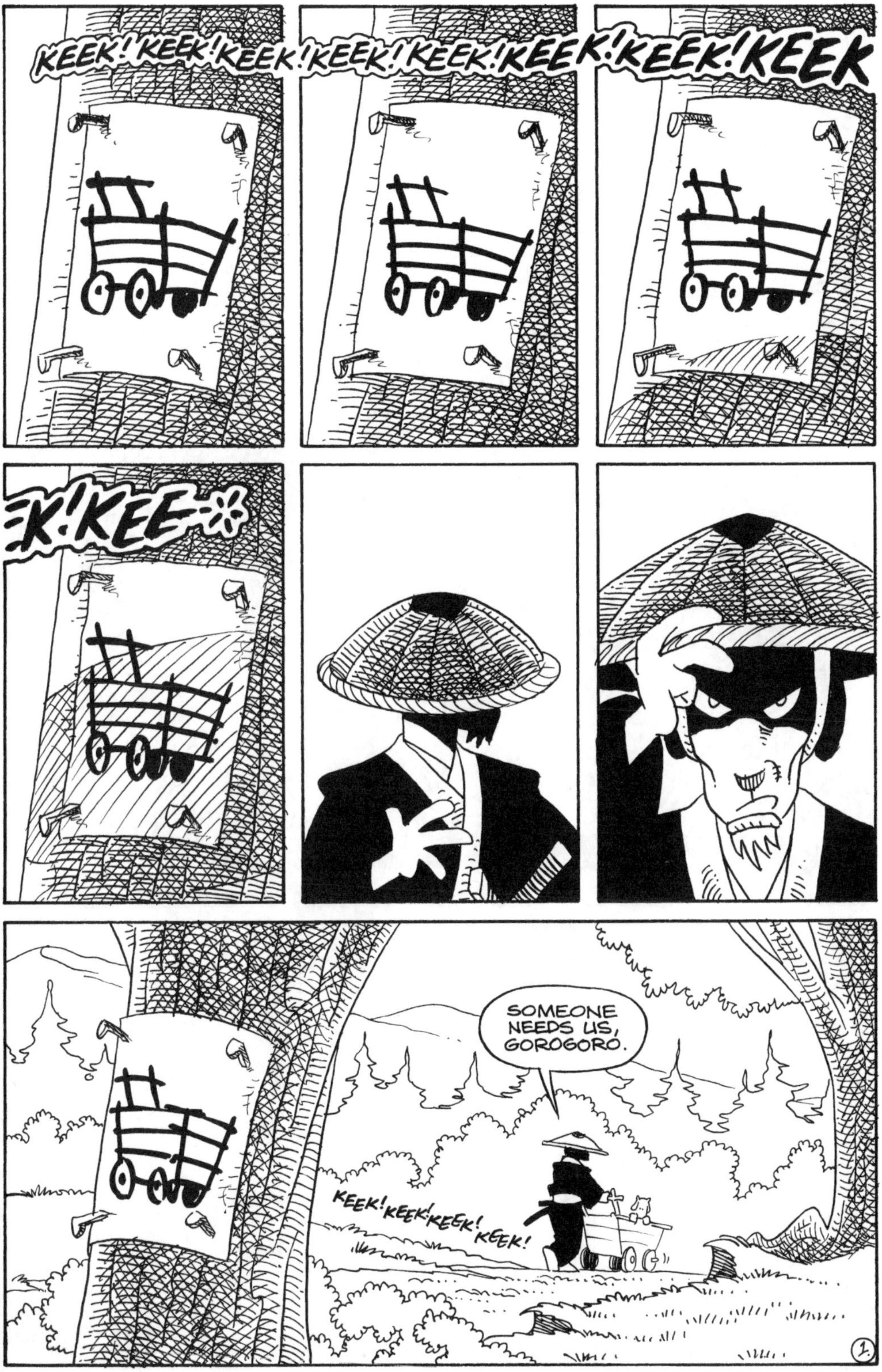
KEEK! KEEK! KEEK! KEEK! KEEK! KEEK! KEEK! KEEK
K! KEE
SOMEONE NEEDS US, GOROGORO.
KEEK! KEEK! KEEK! KEEK!
1

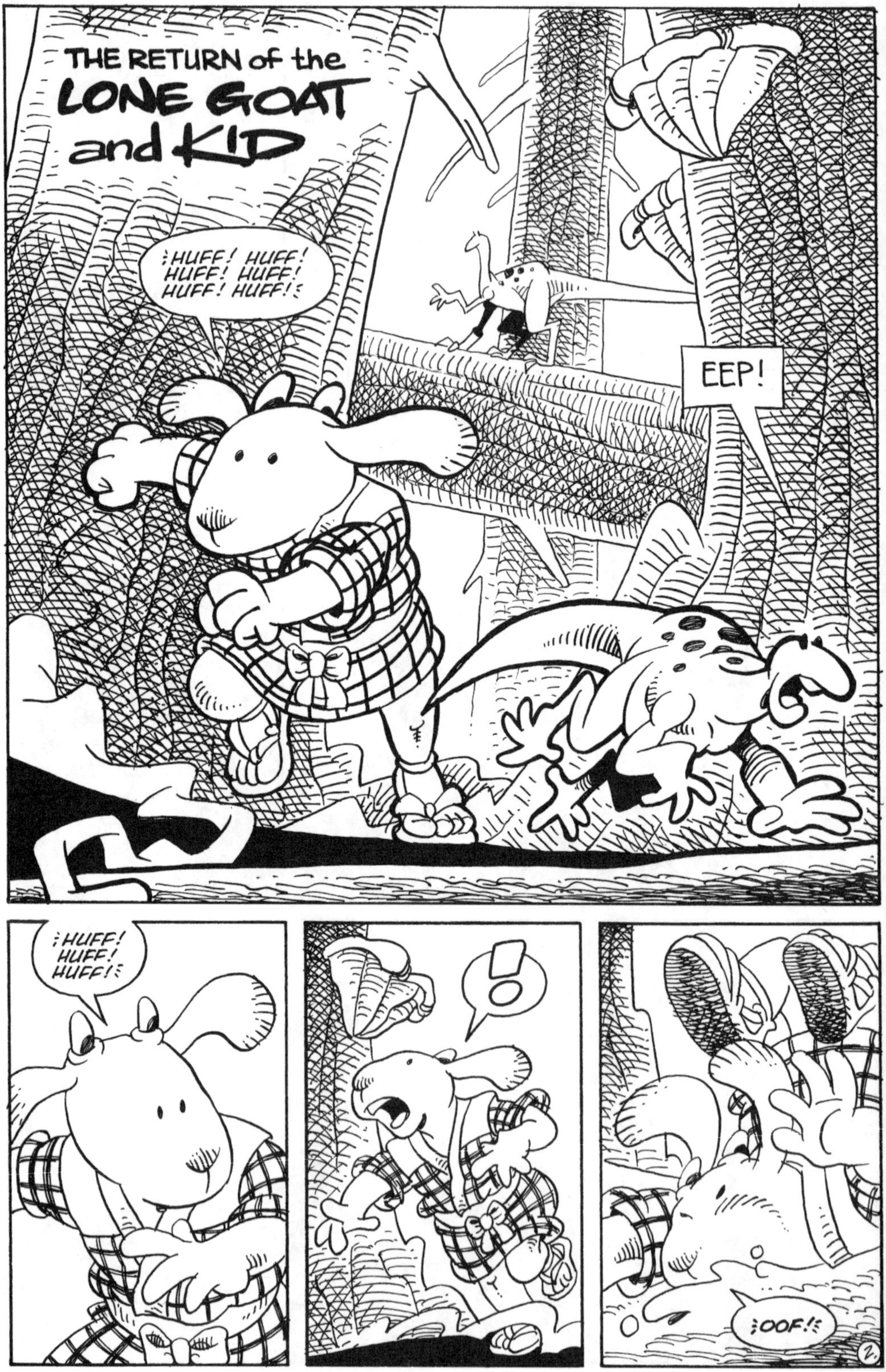
THE RETURN of the LONE GOAT and KID
HUFF! HUFF! HUFF! HUFF! HUFF! HUFF!
EEP!
HUFF! HUFF! HUFF!
!
OOF!

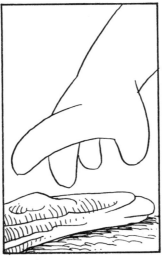

¡HUFF! HUFF!: SO--THERE YOU ARE, YOU BRAT!

¡HUFF! HUFF!: DO YOU THINK YOU ¡HUFF!: CAN FIGHT ME OFF WITH THAT STICK?

WE KNOW MERCHANTS HIRED YOUR FATHER TO ASSASSINATE OUR BOSSES.

HE MAY HAVE KILLED ONE OF THEM, BUT I'M TAKING YOU TO THE OTHER.

WE'LL TAKE CARE OF THOSE MERCHANTS LATER-- BAH! ALL THEY THINK ABOUT IS MONEY.

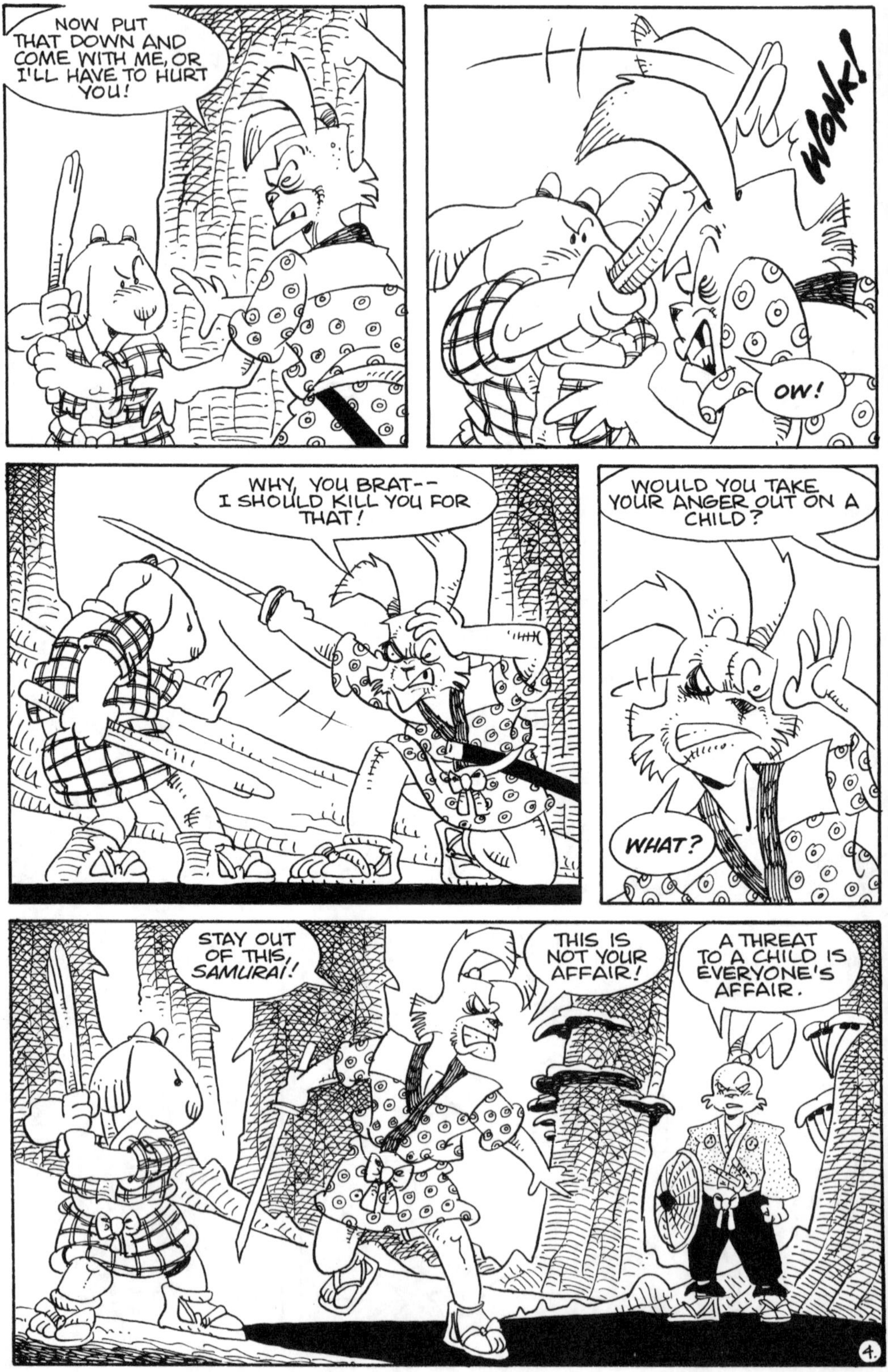
NOW PUT THAT DOWN AND COME WITH ME, OR I'LL HAVE TO HURT YOU!
WONK!
OW!
WHY, YOU BRAT-- I SHOULD KILL YOU FOR THAT!
WOULD YOU TAKE YOUR ANGER OUT ON A CHILD?
WHAT?
STAY OUT OF THIS, SAMURAI!
THIS IS NOT YOUR AFFAIR!
A THREAT TO A CHILD IS EVERYONE'S AFFAIR.
4.

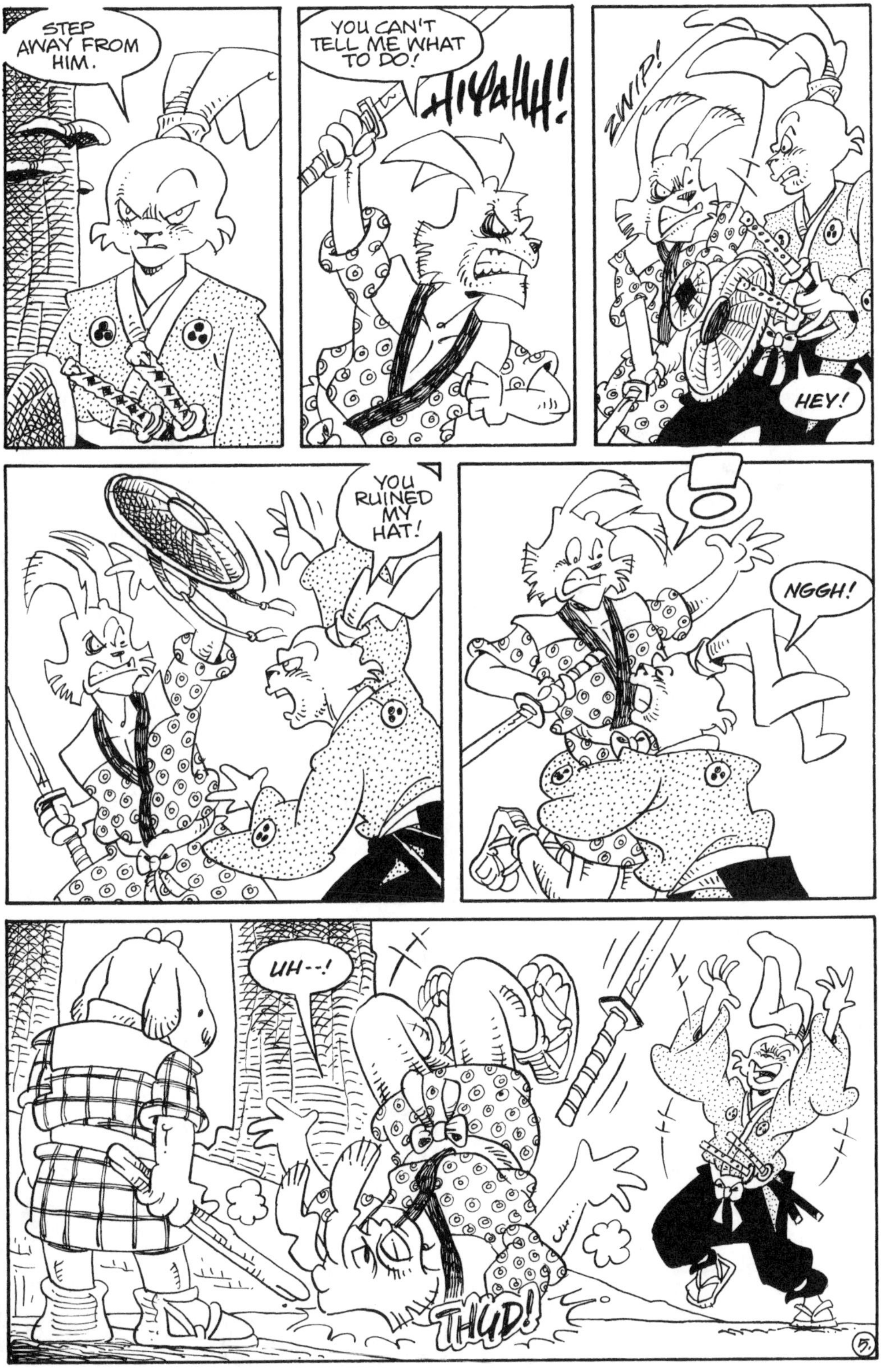
STEP AWAY FROM HIM.
YOU CAN'T TELL ME WHAT TO DO!
HIYAHH!
ZWIP!
HEY!
YOU RUINED MY HAT!
NGGH!
UH--!
THUD!
5.

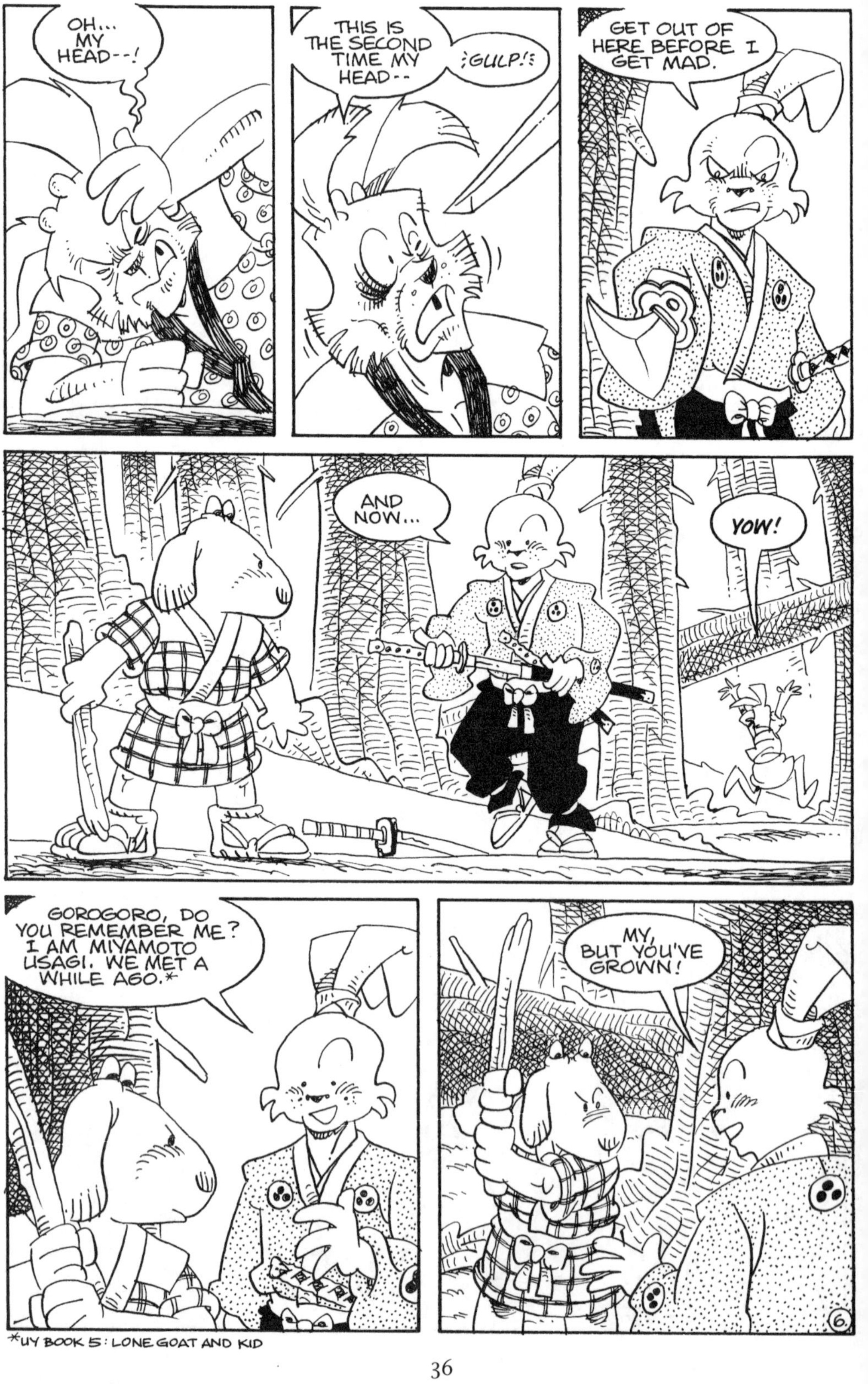
OH... MY HEAD--!
THIS IS THE SECOND TIME MY HEAD--
GULP!
GET OUT OF HERE BEFORE I GET MAD.
AND NOW...
YOW!
GORORGORO, DO YOU REMEMBER ME? I AM MIYAMOTO USAGI. WE MET A WHILE AGO.*
MY, BUT YOU'VE GROWN!
6.

*UY BOOK 5: LONE GOAT AND KID

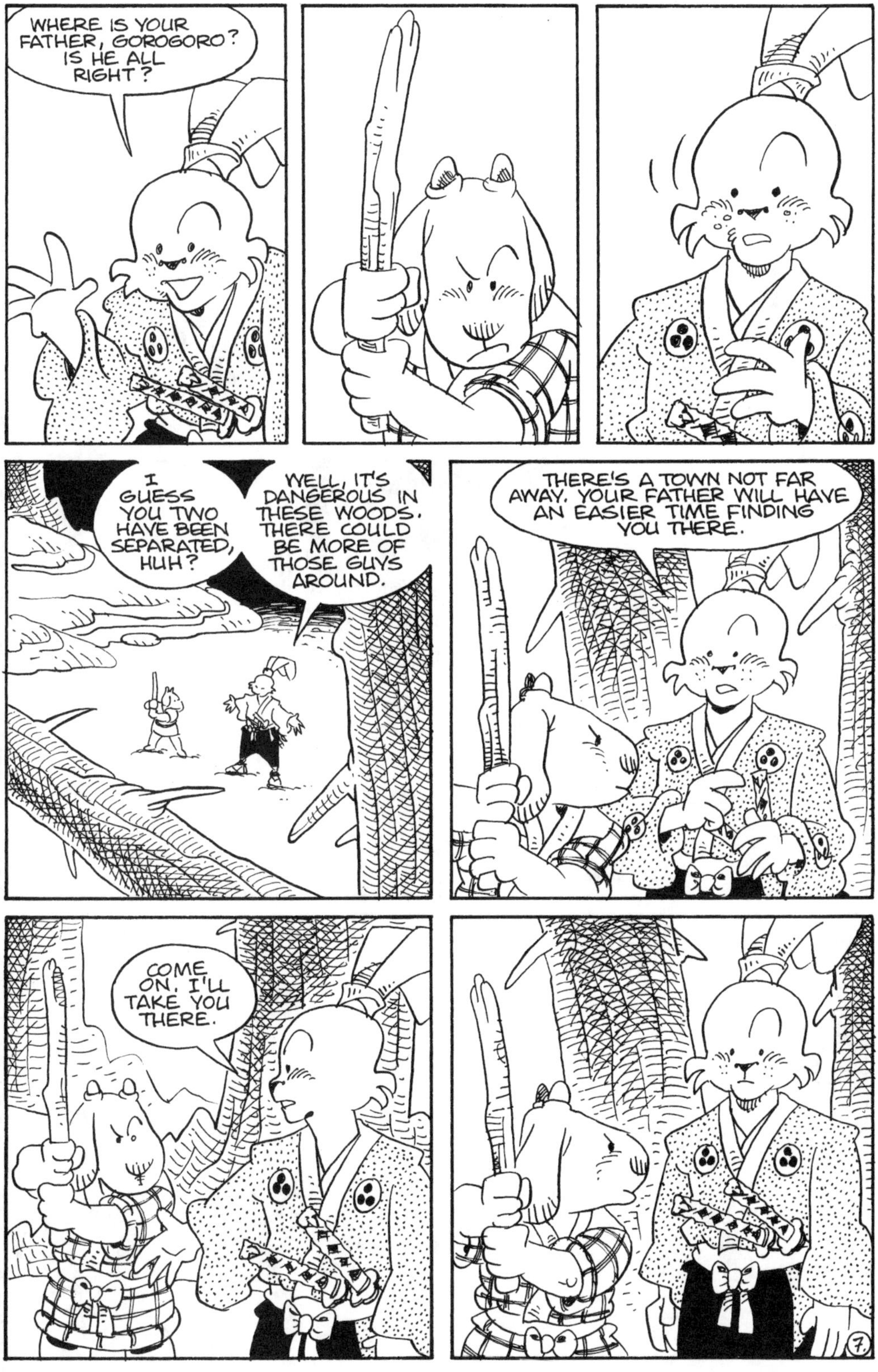
WHERE IS YOUR FATHER, GOROGORO? IS HE ALL RIGHT?
I GUESS YOU TWO HAVE BEEN SEPARATED, HUH?
WELL, IT'S DANGEROUS IN THESE WOODS. THERE COULD BE MORE OF THOSE GUYS AROUND.
THERE'S A TOWN NOT FAR AWAY. YOUR FATHER WILL HAVE AN EASIER TIME FINDING YOU THERE.
COME ON. I'LL TAKE YOU THERE.
7

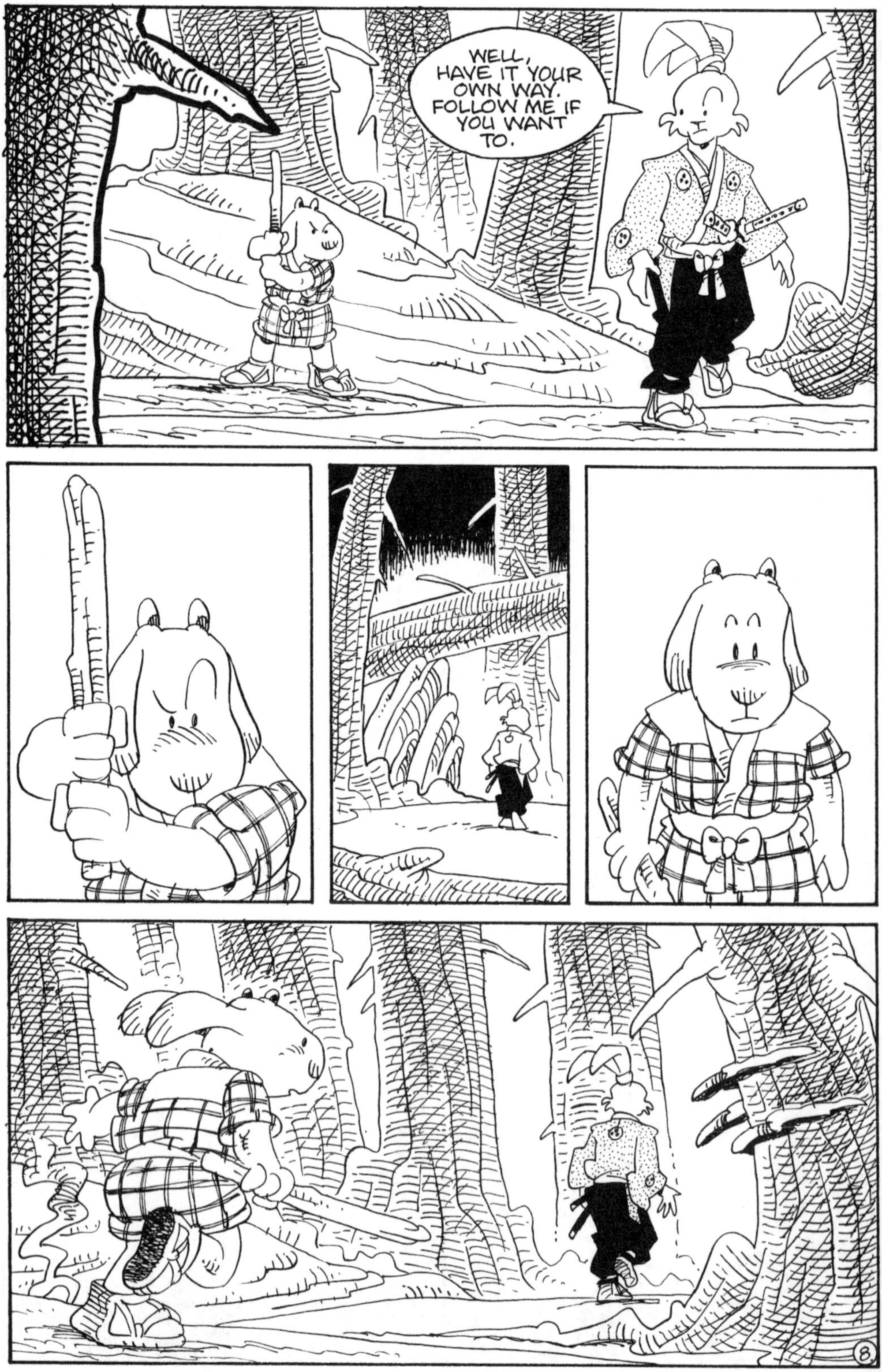
WELL, HAVE IT YOUR OWN WAY. FOLLOW ME IF YOU WANT TO.
8

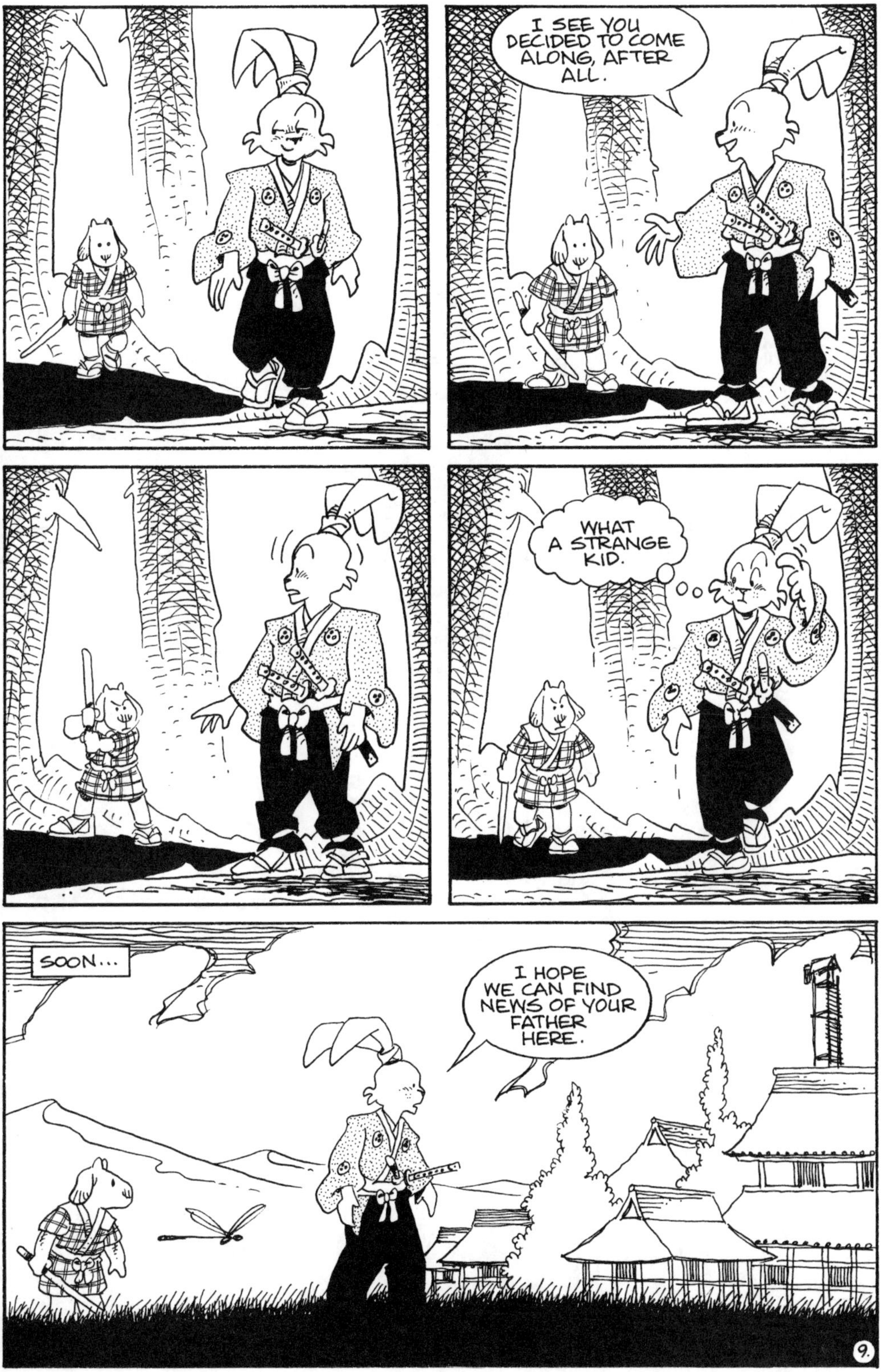
I SEE YOU DECIDED TO COME ALONG, AFTER ALL.
WHAT A STRANGE KID.
SOON...
I HOPE WE CAN FIND NEWS OF YOUR FATHER HERE.
9.

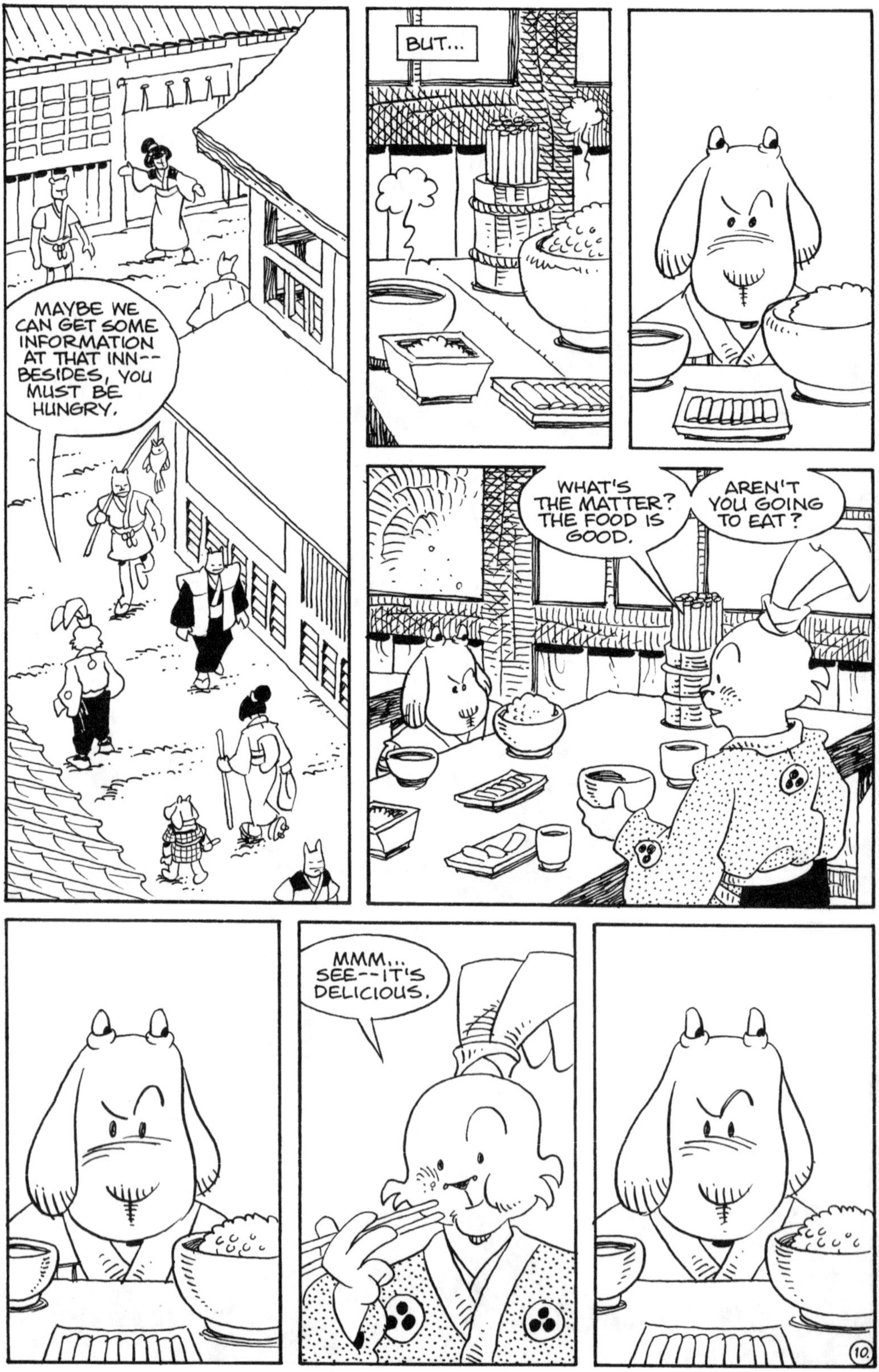
MAYBE WE CAN GET SOME INFORMATION AT THAT INN-- BESIDES, YOU MUST BE HUNGRY.
BUT...
WHAT'S THE MATTER? THE FOOD IS GOOD.
AREN'T YOU GOING TO EAT?
MMM... SEE--IT'S DELICIOUS.
10.

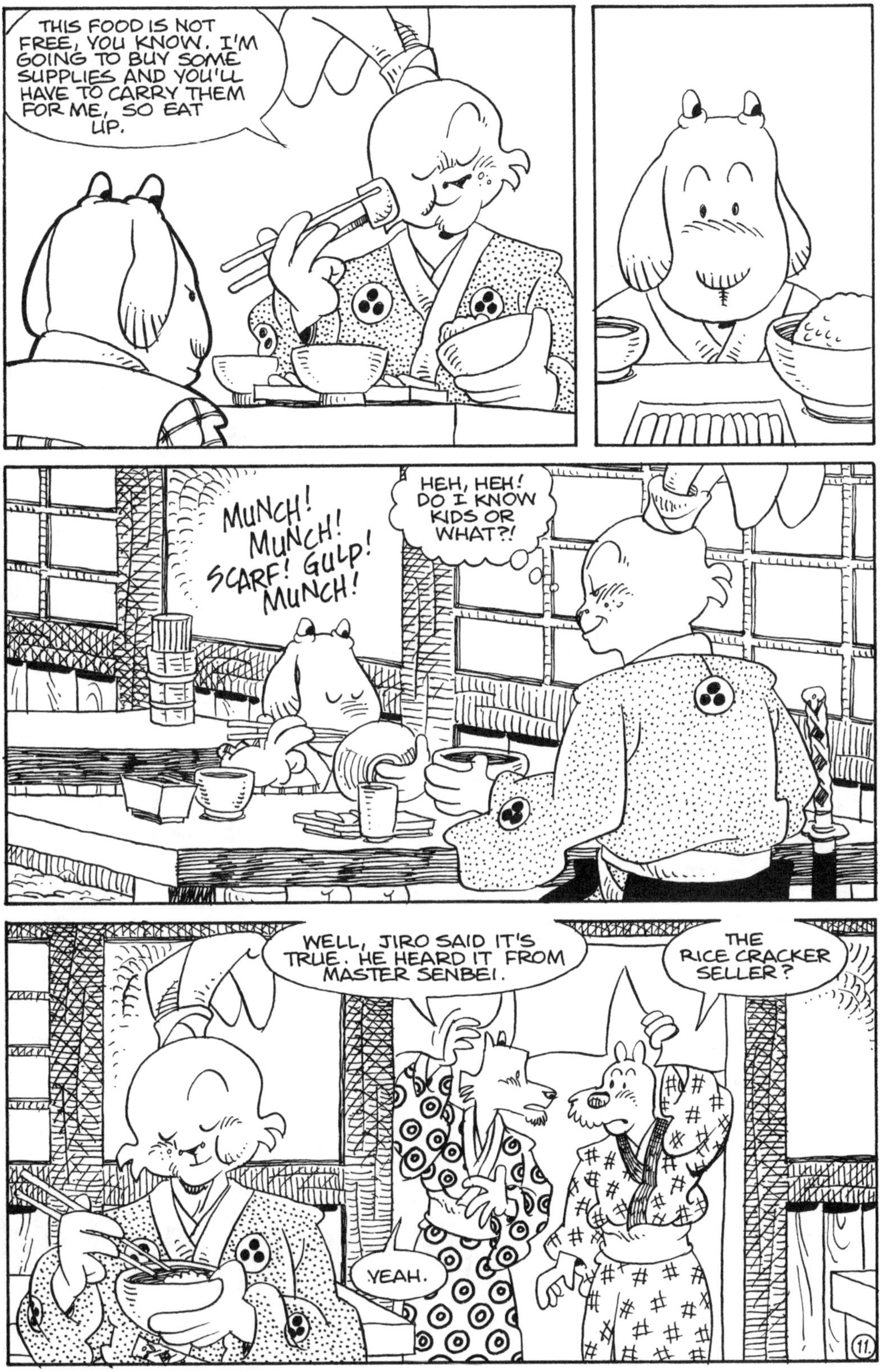
THIS FOOD IS NOT FREE, YOU KNOW. I'M GOING TO BUY SOME SUPPLIES AND YOU'LL HAVE TO CARRY THEM FOR ME, SO EAT UP.
MUNCH! MUNCH! SCARF! GULP! MUNCH!
HEH, HEH! DO I KNOW KIDS OR WHAT?!
WELL, JIRO SAID IT'S TRUE. HE HEARD IT FROM MASTER SENBEI.
THE RICE CRACKER SELLER?
YEAH.
11

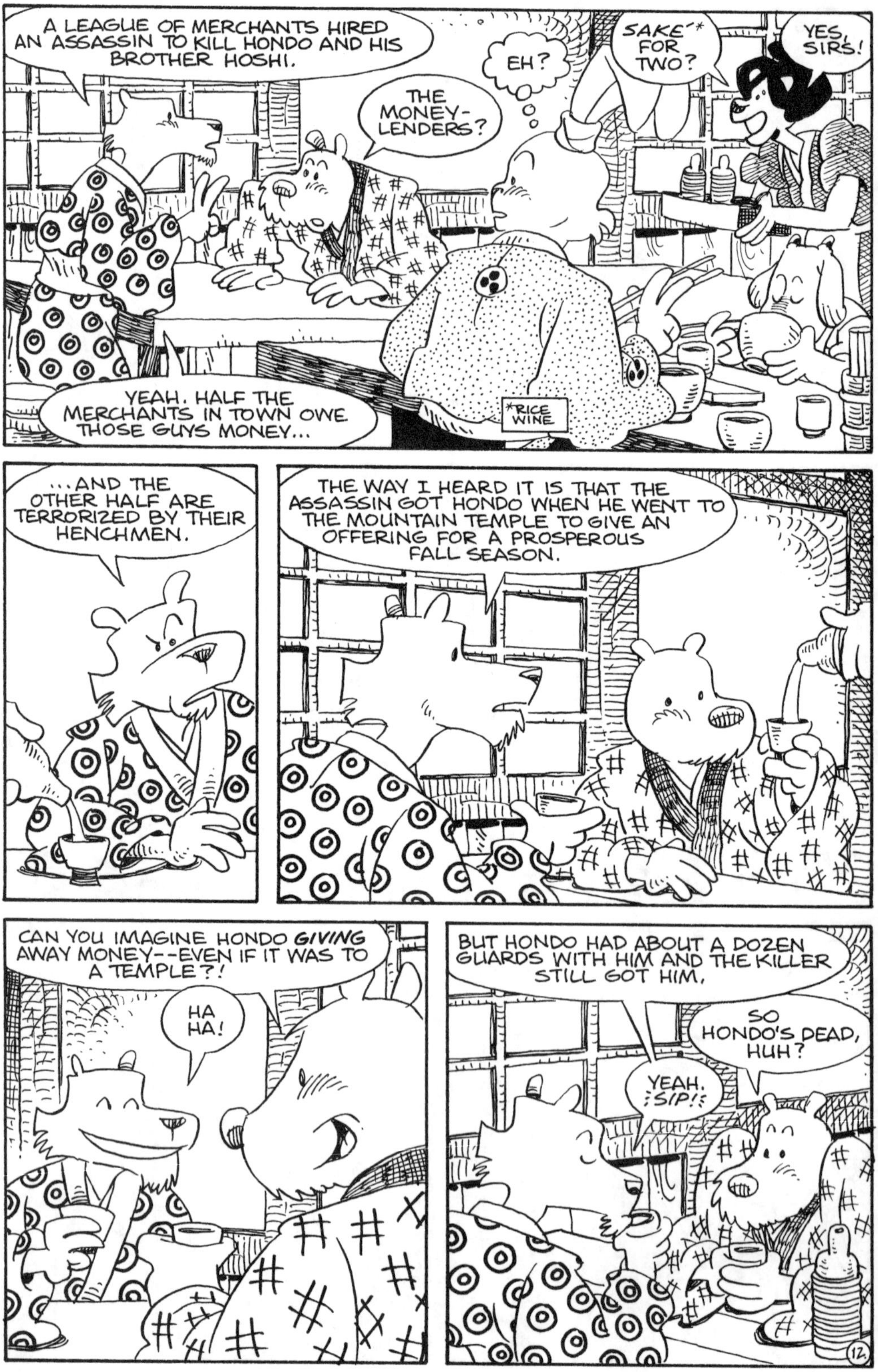
A LEAGUE OF MERCHANTS HIRED AN ASSASSIN TO KILL HONDO AND HIS BROTHER HOSHI.
THE MONEY-LENDERS?
EH?
SAKE'* FOR TWO?
YES, SIRS!
YEAH. HALF THE MERCHANTS IN TOWN OWE THOSE GUYS MONEY...
*RICE WINE
...AND THE OTHER HALF ARE TERRORIZED BY THEIR HENCHMEN.
THE WAY I HEARD IT IS THAT THE ASSASSIN GOT HONDO WHEN HE WENT TO THE MOUNTAIN TEMPLE TO GIVE AN OFFERING FOR A PROSPEROUS FALL SEASON.
CAN YOU IMAGINE HONDO GIVING AWAY MONEY--EVEN IF IT WAS TO A TEMPLE?!
HA HA!
BUT HONDO HAD ABOUT A DOZEN GUARDS WITH HIM AND THE KILLER STILL GOT HIM.
SO HONDO'S DEAD, HUH?
YEAH. SIP!
12

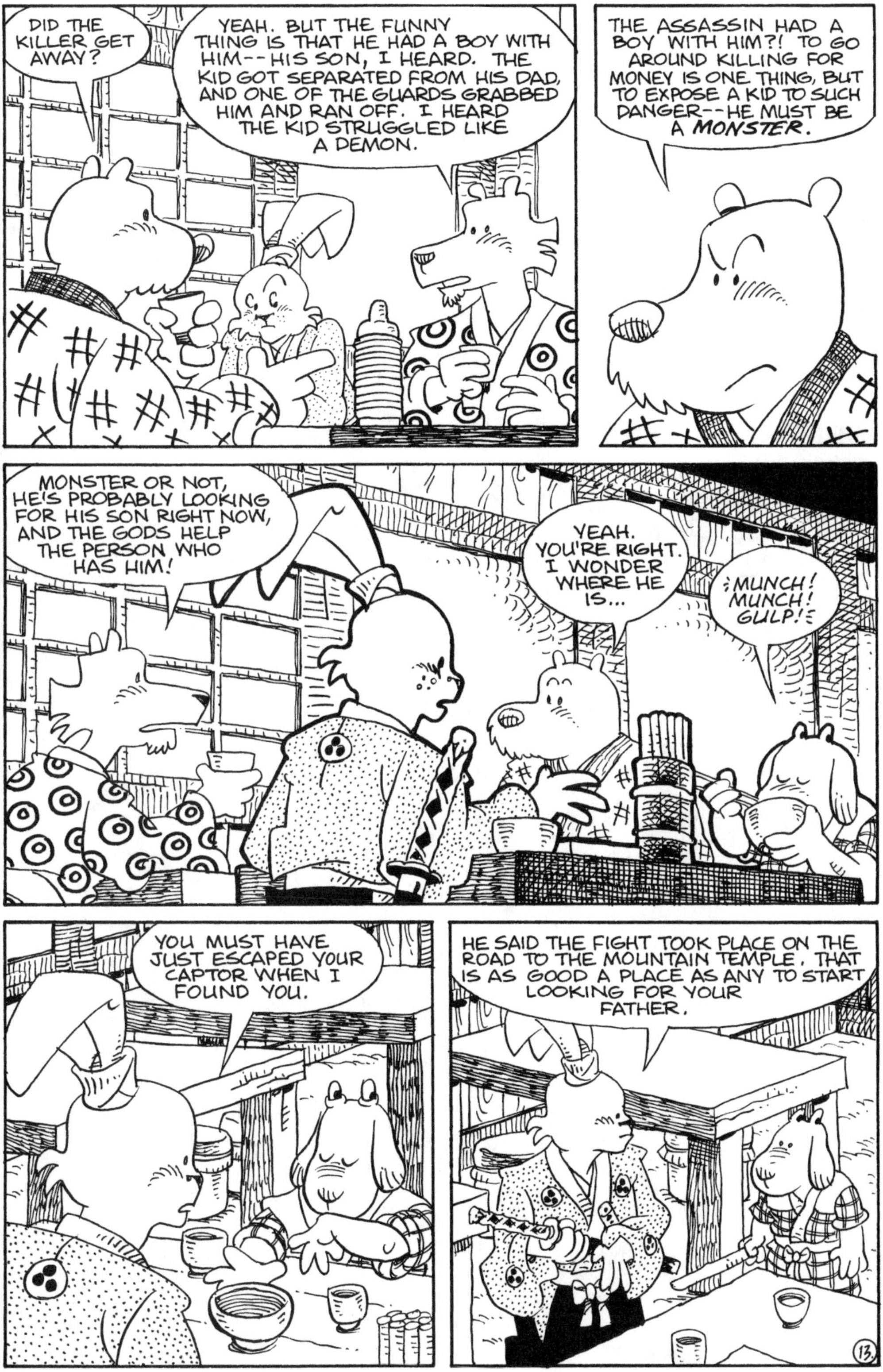
DID THE KILLER GET AWAY?
YEAH. BUT THE FUNNY THING IS THAT HE HAD A BOY WITH HIM--HIS SON, I HEARD. THE KID GOT SEPARATED FROM HIS DAD, AND ONE OF THE GUARDS GRABBED HIM AND RAN OFF. I HEARD THE KID STRUGGLED LIKE A DEMON.
THE ASSASSIN HAD A BOY WITH HIM?! TO GO AROUND KILLING FOR MONEY IS ONE THING, BUT TO EXPOSE A KID TO SUCH DANGER--HE MUST BE A *MONSTER*.
MONSTER OR NOT, HE'S PROBABLY LOOKING FOR HIS SON RIGHT NOW, AND THE GODS HELP THE PERSON WHO HAS HIM!
YEAH. YOU'RE RIGHT. I WONDER WHERE HE IS...
MUNCH! MUNCH! GULP!
YOU MUST HAVE JUST ESCAPED YOUR CAPTOR WHEN I FOUND YOU.
HE SAID THE FIGHT TOOK PLACE ON THE ROAD TO THE MOUNTAIN TEMPLE. THAT IS AS GOOD A PLACE AS ANY TO START LOOKING FOR YOUR FATHER.
13

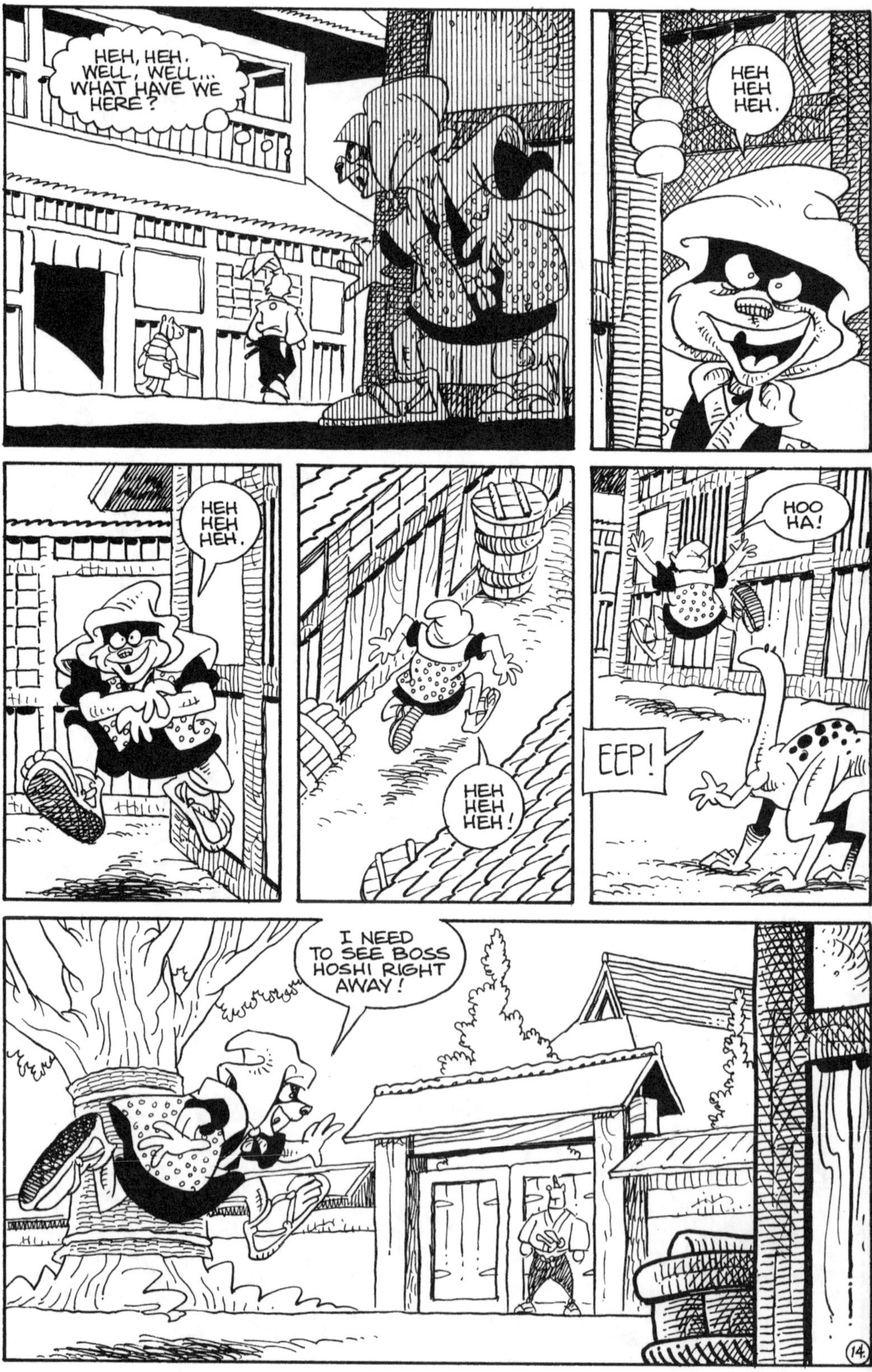
HEH, HEH. WELL, WELL... WHAT HAVE WE HERE?
HEH HEH HEH.
HEH HEH HEH.
HEH HEH HEH!
HOO HA!
EEP!
I NEED TO SEE BOSS HOSHI RIGHT AWAY!
14

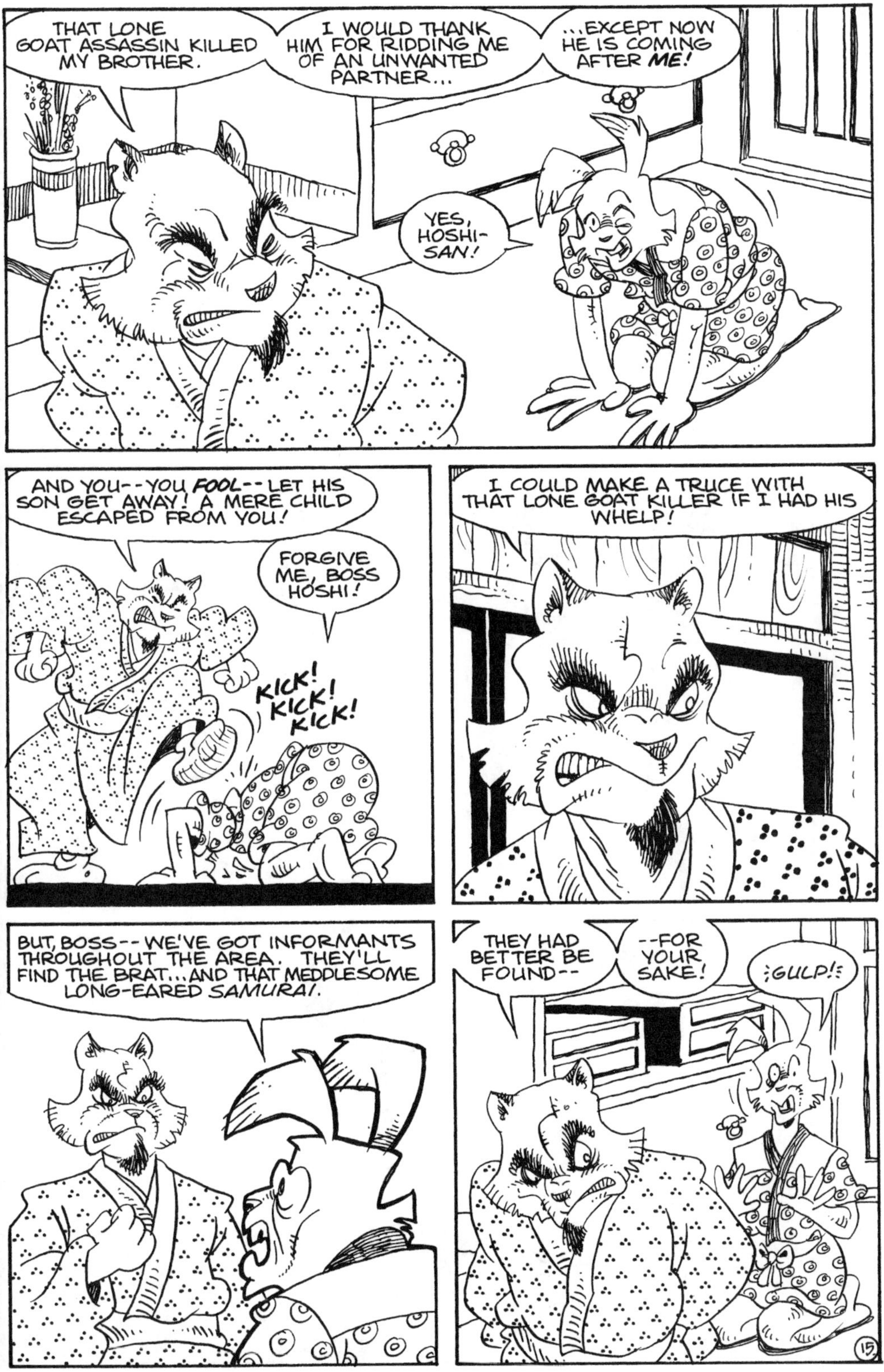
THAT LONE GOAT ASSASSIN KILLED MY BROTHER.
I WOULD THANK HIM FOR RIDDING ME OF AN UNWANTED PARTNER...
...EXCEPT NOW HE IS COMING AFTER *ME!*
YES, HOSHI-SAN!
AND YOU--YOU *FOOL*--LET HIS SON GET AWAY! A MERE CHILD ESCAPED FROM YOU!
FORGIVE ME, BOSS HOSHI!
KICK! KICK! KICK!
I COULD MAKE A TRUCE WITH THAT LONE GOAT KILLER IF I HAD HIS WHELP!
BUT, BOSS--WE'VE GOT INFORMANTS THROUGHOUT THE AREA. THEY'LL FIND THE BRAT...AND THAT MEDDLESOME LONG-EARED *SAMURAI*.
THEY HAD BETTER BE FOUND--
--FOR YOUR SAKE!
GULP!
15

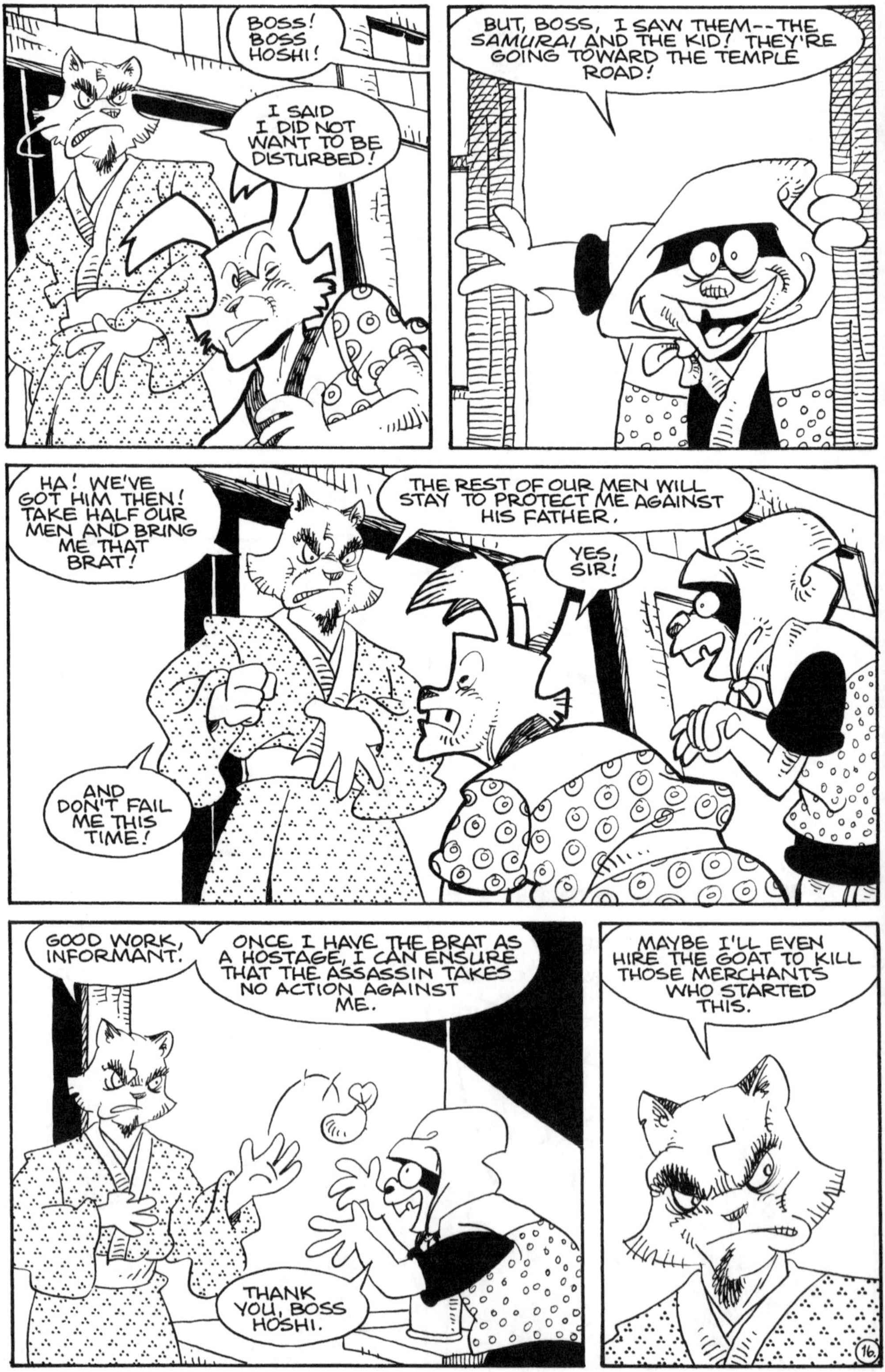
BOSS! BOSS HOSHI!
I SAID I DID NOT WANT TO BE DISTURBED!
BUT, BOSS, I SAW THEM--THE SAMURAI AND THE KID! THEY'RE GOING TOWARD THE TEMPLE ROAD!
HA! WE'VE GOT HIM THEN! TAKE HALF OUR MEN AND BRING ME THAT BRAT!
THE REST OF OUR MEN WILL STAY TO PROTECT ME AGAINST HIS FATHER.
YES, SIR!
AND DON'T FAIL ME THIS TIME!
GOOD WORK, INFORMANT.
ONCE I HAVE THE BRAT AS A HOSTAGE, I CAN ENSURE THAT THE ASSASSIN TAKES NO ACTION AGAINST ME.
THANK YOU, BOSS HOSHI.
MAYBE I'LL EVEN HIRE THE GOAT TO KILL THOSE MERCHANTS WHO STARTED THIS.
16

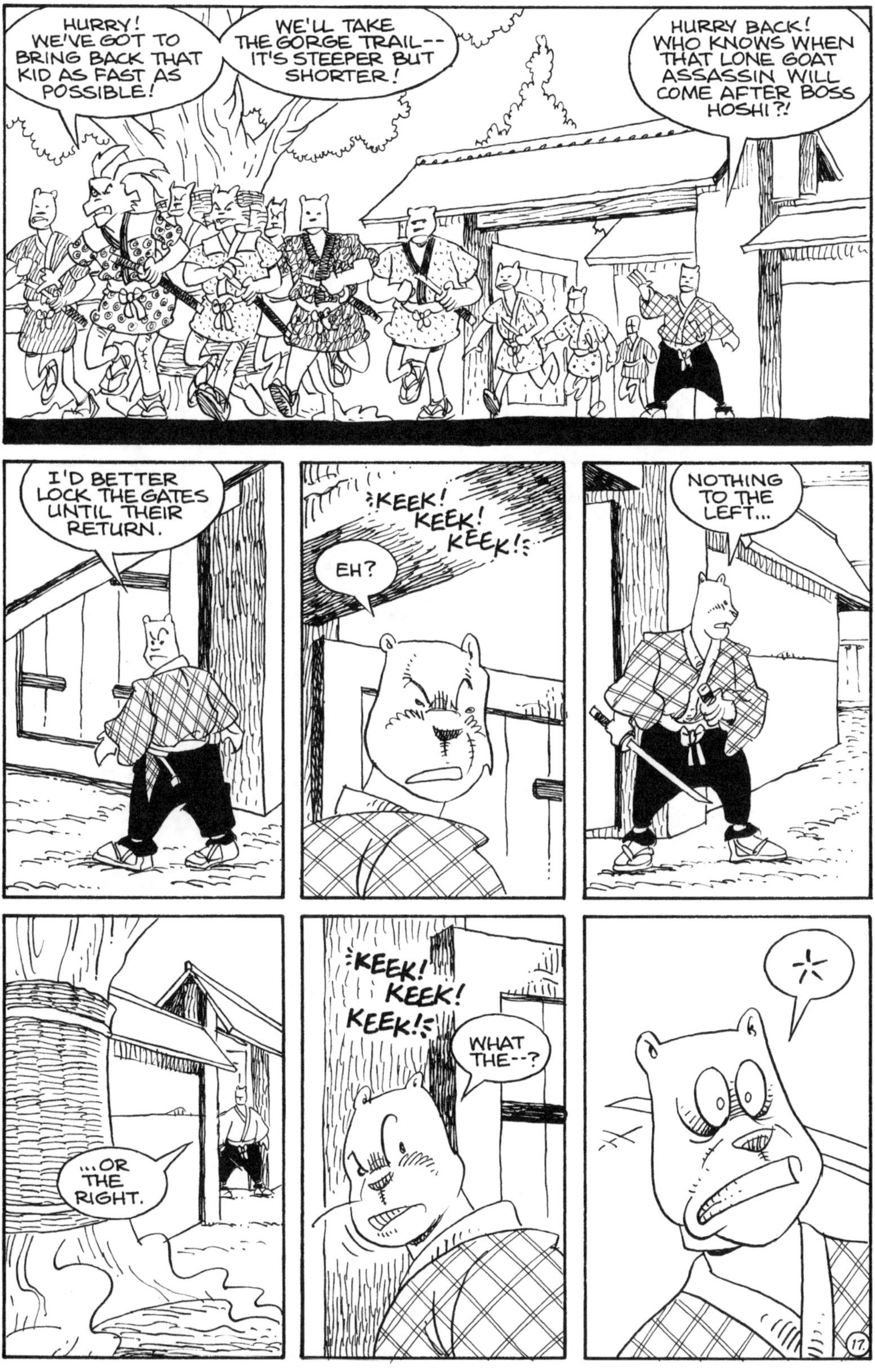
HURRY! WE'VE GOT TO BRING BACK THAT KID AS FAST AS POSSIBLE!
WE'LL TAKE THE GORGE TRAIL-- IT'S STEEPER BUT SHORTER!
HURRY BACK! WHO KNOWS WHEN THAT LONE GOAT ASSASSIN WILL COME AFTER BOSS HOSHI?!
I'D BETTER LOCK THE GATES UNTIL THEIR RETURN.
KEEK! KEEK! KEEK!
EH?
NOTHING TO THE LEFT...
...OR THE RIGHT.
KEEK! KEEK! KEEK!
WHAT THE--?
17.

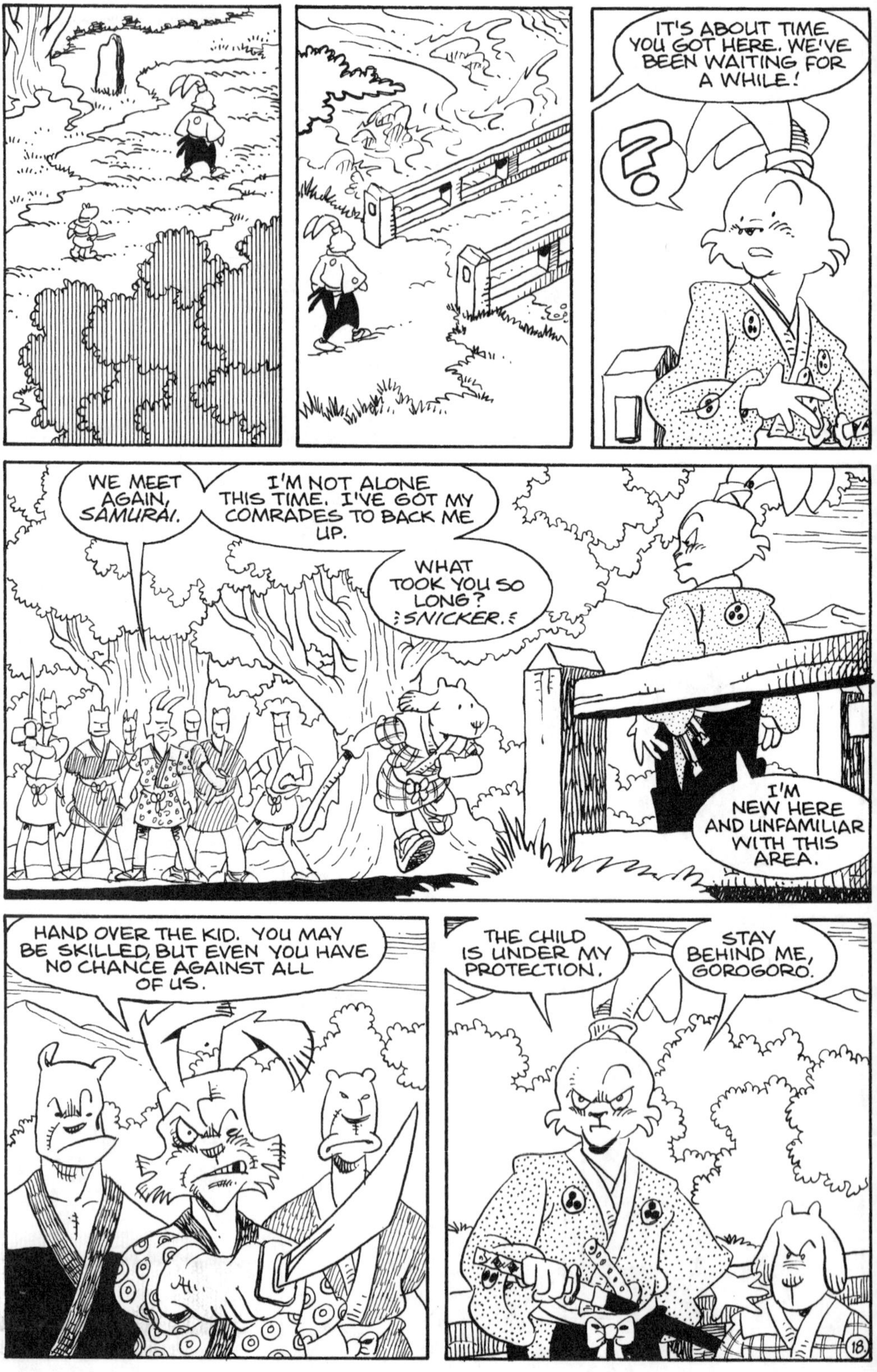
IT'S ABOUT TIME YOU GOT HERE. WE'VE BEEN WAITING FOR A WHILE!
?
WE MEET AGAIN, SAMURAI.
I'M NOT ALONE THIS TIME. I'VE GOT MY COMRADES TO BACK ME UP.
WHAT TOOK YOU SO LONG? SNICKER.
I'M NEW HERE AND UNFAMILIAR WITH THIS AREA.
HAND OVER THE KID. YOU MAY BE SKILLED, BUT EVEN YOU HAVE NO CHANCE AGAINST ALL OF US.
THE CHILD IS UNDER MY PROTECTION.
STAY BEHIND ME, GOROGORO.
18

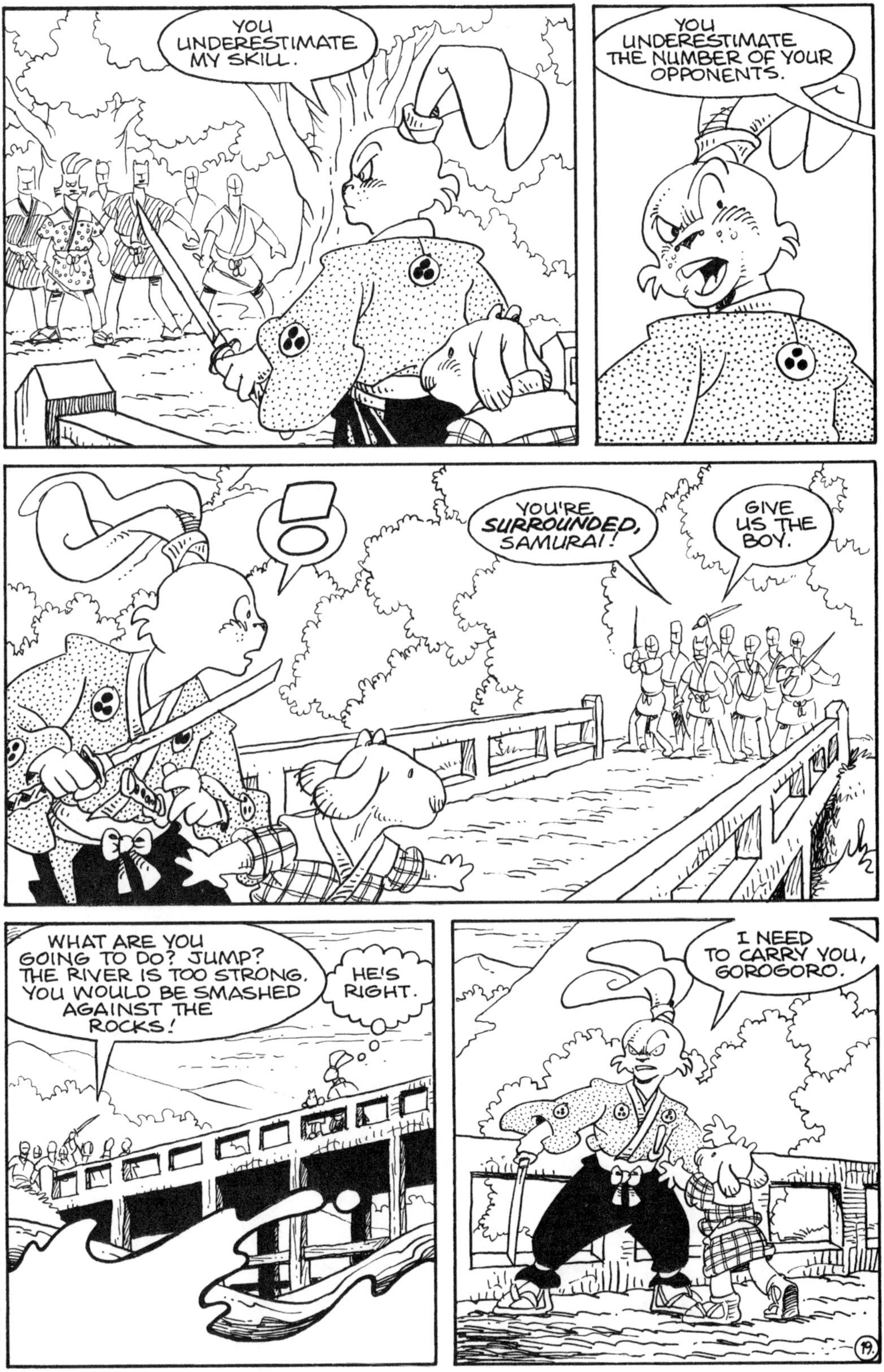
YOU UNDERESTIMATE MY SKILL.
YOU UNDERESTIMATE THE NUMBER OF YOUR OPPONENTS.
YOU'RE **SURROUNDED**, SAMURAI!
GIVE US THE BOY.
WHAT ARE YOU GOING TO DO? JUMP? THE RIVER IS TOO STRONG. YOU WOULD BE SMASHED AGAINST THE ROCKS!
HE'S RIGHT.
I NEED TO CARRY YOU, GOROGORO.
19.

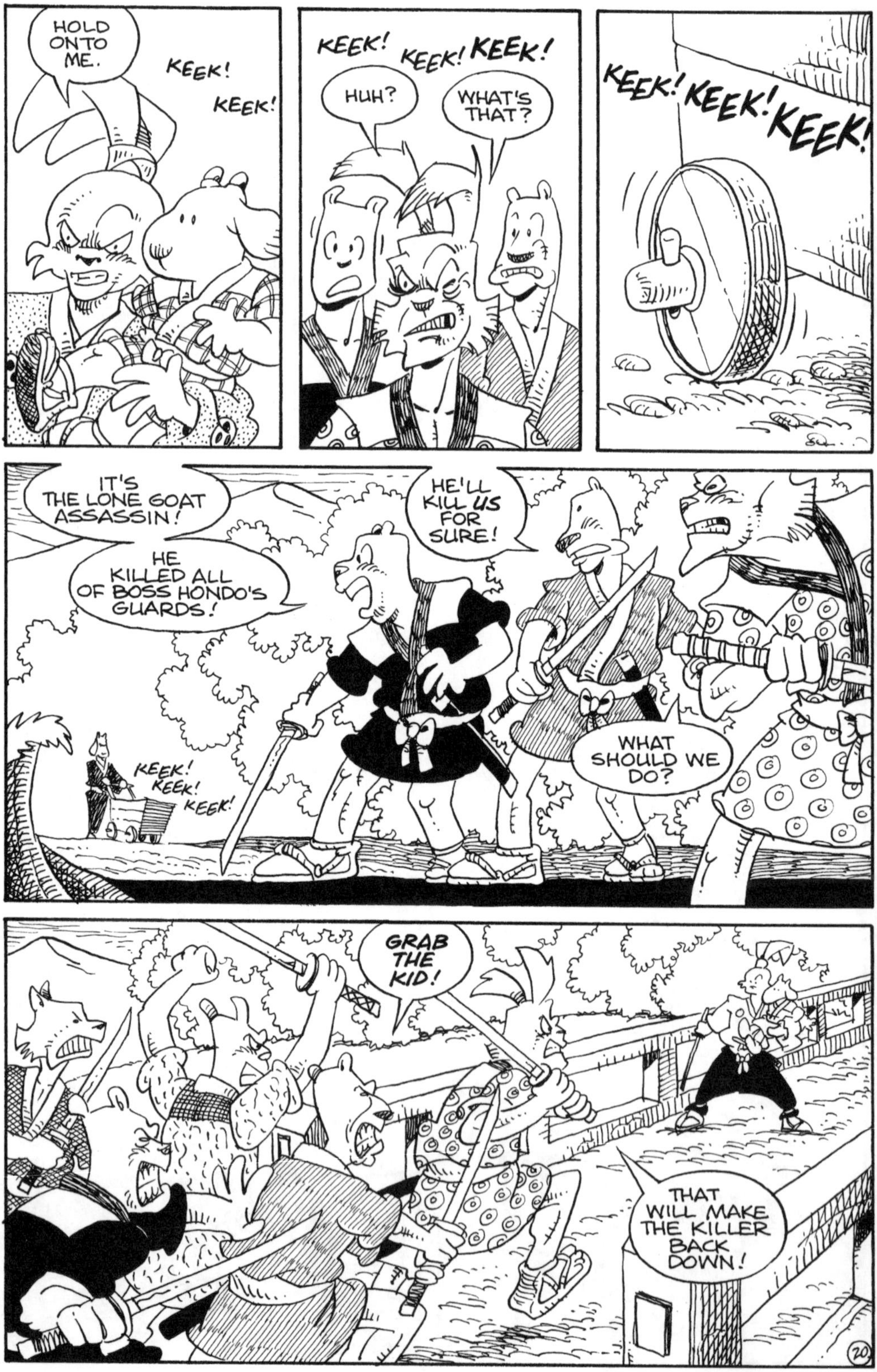
HOLD ONTO ME.
KEEK!
KEEK!
KEEK!
KEEK! KEEK!
HUH?
WHAT'S THAT?
KEEK! KEEK! KEEK!
IT'S THE LONE GOAT ASSASSIN!
HE KILLED ALL OF BOSS HONDO'S GUARDS!
HE'LL KILL US FOR SURE!
KEEK! KEEK! KEEK!
WHAT SHOULD WE DO?
GRAB THE KID!
THAT WILL MAKE THE KILLER BACK DOWN!
20

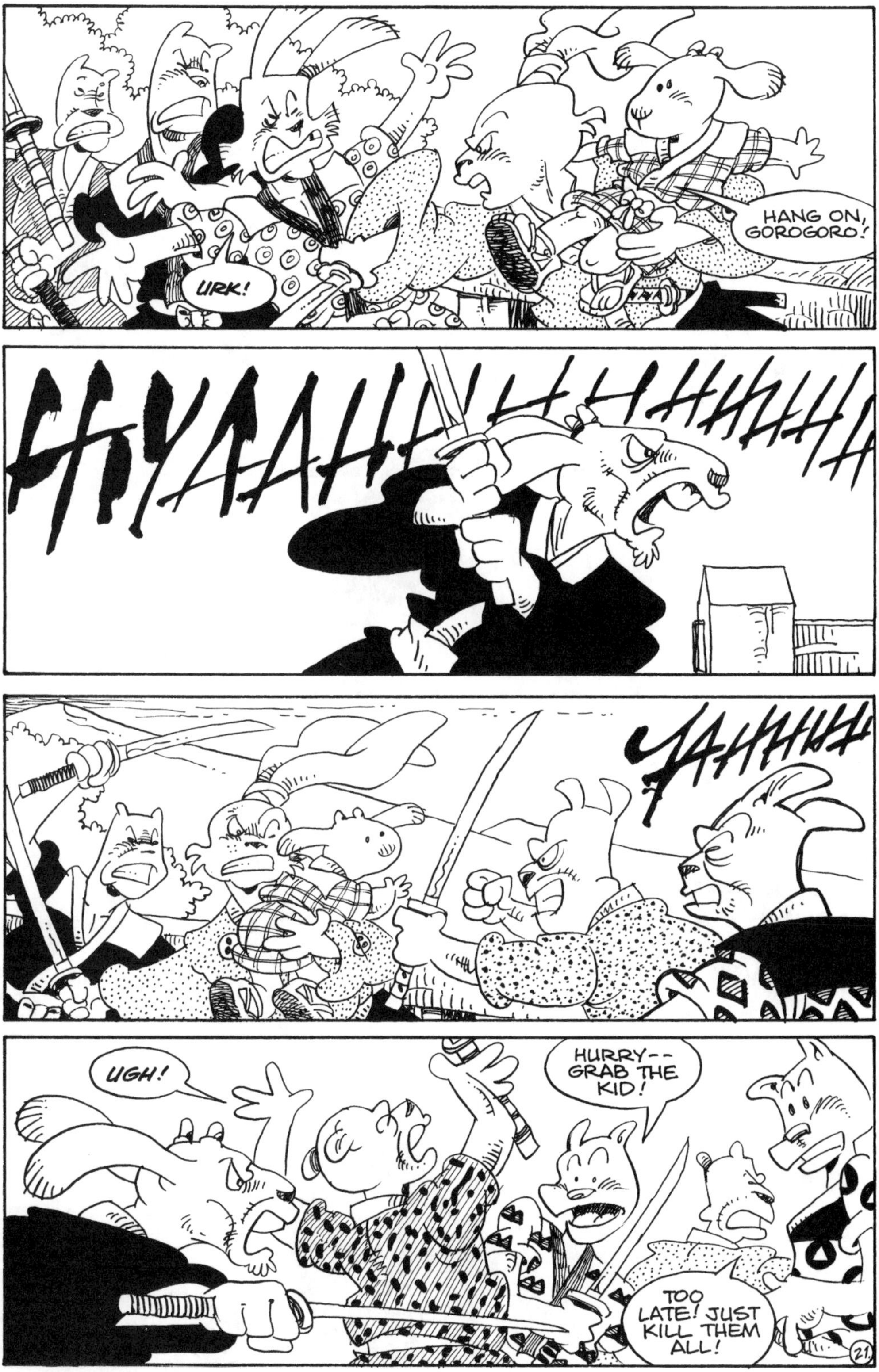
URK!
HANG ON, GORO GORO!
HYAAHHHHHHHHHHH
YAHHHH
UGH!
HURRY-- GRAB THE KID!
TOO LATE! JUST KILL THEM ALL!
21

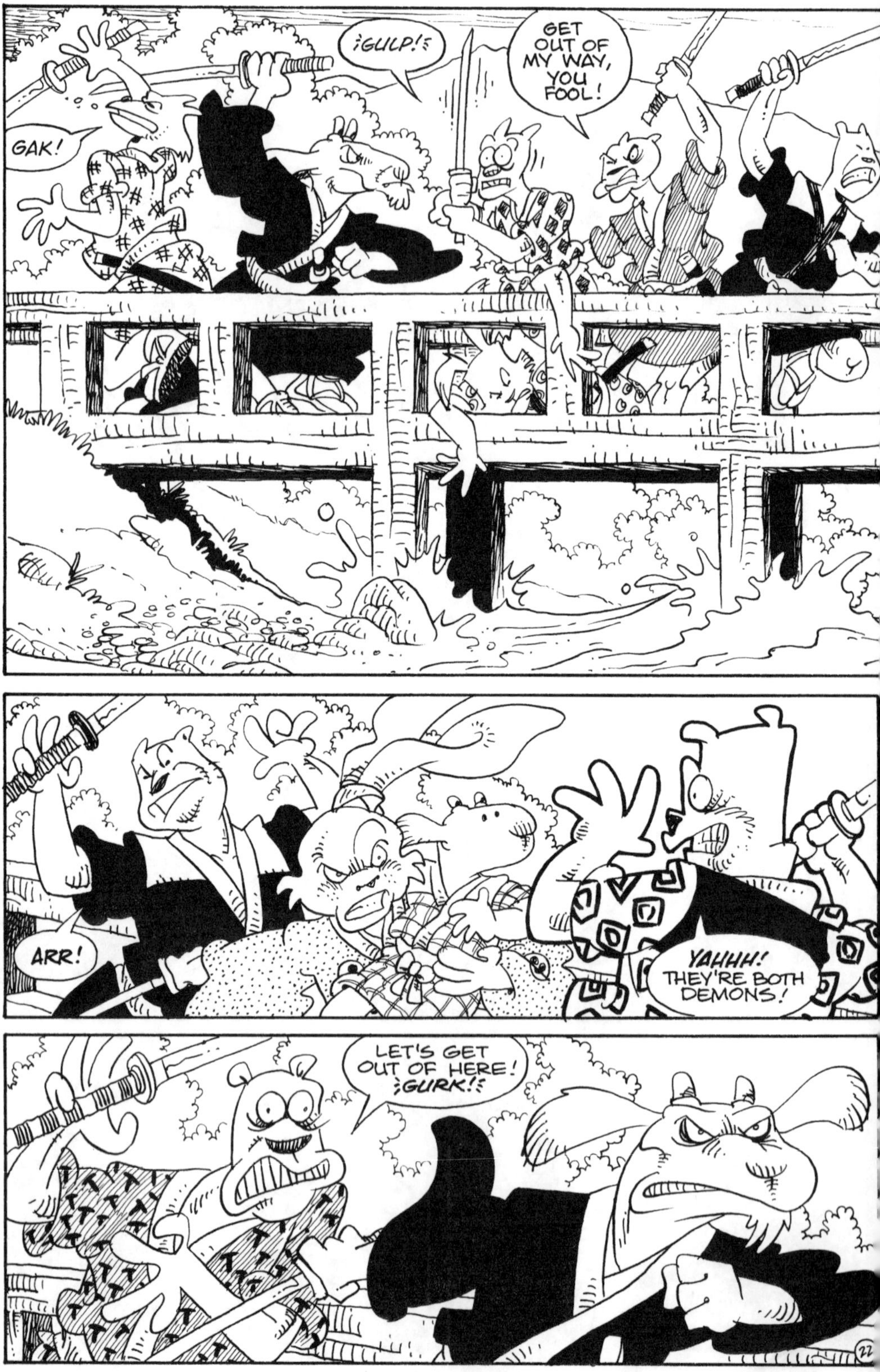
GAK!
¡GULP!
GET OUT OF MY WAY, YOU FOOL!
ARR!
YAHHH! THEY'RE BOTH DEMONS!
LET'S GET OUT OF HERE! ¡GURK!
22

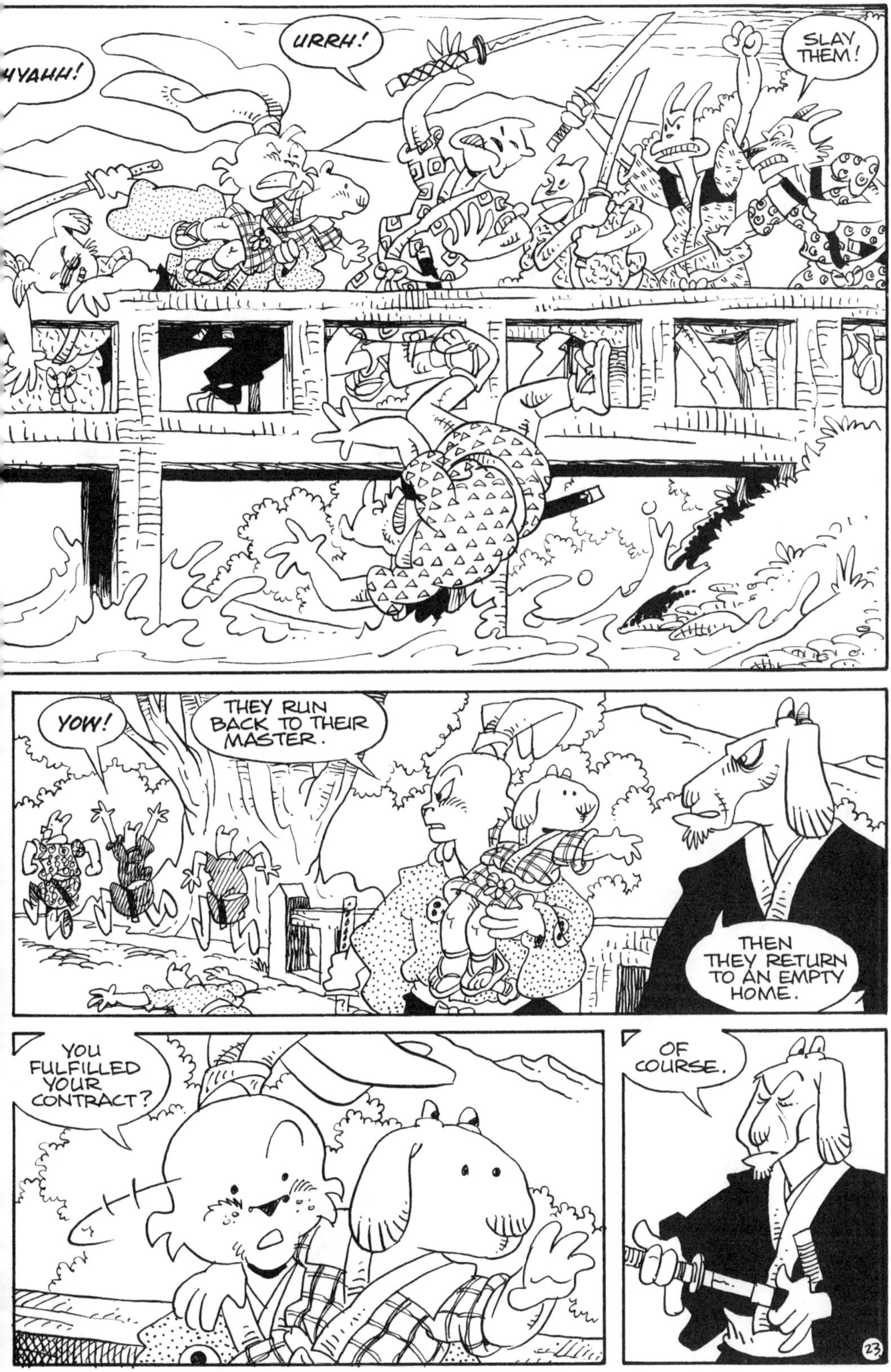
HYAHH!
URRH!
SLAY THEM!
YOW!
THEY RUN BACK TO THEIR MASTER.
THEN THEY RETURN TO AN EMPTY HOME.
YOU FULFILLED YOUR CONTRACT?
OF COURSE.
23

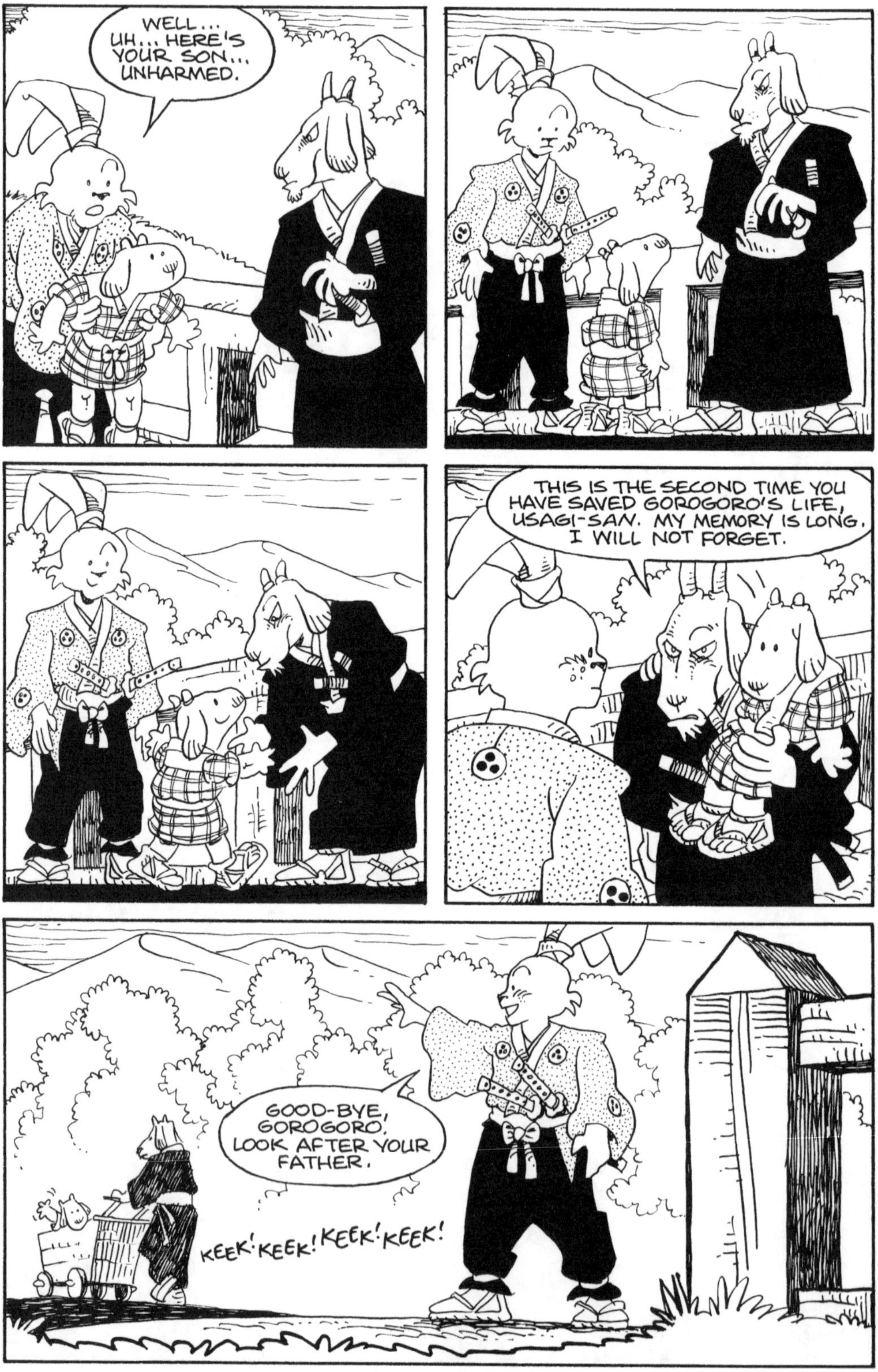
WELL... UH... HERE'S YOUR SON... UNHARMED.
THIS IS THE SECOND TIME YOU HAVE SAVED GOROGORO'S LIFE, USAGI-SAN. MY MEMORY IS LONG. I WILL NOT FORGET.
GOOD-BYE, GOROGORO. LOOK AFTER YOUR FATHER.
KEEK! KEEK! KEEK! KEEK!

THE END.

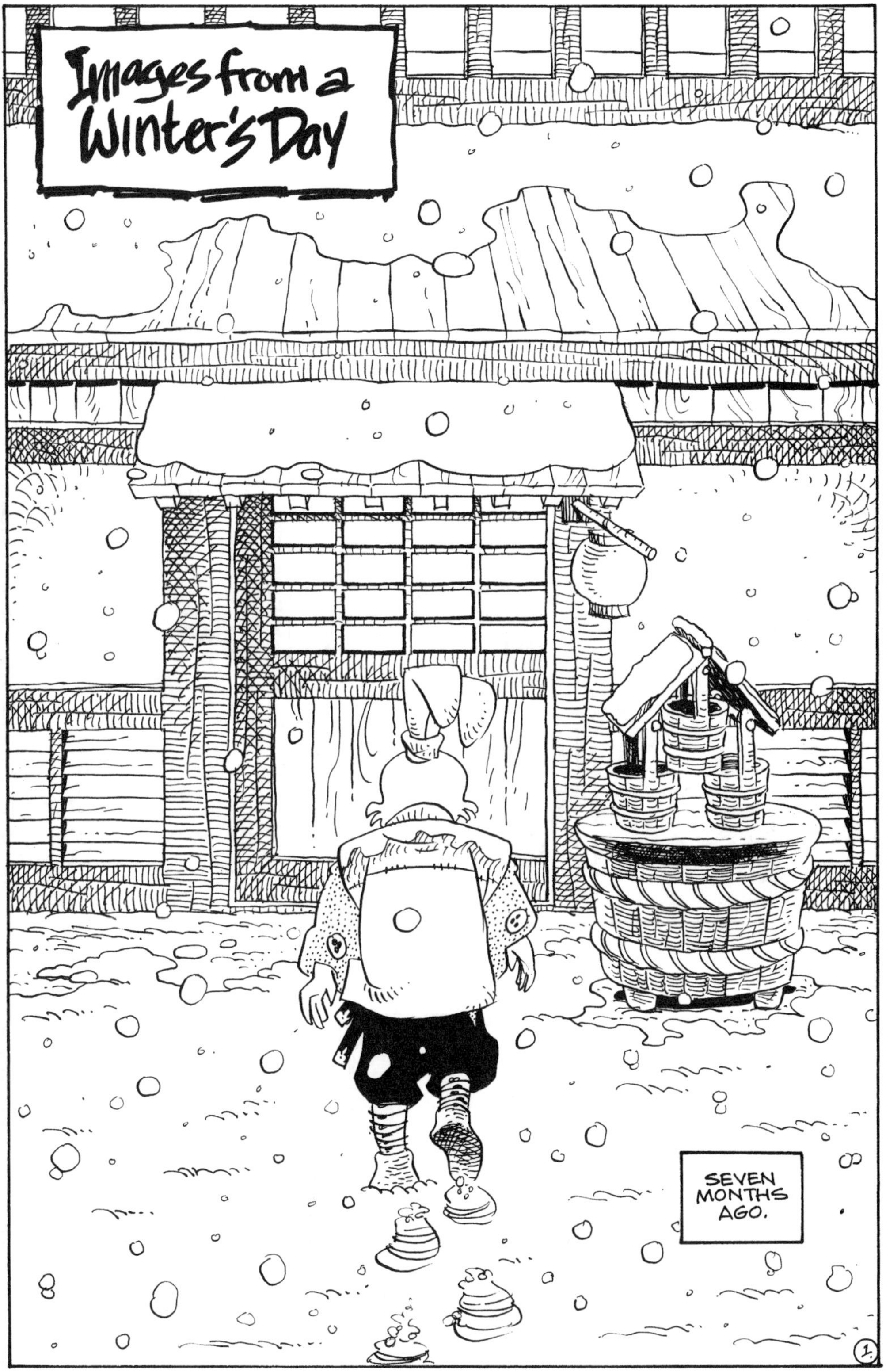
Images from a Winter's Day
SEVEN MONTHS AGO.

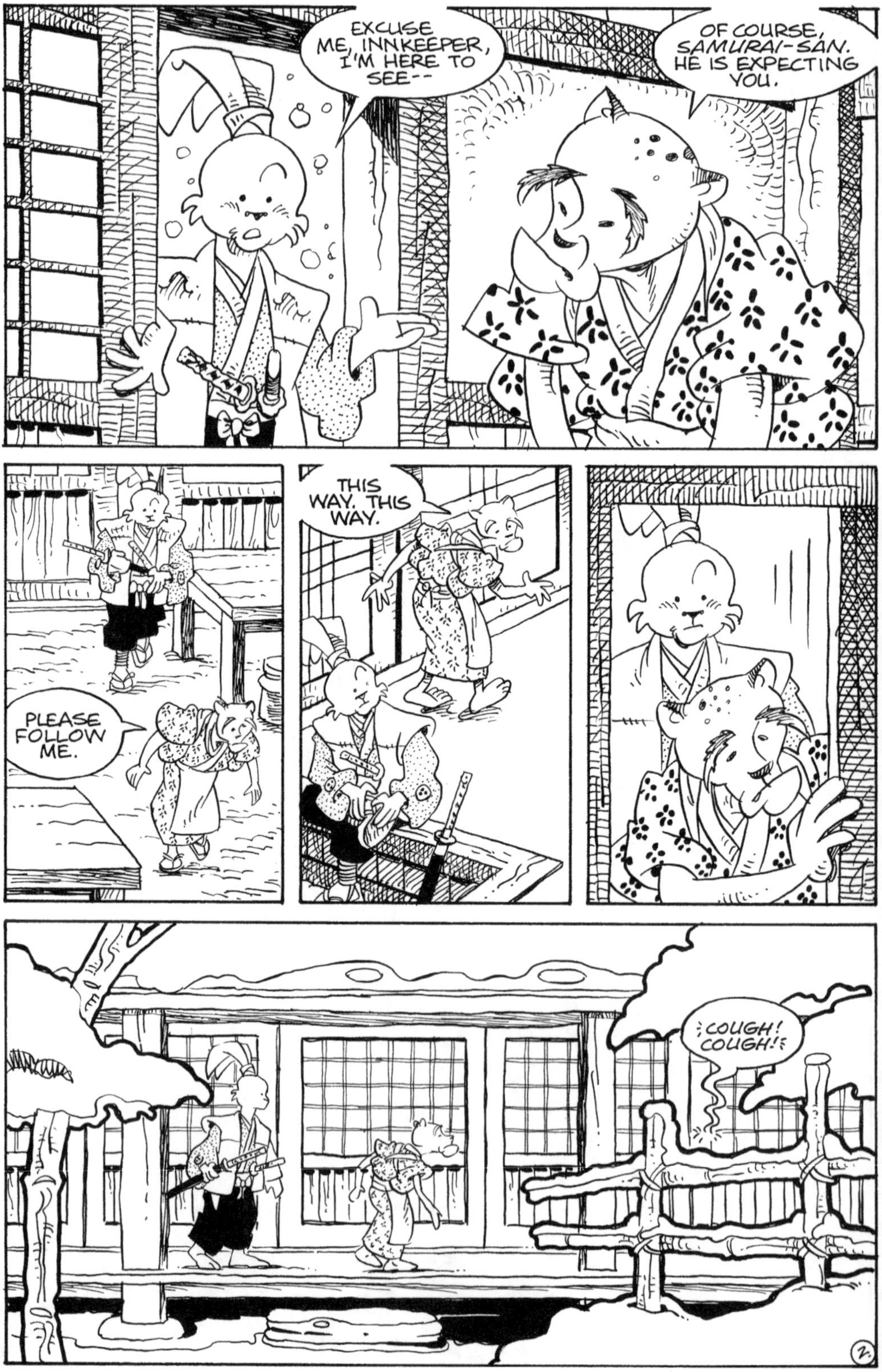
EXCUSE ME, INNKEEPER, I'M HERE TO SEE--
OF COURSE, SAMURAI-SAN. HE IS EXPECTING YOU.
PLEASE FOLLOW ME.
THIS WAY. THIS WAY.
COUGH! COUGH!
2.

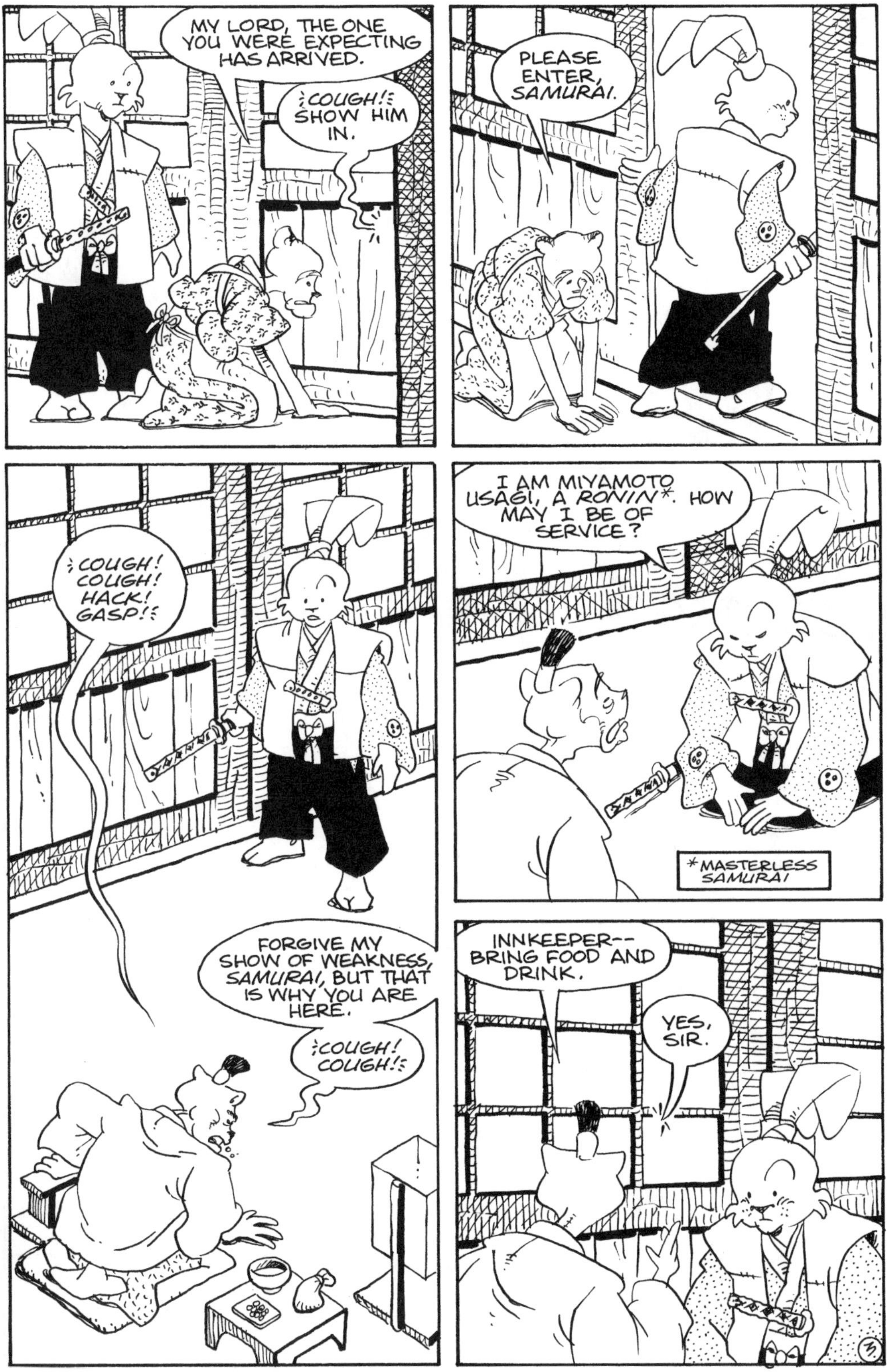
MY LORD, THE ONE YOU WERE EXPECTING HAS ARRIVED.
COUGH! SHOW HIM IN.
PLEASE ENTER, SAMURAI.
COUGH! COUGH! HACK! GASP!
FORGIVE MY SHOW OF WEAKNESS, SAMURAI, BUT THAT IS WHY YOU ARE HERE.
COUGH! COUGH!
I AM MIYAMOTO USAGI, A RONIN*. HOW MAY I BE OF SERVICE?
*MASTERLESS SAMURAI
INNKEEPER-- BRING FOOD AND DRINK.
YES, SIR.

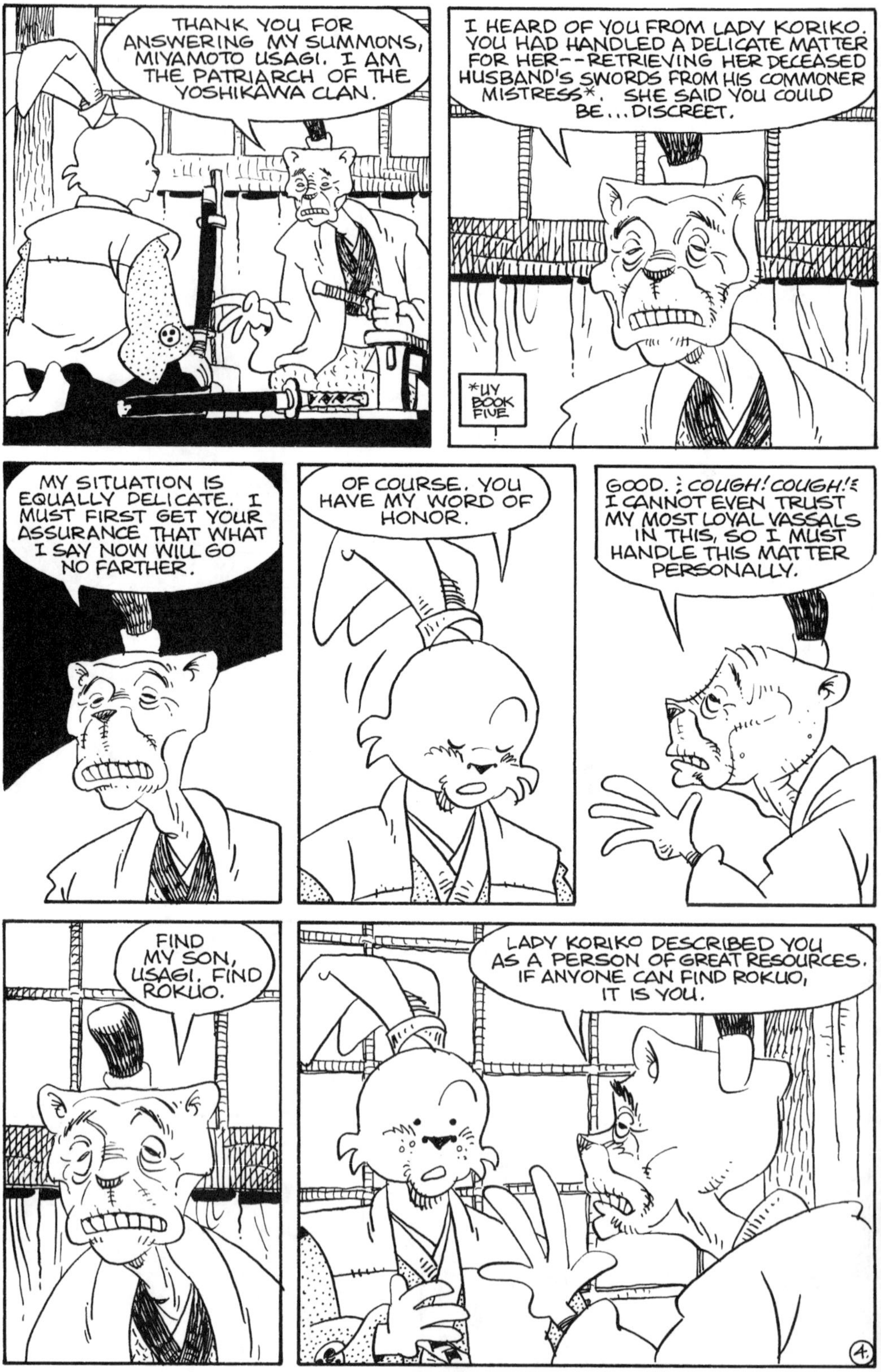

THANK YOU FOR ANSWERING MY SUMMONS, MIYAMOTO USAGI. I AM THE PATRIARCH OF THE YOSHIKAWA CLAN.
I HEARD OF YOU FROM LADY KORIKO. YOU HAD HANDLED A DELICATE MATTER FOR HER--RETRIEVING HER DECEASED HUSBAND'S SWORDS FROM HIS COMMONER MISTRESS*. SHE SAID YOU COULD BE...DISCREET.
*UY BOOK FIVE
MY SITUATION IS EQUALLY DELICATE. I MUST FIRST GET YOUR ASSURANCE THAT WHAT I SAY NOW WILL GO NO FARTHER.
OF COURSE. YOU HAVE MY WORD OF HONOR.
GOOD. COUGH! COUGH! I CANNOT EVEN TRUST MY MOST LOYAL VASSALS IN THIS, SO I MUST HANDLE THIS MATTER PERSONALLY.
FIND MY SON, USAGI. FIND ROKUO.
LADY KORIKO DESCRIBED YOU AS A PERSON OF GREAT RESOURCES. IF ANYONE CAN FIND ROKUO, IT IS YOU.
4

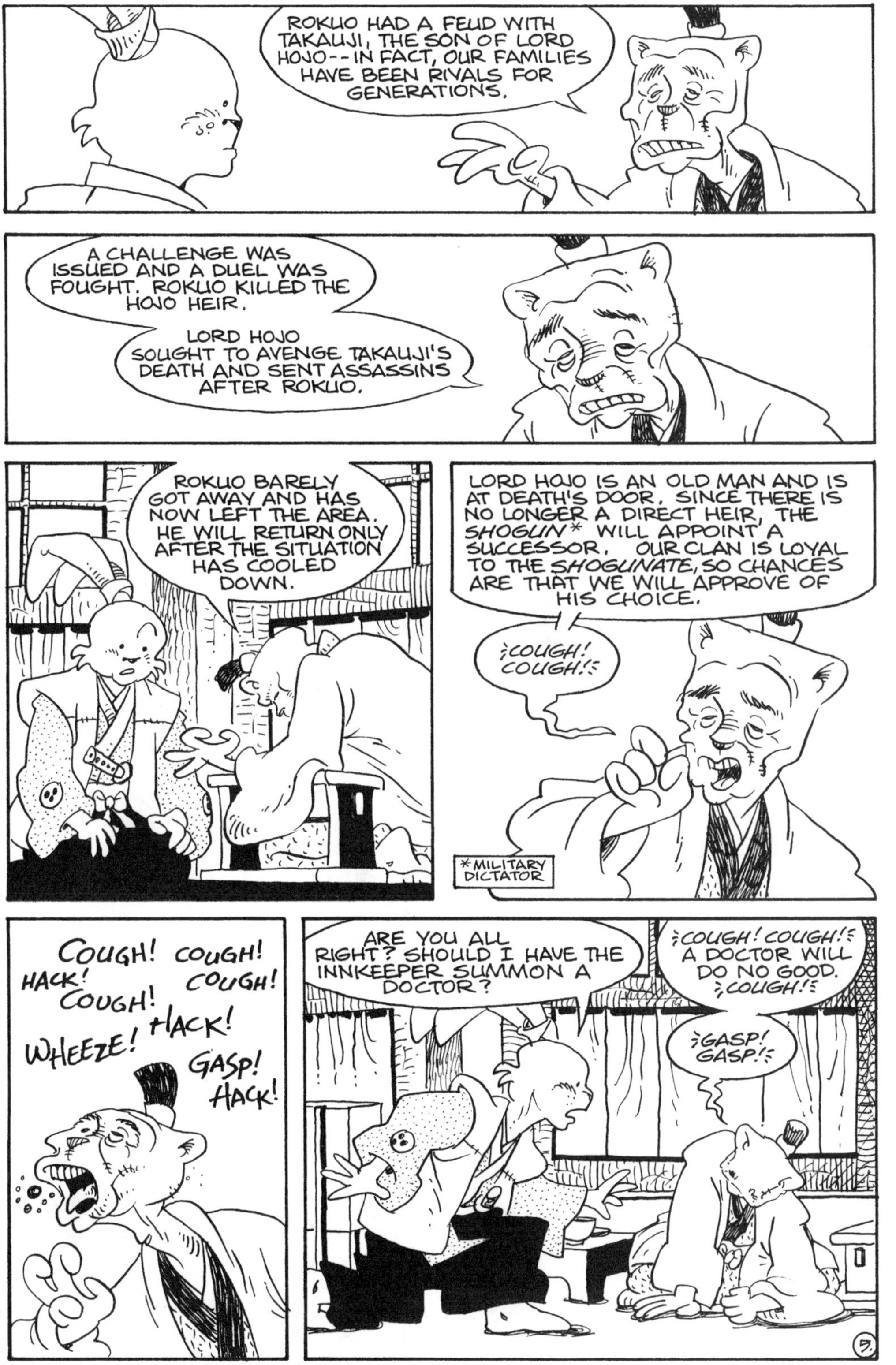
ROKUO HAD A FEUD WITH TAKAUJI, THE SON OF LORD HOJO--IN FACT, OUR FAMILIES HAVE BEEN RIVALS FOR GENERATIONS.
A CHALLENGE WAS ISSUED AND A DUEL WAS FOUGHT. ROKUO KILLED THE HOJO HEIR.
LORD HOJO SOUGHT TO AVENGE TAKAUJI'S DEATH AND SENT ASSASSINS AFTER ROKUO.
ROKUO BARELY GOT AWAY AND HAS NOW LEFT THE AREA. HE WILL RETURN ONLY AFTER THE SITUATION HAS COOLED DOWN.
LORD HOJO IS AN OLD MAN AND IS AT DEATH'S DOOR. SINCE THERE IS NO LONGER A DIRECT HEIR, THE SHOGUN* WILL APPOINT A SUCCESSOR. OUR CLAN IS LOYAL TO THE SHOGUNATE, SO CHANCES ARE THAT WE WILL APPROVE OF HIS CHOICE.
COUGH! COUGH!
*MILITARY DICTATOR
COUGH! COUGH! HACK! COUGH! COUGH! HACK! WHEEZE! GASP! HACK!
ARE YOU ALL RIGHT? SHOULD I HAVE THE INNKEEPER SUMMON A DOCTOR?
COUGH! COUGH! A DOCTOR WILL DO NO GOOD. COUGH!
GASP! GASP!
7.

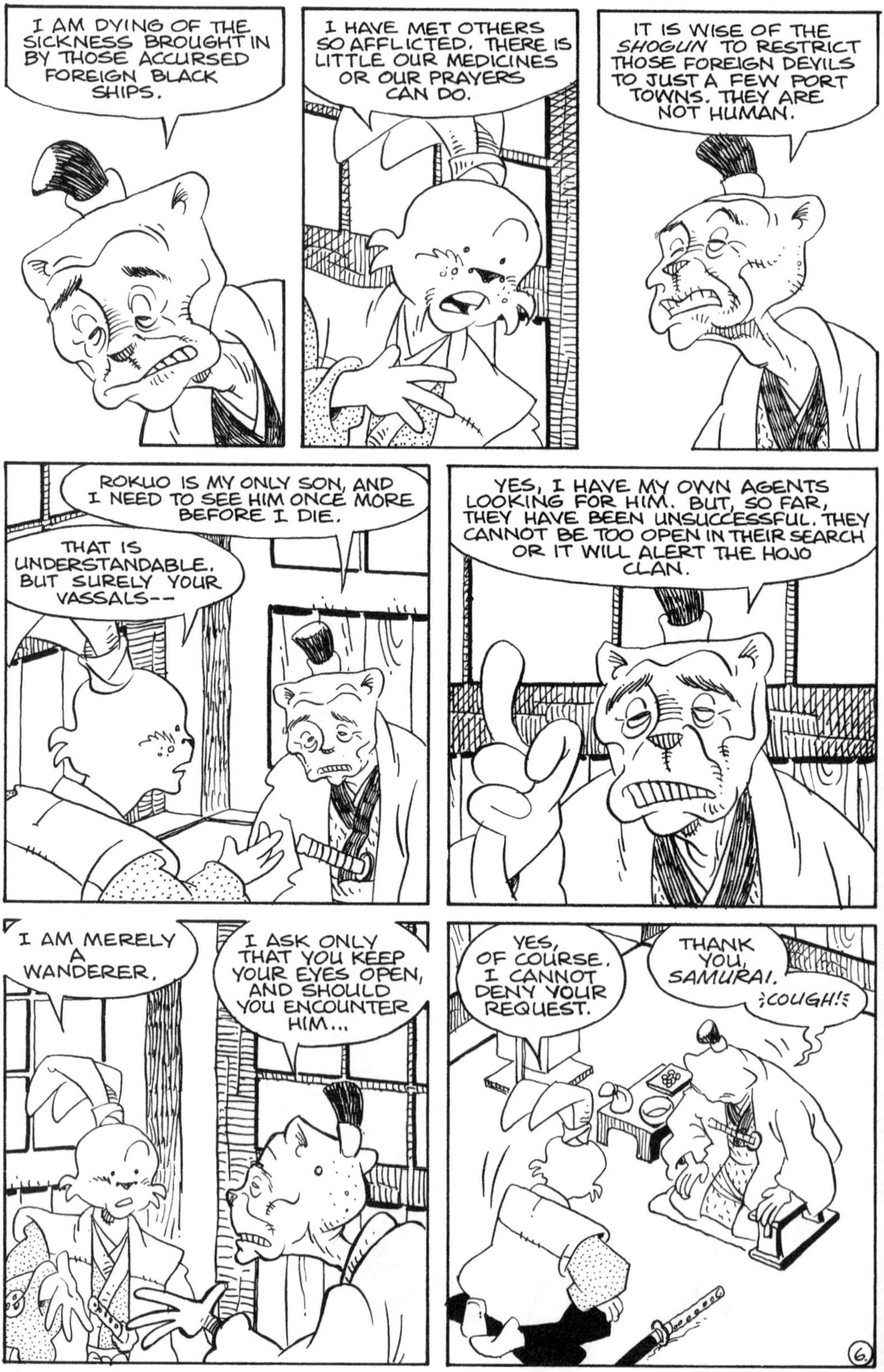
I AM DYING OF THE SICKNESS BROUGHT IN BY THOSE ACCURSED FOREIGN BLACK SHIPS.
I HAVE MET OTHERS SO AFFLICTED. THERE IS LITTLE OUR MEDICINES OR OUR PRAYERS CAN DO.
IT IS WISE OF THE *SHOGUN* TO RESTRICT THOSE FOREIGN DEVILS TO JUST A FEW PORT TOWNS. THEY ARE NOT HUMAN.
ROKUO IS MY ONLY SON, AND I NEED TO SEE HIM ONCE MORE BEFORE I DIE.
THAT IS UNDERSTANDABLE. BUT SURELY YOUR VASSALS--
YES, I HAVE MY OWN AGENTS LOOKING FOR HIM. BUT, SO FAR, THEY HAVE BEEN UNSUCCESSFUL. THEY CANNOT BE TOO OPEN IN THEIR SEARCH OR IT WILL ALERT THE HOJO CLAN.
I AM MERELY A WANDERER.
I ASK ONLY THAT YOU KEEP YOUR EYES OPEN, AND SHOULD YOU ENCOUNTER HIM...
YES, OF COURSE. I CANNOT DENY YOUR REQUEST.
THANK YOU, SAMURAI.
COUGH!
6.

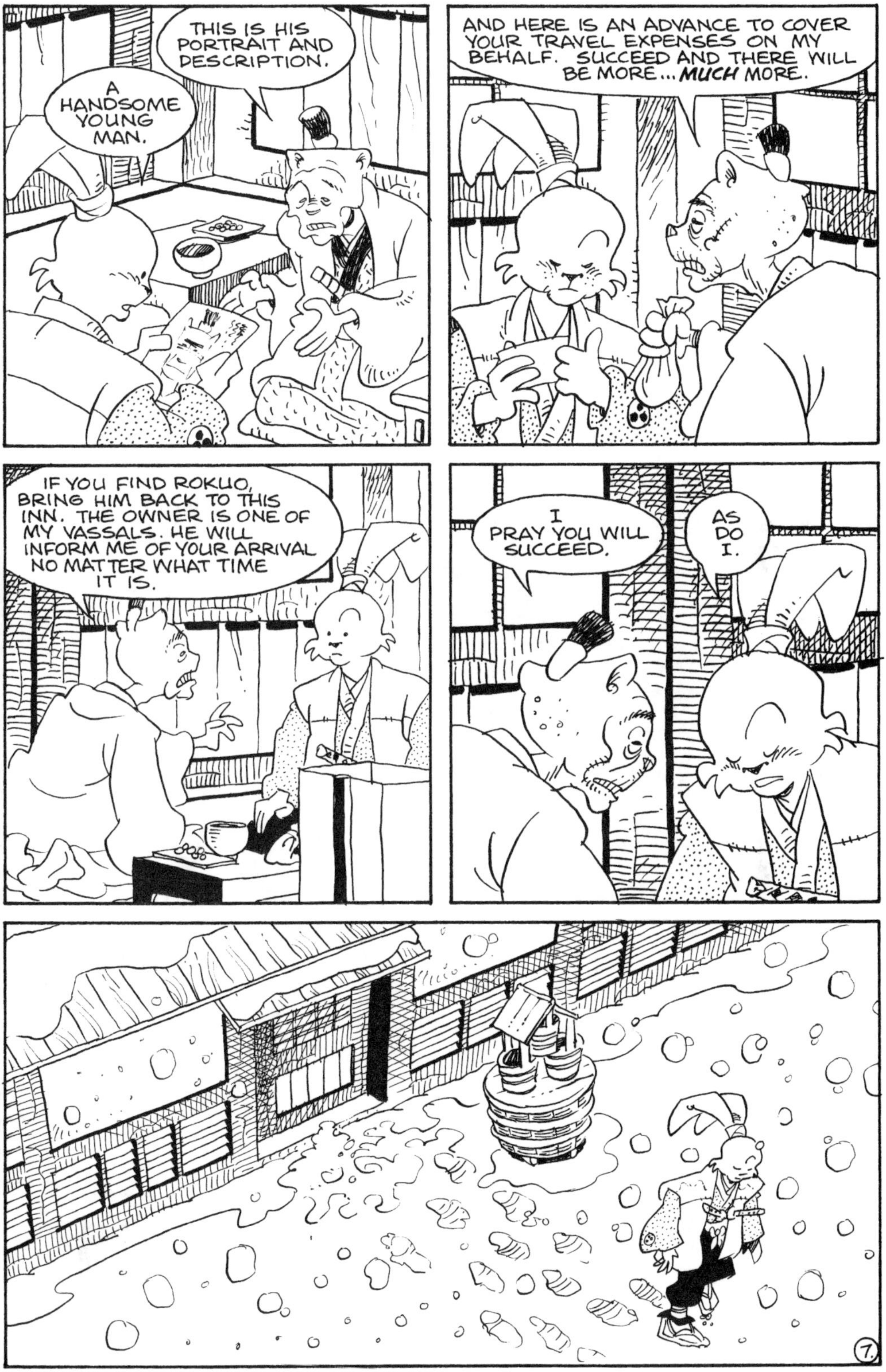
THIS IS HIS PORTRAIT AND DESCRIPTION.
A HANDSOME YOUNG MAN.
AND HERE IS AN ADVANCE TO COVER YOUR TRAVEL EXPENSES ON MY BEHALF. SUCCEED AND THERE WILL BE MORE... *MUCH* MORE.
IF YOU FIND ROKUO, BRING HIM BACK TO THIS INN. THE OWNER IS ONE OF MY VASSALS. HE WILL INFORM ME OF YOUR ARRIVAL NO MATTER WHAT TIME IT IS.
I PRAY YOU WILL SUCCEED.
AS DO I.
7.

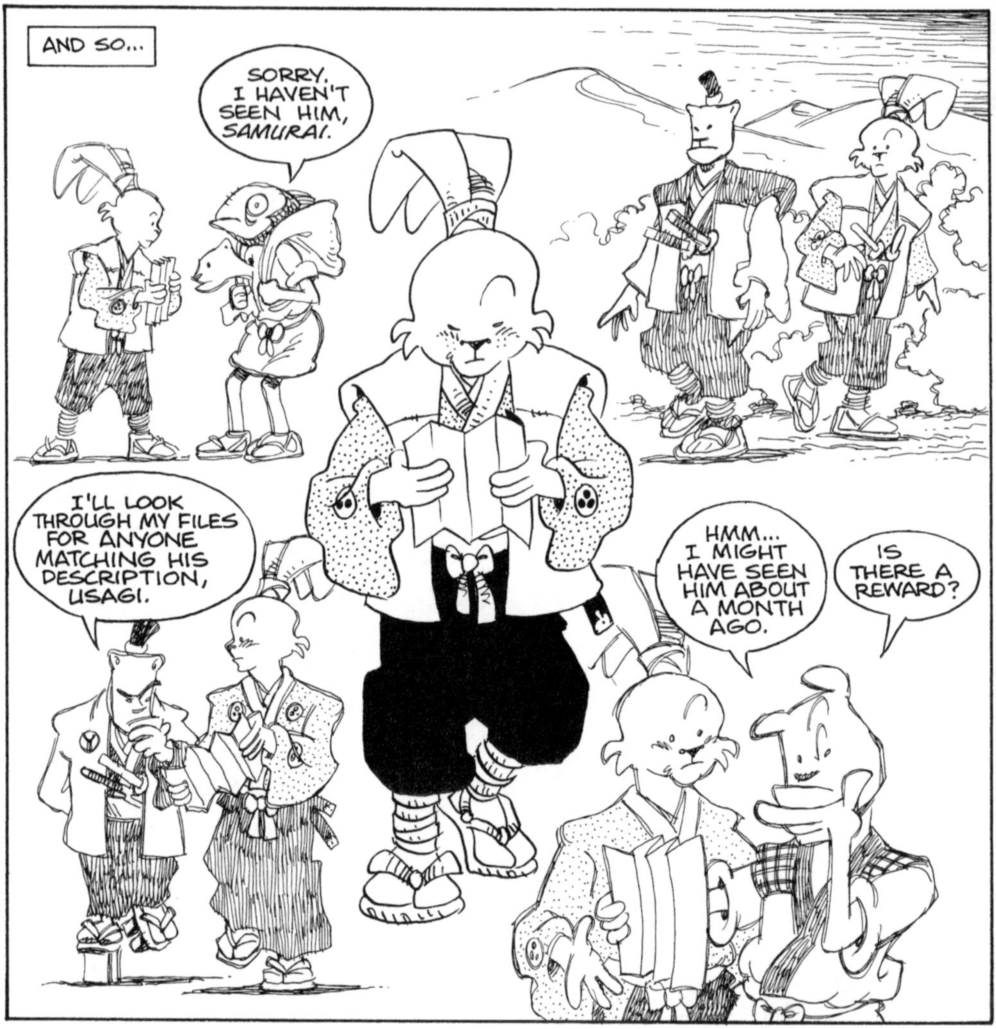
AND SO...
SORRY. I HAVEN'T SEEN HIM, SAMURAI.
I'LL LOOK THROUGH MY FILES FOR ANYONE MATCHING HIS DESCRIPTION, USAGI.
HMM... I MIGHT HAVE SEEN HIM ABOUT A MONTH AGO.
IS THERE A REWARD?

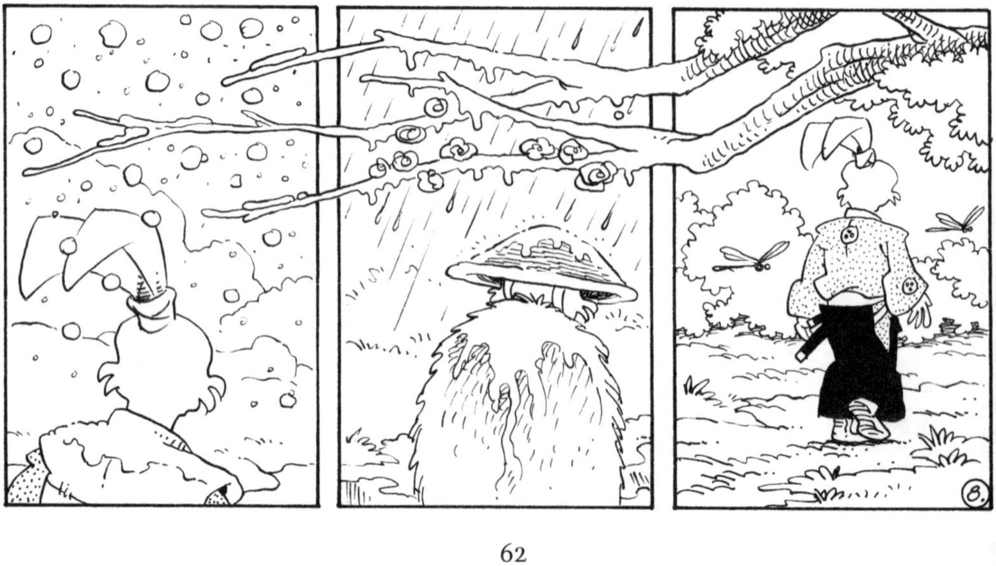
8.

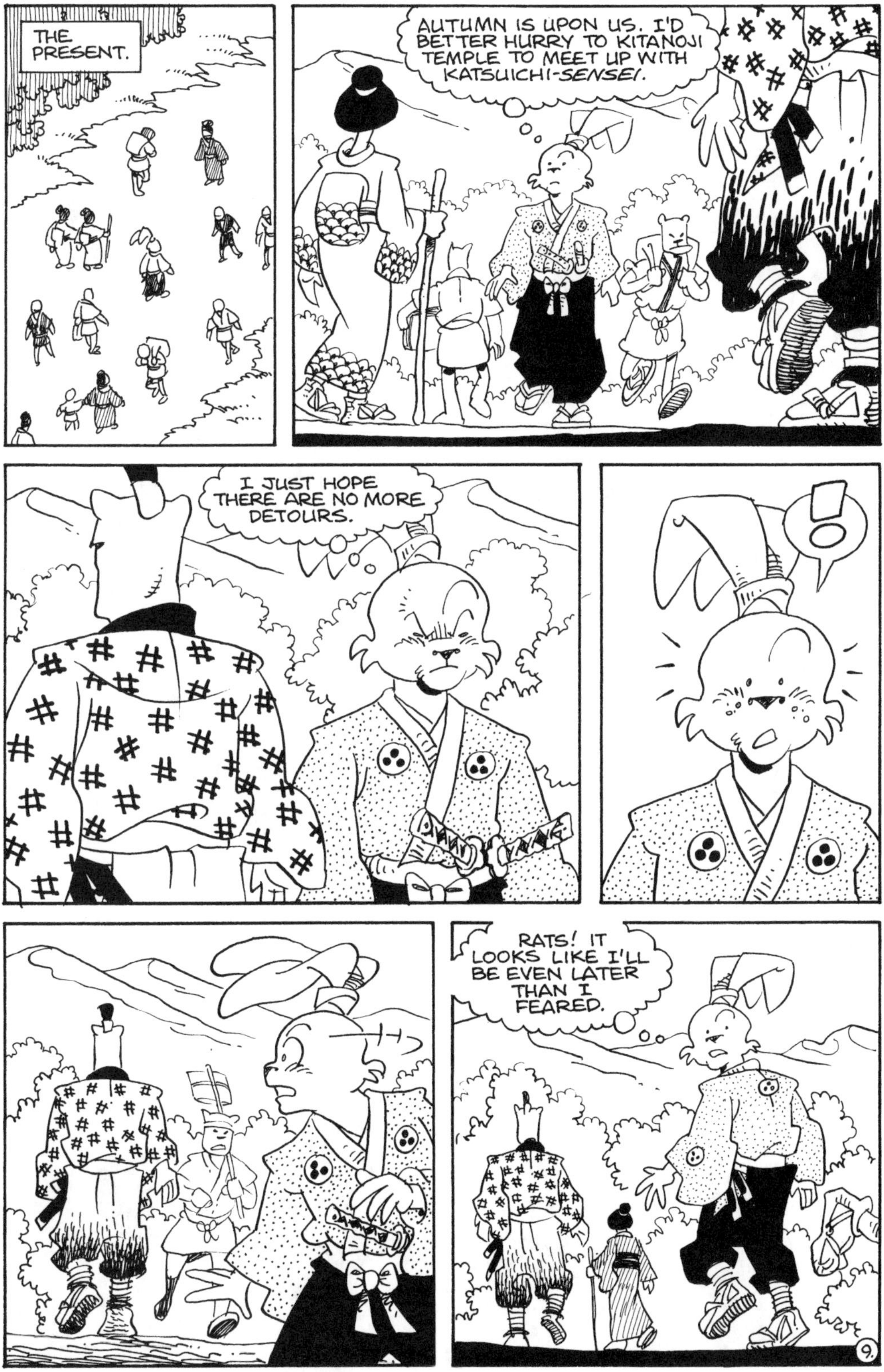
THE PRESENT.
AUTUMN IS UPON US. I'D BETTER HURRY TO KITANOJI TEMPLE TO MEET UP WITH KATSUICHI-SENSEI.
I JUST HOPE THERE ARE NO MORE DETOURS.
!
RATS! IT LOOKS LIKE I'LL BE EVEN LATER THAN I FEARED.
9.

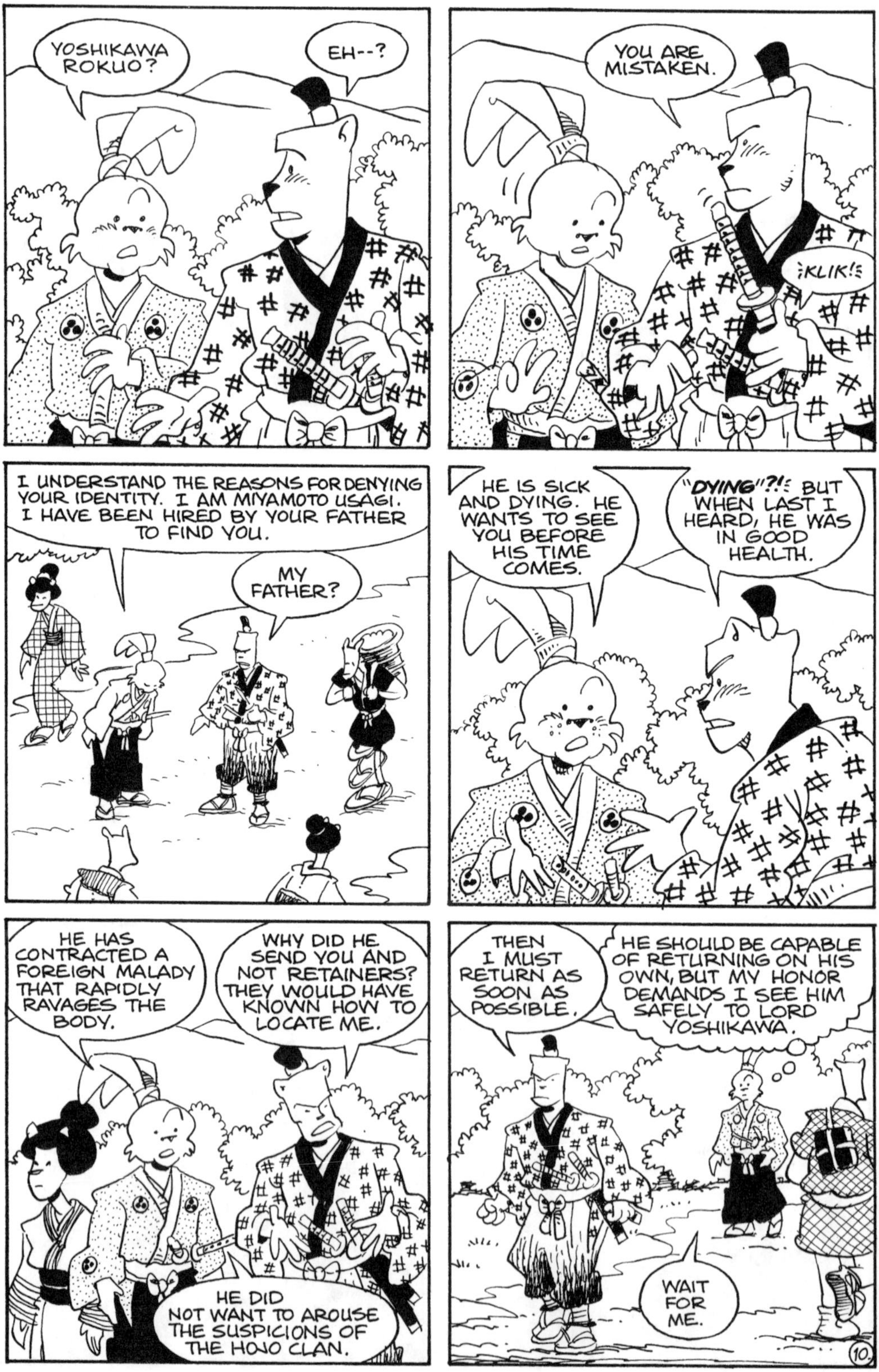
YOSHIKAWA ROKUO?
EH--?
YOU ARE MISTAKEN.
KLIK!
I UNDERSTAND THE REASONS FOR DENYING YOUR IDENTITY. I AM MIYAMOTO USAGI. I HAVE BEEN HIRED BY YOUR FATHER TO FIND YOU.
MY FATHER?
HE IS SICK AND DYING. HE WANTS TO SEE YOU BEFORE HIS TIME COMES.
"DYING"?! BUT WHEN LAST I HEARD, HE WAS IN GOOD HEALTH.
HE HAS CONTRACTED A FOREIGN MALADY THAT RAPIDLY RAVAGES THE BODY.
WHY DID HE SEND YOU AND NOT RETAINERS? THEY WOULD HAVE KNOWN HOW TO LOCATE ME.
HE DID NOT WANT TO AROUSE THE SUSPICIONS OF THE HOJO CLAN.
THEN I MUST RETURN AS SOON AS POSSIBLE.
HE SHOULD BE CAPABLE OF RETURNING ON HIS OWN, BUT MY HONOR DEMANDS I SEE HIM SAFELY TO LORD YOSHIKAWA.
WAIT FOR ME.
10.

DAYS PASS WITHOUT INCIDENT.

THE DANGER WILL BE GREATER AS WE NEAR YOUR BORDERS.

THOSE *SAMURAI* WEAR THE TRIPLE DIAMOND CREST OF THE HOJO CLAN.

GLUG! GLUG!

HEY! SAVE SOME OF THAT *SAKE** FOR US!

...SO I LOOKED UNDER THE COVERS...

THEY MUST HAVE NOTICED US. TO LEAVE THE ROAD NOW WOULD AROUSE THEIR SUSPICIONS. BETTER TO BRAZEN IT OUT.

*RICE WINE

...AND IT TURNED OUT TO BE A FISH!

HA! HA! HA! HA! HA! HA!

HA! HA! HA! HA!

HA! HA! HA! GLUG! GULP!

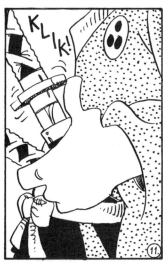

KLIK!

11

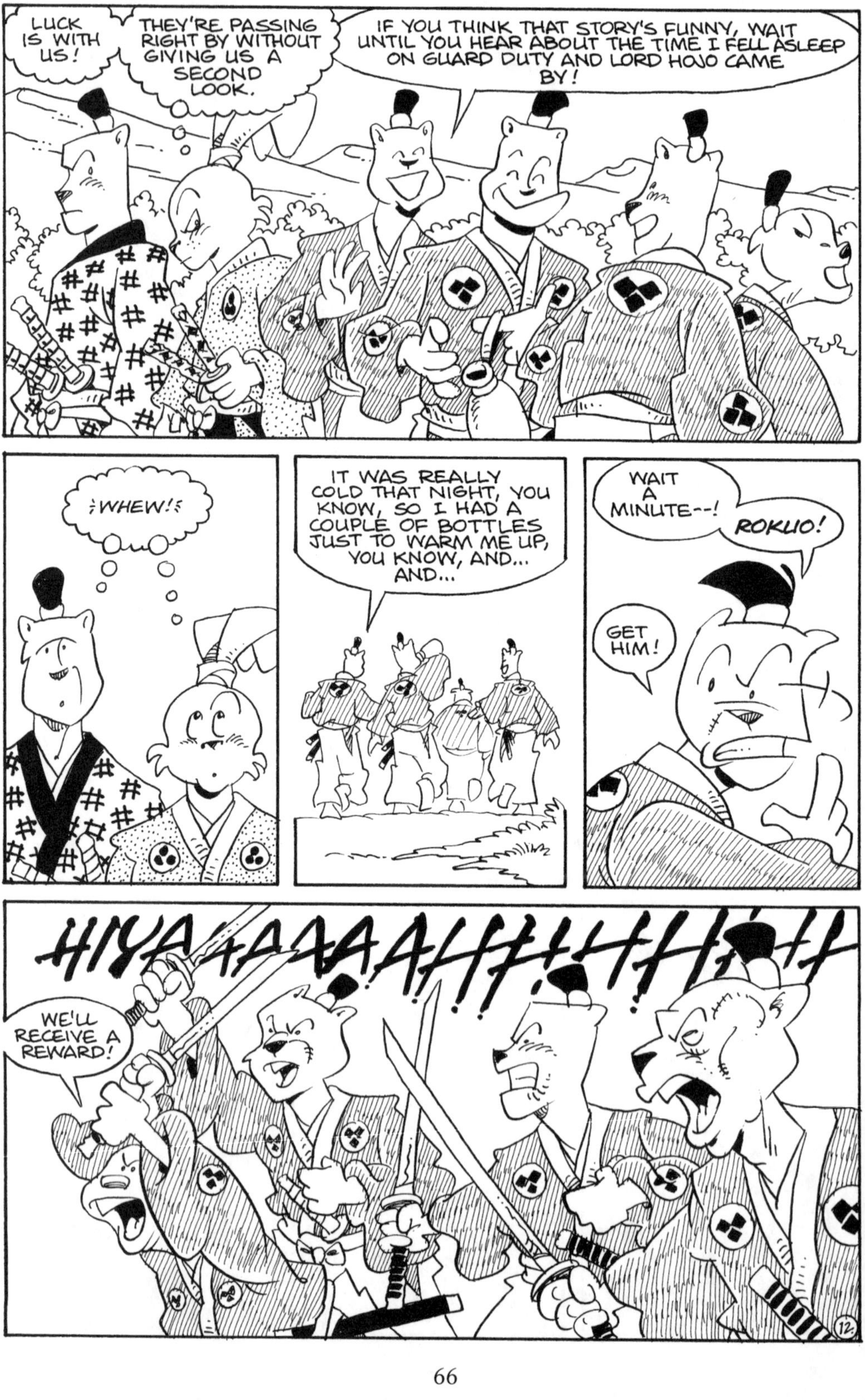
LUCK IS WITH US!
THEY'RE PASSING RIGHT BY WITHOUT GIVING US A SECOND LOOK.
IF YOU THINK THAT STORY'S FUNNY, WAIT UNTIL YOU HEAR ABOUT THE TIME I FELL ASLEEP ON GUARD DUTY AND LORD HOJO CAME BY!
WHEW!
IT WAS REALLY COLD THAT NIGHT, YOU KNOW, SO I HAD A COUPLE OF BOTTLES JUST TO WARM ME UP, YOU KNOW, AND... AND...
WAIT A MINUTE--!
ROKUO!
GET HIM!
HIYAAAAAAHHHHHHHH!!!
WE'LL RECEIVE A REWARD!
12.

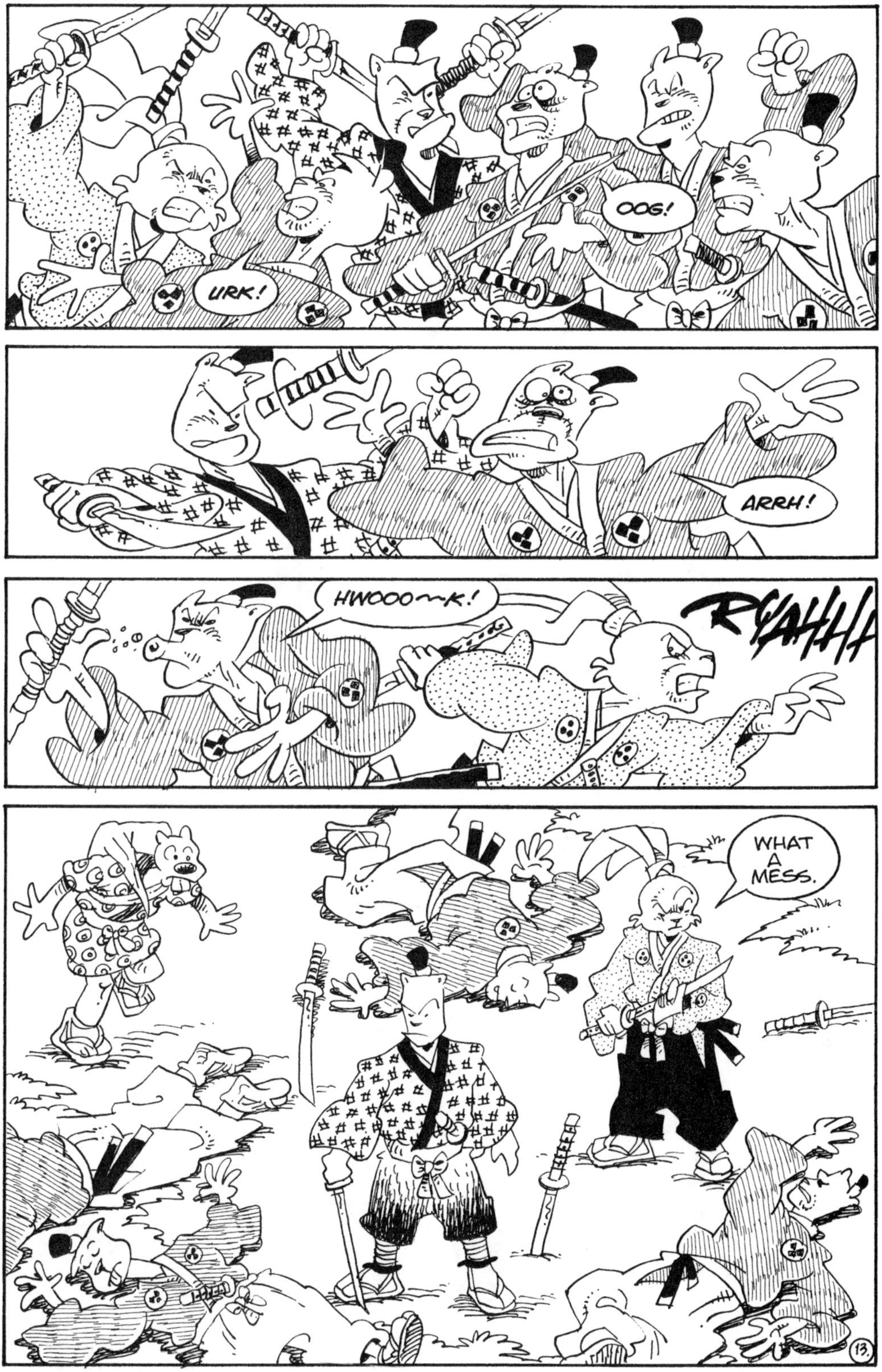
URK!
OOG!
ARRH!
HWOOO~K!
RYAHHA
WHAT A MESS.
13.

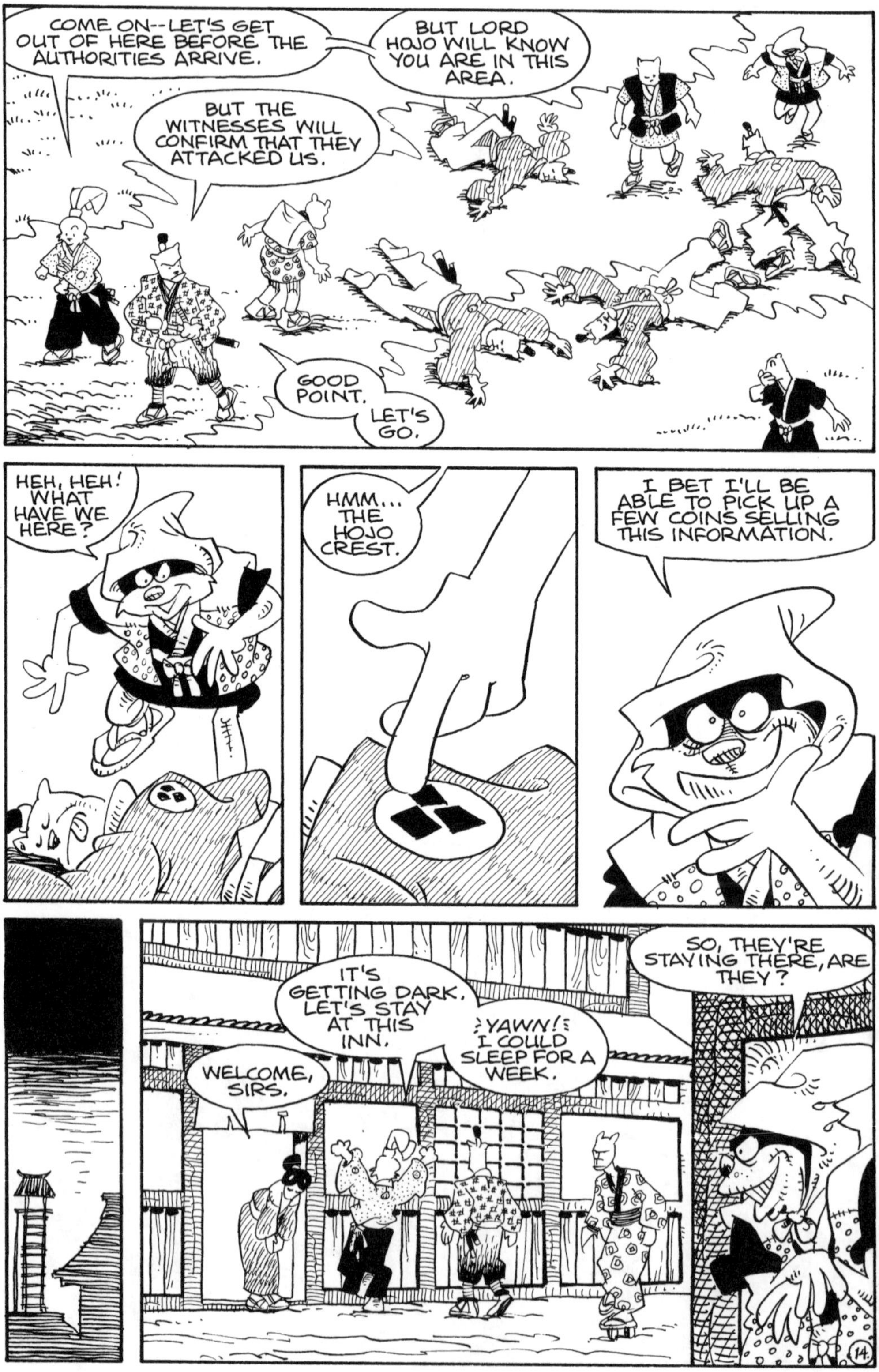
COME ON--LET'S GET OUT OF HERE BEFORE THE AUTHORITIES ARRIVE.
BUT LORD HOJO WILL KNOW YOU ARE IN THIS AREA.
BUT THE WITNESSES WILL CONFIRM THAT THEY ATTACKED US.
GOOD POINT.
LET'S GO.
HEH, HEH! WHAT HAVE WE HERE?
HMM... THE HOJO CREST.
I BET I'LL BE ABLE TO PICK UP A FEW COINS SELLING THIS INFORMATION.
IT'S GETTING DARK. LET'S STAY AT THIS INN.
WELCOME, SIRS.
YAWN! I COULD SLEEP FOR A WEEK.
SO, THEY'RE STAYING THERE, ARE THEY?
14.

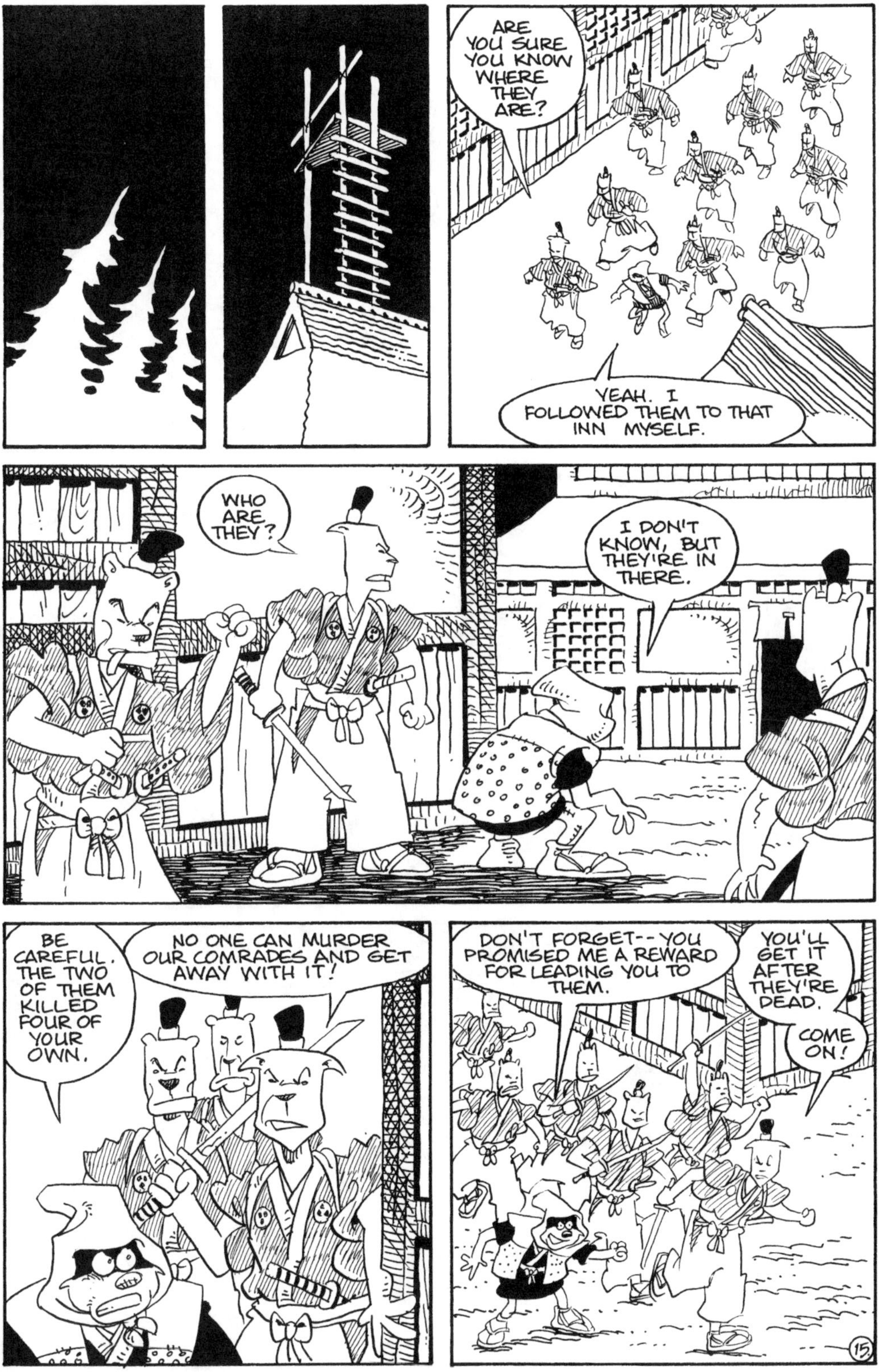
ARE YOU SURE YOU KNOW WHERE THEY ARE?
YEAH. I FOLLOWED THEM TO THAT INN MYSELF.
WHO ARE THEY?
I DON'T KNOW, BUT THEY'RE IN THERE.
BE CAREFUL. THE TWO OF THEM KILLED FOUR OF YOUR OWN.
NO ONE CAN MURDER OUR COMRADES AND GET AWAY WITH IT!
DON'T FORGET-- YOU PROMISED ME A REWARD FOR LEADING YOU TO THEM.
YOU'LL GET IT AFTER THEY'RE DEAD.
COME ON!
15

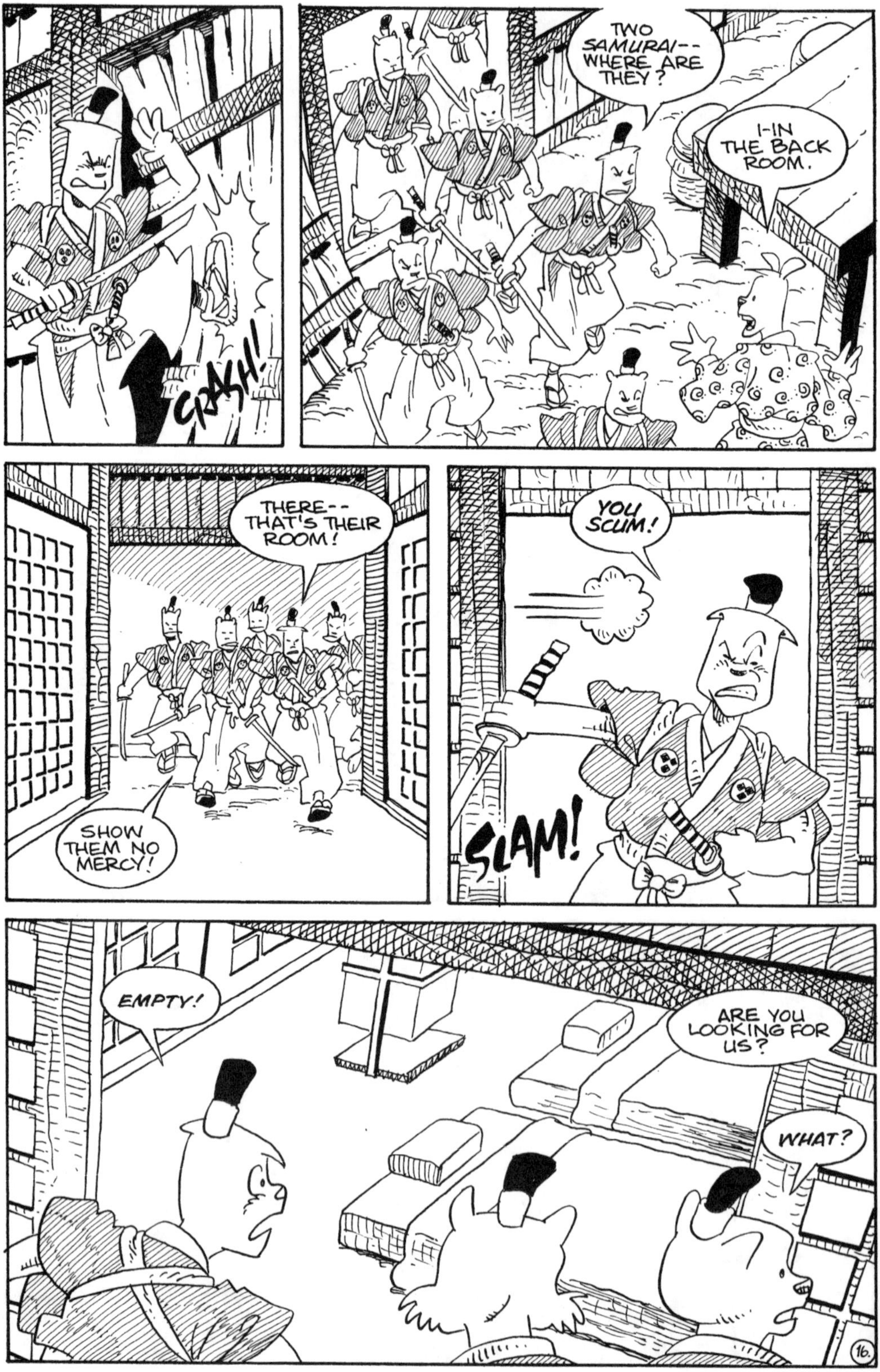
CRASH!
TWO SAMURAI-- WHERE ARE THEY?
I-IN THE BACK ROOM.
THERE-- THAT'S THEIR ROOM!
SHOW THEM NO MERCY!
YOU SCUM!
SLAM!
EMPTY!
ARE YOU LOOKING FOR US?
WHAT?
16.

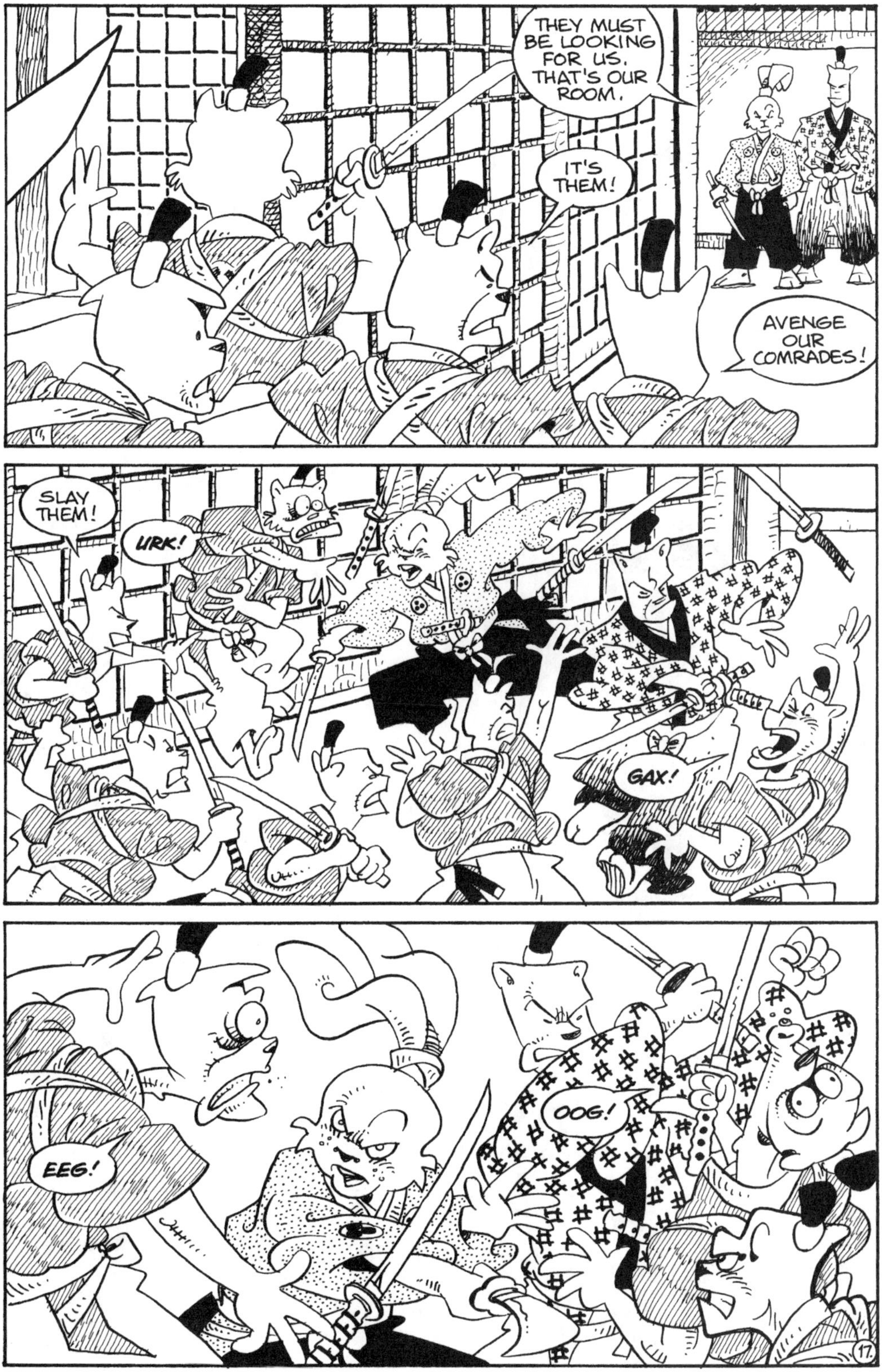
THEY MUST BE LOOKING FOR US. THAT'S OUR ROOM.
IT'S THEM!
AVENGE OUR COMRADES!
SLAY THEM!
URK!
GAX!
EEG!
OOG!
17.

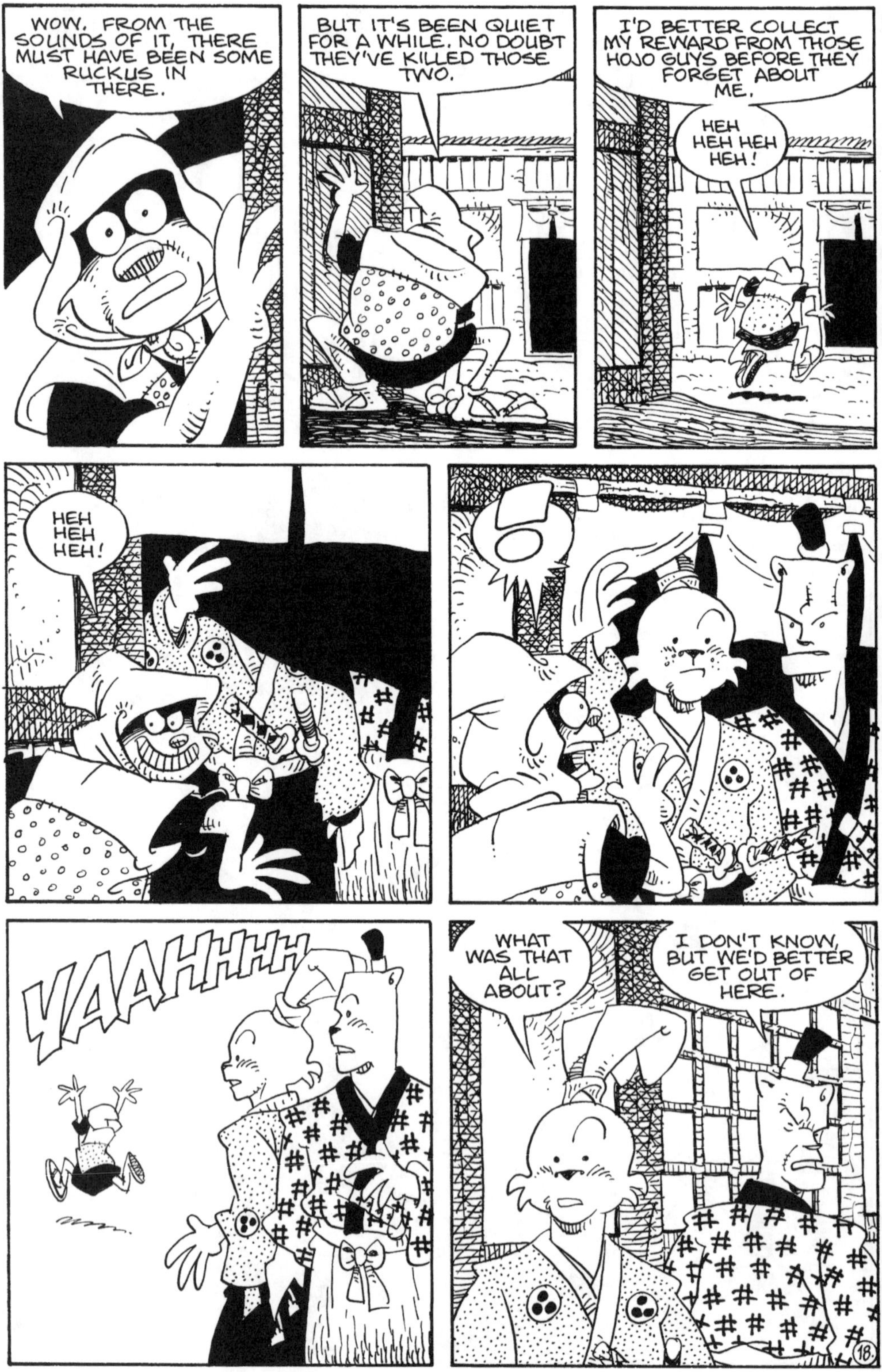
WOW. FROM THE SOUNDS OF IT, THERE MUST HAVE BEEN SOME RUCKUS IN THERE.
BUT IT'S BEEN QUIET FOR A WHILE. NO DOUBT THEY'VE KILLED THOSE TWO.
I'D BETTER COLLECT MY REWARD FROM THOSE HOJO GUYS BEFORE THEY FORGET ABOUT ME.
HEH HEH HEH HEH!
HEH HEH HEH!
YAAHHHH
WHAT WAS THAT ALL ABOUT?
I DON'T KNOW, BUT WE'D BETTER GET OUT OF HERE.
18

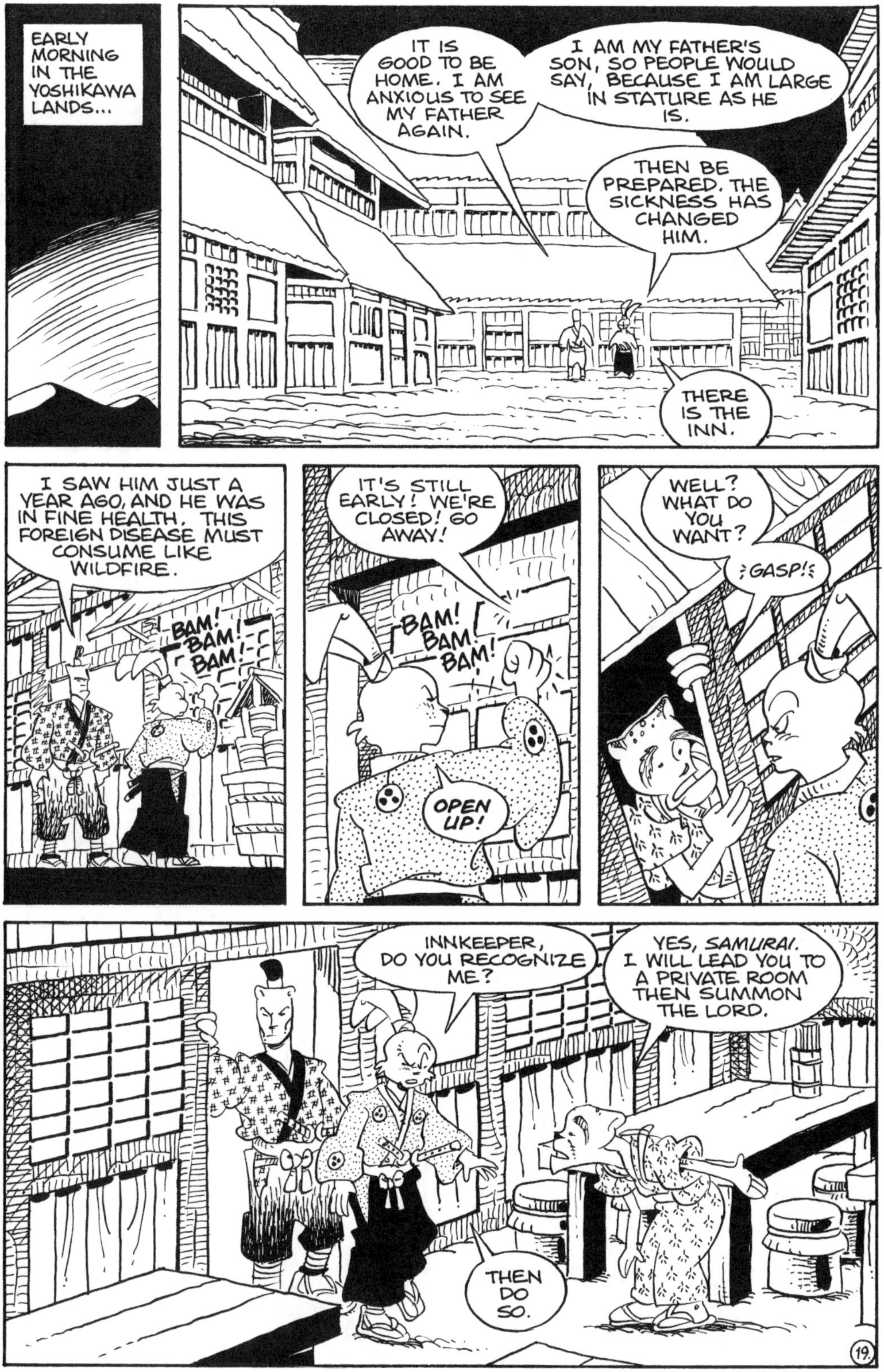
EARLY MORNING IN THE YOSHIKAWA LANDS...
IT IS GOOD TO BE HOME. I AM ANXIOUS TO SEE MY FATHER AGAIN.
I AM MY FATHER'S SON, SO PEOPLE WOULD SAY, BECAUSE I AM LARGE IN STATURE AS HE IS.
THEN BE PREPARED. THE SICKNESS HAS CHANGED HIM.
THERE IS THE INN.
I SAW HIM JUST A YEAR AGO, AND HE WAS IN FINE HEALTH. THIS FOREIGN DISEASE MUST CONSUME LIKE WILDFIRE.
BAM! BAM! BAM!
IT'S STILL EARLY! WE'RE CLOSED! GO AWAY!
BAM! BAM! BAM!
OPEN UP!
WELL? WHAT DO YOU WANT?
GASP!
INNKEEPER, DO YOU RECOGNIZE ME?
YES, SAMURAI. I WILL LEAD YOU TO A PRIVATE ROOM THEN SUMMON THE LORD.
THEN DO SO.
19

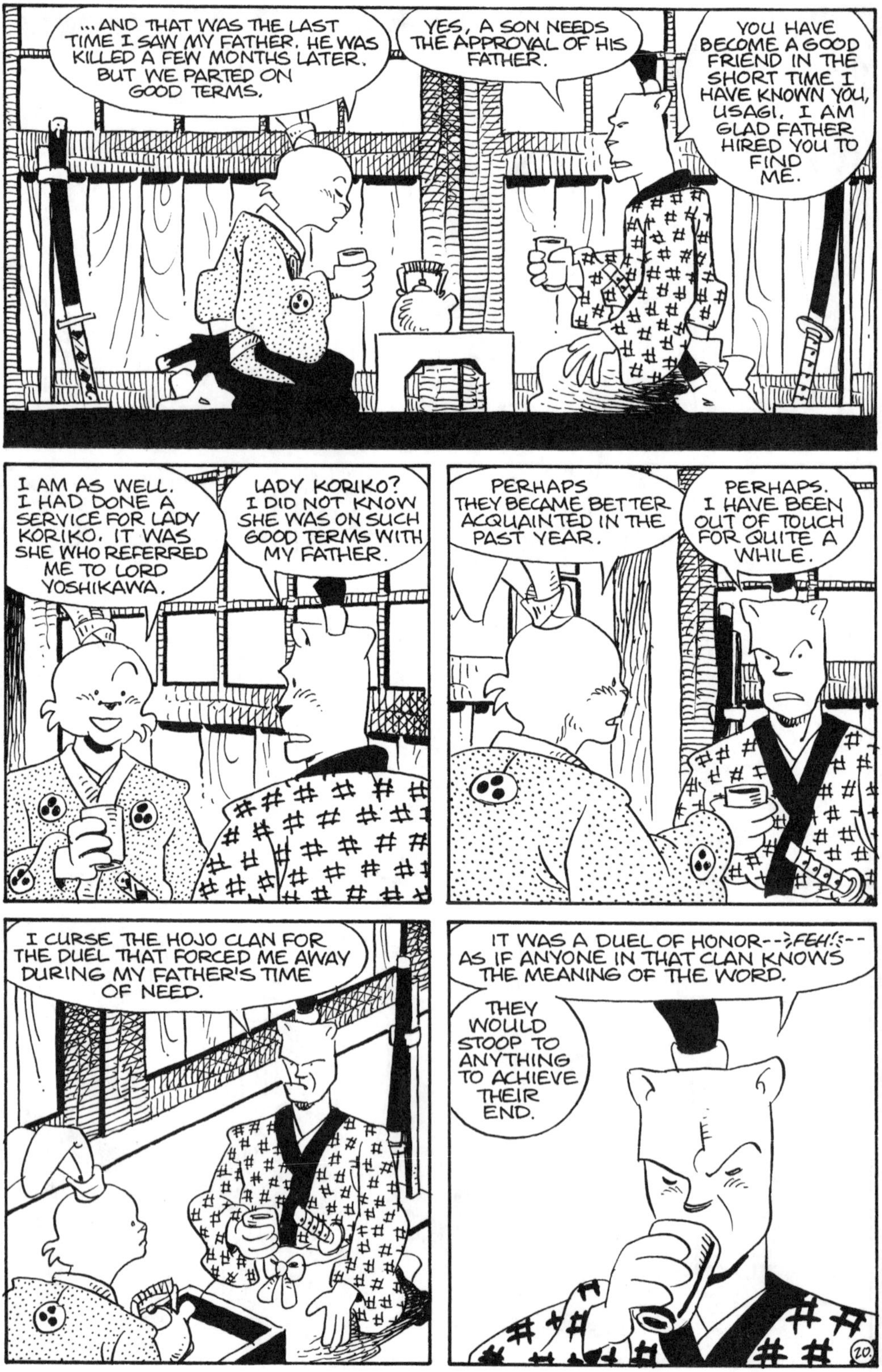
...AND THAT WAS THE LAST TIME I SAW MY FATHER. HE WAS KILLED A FEW MONTHS LATER. BUT WE PARTED ON GOOD TERMS.
YES, A SON NEEDS THE APPROVAL OF HIS FATHER.
YOU HAVE BECOME A GOOD FRIEND IN THE SHORT TIME I HAVE KNOWN YOU, USAGI. I AM GLAD FATHER HIRED YOU TO FIND ME.
I AM AS WELL. I HAD DONE A SERVICE FOR LADY KORIKO. IT WAS SHE WHO REFERRED ME TO LORD YOSHIKAWA.
LADY KORIKO? I DID NOT KNOW SHE WAS ON SUCH GOOD TERMS WITH MY FATHER.
PERHAPS THEY BECAME BETTER ACQUAINTED IN THE PAST YEAR.
PERHAPS. I HAVE BEEN OUT OF TOUCH FOR QUITE A WHILE.
I CURSE THE HOJO CLAN FOR THE DUEL THAT FORCED ME AWAY DURING MY FATHER'S TIME OF NEED.
IT WAS A DUEL OF HONOR-- FEH!-- AS IF ANYONE IN THAT CLAN KNOWS THE MEANING OF THE WORD.
THEY WOULD STOOP TO ANYTHING TO ACHIEVE THEIR END.
20.

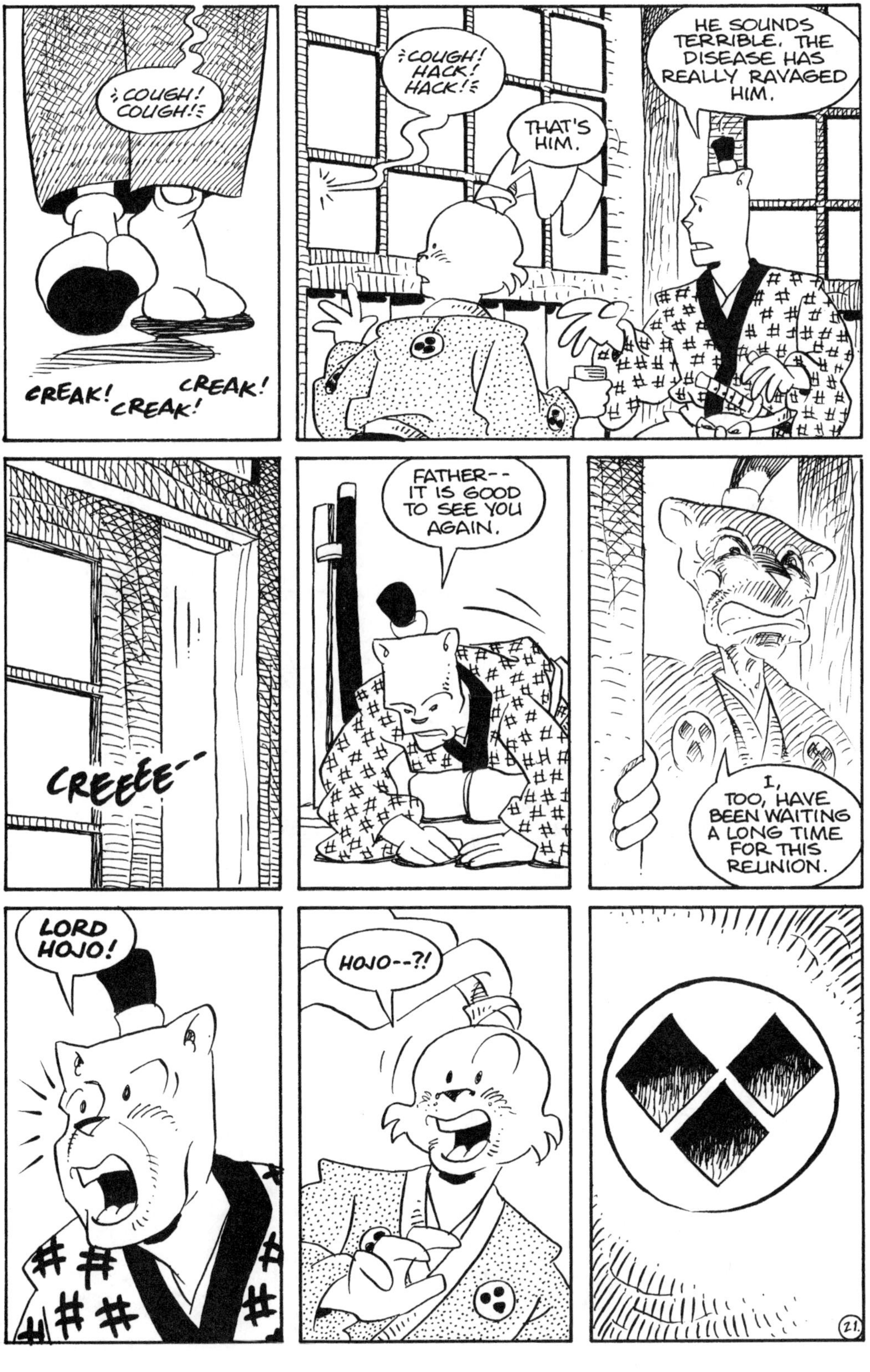
COUGH! COUGH!
CREAK! CREAK! CREAK!
COUGH! HACK! HACK!
THAT'S HIM.
HE SOUNDS TERRIBLE. THE DISEASE HAS REALLY RAVAGED HIM.
CREEEE--
FATHER-- IT IS GOOD TO SEE YOU AGAIN.
I, TOO, HAVE BEEN WAITING A LONG TIME FOR THIS REUNION.
LORD HOJO!
HOJO--?!
21.

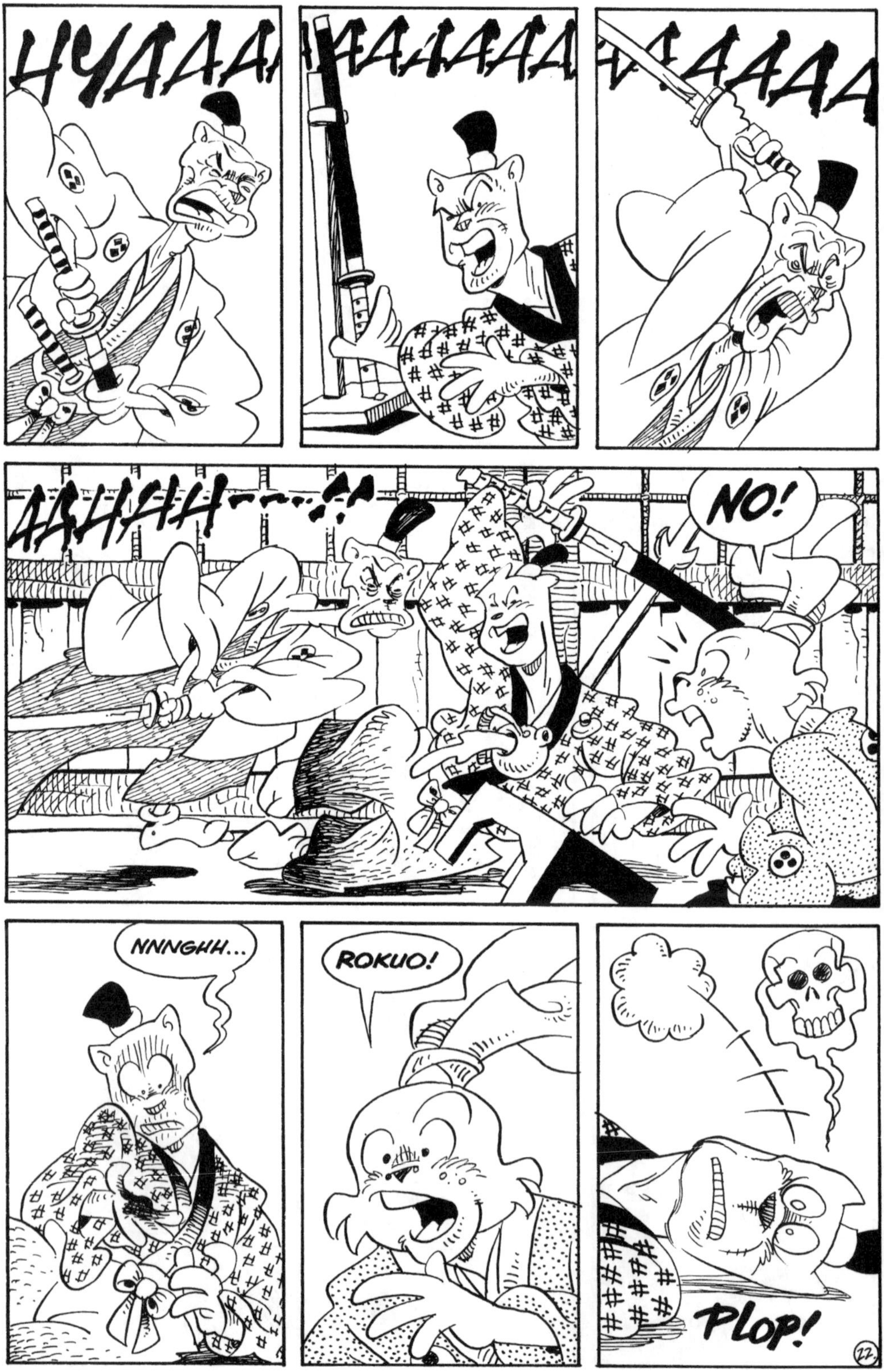
HYAAAAAAAAAAAAAAAAAAAAAAAAAHHH---!!
NO!
NNNGHH...
ROKUO!
PLOP!
22

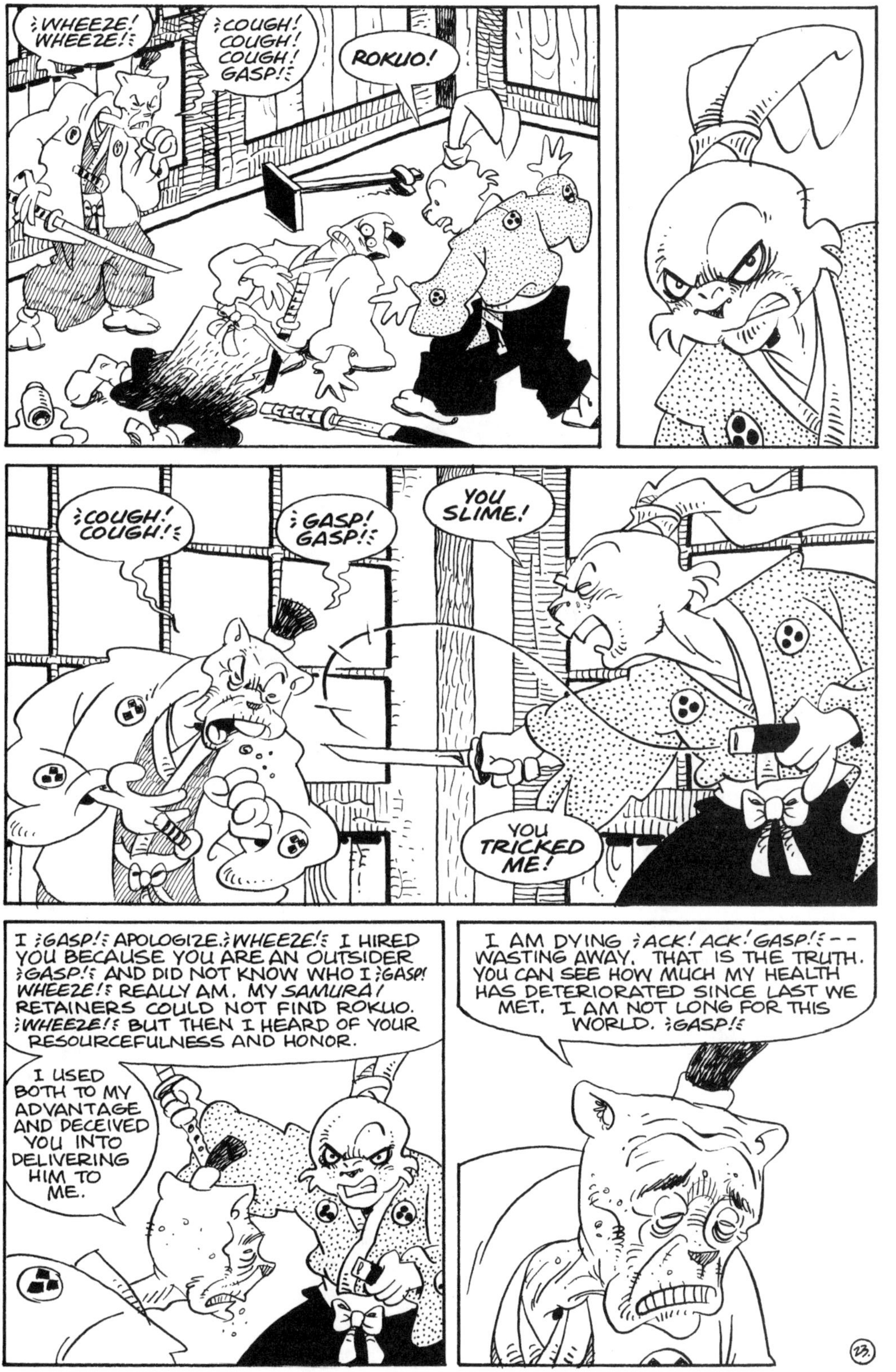
WHEEZE! WHEEZE!
COUGH! COUGH! COUGH! GASP!
ROKUO!
COUGH! COUGH!
GASP! GASP!
YOU SLIME!
YOU TRICKED ME!
I GASP! APOLOGIZE. WHEEZE! I HIRED YOU BECAUSE YOU ARE AN OUTSIDER GASP! AND DID NOT KNOW WHO I GASP! WHEEZE! REALLY AM. MY SAMURAI RETAINERS COULD NOT FIND ROKUO. WHEEZE! BUT THEN I HEARD OF YOUR RESOURCEFULNESS AND HONOR.
I USED BOTH TO MY ADVANTAGE AND DECEIVED YOU INTO DELIVERING HIM TO ME.
I AM DYING ACK! ACK! GASP! -- WASTING AWAY. THAT IS THE TRUTH. YOU CAN SEE HOW MUCH MY HEALTH HAS DETERIORATED SINCE LAST WE MET. I AM NOT LONG FOR THIS WORLD. GASP!
23.

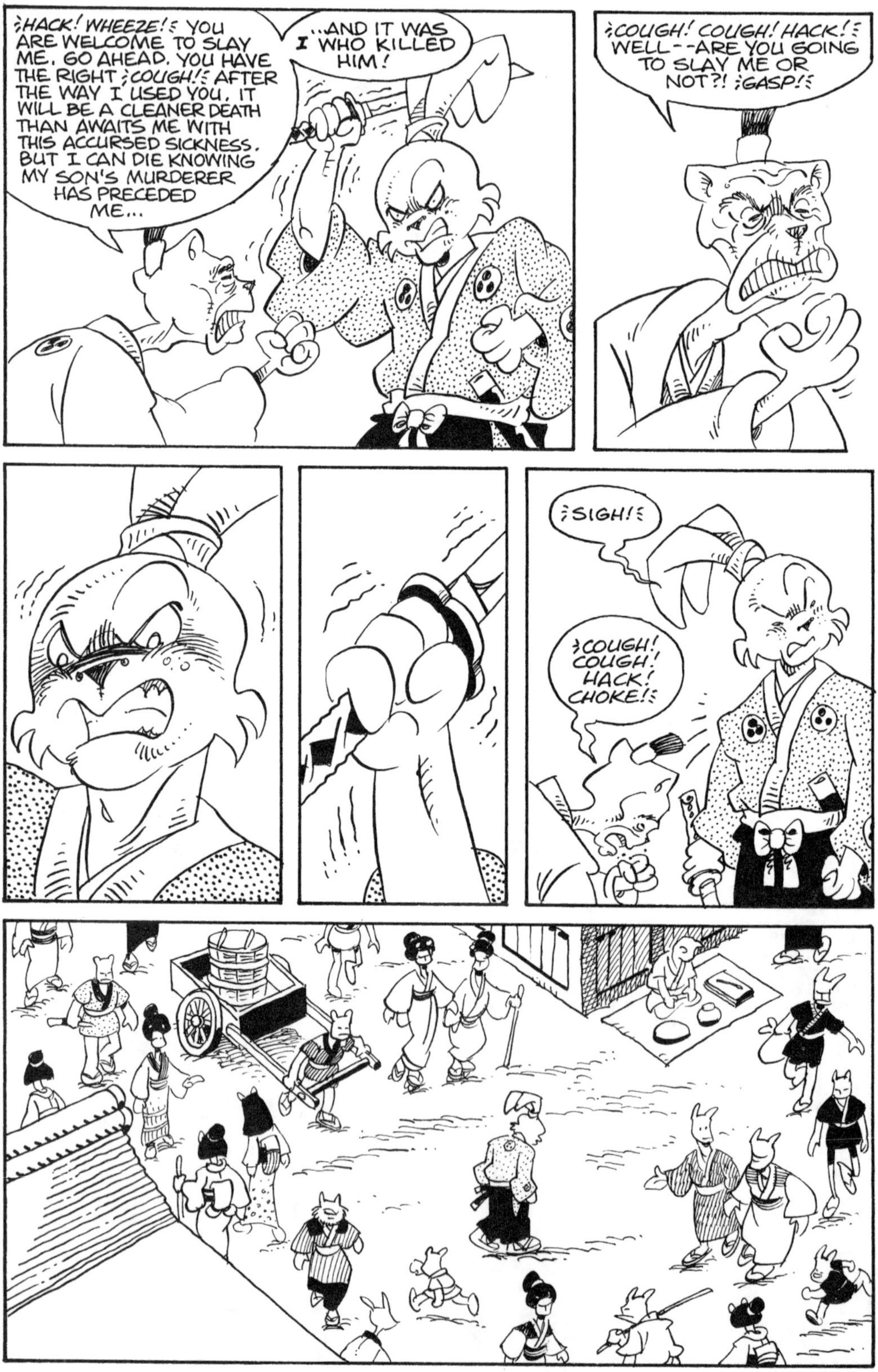

;HACK! WHEEZE!; YOU ARE WELCOME TO SLAY ME. GO AHEAD. YOU HAVE THE RIGHT ;COUGH!; AFTER THE WAY I USED YOU, IT WILL BE A CLEANER DEATH THAN AWAITS ME WITH THIS ACCURSED SICKNESS. BUT I CAN DIE KNOWING MY SON'S MURDERER HAS PRECEDED ME...
...AND IT WAS I WHO KILLED HIM!
;COUGH! COUGH! HACK!; WELL--ARE YOU GOING TO SLAY ME OR NOT?! ;GASP!;
;SIGH!;
;COUGH! COUGH! HACK! CHOKE!;

THE END.

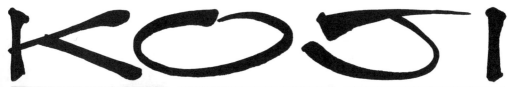

KOJI

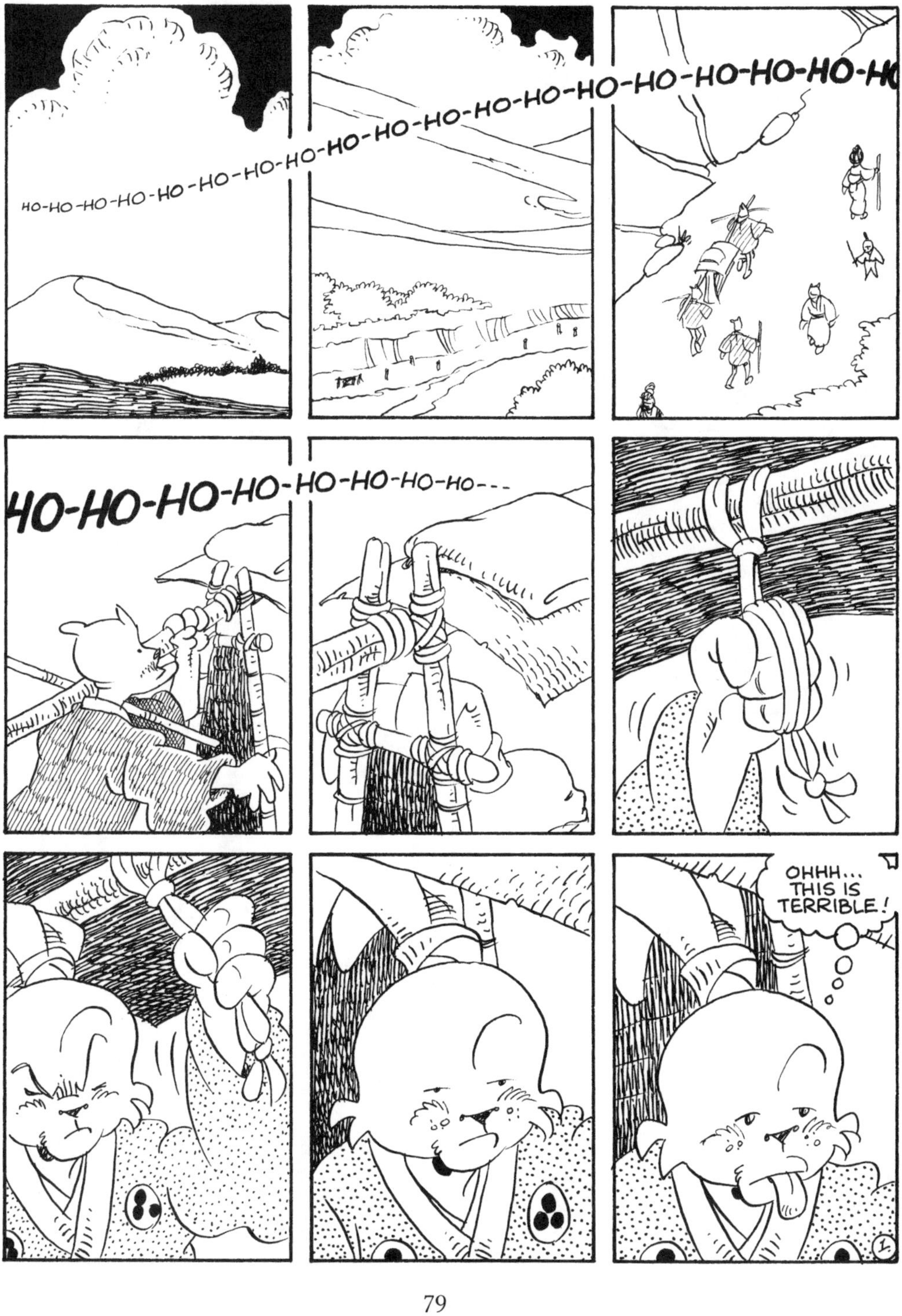
HO-HO-HO-HO-HO-HO-HO-HO-HO-HO-HO-HO-HO-HO-HO-HO-HO-HO-HO-HO-HO-HO-HO-HO-HO-HO-HO-HO-HO-HO-HO-HO-ho---
OHHH... THIS IS TERRIBLE!
1.

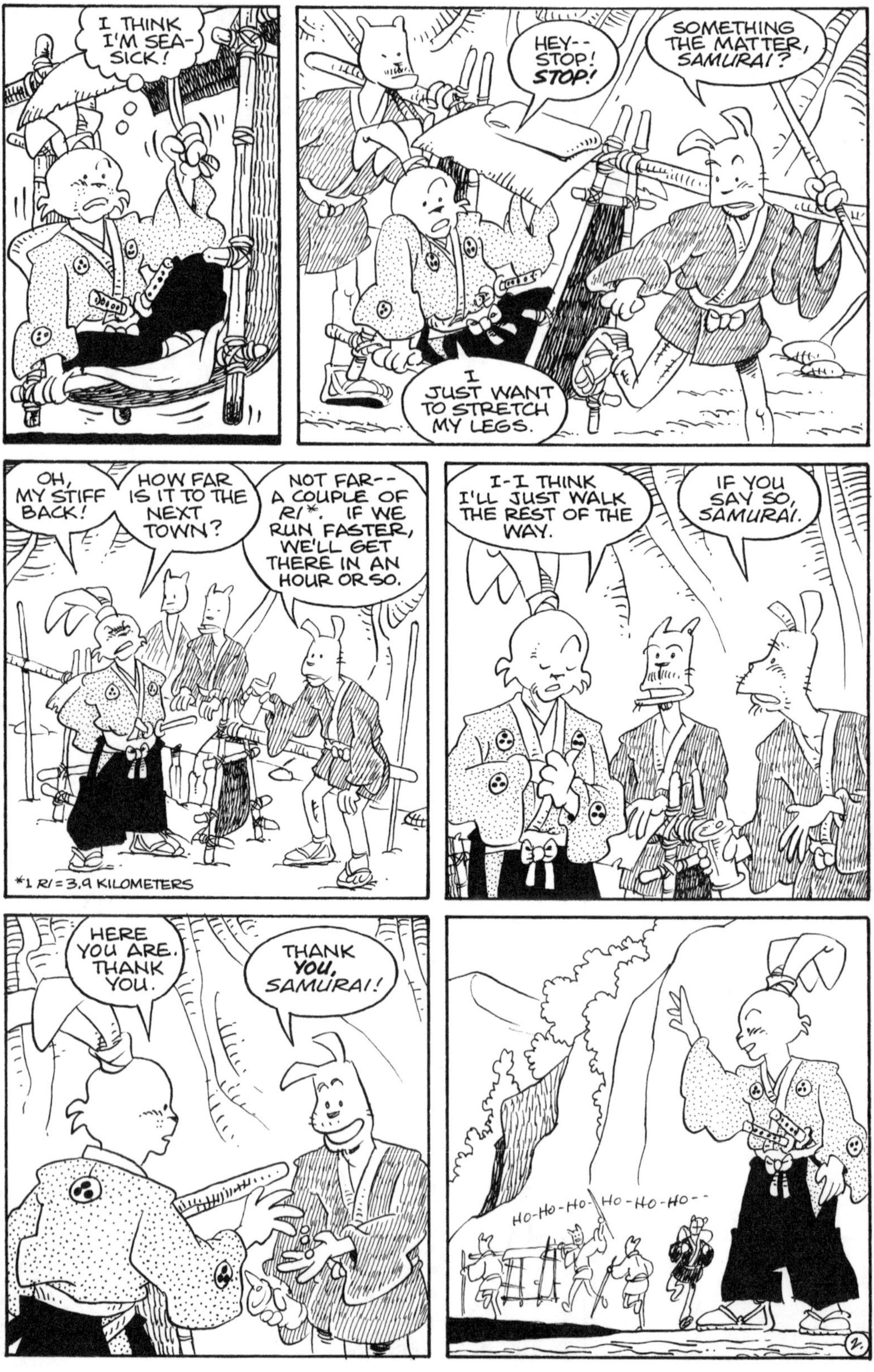
I THINK I'M SEA-SICK!
HEY-- STOP! STOP!
SOMETHING THE MATTER, SAMURAI?
I JUST WANT TO STRETCH MY LEGS.
OH, MY STIFF BACK!
HOW FAR IS IT TO THE NEXT TOWN?
NOT FAR-- A COUPLE OF RI*. IF WE RUN FASTER, WE'LL GET THERE IN AN HOUR OR SO.
*1 RI = 3.9 KILOMETERS
I-I THINK I'LL JUST WALK THE REST OF THE WAY.
IF YOU SAY SO, SAMURAI.
HERE YOU ARE. THANK YOU.
THANK YOU, SAMURAI!
HO-HO-HO- HO-HO-HO--
2.

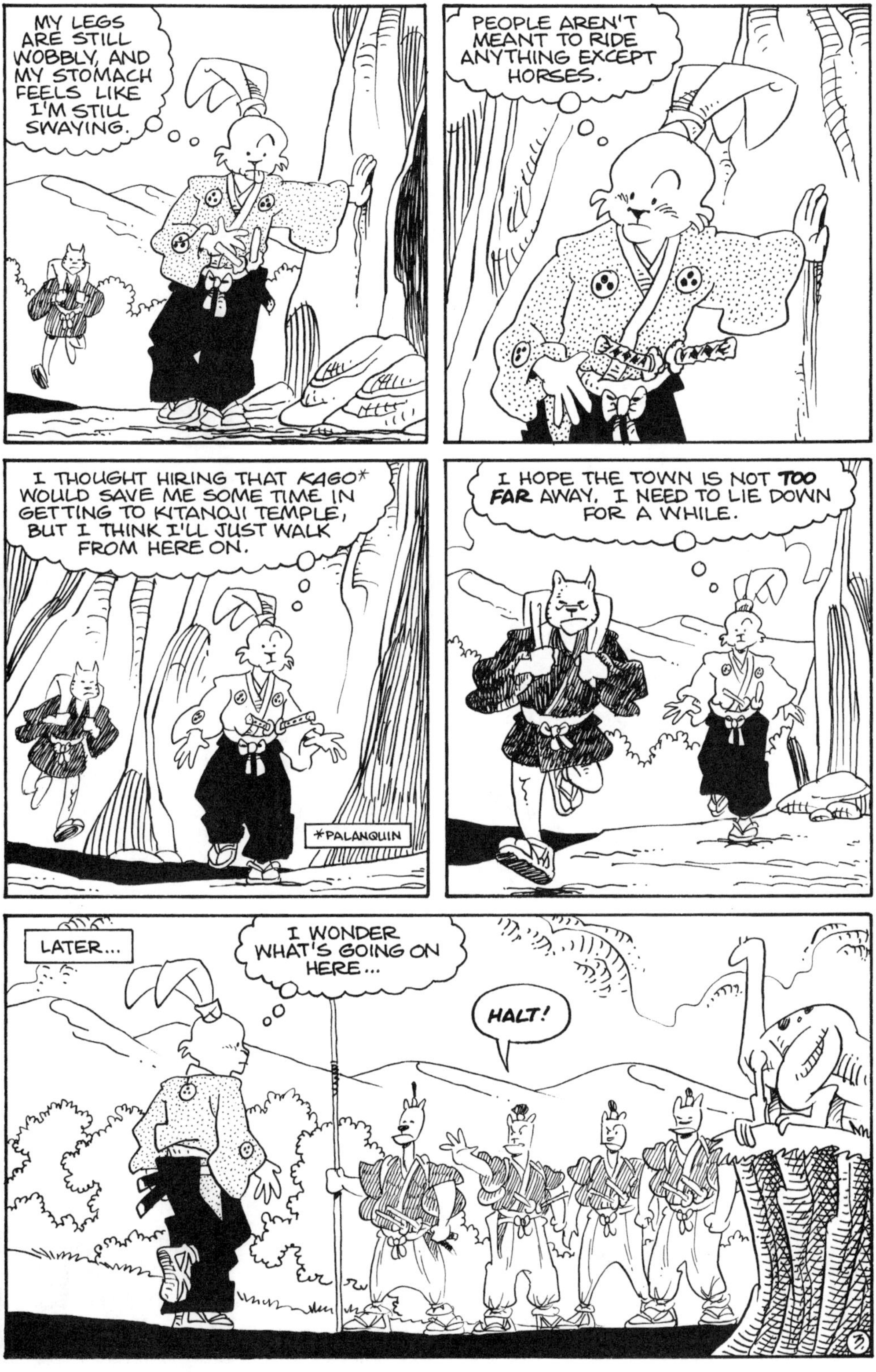
MY LEGS ARE STILL WOBBLY, AND MY STOMACH FEELS LIKE I'M STILL SWAYING.
PEOPLE AREN'T MEANT TO RIDE ANYTHING EXCEPT HORSES.
I THOUGHT HIRING THAT KAGO* WOULD SAVE ME SOME TIME IN GETTING TO KITANOJI TEMPLE, BUT I THINK I'LL JUST WALK FROM HERE ON.
*PALANQUIN
I HOPE THE TOWN IS NOT TOO FAR AWAY. I NEED TO LIE DOWN FOR A WHILE.
LATER...
I WONDER WHAT'S GOING ON HERE...
HALT!

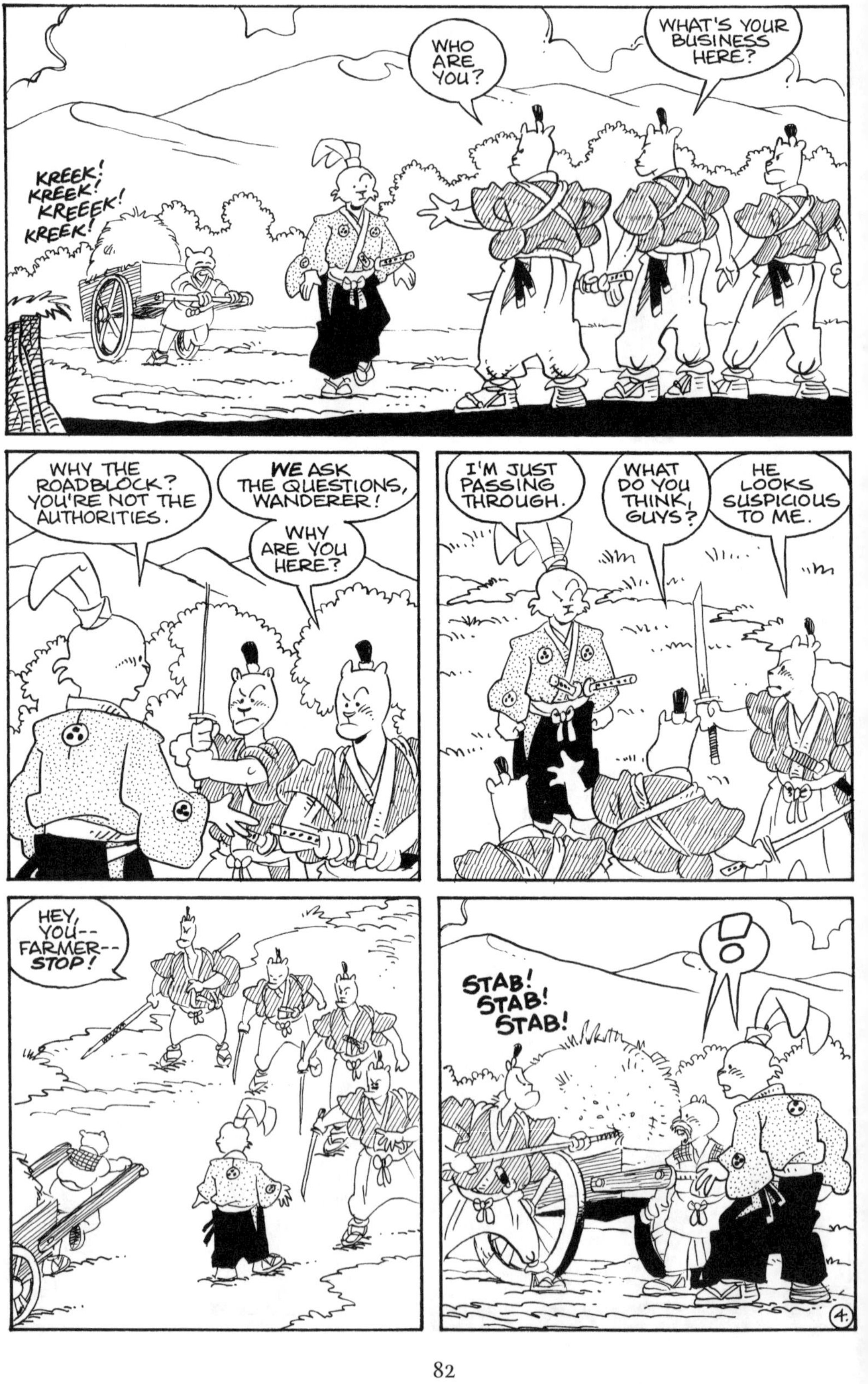
WHO ARE YOU?
WHAT'S YOUR BUSINESS HERE?
KREEK! KREEK! KREEEK! KREEK!
WHY THE ROADBLOCK? YOU'RE NOT THE AUTHORITIES.
WE ASK THE QUESTIONS, WANDERER!
WHY ARE YOU HERE?
I'M JUST PASSING THROUGH.
WHAT DO YOU THINK, GUYS?
HE LOOKS SUSPICIOUS TO ME.
HEY, YOU-- FARMER-- STOP!
STAB! STAB! STAB!
!
4.

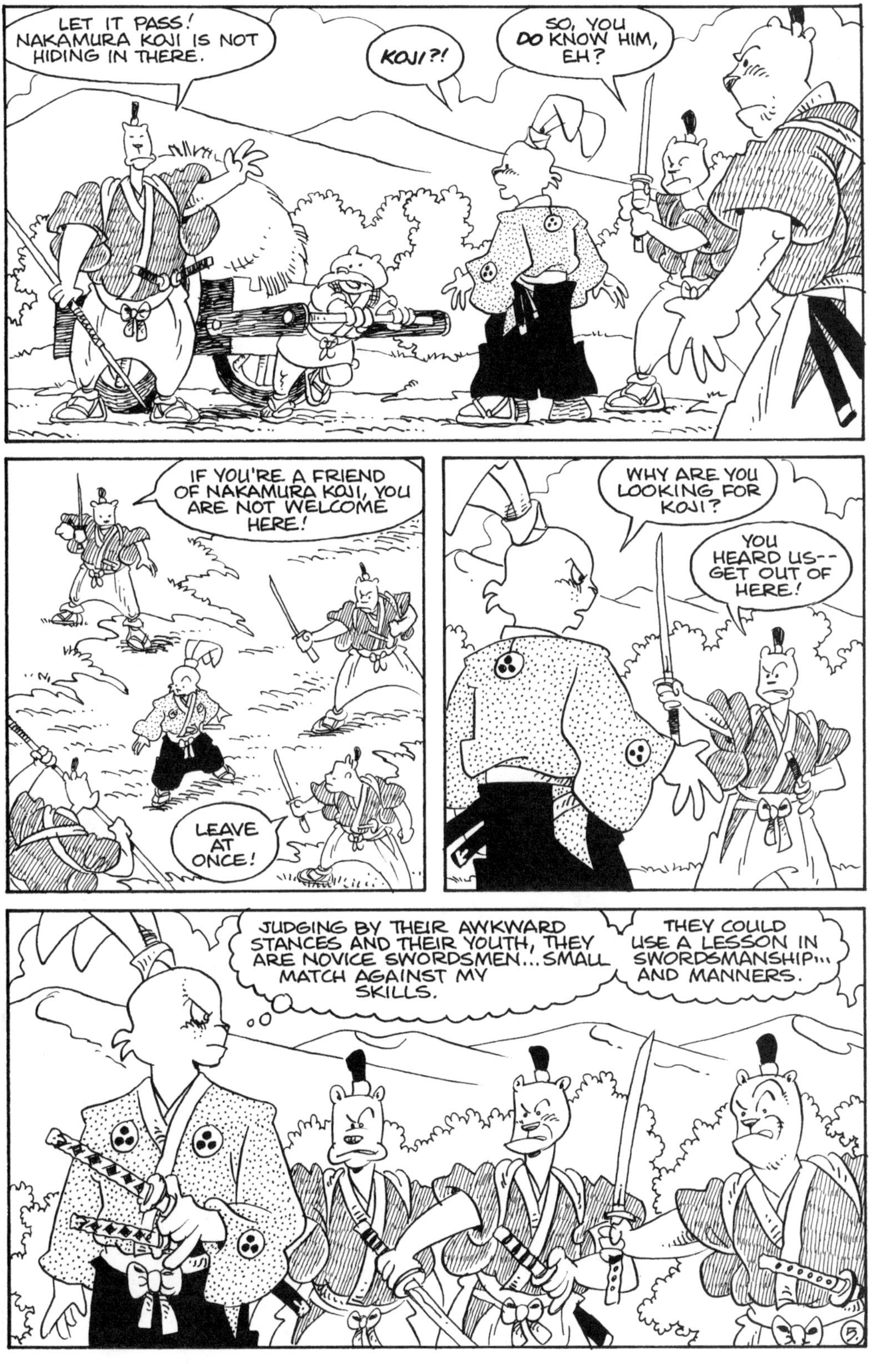
LET IT PASS! NAKAMURA KOJI IS NOT HIDING IN THERE.
KOJI?!
SO, YOU DO KNOW HIM, EH?
IF YOU'RE A FRIEND OF NAKAMURA KOJI, YOU ARE NOT WELCOME HERE!
LEAVE AT ONCE!
WHY ARE YOU LOOKING FOR KOJI?
YOU HEARD US--GET OUT OF HERE!
JUDGING BY THEIR AWKWARD STANCES AND THEIR YOUTH, THEY ARE NOVICE SWORDSMEN... SMALL MATCH AGAINST MY SKILLS.
THEY COULD USE A LESSON IN SWORDSMANSHIP... AND MANNERS.
5.

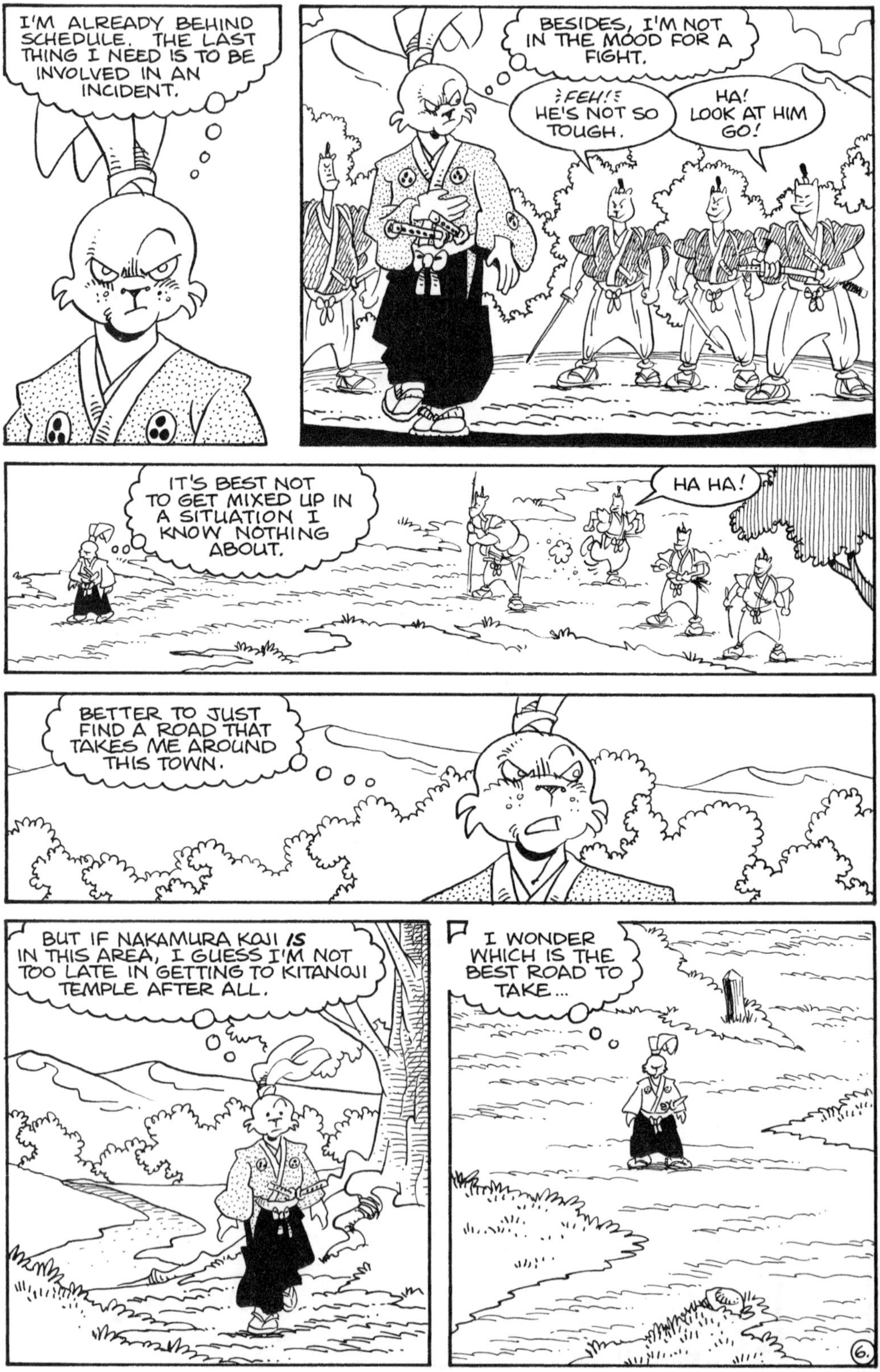
I'M ALREADY BEHIND SCHEDULE. THE LAST THING I NEED IS TO BE INVOLVED IN AN INCIDENT.
BESIDES, I'M NOT IN THE MOOD FOR A FIGHT.
FEH! HE'S NOT SO TOUGH.
HA! LOOK AT HIM GO!
IT'S BEST NOT TO GET MIXED UP IN A SITUATION I KNOW NOTHING ABOUT.
HA HA!
BETTER TO JUST FIND A ROAD THAT TAKES ME AROUND THIS TOWN.
BUT IF NAKAMURA KOJI *IS* IN THIS AREA, I GUESS I'M NOT TOO LATE IN GETTING TO KITANOJI TEMPLE AFTER ALL.
I WONDER WHICH IS THE BEST ROAD TO TAKE...
6.

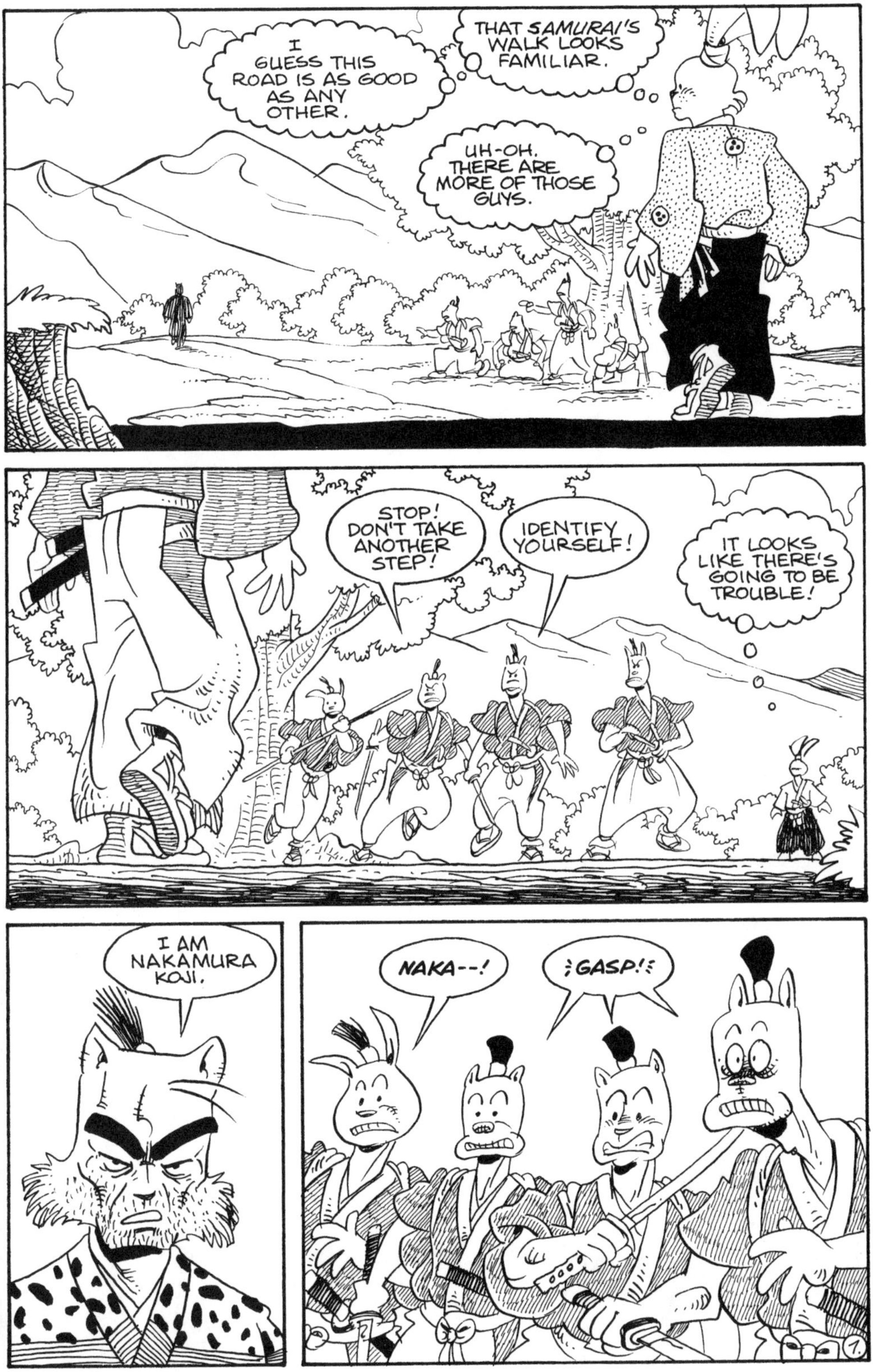
I GUESS THIS ROAD IS AS GOOD AS ANY OTHER.
THAT SAMURAI'S WALK LOOKS FAMILIAR.
UH-OH. THERE ARE MORE OF THOSE GUYS.
STOP! DON'T TAKE ANOTHER STEP!
IDENTIFY YOURSELF!
IT LOOKS LIKE THERE'S GOING TO BE TROUBLE!
I AM NAKAMURA KOJI.
NAKA--!
GASP!
1.

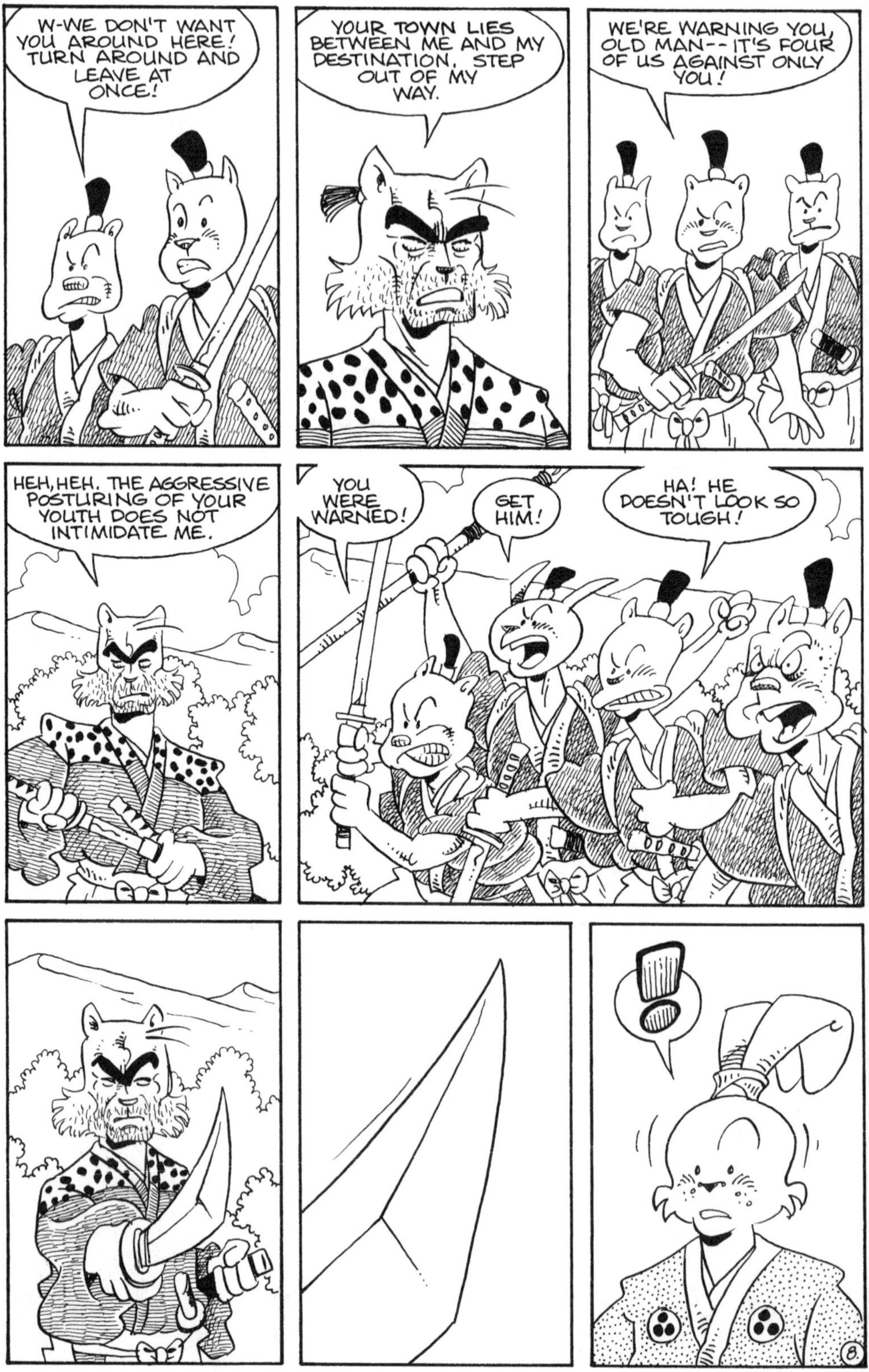
W-WE DON'T WANT YOU AROUND HERE! TURN AROUND AND LEAVE AT ONCE!
YOUR TOWN LIES BETWEEN ME AND MY DESTINATION. STEP OUT OF MY WAY.
WE'RE WARNING YOU, OLD MAN-- IT'S FOUR OF US AGAINST ONLY YOU!
HEH, HEH. THE AGGRESSIVE POSTURING OF YOUR YOUTH DOES NOT INTIMIDATE ME.
YOU WERE WARNED!
GET HIM!
HA! HE DOESN'T LOOK SO TOUGH!
!
8

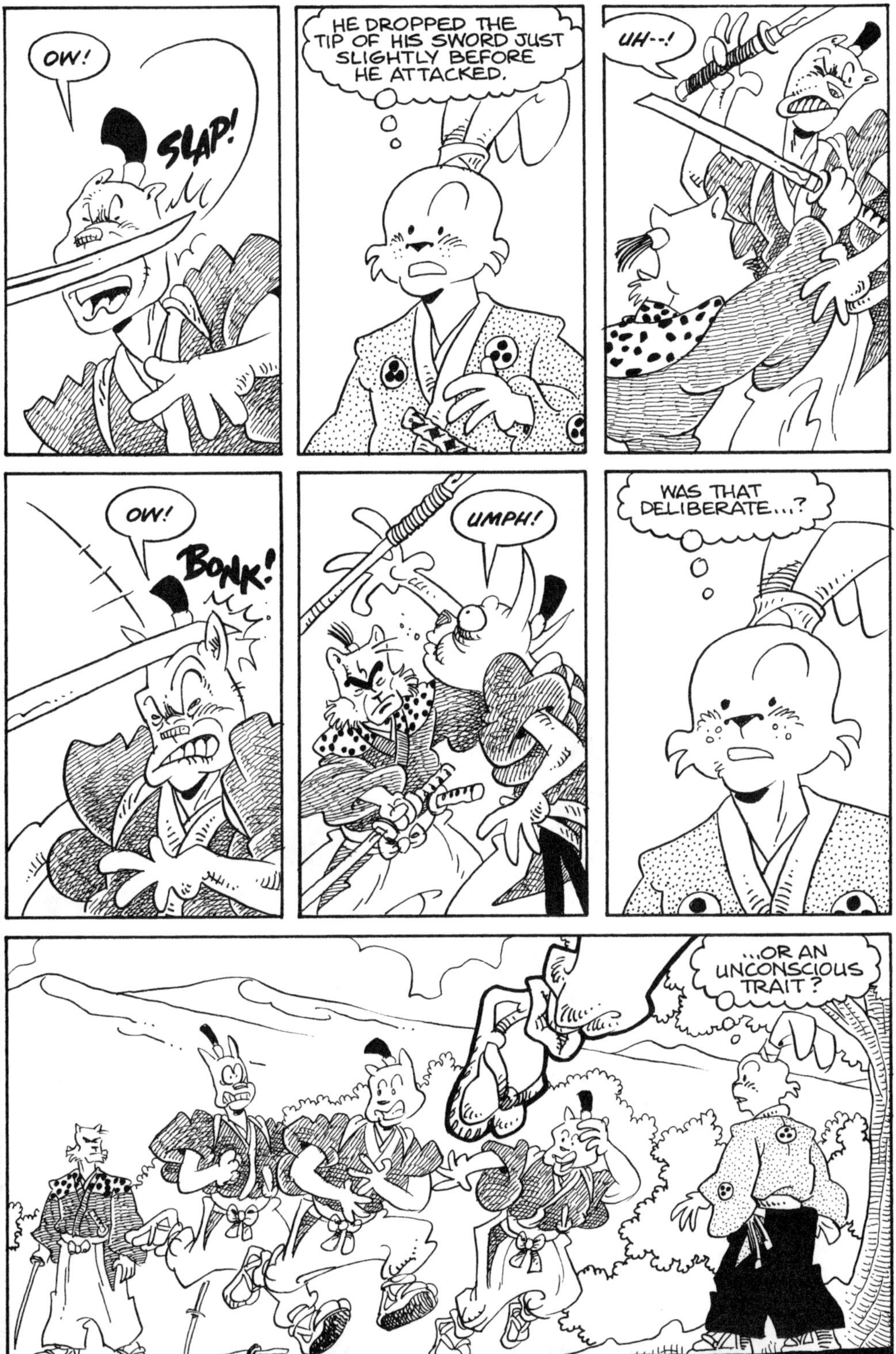
OW!
SLAP!
HE DROPPED THE TIP OF HIS SWORD JUST SLIGHTLY BEFORE HE ATTACKED.
UH--!
OW!
BONK!
UMPH!
WAS THAT DELIBERATE...?
...OR AN UNCONSCIOUS TRAIT?
9.

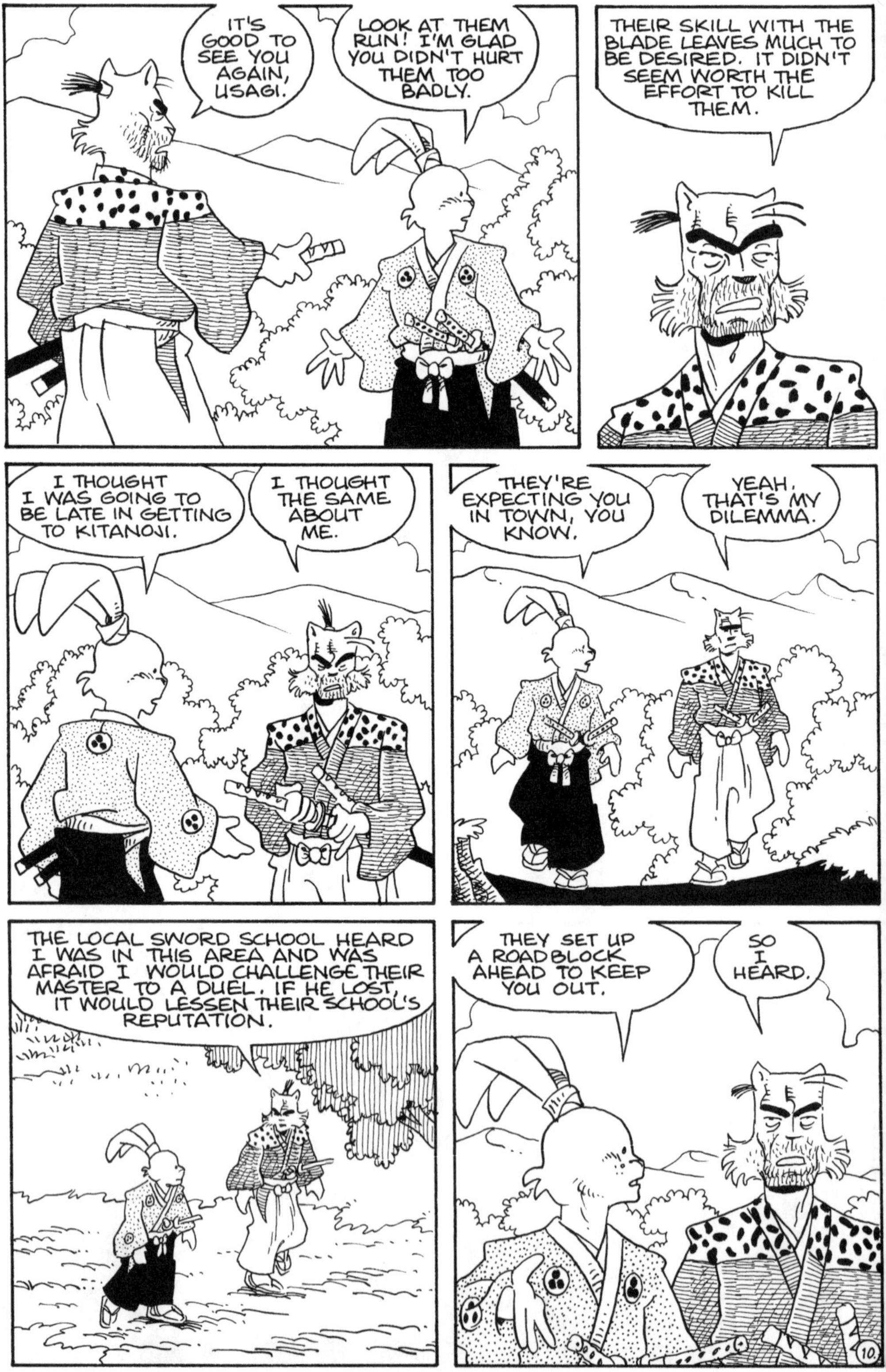
IT'S GOOD TO SEE YOU AGAIN, USAGI.
LOOK AT THEM RUN! I'M GLAD YOU DIDN'T HURT THEM TOO BADLY.
THEIR SKILL WITH THE BLADE LEAVES MUCH TO BE DESIRED. IT DIDN'T SEEM WORTH THE EFFORT TO KILL THEM.
I THOUGHT I WAS GOING TO BE LATE IN GETTING TO KITANOJI.
I THOUGHT THE SAME ABOUT ME.
THEY'RE EXPECTING YOU IN TOWN, YOU KNOW.
YEAH. THAT'S MY DILEMMA.
THE LOCAL SWORD SCHOOL HEARD I WAS IN THIS AREA AND WAS AFRAID I WOULD CHALLENGE THEIR MASTER TO A DUEL. IF HE LOST, IT WOULD LESSEN THEIR SCHOOL'S REPUTATION.
THEY SET UP A ROADBLOCK AHEAD TO KEEP YOU OUT.
SO I HEARD.
10.

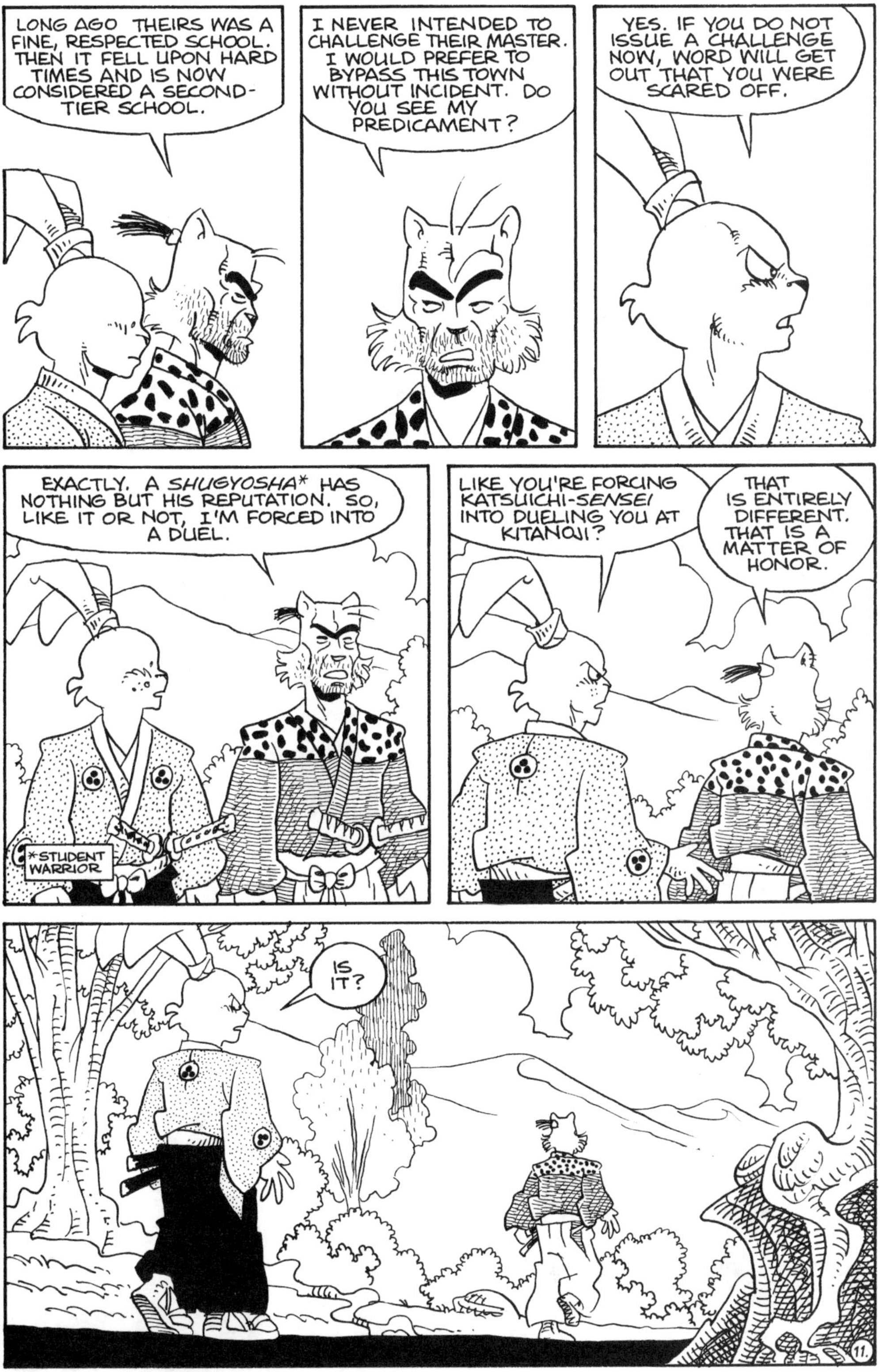
LONG AGO THEIRS WAS A FINE, RESPECTED SCHOOL. THEN IT FELL UPON HARD TIMES AND IS NOW CONSIDERED A SECOND-TIER SCHOOL.
I NEVER INTENDED TO CHALLENGE THEIR MASTER. I WOULD PREFER TO BYPASS THIS TOWN WITHOUT INCIDENT. DO YOU SEE MY PREDICAMENT?
YES. IF YOU DO NOT ISSUE A CHALLENGE NOW, WORD WILL GET OUT THAT YOU WERE SCARED OFF.
EXACTLY. A *SHUGYOSHA** HAS NOTHING BUT HIS REPUTATION. SO, LIKE IT OR NOT, I'M FORCED INTO A DUEL.
*STUDENT WARRIOR
LIKE YOU'RE FORCING KATSUICHI-*SENSEI* INTO DUELING YOU AT KITANOJI?
THAT IS ENTIRELY DIFFERENT. THAT IS A MATTER OF HONOR.
IS IT?
11.

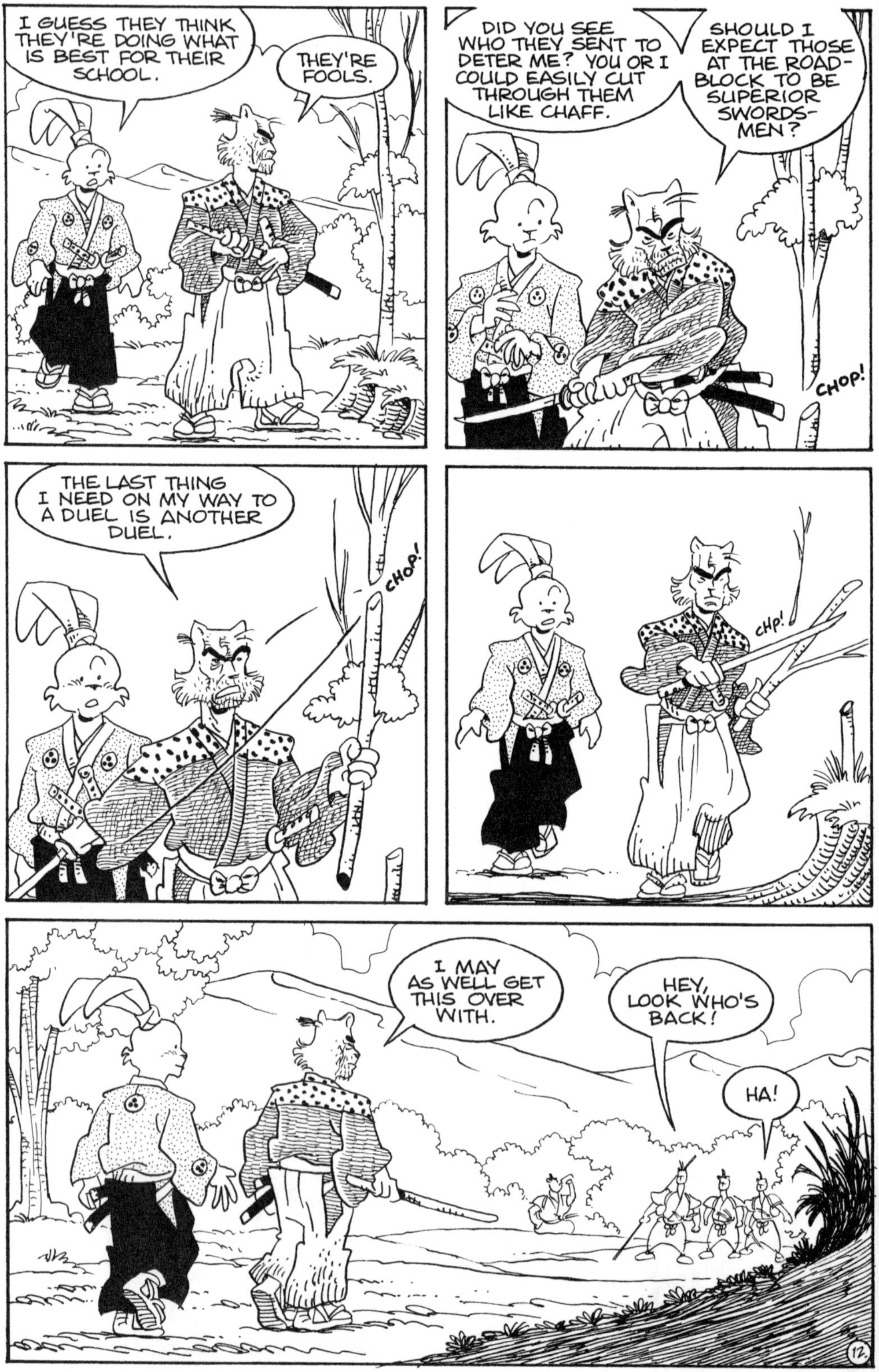
I GUESS THEY THINK THEY'RE DOING WHAT IS BEST FOR THEIR SCHOOL.
THEY'RE FOOLS.
DID YOU SEE WHO THEY SENT TO DETER ME? YOU OR I COULD EASILY CUT THROUGH THEM LIKE CHAFF.
SHOULD I EXPECT THOSE AT THE ROAD-BLOCK TO BE SUPERIOR SWORDS-MEN?
CHOP!
THE LAST THING I NEED ON MY WAY TO A DUEL IS ANOTHER DUEL.
CHOP!
CHP!
I MAY AS WELL GET THIS OVER WITH.
HEY, LOOK WHO'S BACK!
HA!
12.

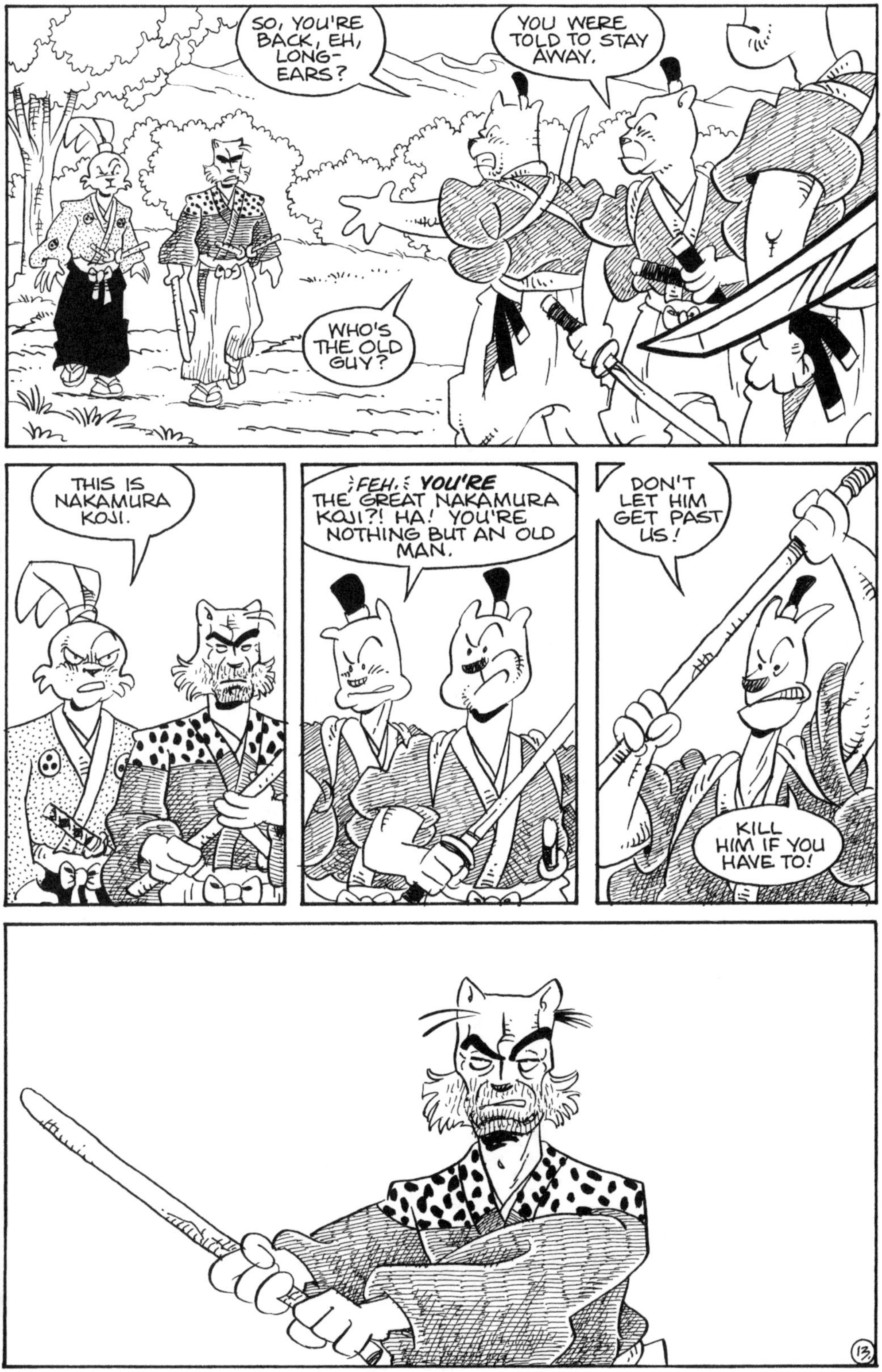
SO, YOU'RE BACK, EH, LONG-EARS?
YOU WERE TOLD TO STAY AWAY.
WHO'S THE OLD GUY?
THIS IS NAKAMURA KOJI.
FEH. YOU'RE THE GREAT NAKAMURA KOJI?! HA! YOU'RE NOTHING BUT AN OLD MAN.
DON'T LET HIM GET PAST US!
KILL HIM IF YOU HAVE TO!
13

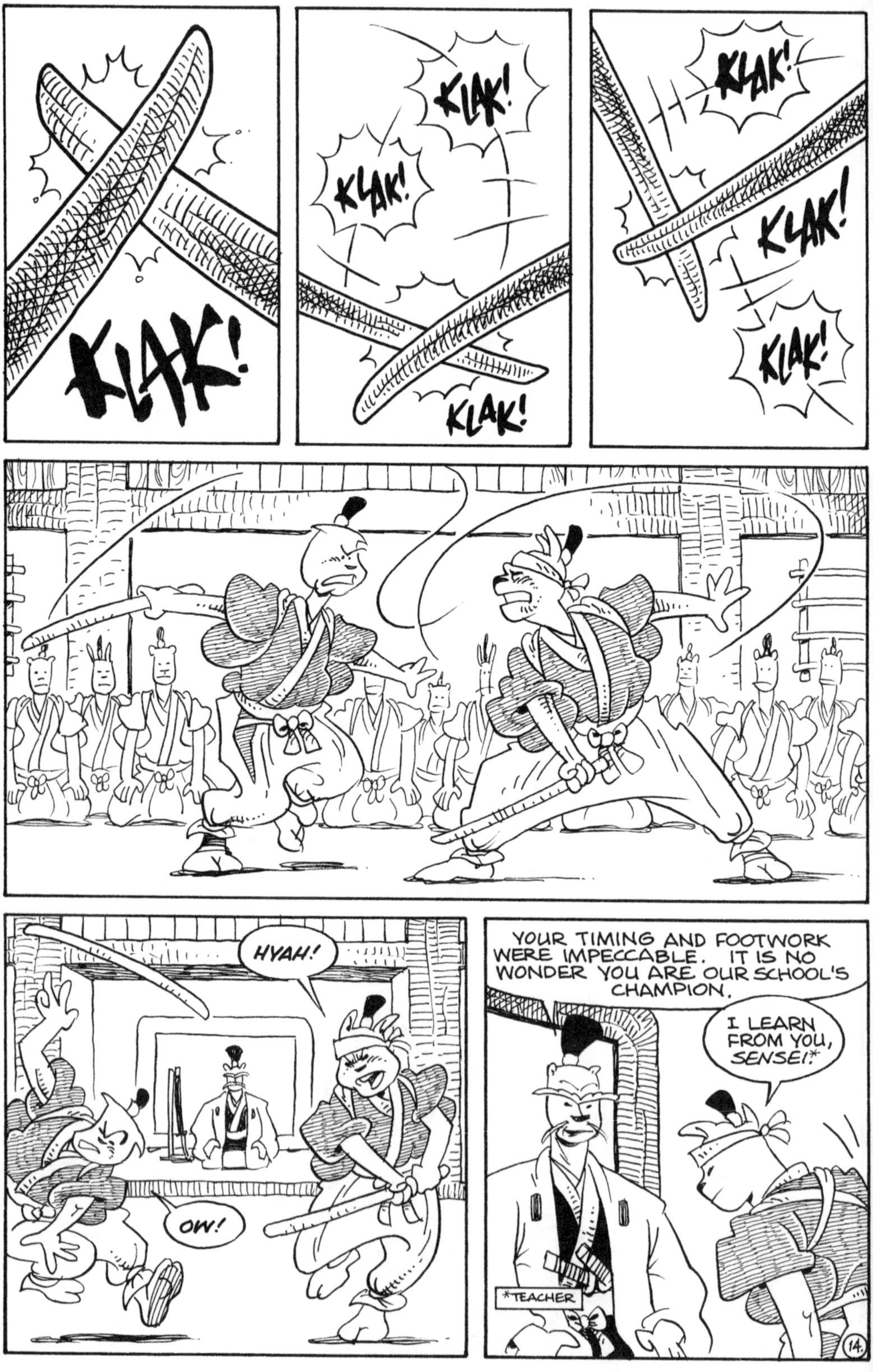
KLAK!
KLAK!
KLAK!
KLAK!
KLAK!
KLAK!
KLAK!
HYAH!
OW!
YOUR TIMING AND FOOTWORK WERE IMPECCABLE. IT IS NO WONDER YOU ARE OUR SCHOOL'S CHAMPION.
I LEARN FROM YOU, SENSEI!*
*TEACHER
14.

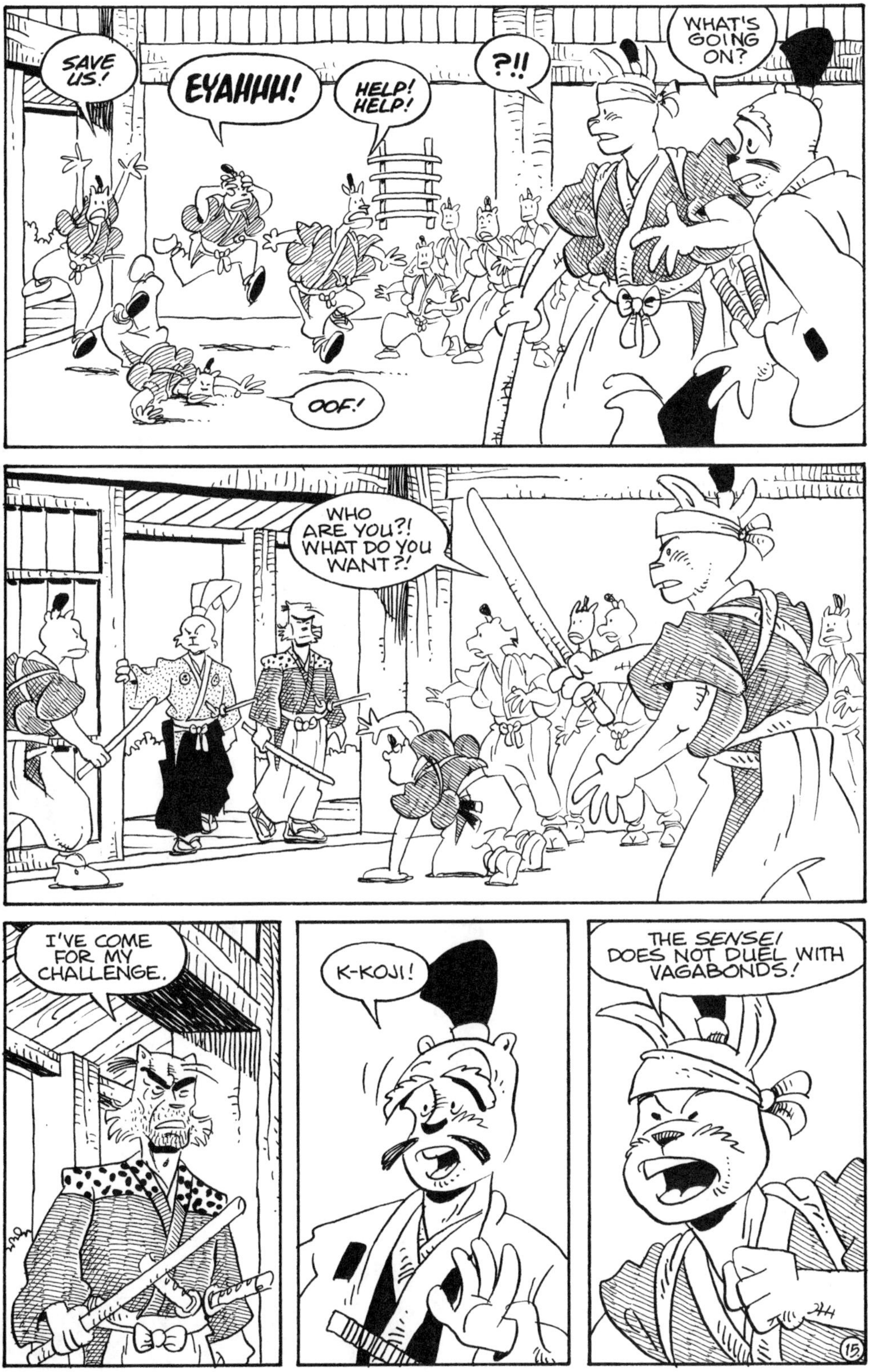
SAVE US!
EYAHHH!
HELP! HELP!
?!!
WHAT'S GOING ON?
OOF!
WHO ARE YOU?! WHAT DO YOU WANT?!
I'VE COME FOR MY CHALLENGE.
K-KOJI!
THE SENSEI DOES NOT DUEL WITH VAGABONDS!
15

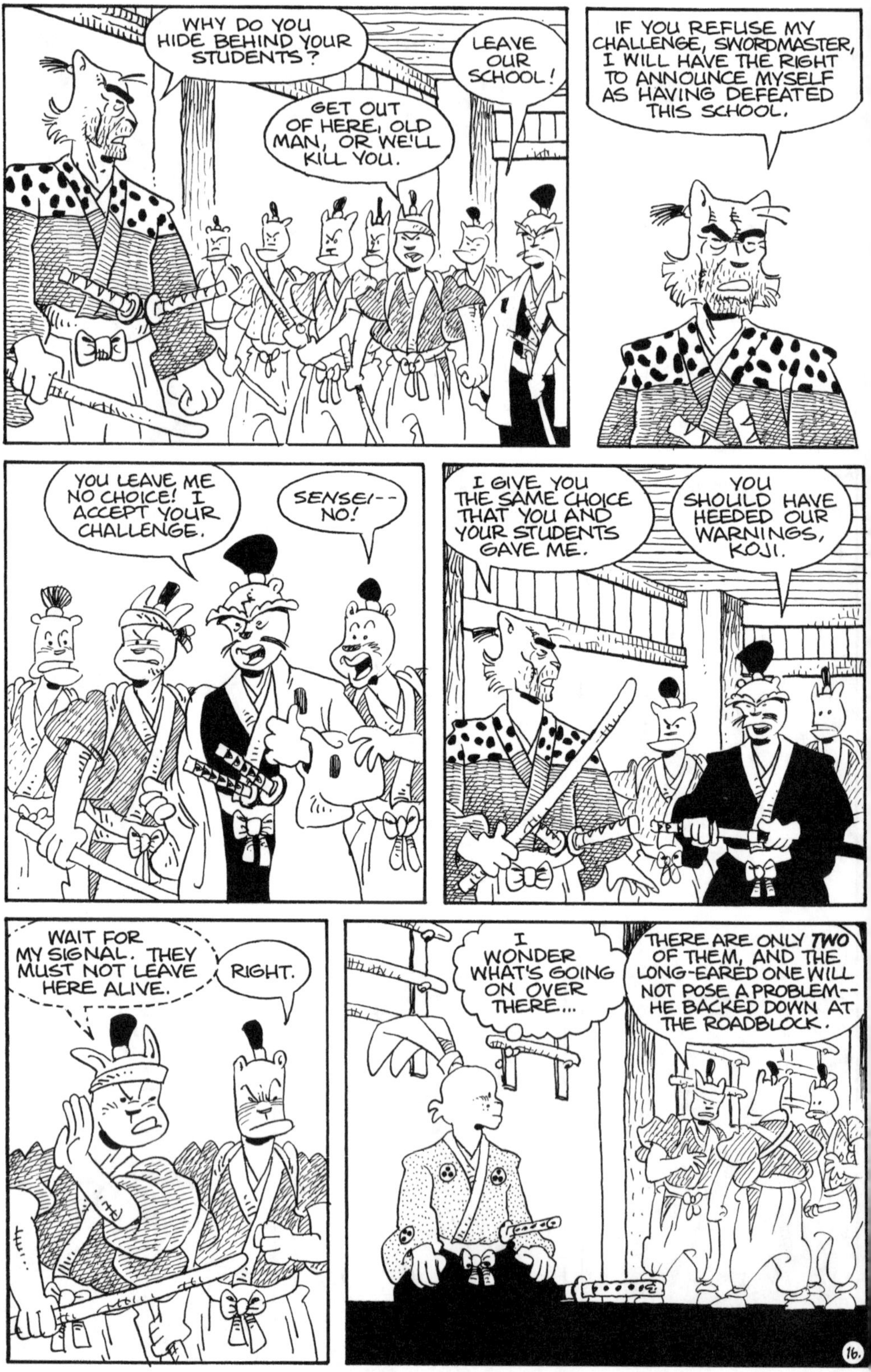
WHY DO YOU HIDE BEHIND YOUR STUDENTS?
LEAVE OUR SCHOOL!
GET OUT OF HERE, OLD MAN, OR WE'LL KILL YOU.
IF YOU REFUSE MY CHALLENGE, SWORDMASTER, I WILL HAVE THE RIGHT TO ANNOUNCE MYSELF AS HAVING DEFEATED THIS SCHOOL.
YOU LEAVE ME NO CHOICE! I ACCEPT YOUR CHALLENGE.
SENSEI-- NO!
I GIVE YOU THE SAME CHOICE THAT YOU AND YOUR STUDENTS GAVE ME.
YOU SHOULD HAVE HEEDED OUR WARNINGS, KOJI.
WAIT FOR MY SIGNAL. THEY MUST NOT LEAVE HERE ALIVE.
RIGHT.
I WONDER WHAT'S GOING ON OVER THERE...
THERE ARE ONLY TWO OF THEM, AND THE LONG-EARED ONE WILL NOT POSE A PROBLEM-- HE BACKED DOWN AT THE ROADBLOCK.
16.

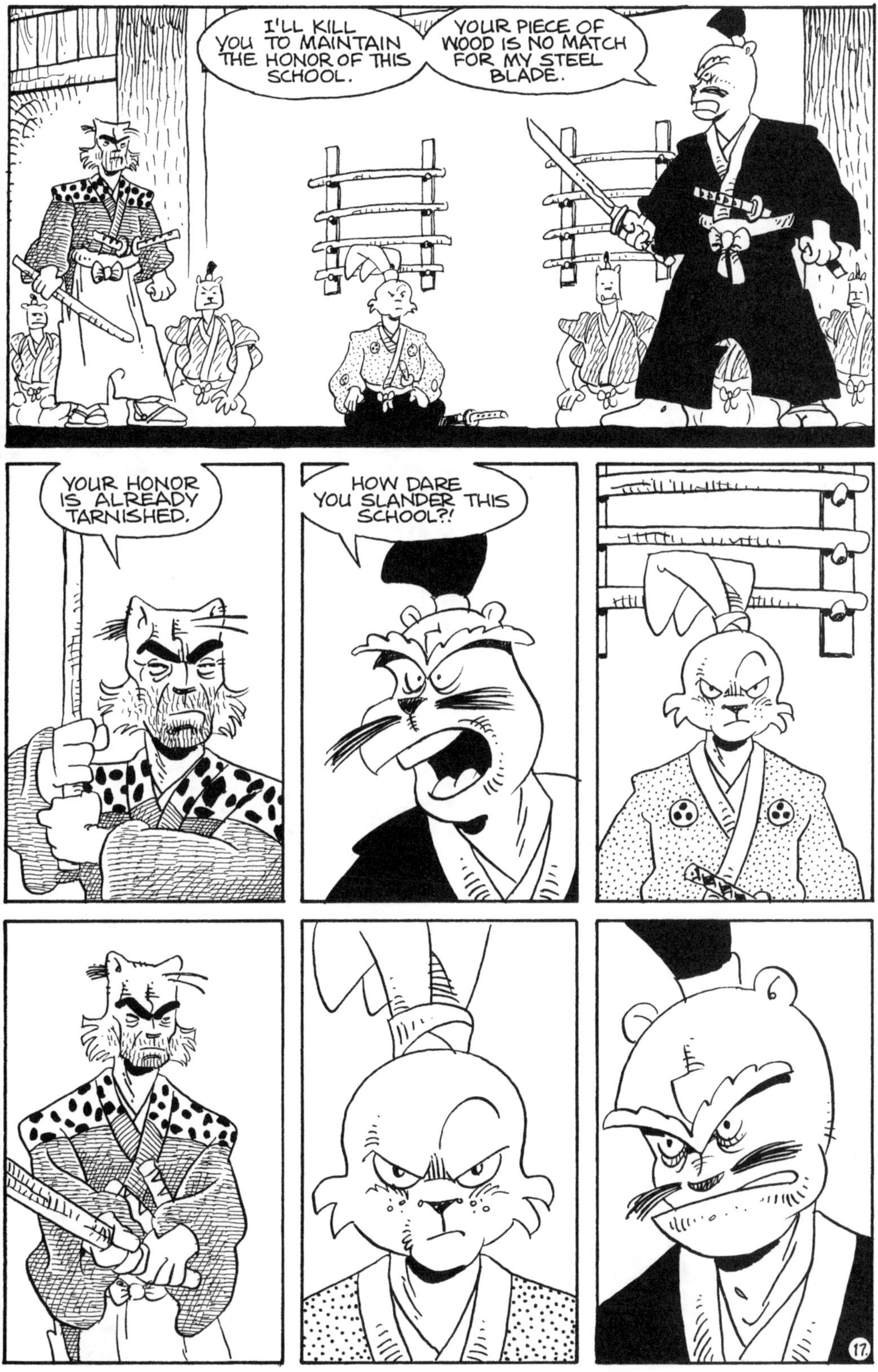
I'LL KILL YOU TO MAINTAIN THE HONOR OF THIS SCHOOL.
YOUR PIECE OF WOOD IS NO MATCH FOR MY STEEL BLADE.
YOUR HONOR IS ALREADY TARNISHED.
HOW DARE YOU SLANDER THIS SCHOOL?!
17.

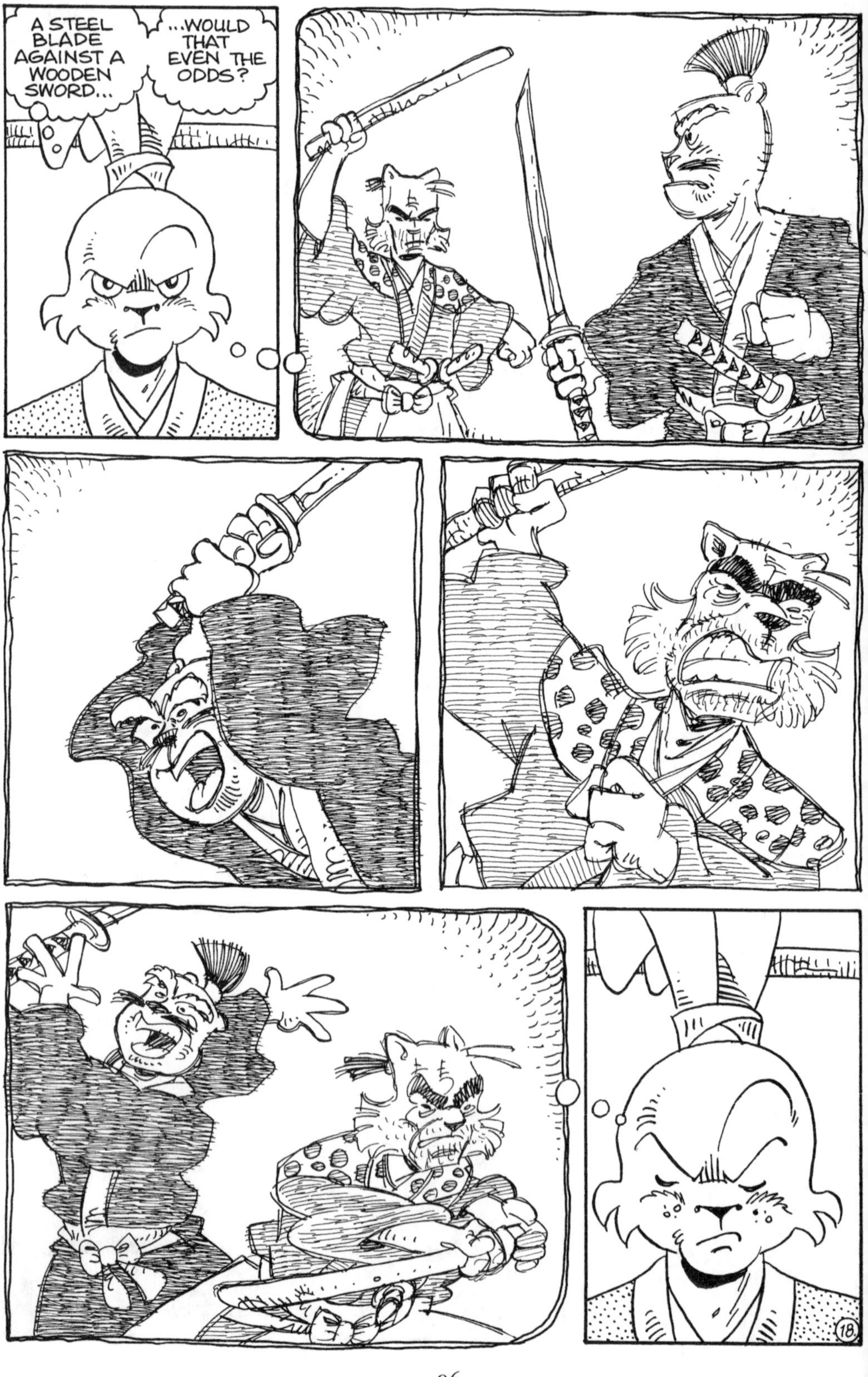
A STEEL BLADE AGAINST A WOODEN SWORD...
...WOULD THAT EVEN THE ODDS?
18

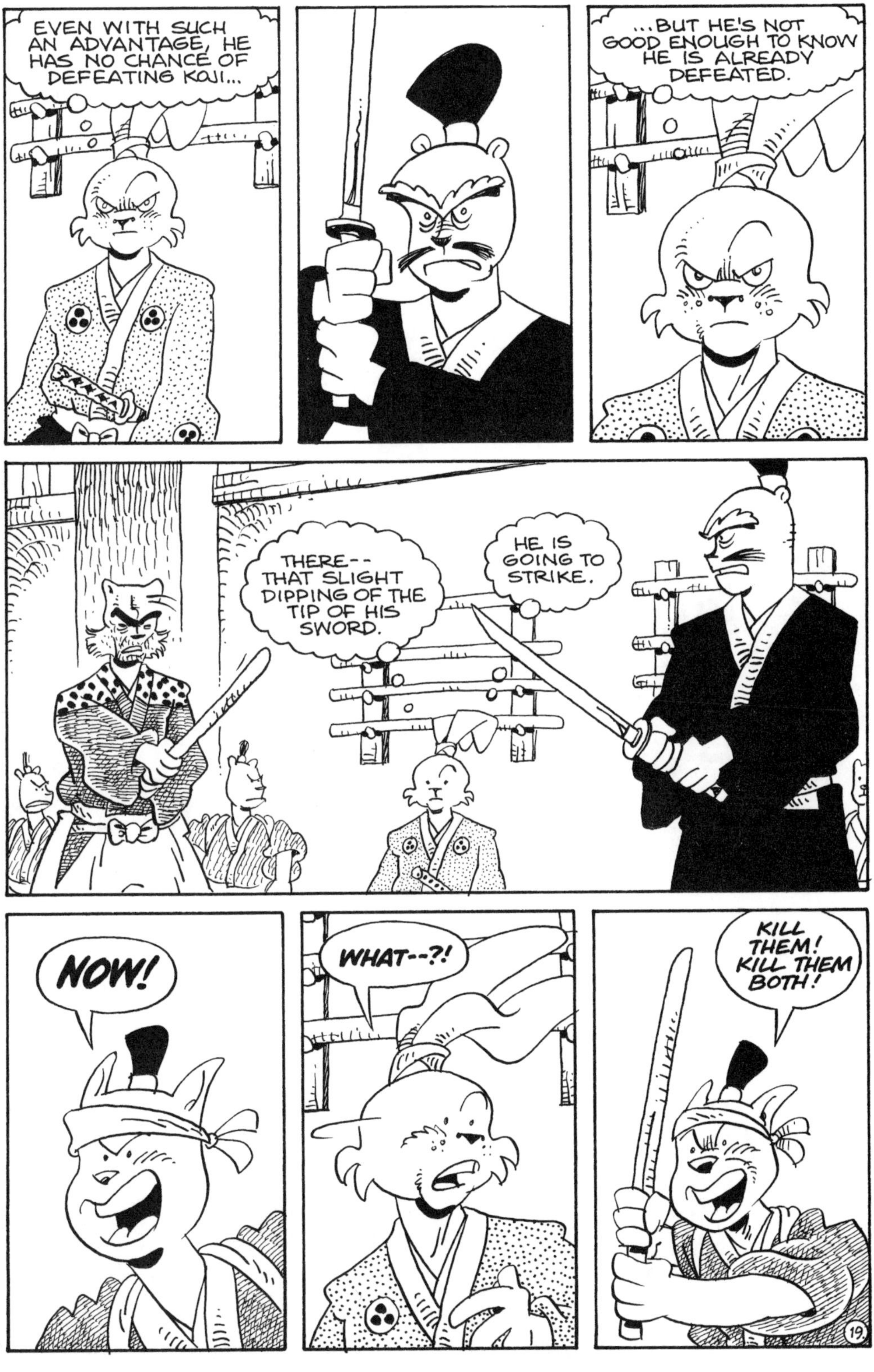

EVEN WITH SUCH AN ADVANTAGE, HE HAS NO CHANCE OF DEFEATING KOJI...
...BUT HE'S NOT GOOD ENOUGH TO KNOW HE IS ALREADY DEFEATED.
THERE-- THAT SLIGHT DIPPING OF THE TIP OF HIS SWORD.
HE IS GOING TO STRIKE.
NOW!
WHAT--?!
KILL THEM! KILL THEM BOTH!
19

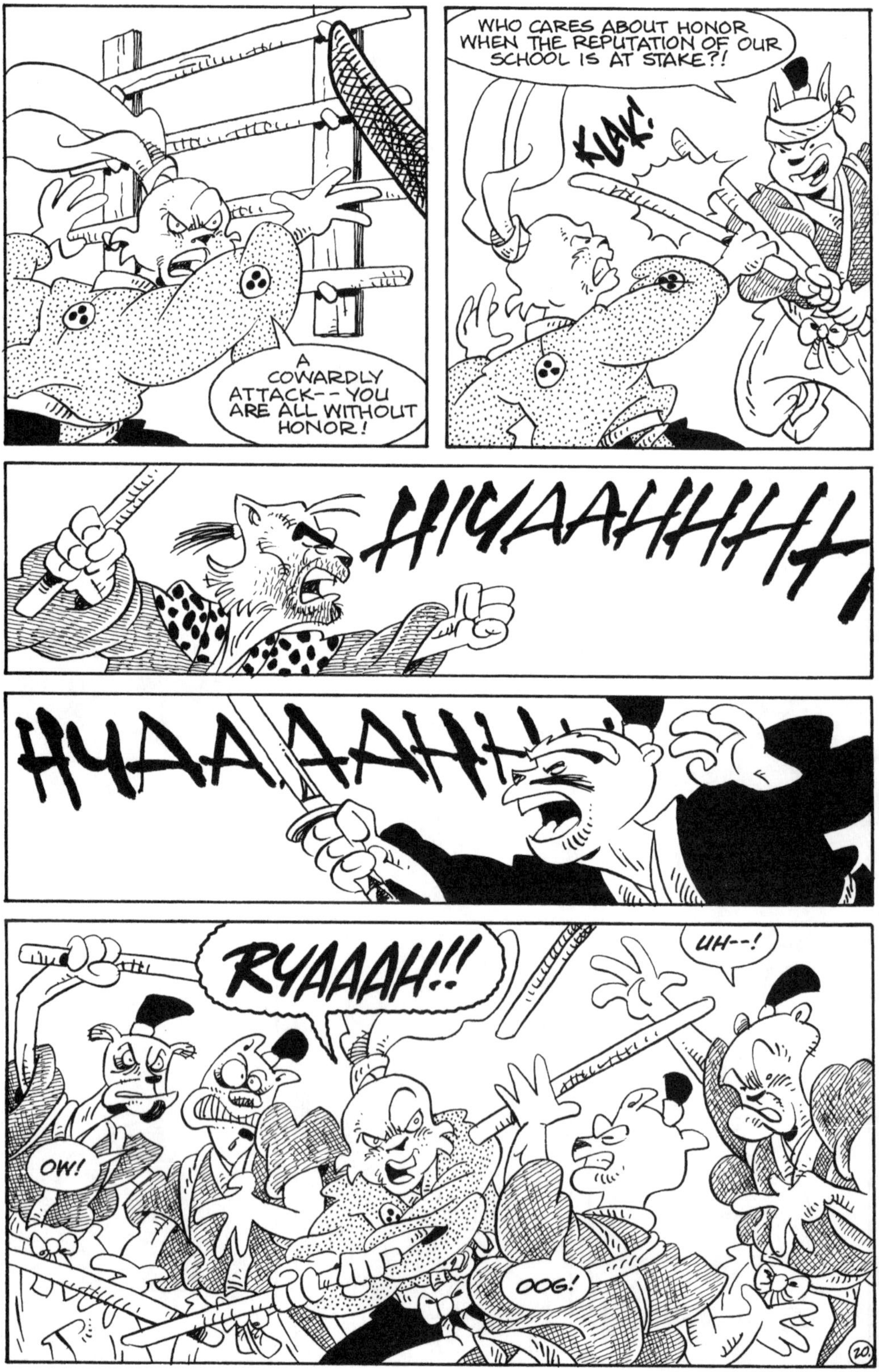
A COWARDLY ATTACK-- YOU ARE ALL WITHOUT HONOR!
WHO CARES ABOUT HONOR WHEN THE REPUTATION OF OUR SCHOOL IS AT STAKE?!
KLAK!
HIYAAHHHH
HYAAAAHH
RYAAAH!!
UH--!
OW!
OOG!
20.

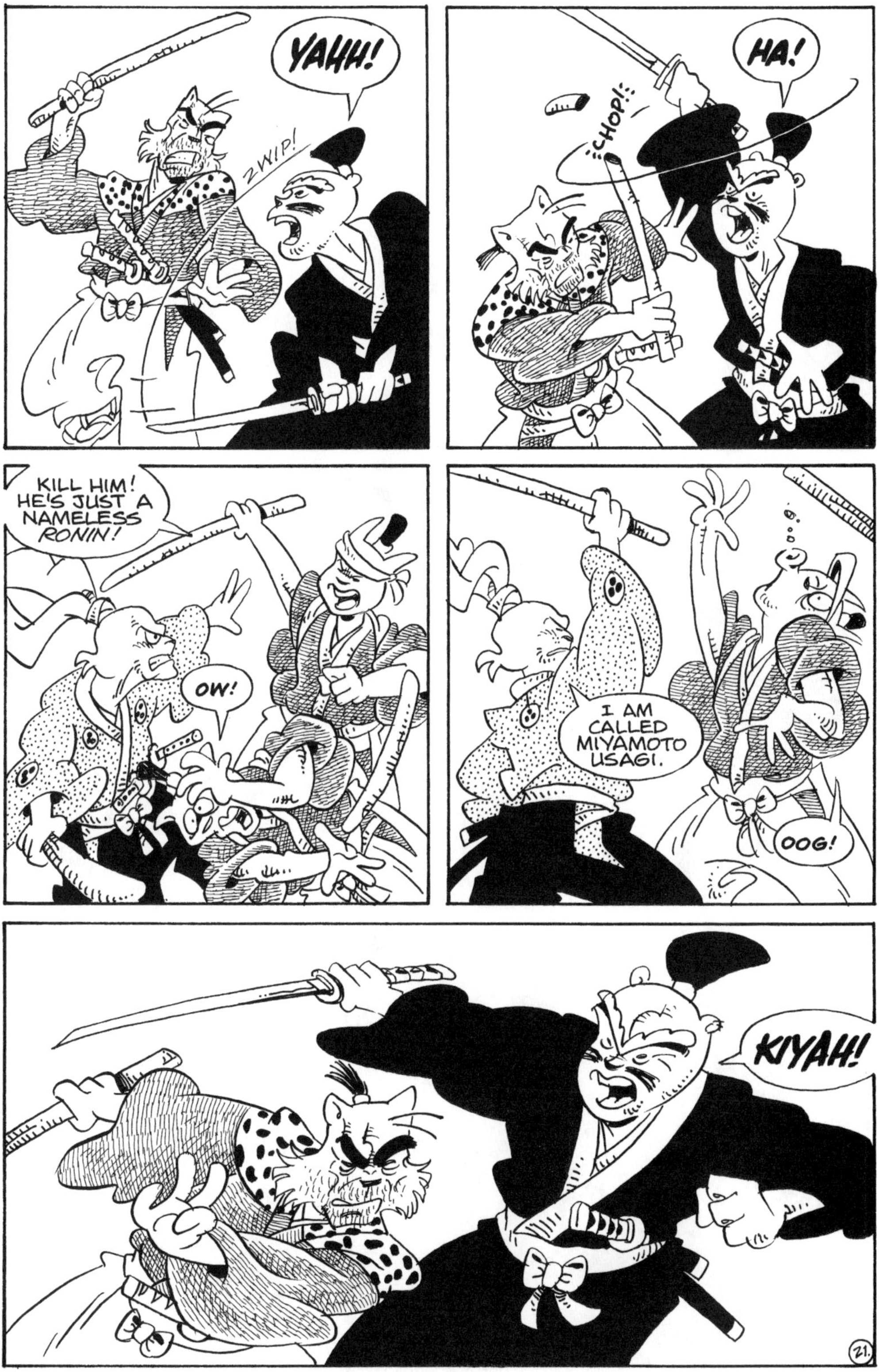
YAHH!
ZWIP!
HA!
CHOP!
KILL HIM! HE'S JUST A NAMELESS RONIN!
OW!
I AM CALLED MIYAMOTO USAGI.
OOG!
KIYAH!
21.

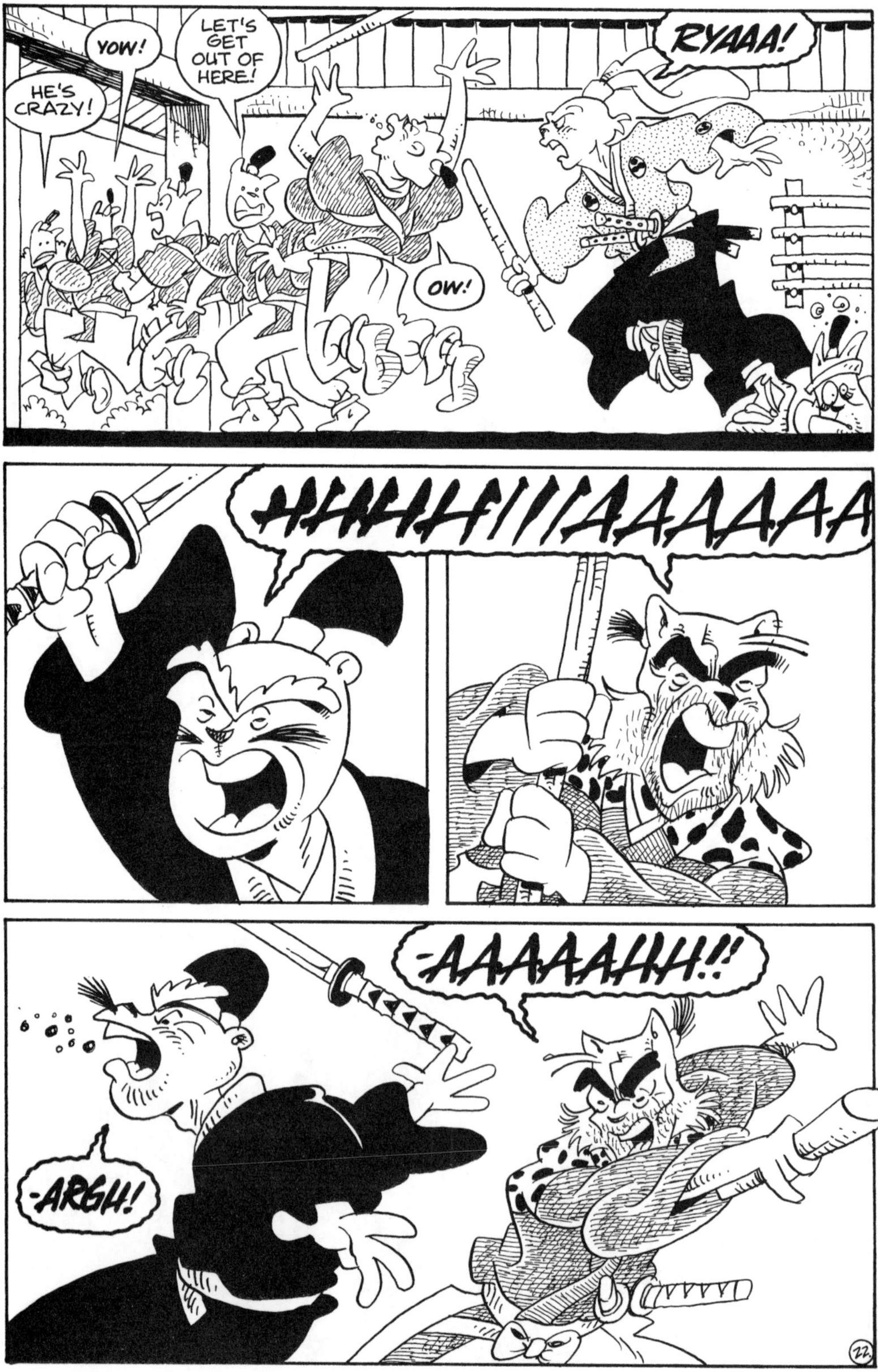
HE'S CRAZY!
YOW!
LET'S GET OUT OF HERE!
RYAAA!
OW!
HHHHIIIAAAAAAA
-AAAAAHH!!
-ARGH!
22

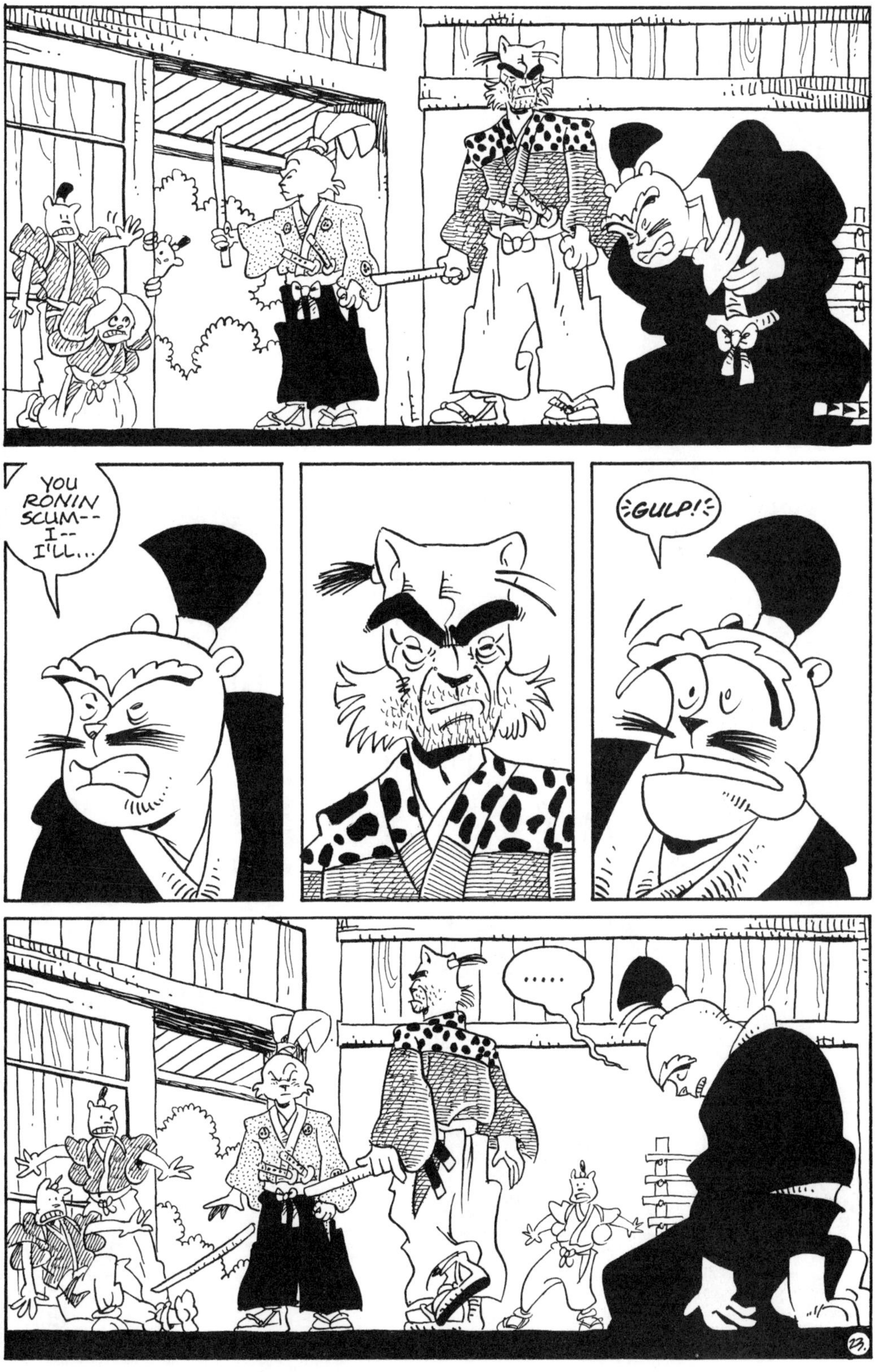
YOU RONIN SCUM-- I-- I'LL...
GULP!
.....
23.

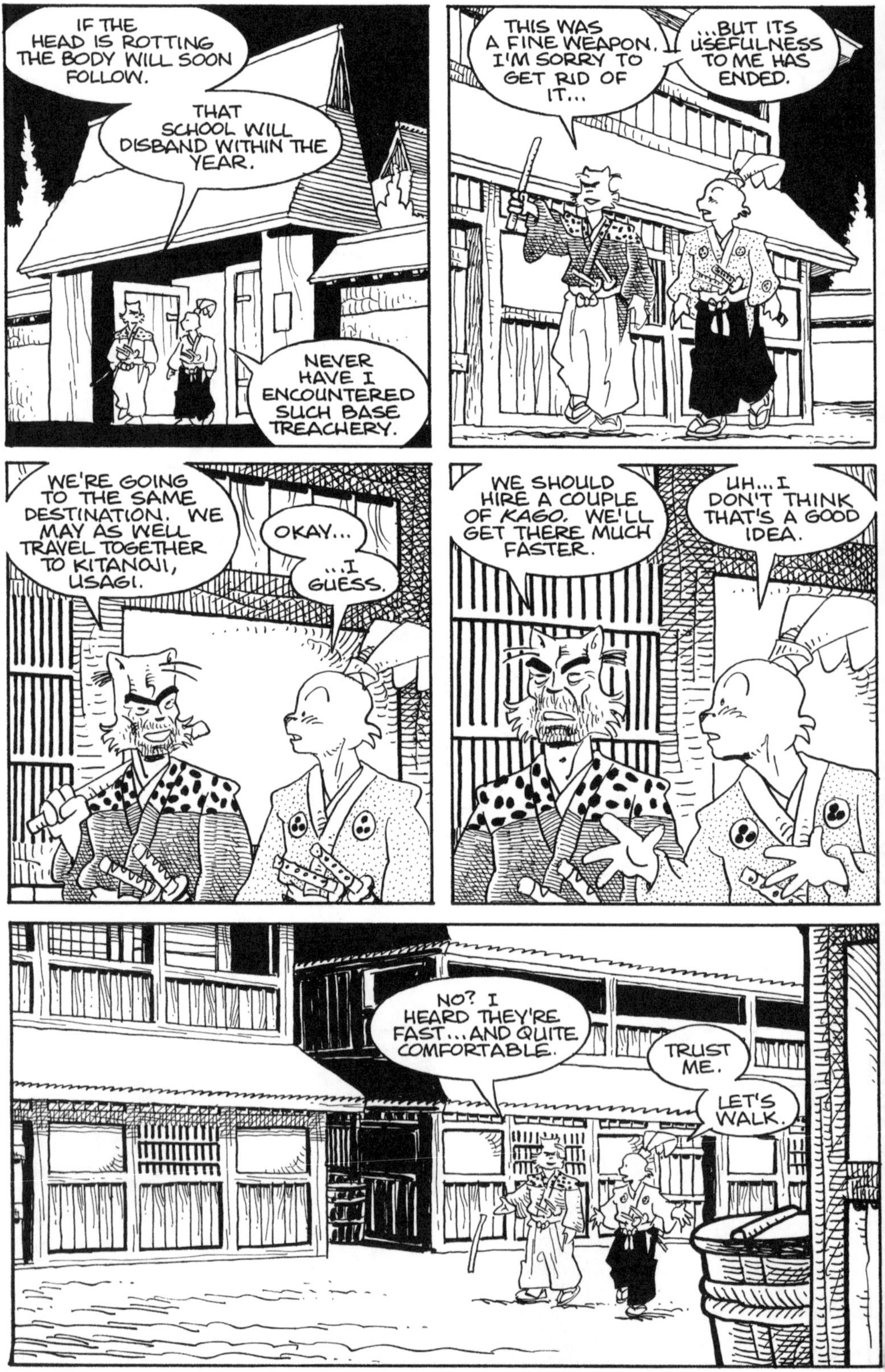
IF THE HEAD IS ROTTING THE BODY WILL SOON FOLLOW.
THAT SCHOOL WILL DISBAND WITHIN THE YEAR.
NEVER HAVE I ENCOUNTERED SUCH BASE TREACHERY.
THIS WAS A FINE WEAPON. I'M SORRY TO GET RID OF IT...
...BUT ITS USEFULNESS TO ME HAS ENDED.
WE'RE GOING TO THE SAME DESTINATION. WE MAY AS WELL TRAVEL TOGETHER TO KITANOJI, USAGI.
OKAY...
...I GUESS.
WE SHOULD HIRE A COUPLE OF *KAGO*. WE'LL GET THERE MUCH FASTER.
UH...I DON'T THINK THAT'S A GOOD IDEA.
NO? I HEARD THEY'RE FAST...AND QUITE COMFORTABLE.
TRUST ME.
LET'S WALK.

THE END

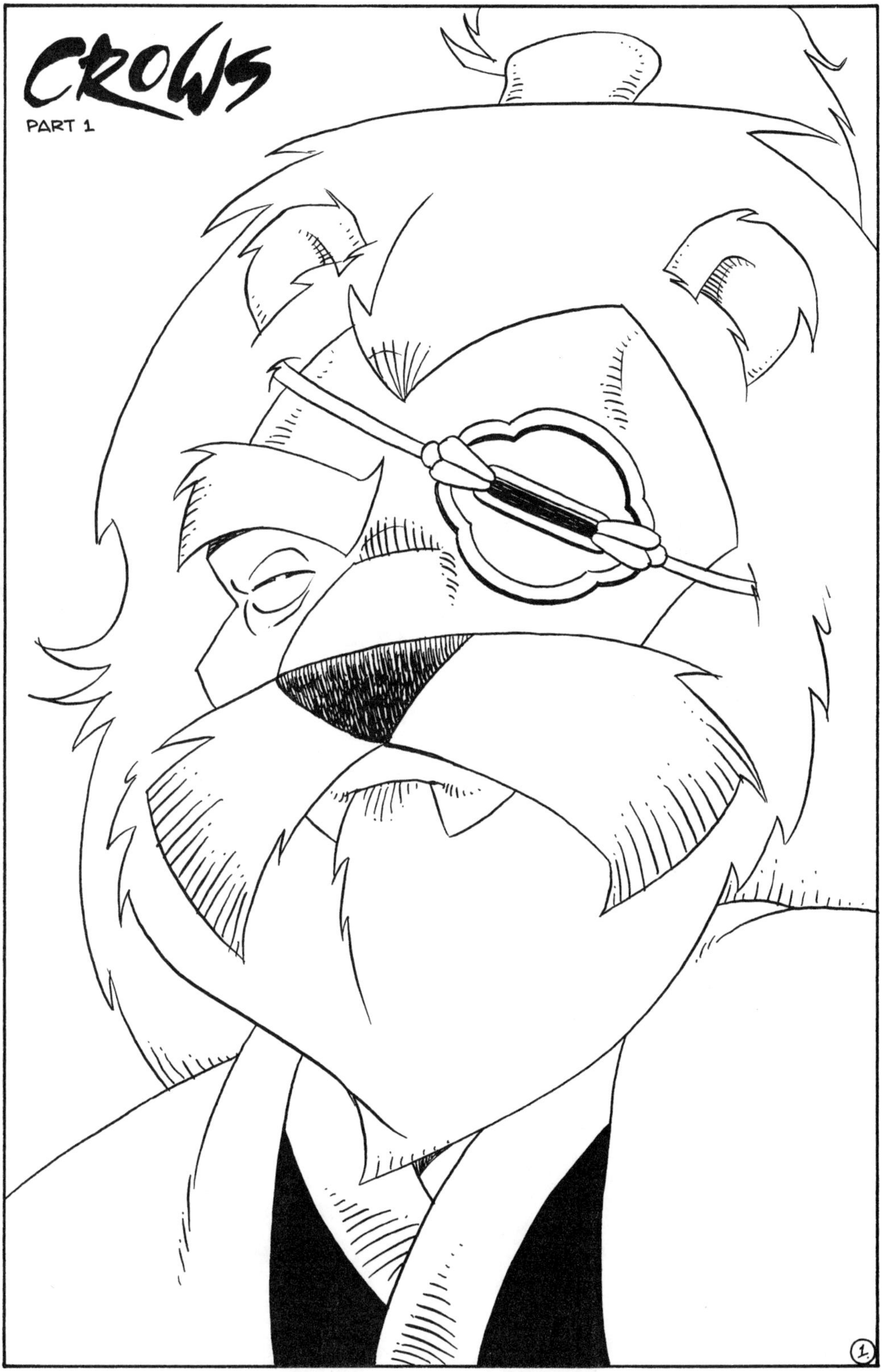
CROWS
PART 1
1

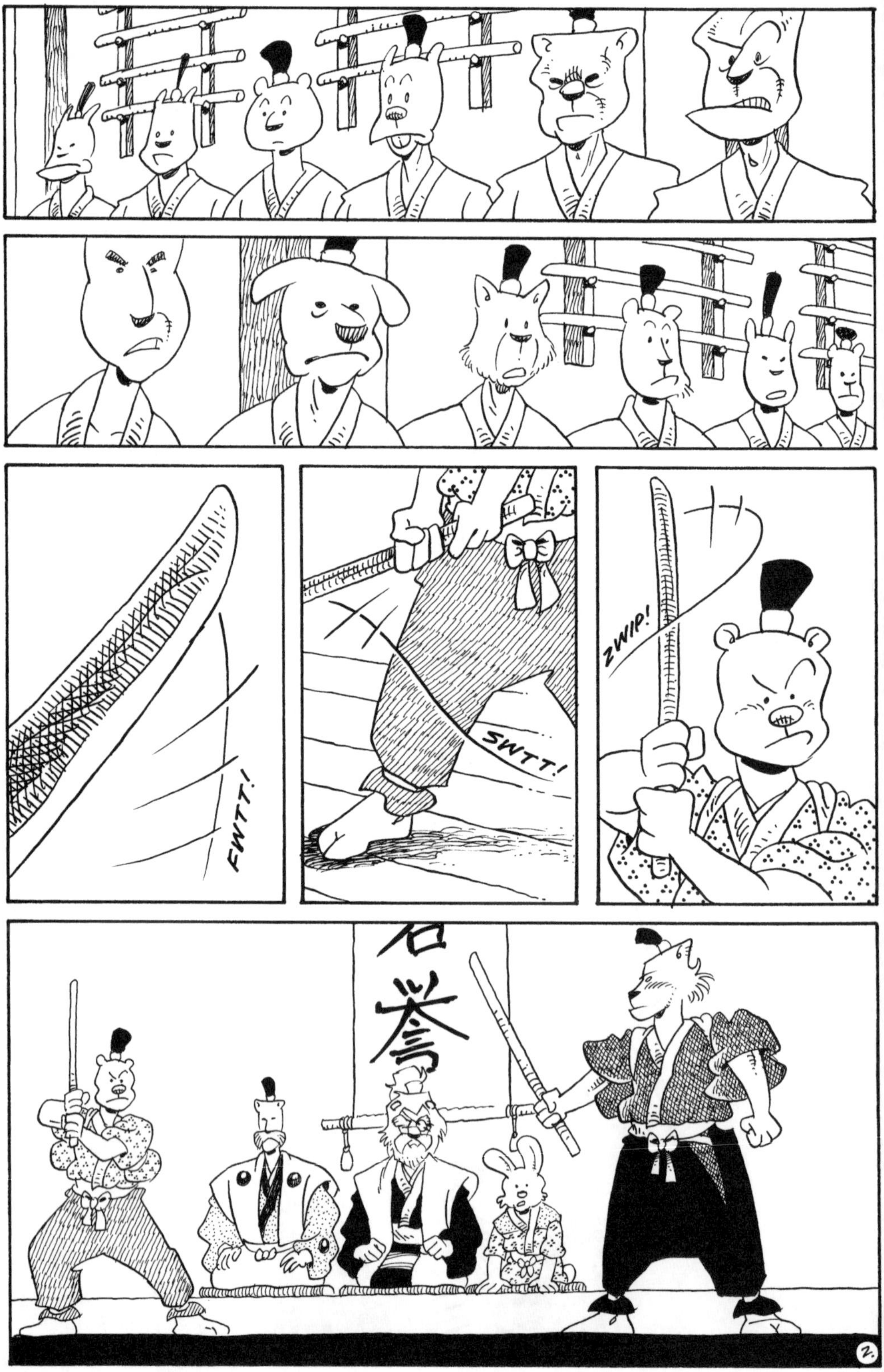
FWTT!
SWTT!
ZWIP!
誉

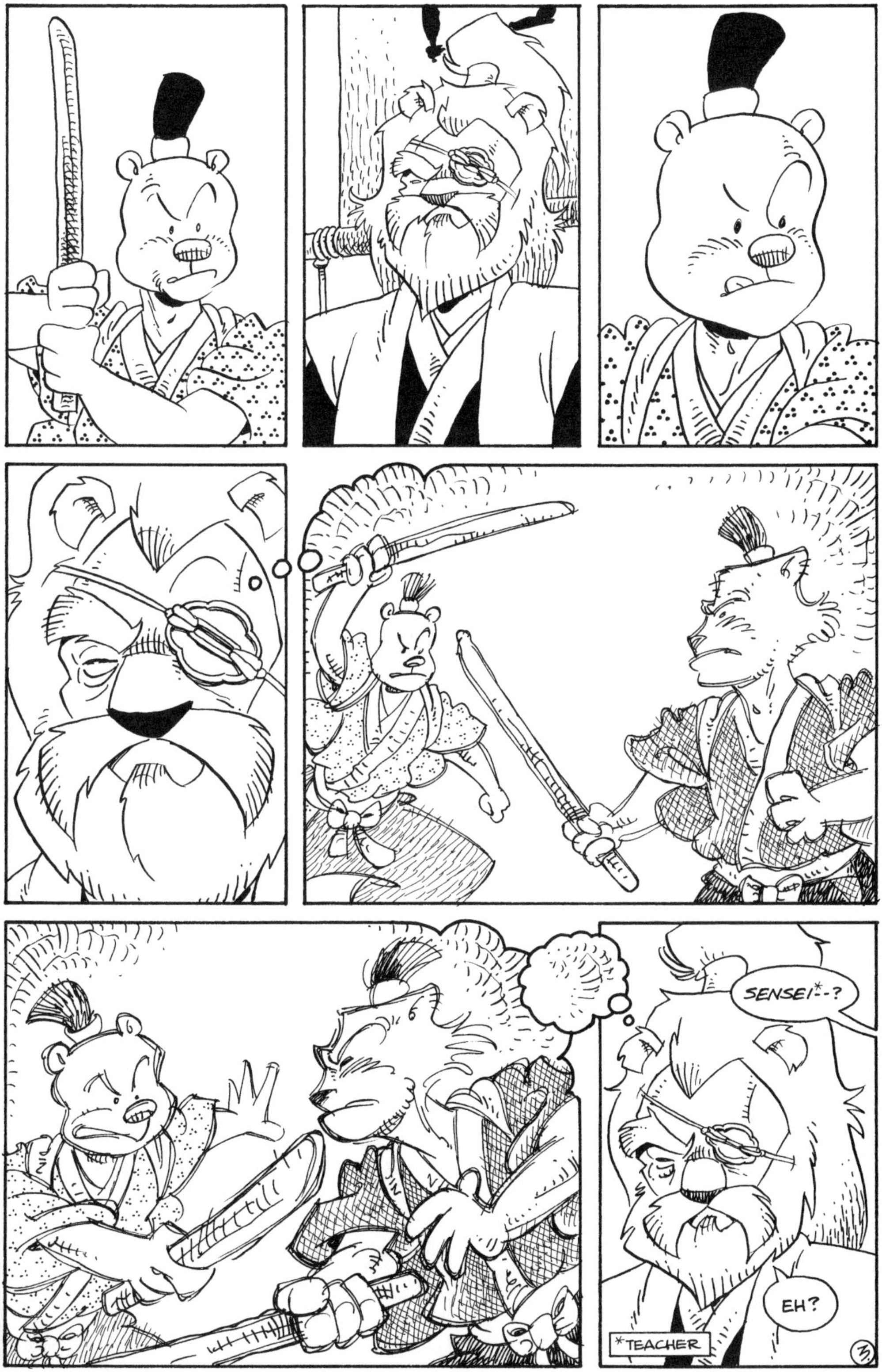
SENSEI*--?
EH?
*TEACHER

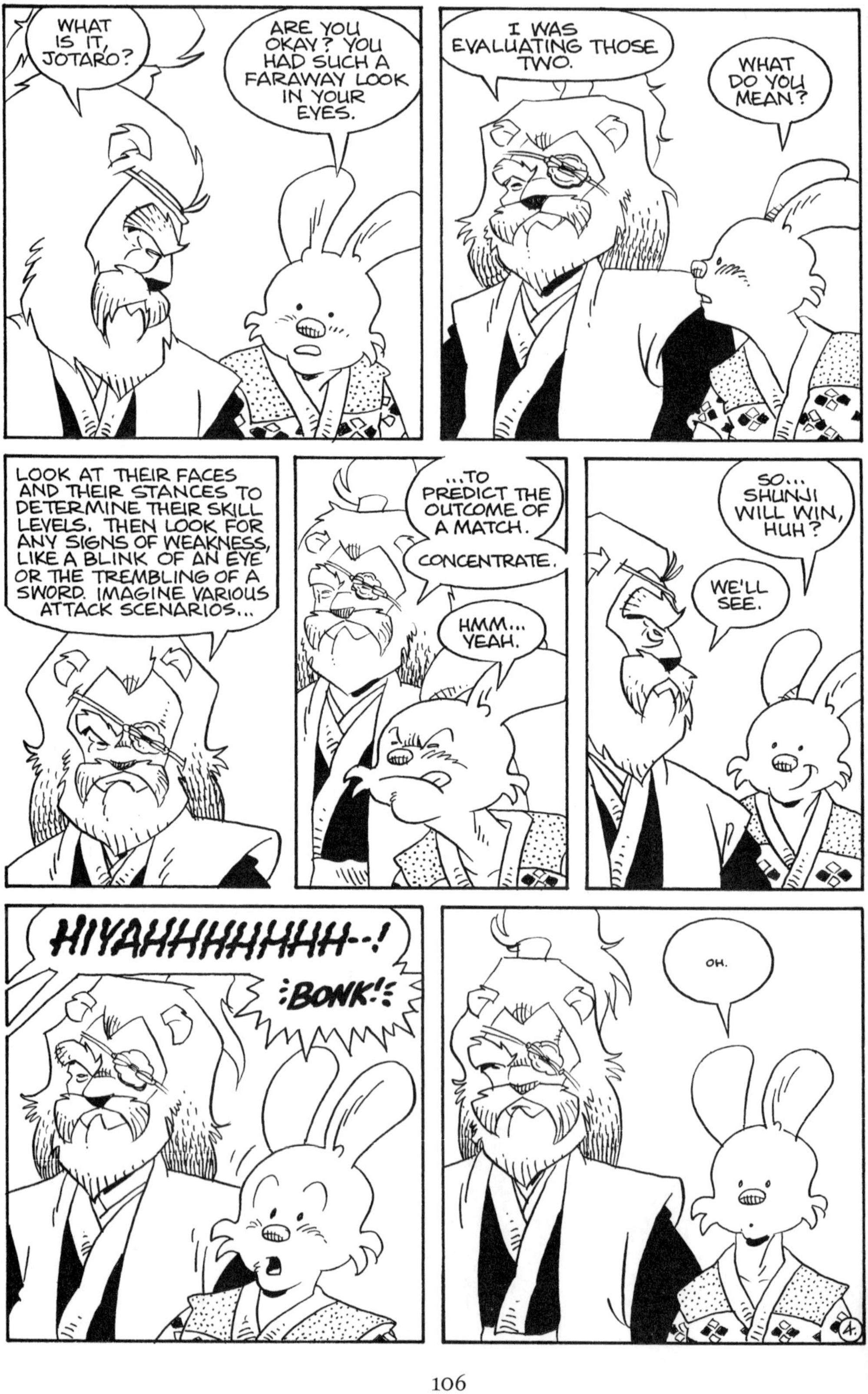
WHAT IS IT, JOTARO?
ARE YOU OKAY? YOU HAD SUCH A FARAWAY LOOK IN YOUR EYES.
I WAS EVALUATING THOSE TWO.
WHAT DO YOU MEAN?
LOOK AT THEIR FACES AND THEIR STANCES TO DETERMINE THEIR SKILL LEVELS. THEN LOOK FOR ANY SIGNS OF WEAKNESS, LIKE A BLINK OF AN EYE OR THE TREMBLING OF A SWORD. IMAGINE VARIOUS ATTACK SCENARIOS...
...TO PREDICT THE OUTCOME OF A MATCH.
CONCENTRATE.
HMM... YEAH.
SO... SHUNJI WILL WIN, HUH?
WE'LL SEE.
HIYAHHHHHHHH--!
BONK!
OH.
4.

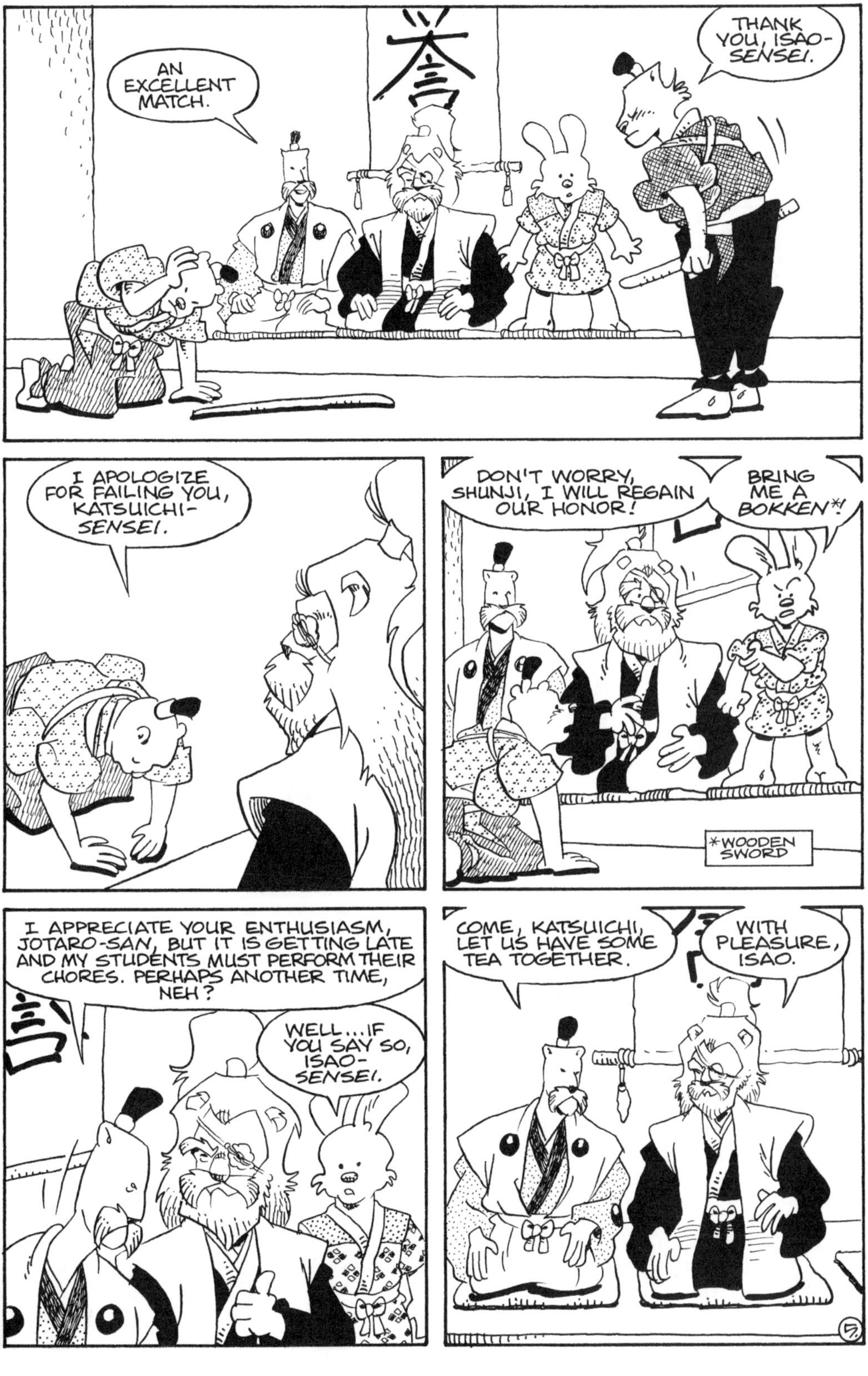
AN EXCELLENT MATCH.
THANK YOU, ISAO-SENSEI.
I APOLOGIZE FOR FAILING YOU, KATSUICHI-SENSEI.
DON'T WORRY, SHUNJI, I WILL REGAIN OUR HONOR!
BRING ME A BOKKEN*!
*WOODEN SWORD
I APPRECIATE YOUR ENTHUSIASM, JOTARO-SAN, BUT IT IS GETTING LATE AND MY STUDENTS MUST PERFORM THEIR CHORES. PERHAPS ANOTHER TIME, NEH?
WELL...IF YOU SAY SO, ISAO-SENSEI.
COME, KATSUICHI, LET US HAVE SOME TEA TOGETHER.
WITH PLEASURE, ISAO.
5

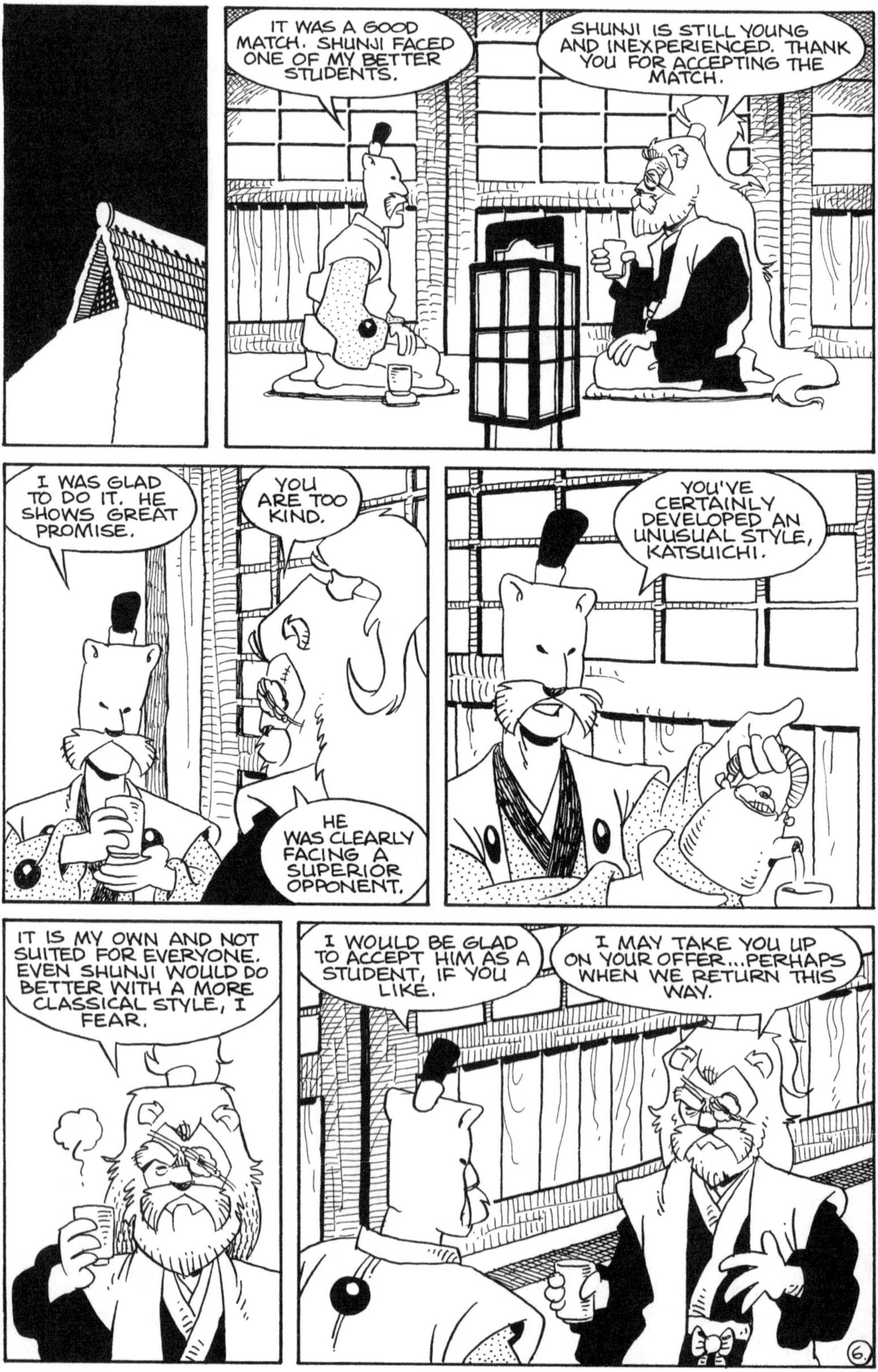
IT WAS A GOOD MATCH. SHUNJI FACED ONE OF MY BETTER STUDENTS.
SHUNJI IS STILL YOUNG AND INEXPERIENCED. THANK YOU FOR ACCEPTING THE MATCH.
I WAS GLAD TO DO IT. HE SHOWS GREAT PROMISE.
YOU ARE TOO KIND.
HE WAS CLEARLY FACING A SUPERIOR OPPONENT.
YOU'VE CERTAINLY DEVELOPED AN UNUSUAL STYLE, KATSUICHI.
IT IS MY OWN AND NOT SUITED FOR EVERYONE. EVEN SHUNJI WOULD DO BETTER WITH A MORE CLASSICAL STYLE, I FEAR.
I WOULD BE GLAD TO ACCEPT HIM AS A STUDENT, IF YOU LIKE.
I MAY TAKE YOU UP ON YOUR OFFER...PERHAPS WHEN WE RETURN THIS WAY.
6.

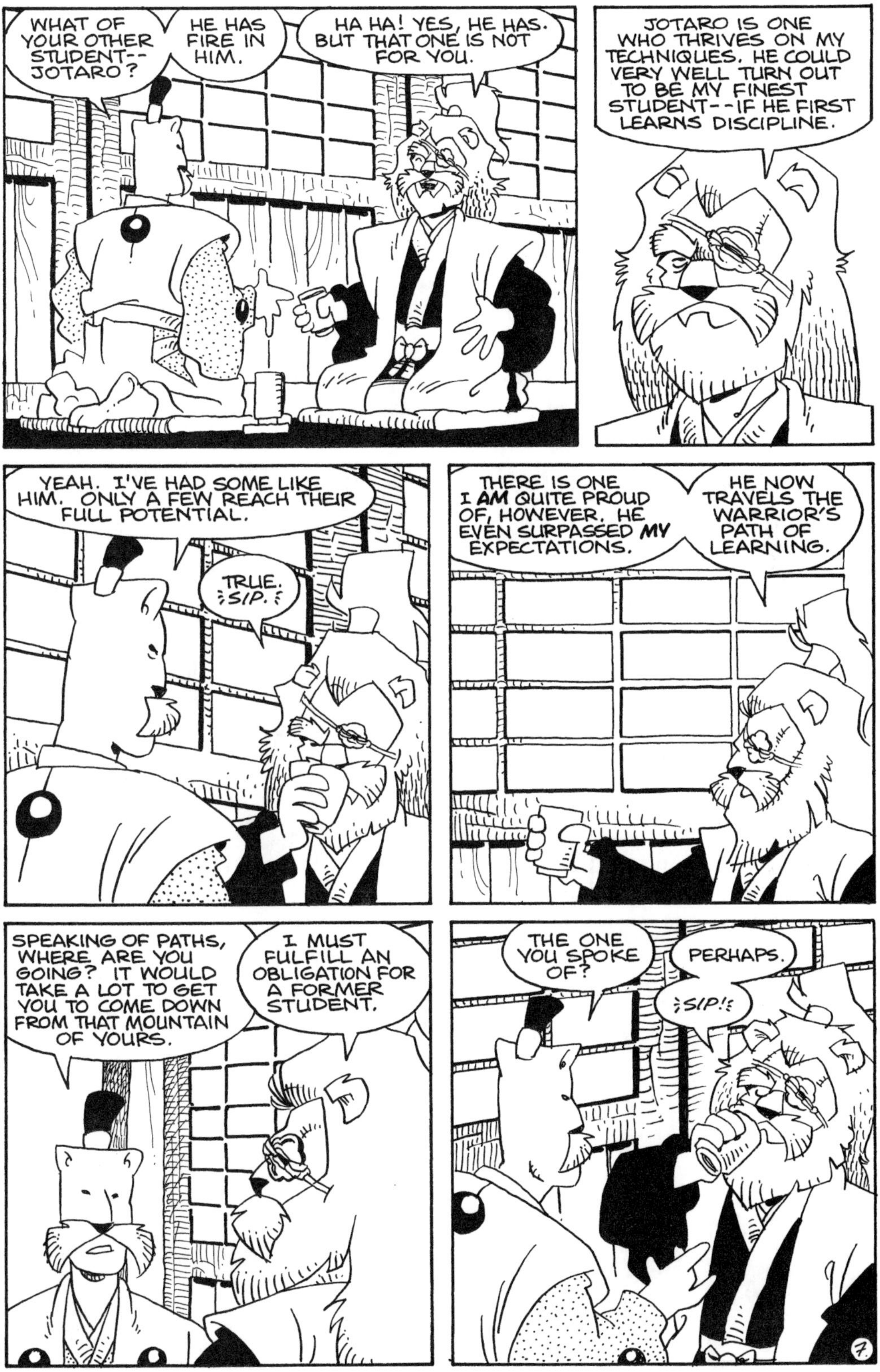
WHAT OF YOUR OTHER STUDENT--JOTARO?
HE HAS FIRE IN HIM.
HA HA! YES, HE HAS. BUT THAT ONE IS NOT FOR YOU.
JOTARO IS ONE WHO THRIVES ON MY TECHNIQUES. HE COULD VERY WELL TURN OUT TO BE MY FINEST STUDENT--IF HE FIRST LEARNS DISCIPLINE.
YEAH. I'VE HAD SOME LIKE HIM. ONLY A FEW REACH THEIR FULL POTENTIAL.
TRUE. SIP.
THERE IS ONE I AM QUITE PROUD OF, HOWEVER. HE EVEN SURPASSED MY EXPECTATIONS.
HE NOW TRAVELS THE WARRIOR'S PATH OF LEARNING.
SPEAKING OF PATHS, WHERE ARE YOU GOING? IT WOULD TAKE A LOT TO GET YOU TO COME DOWN FROM THAT MOUNTAIN OF YOURS.
I MUST FULFILL AN OBLIGATION FOR A FORMER STUDENT.
THE ONE YOU SPOKE OF?
PERHAPS.
SIP!
7

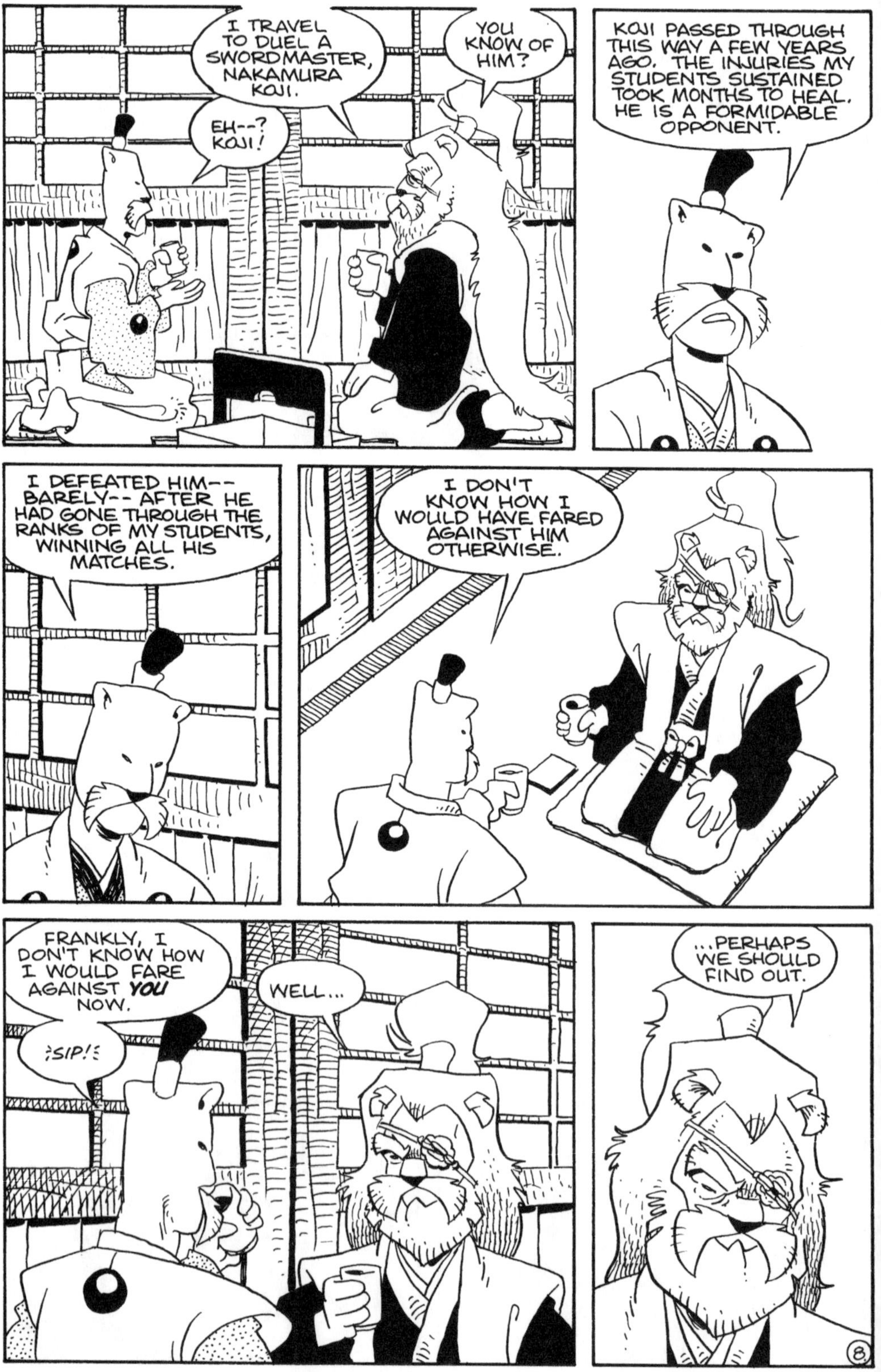
I TRAVEL TO DUEL A SWORDMASTER, NAKAMURA KOJI.
EH--? KOJI!
YOU KNOW OF HIM?
KOJI PASSED THROUGH THIS WAY A FEW YEARS AGO. THE INJURIES MY STUDENTS SUSTAINED TOOK MONTHS TO HEAL. HE IS A FORMIDABLE OPPONENT.
I DEFEATED HIM-- BARELY-- AFTER HE HAD GONE THROUGH THE RANKS OF MY STUDENTS, WINNING ALL HIS MATCHES.
I DON'T KNOW HOW I WOULD HAVE FARED AGAINST HIM OTHERWISE.
FRANKLY, I DON'T KNOW HOW I WOULD FARE AGAINST ***YOU*** NOW.
¡SIP!
WELL...
...PERHAPS WE SHOULD FIND OUT.
8

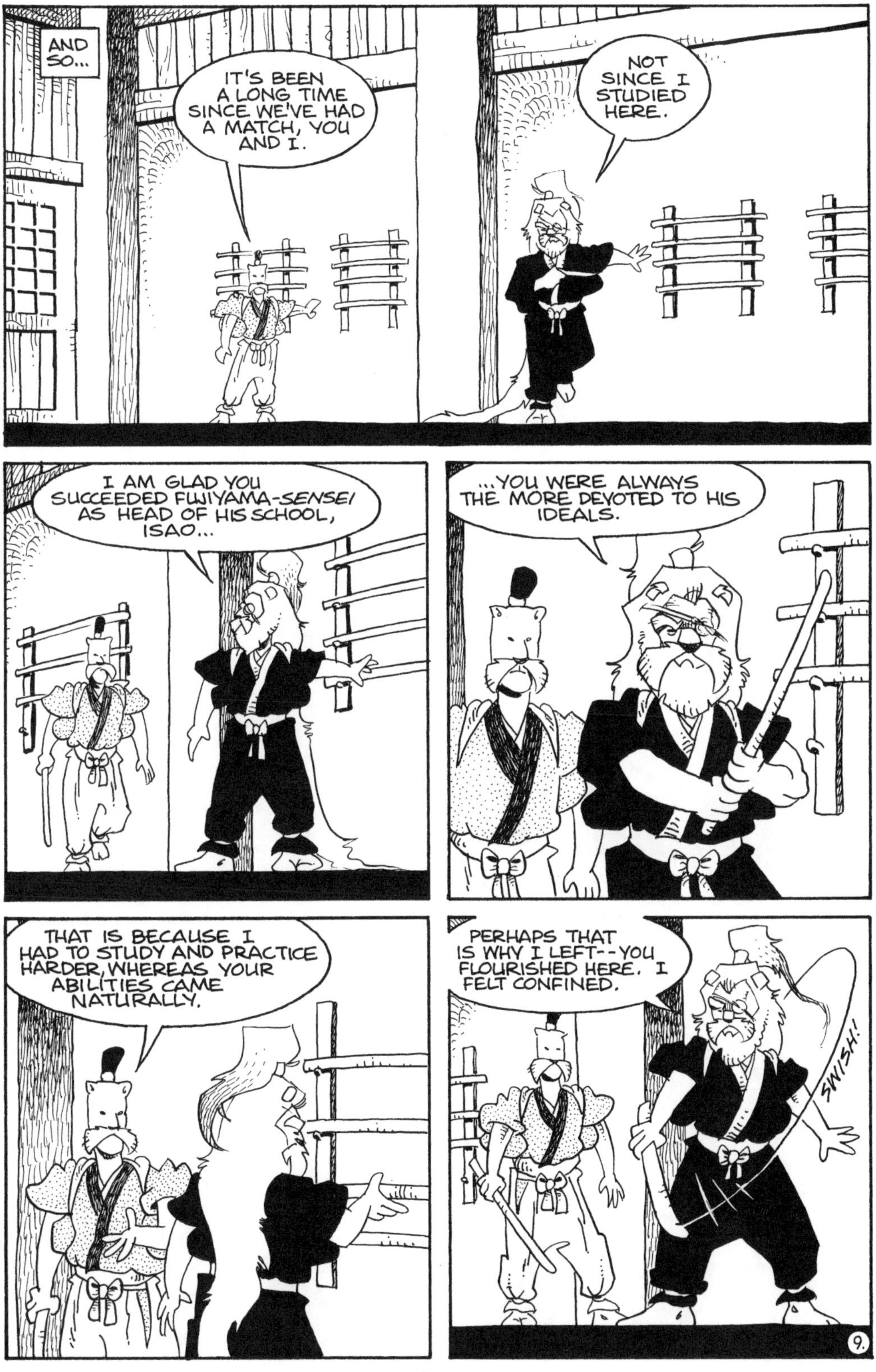
AND SO...
IT'S BEEN A LONG TIME SINCE WE'VE HAD A MATCH, YOU AND I.
NOT SINCE I STUDIED HERE.
I AM GLAD YOU SUCCEEDED FUJIYAMA-*SENSEI* AS HEAD OF HIS SCHOOL, ISAO...
...YOU WERE ALWAYS THE MORE DEVOTED TO HIS IDEALS.
THAT IS BECAUSE I HAD TO STUDY AND PRACTICE HARDER, WHEREAS YOUR ABILITIES CAME NATURALLY.
PERHAPS THAT IS WHY I LEFT--YOU FLOURISHED HERE. I FELT CONFINED.
SWISH!
9.

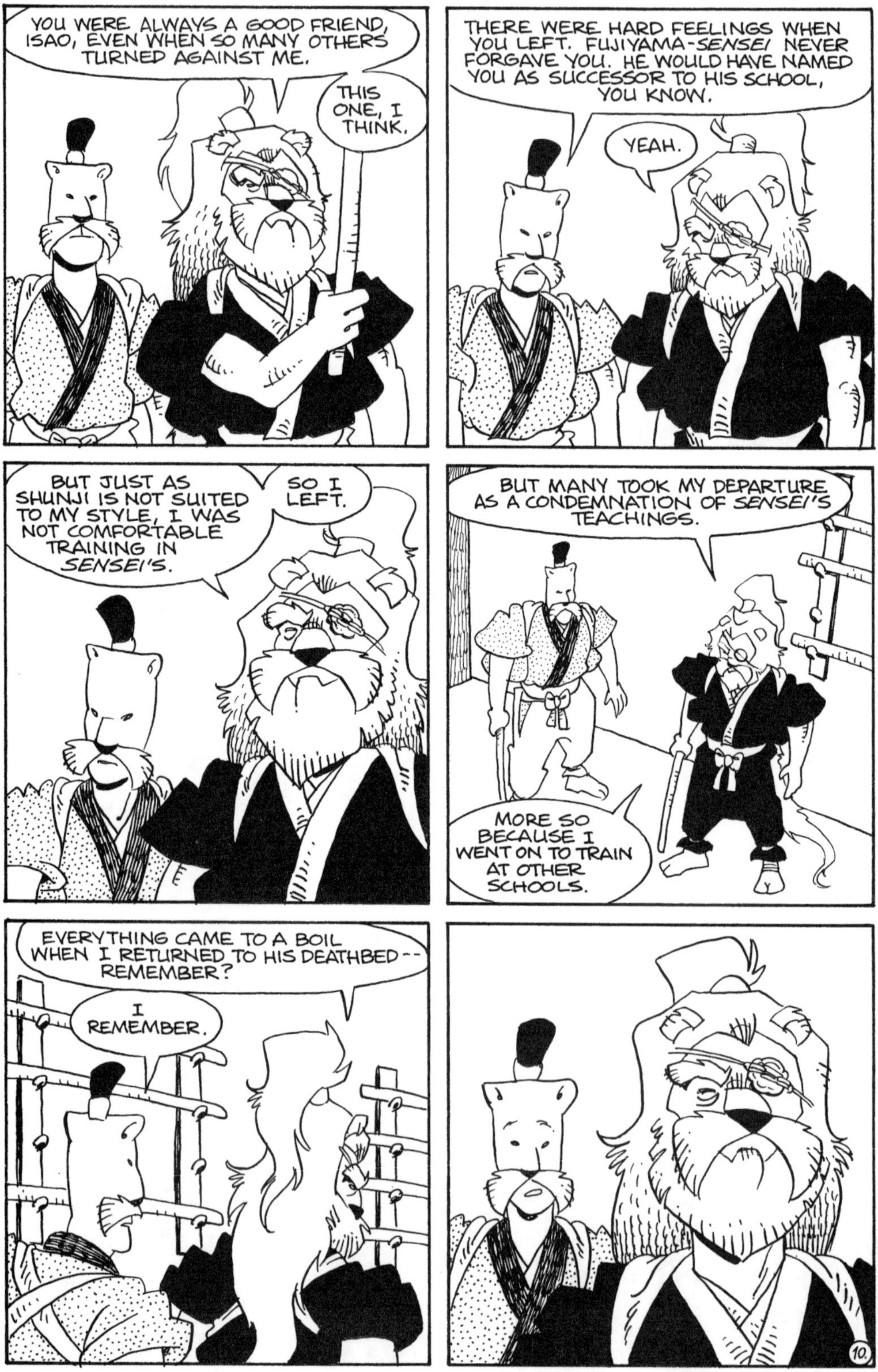
YOU WERE ALWAYS A GOOD FRIEND, ISAO, EVEN WHEN SO MANY OTHERS TURNED AGAINST ME.
THIS ONE, I THINK.
THERE WERE HARD FEELINGS WHEN YOU LEFT. FUJIYAMA-*SENSEI* NEVER FORGAVE YOU. HE WOULD HAVE NAMED YOU AS SUCCESSOR TO HIS SCHOOL, YOU KNOW.
YEAH.
BUT JUST AS SHUNJI IS NOT SUITED TO MY STYLE, I WAS NOT COMFORTABLE TRAINING IN *SENSEI'S*.
SO I LEFT.
BUT MANY TOOK MY DEPARTURE AS A CONDEMNATION OF *SENSEI'S* TEACHINGS.
MORE SO BECAUSE I WENT ON TO TRAIN AT OTHER SCHOOLS.
EVERYTHING CAME TO A BOIL WHEN I RETURNED TO HIS DEATHBED-- REMEMBER?
I REMEMBER.
10.

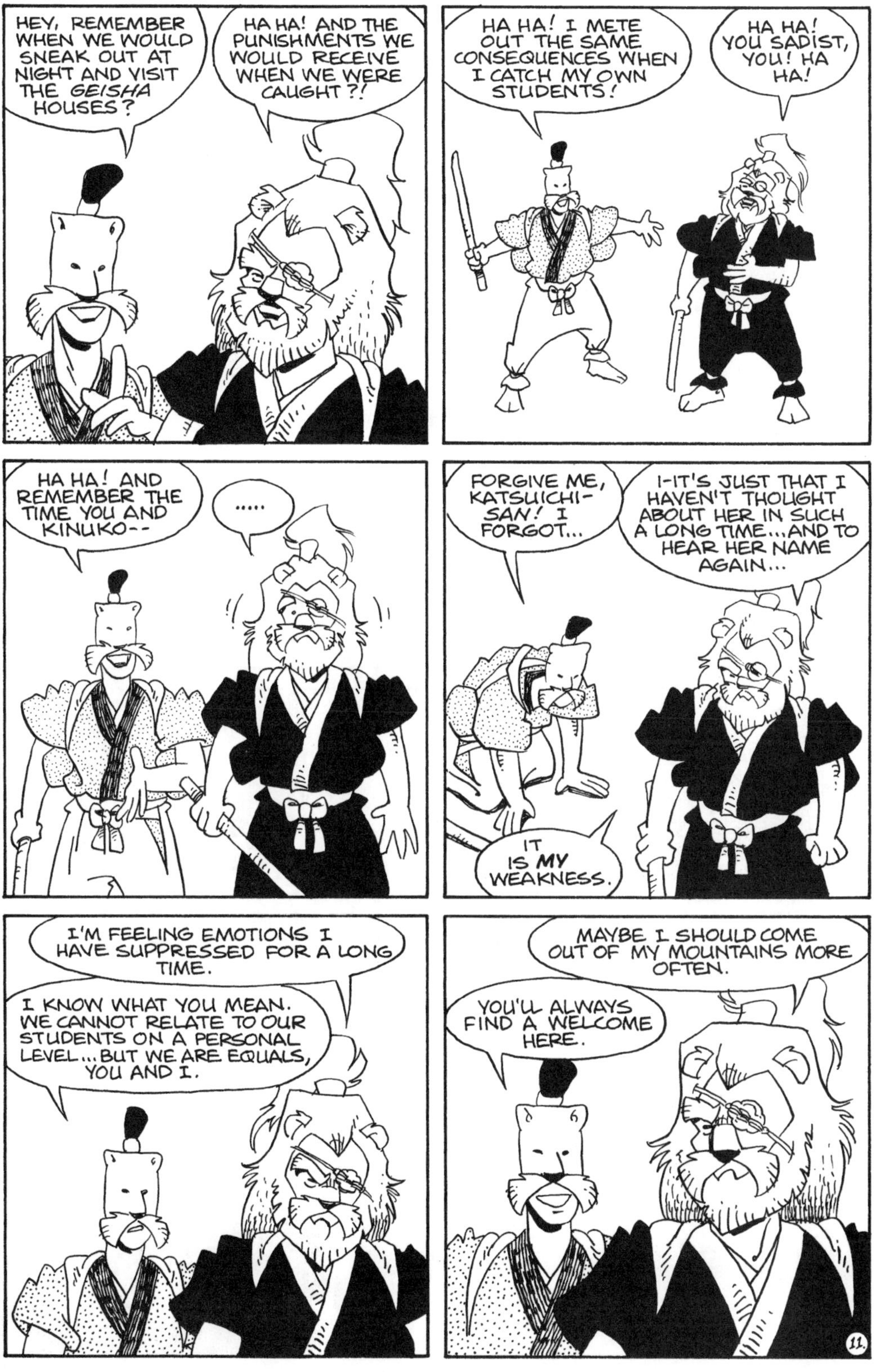
HEY, REMEMBER WHEN WE WOULD SNEAK OUT AT NIGHT AND VISIT THE *GEISHA* HOUSES?
HA HA! AND THE PUNISHMENTS WE WOULD RECEIVE WHEN WE WERE CAUGHT?!
HA HA! I METE OUT THE SAME CONSEQUENCES WHEN I CATCH MY OWN STUDENTS!
HA HA! YOU SADIST, YOU! HA HA!
HA HA! AND REMEMBER THE TIME YOU AND KINUKO--
.....
FORGIVE ME, KATSUICHI-SAN! I FORGOT...
I-IT'S JUST THAT I HAVEN'T THOUGHT ABOUT HER IN SUCH A LONG TIME...AND TO HEAR HER NAME AGAIN...
IT IS **MY** WEAKNESS.
I'M FEELING EMOTIONS I HAVE SUPPRESSED FOR A LONG TIME.
I KNOW WHAT YOU MEAN. WE CANNOT RELATE TO OUR STUDENTS ON A PERSONAL LEVEL...BUT WE ARE EQUALS, YOU AND I.
MAYBE I SHOULD COME OUT OF MY MOUNTAINS MORE OFTEN.
YOU'LL ALWAYS FIND A WELCOME HERE.
11.

ENOUGH TALKING, KABO-*CHAN*--ARE WE GOING TO HAVE A MATCH OR NOT?
CALLING ME BY MY CHILDHOOD NAME ISN'T GOING TO HELP YOU WIN, IT-*CHAN*.
PREPARE YOURSELF.
HHIIYAAHHHHH
12.

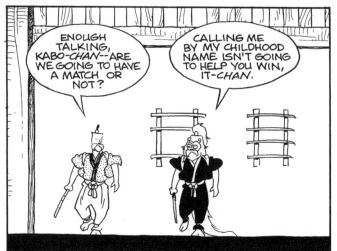

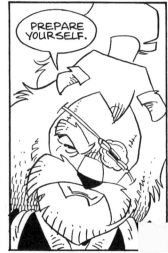

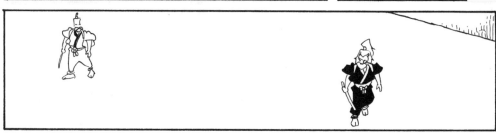

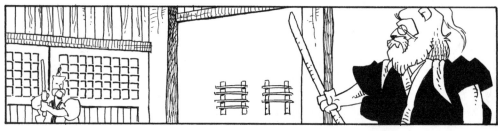

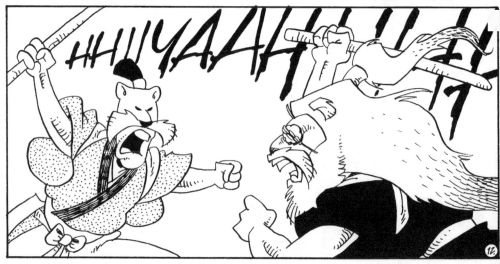

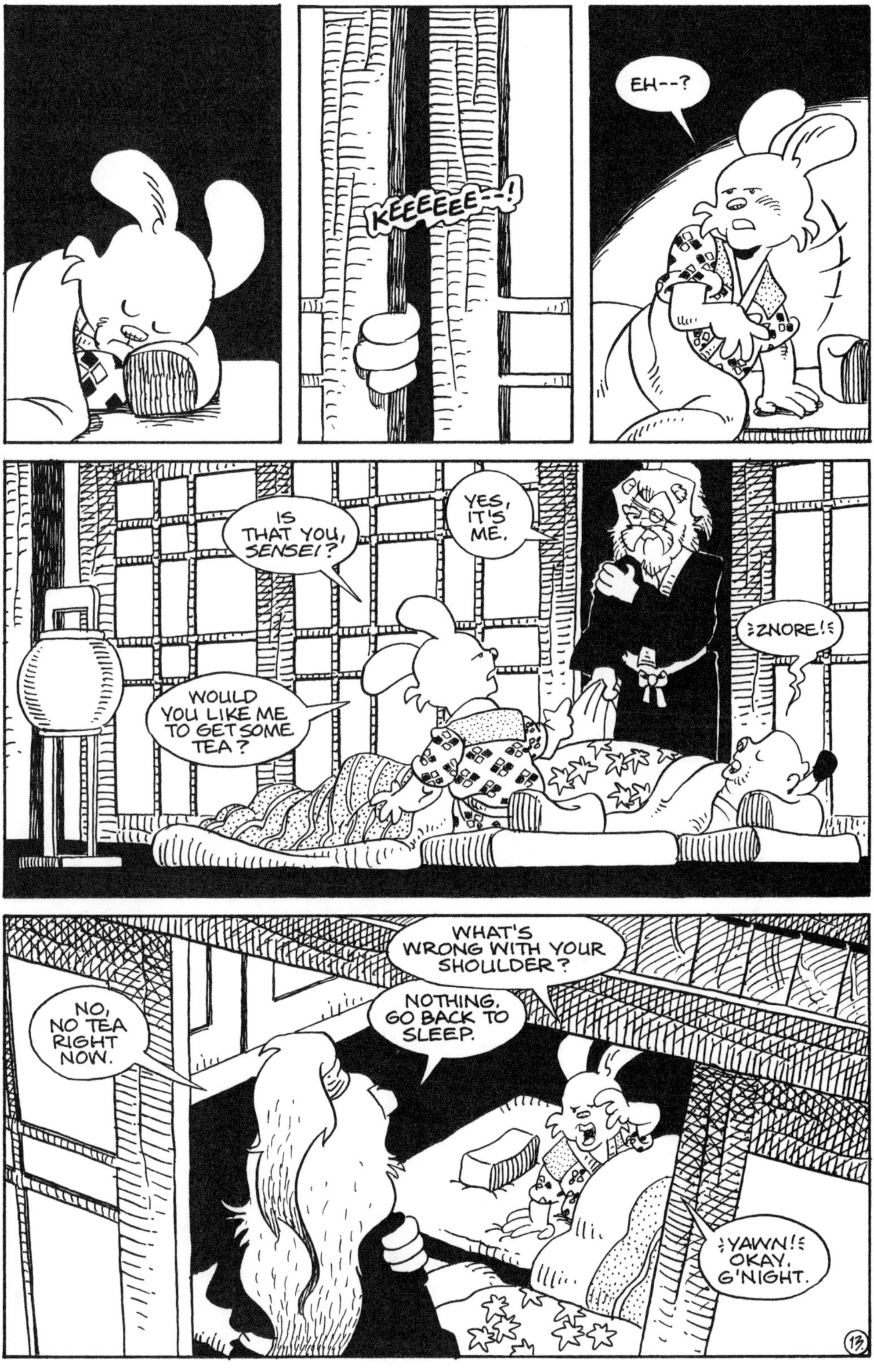
KEEEEEEE--!
EH--?
IS THAT YOU, SENSEI?
YES, IT'S ME.
WOULD YOU LIKE ME TO GET SOME TEA?
ZNORE!
NO, NO TEA RIGHT NOW.
WHAT'S WRONG WITH YOUR SHOULDER?
NOTHING. GO BACK TO SLEEP.
YAWN! OKAY. G'NIGHT.
13

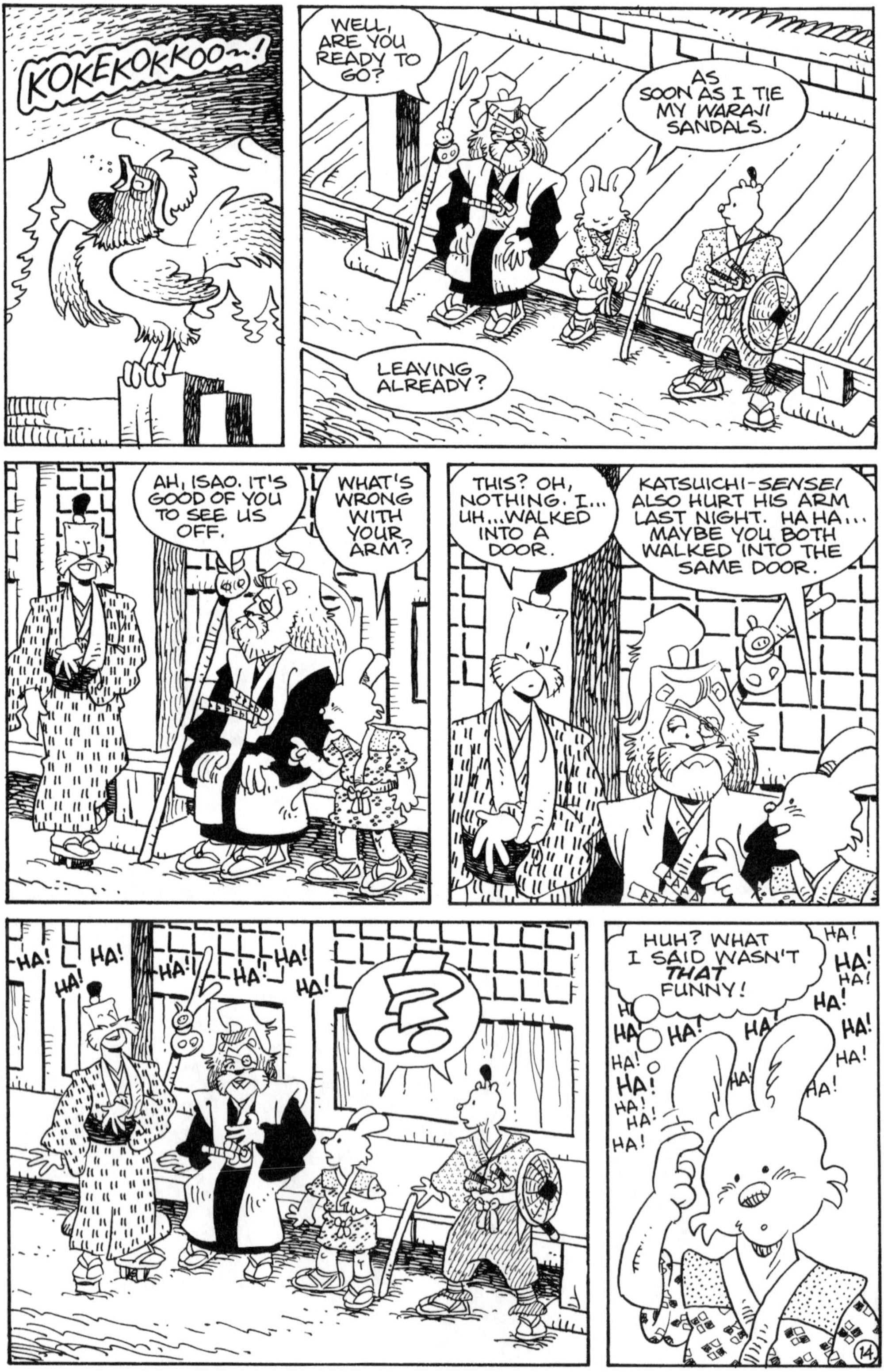
KOKEKOKKOO~!
WELL, ARE YOU READY TO GO?
AS SOON AS I TIE MY WARAJI SANDALS.
LEAVING ALREADY?
AH, ISAO. IT'S GOOD OF YOU TO SEE US OFF.
WHAT'S WRONG WITH YOUR ARM?
THIS? OH, NOTHING. I... UH...WALKED INTO A DOOR.
KATSUICHI-SENSEI ALSO HURT HIS ARM LAST NIGHT. HA HA... MAYBE YOU BOTH WALKED INTO THE SAME DOOR.
HA! HA! HA! HA! HA! HA! HA!
?
HUH? WHAT I SAID WASN'T THAT FUNNY!
HA! HA! HA! HA! HA! HA! HA! HA! HA! HA! HA! HA! HA! HA! HA! HA!
14

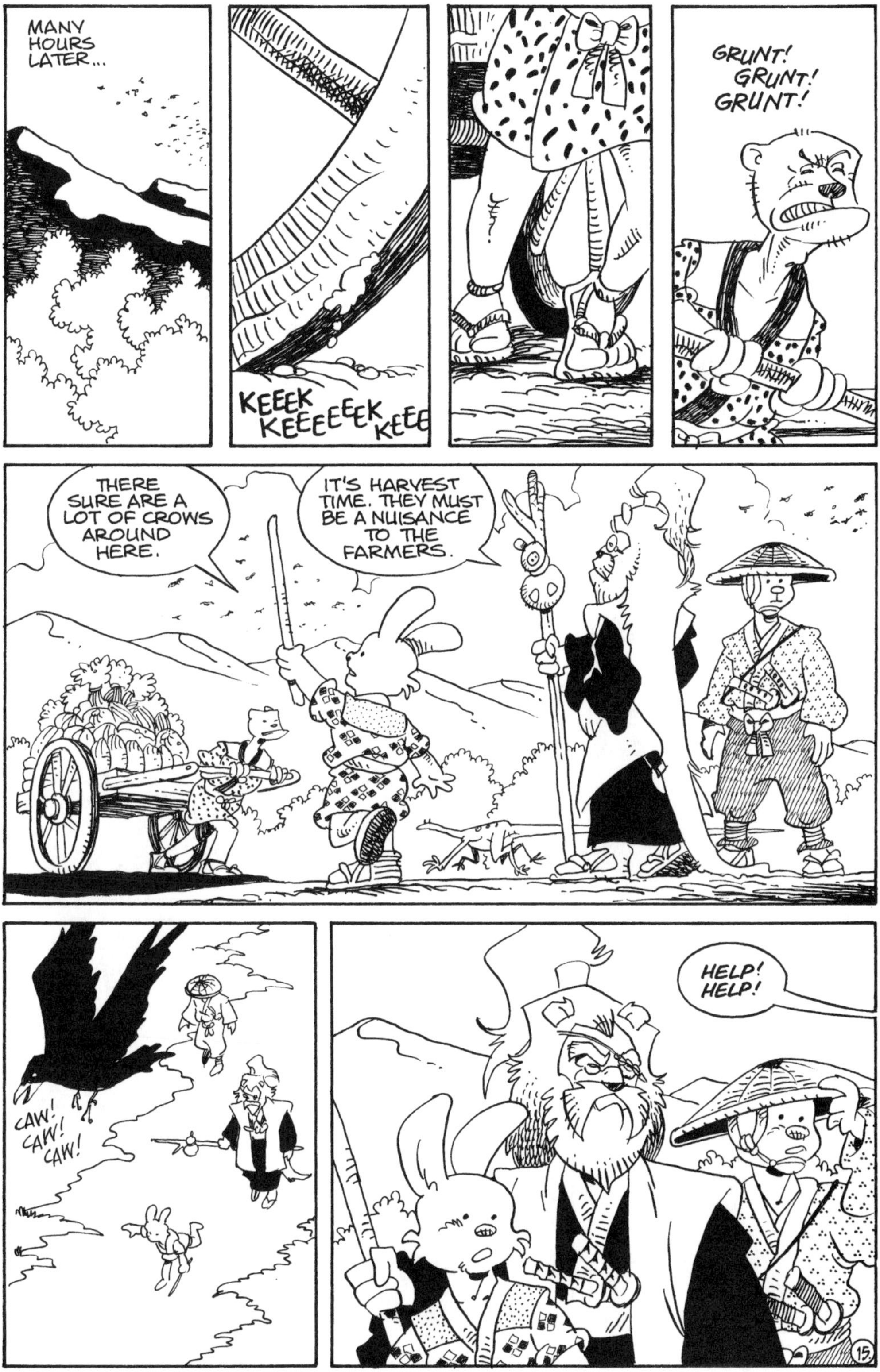
MANY HOURS LATER...
KEEEK KEEEEEEK KEEE
GRUNT! GRUNT! GRUNT!
THERE SURE ARE A LOT OF CROWS AROUND HERE.
IT'S HARVEST TIME. THEY MUST BE A NUISANCE TO THE FARMERS.
CAW! CAW! CAW!
HELP! HELP!
15

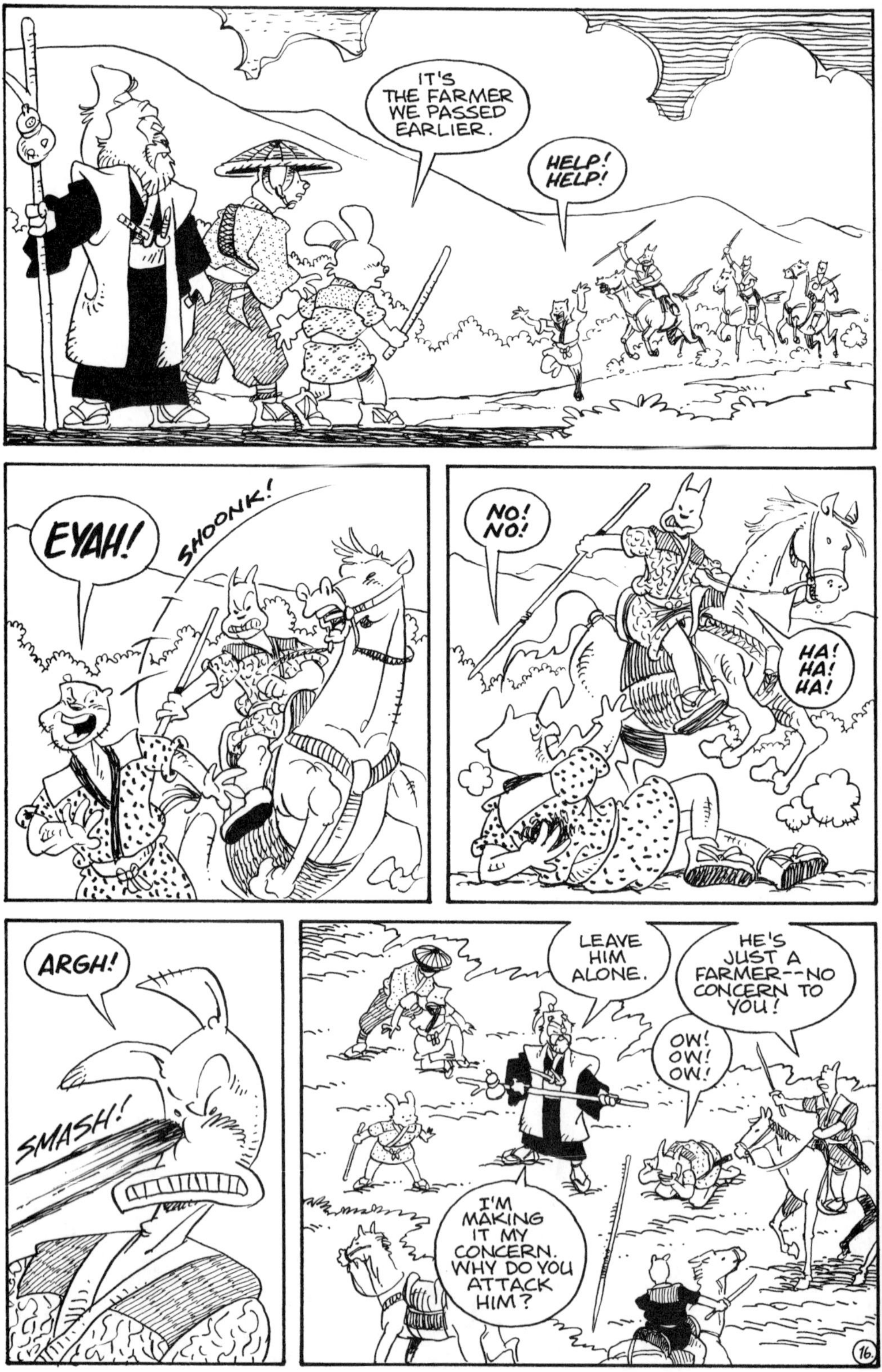
IT'S THE FARMER WE PASSED EARLIER.
HELP! HELP!
EYAH!
SHOONK!
NO! NO!
HA! HA! HA!
ARGH!
SMASH!
LEAVE HIM ALONE.
HE'S JUST A FARMER--NO CONCERN TO YOU!
OW! OW! OW!
I'M MAKING IT MY CONCERN. WHY DO YOU ATTACK HIM?
16.

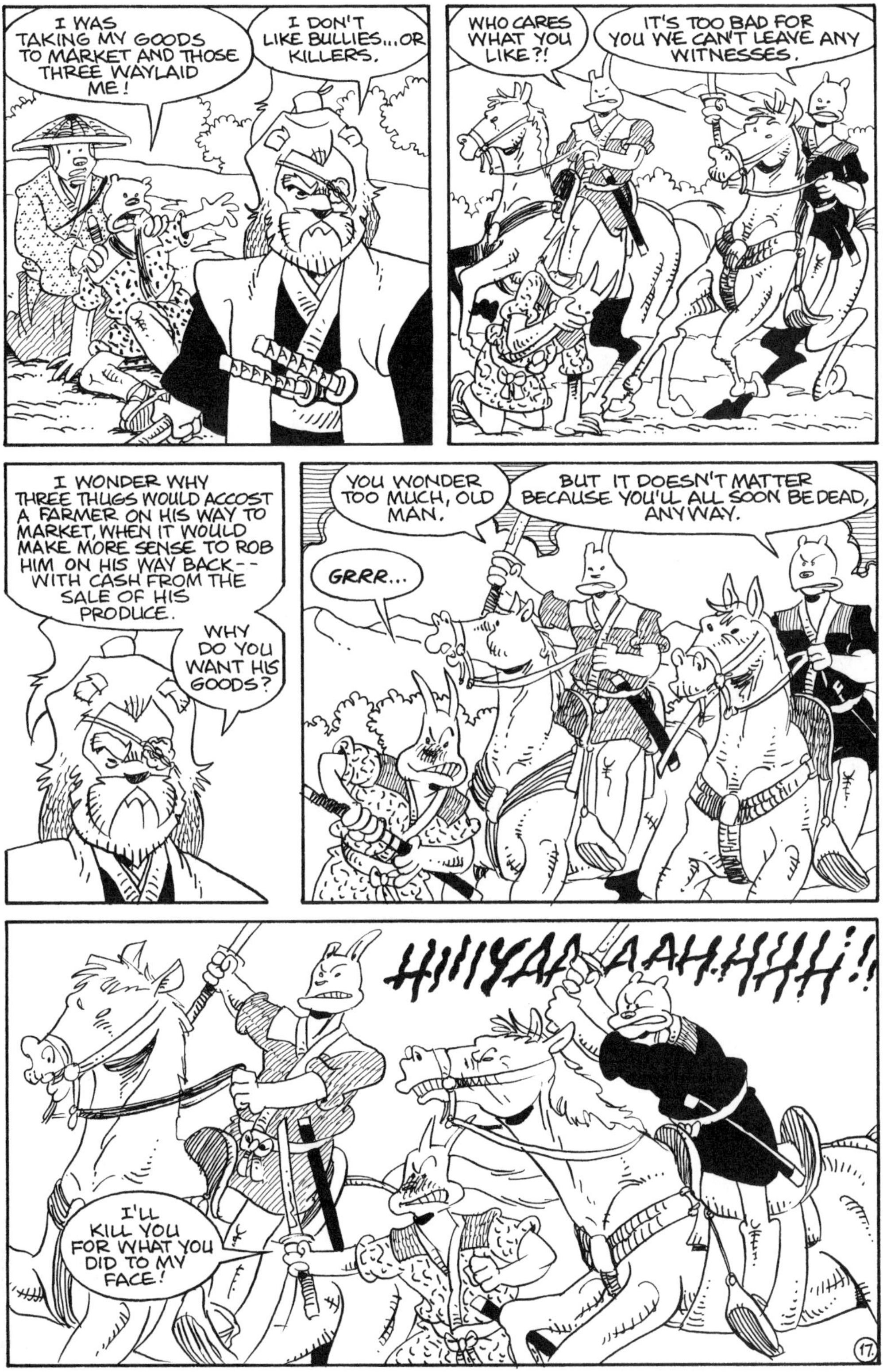
I WAS TAKING MY GOODS TO MARKET AND THOSE THREE WAYLAID ME!
I DON'T LIKE BULLIES...OR KILLERS.
WHO CARES WHAT YOU LIKE?!
IT'S TOO BAD FOR YOU WE CAN'T LEAVE ANY WITNESSES.
I WONDER WHY THREE THUGS WOULD ACCOST A FARMER ON HIS WAY TO MARKET, WHEN IT WOULD MAKE MORE SENSE TO ROB HIM ON HIS WAY BACK-- WITH CASH FROM THE SALE OF HIS PRODUCE.
WHY DO YOU WANT HIS GOODS?
YOU WONDER TOO MUCH, OLD MAN.
BUT IT DOESN'T MATTER BECAUSE YOU'LL ALL SOON BE DEAD, ANYWAY.
GRRR...
HIIIYAAAAAHHHHH!!
I'LL KILL YOU FOR WHAT YOU DID TO MY FACE!
17.

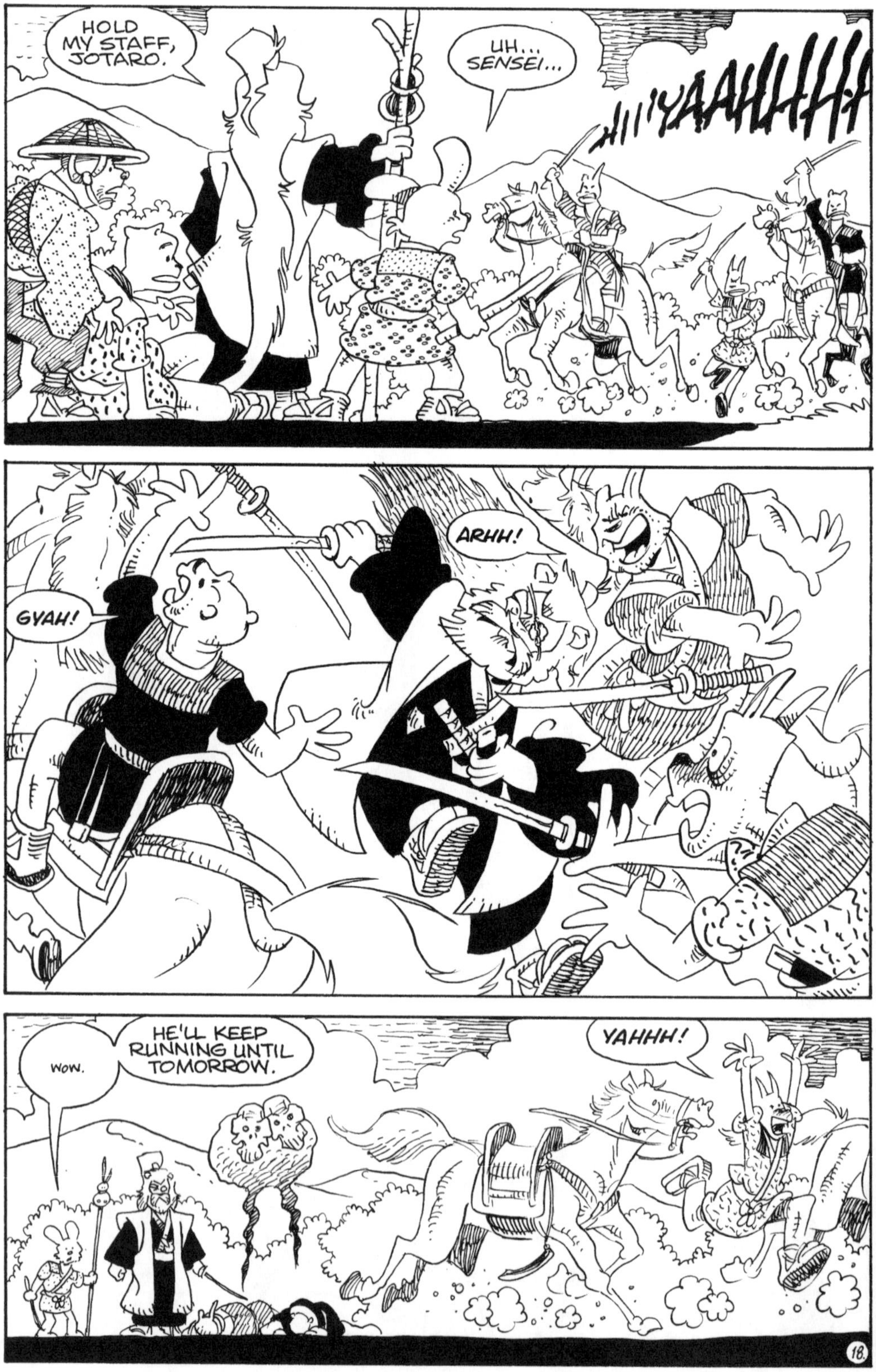
HOLD MY STAFF, JOTARO.
UH... SENSEI...
HIIYAAHHHH
GYAH!
ARHH!
WOW.
HE'LL KEEP RUNNING UNTIL TOMORROW.
YAHHH!
18.

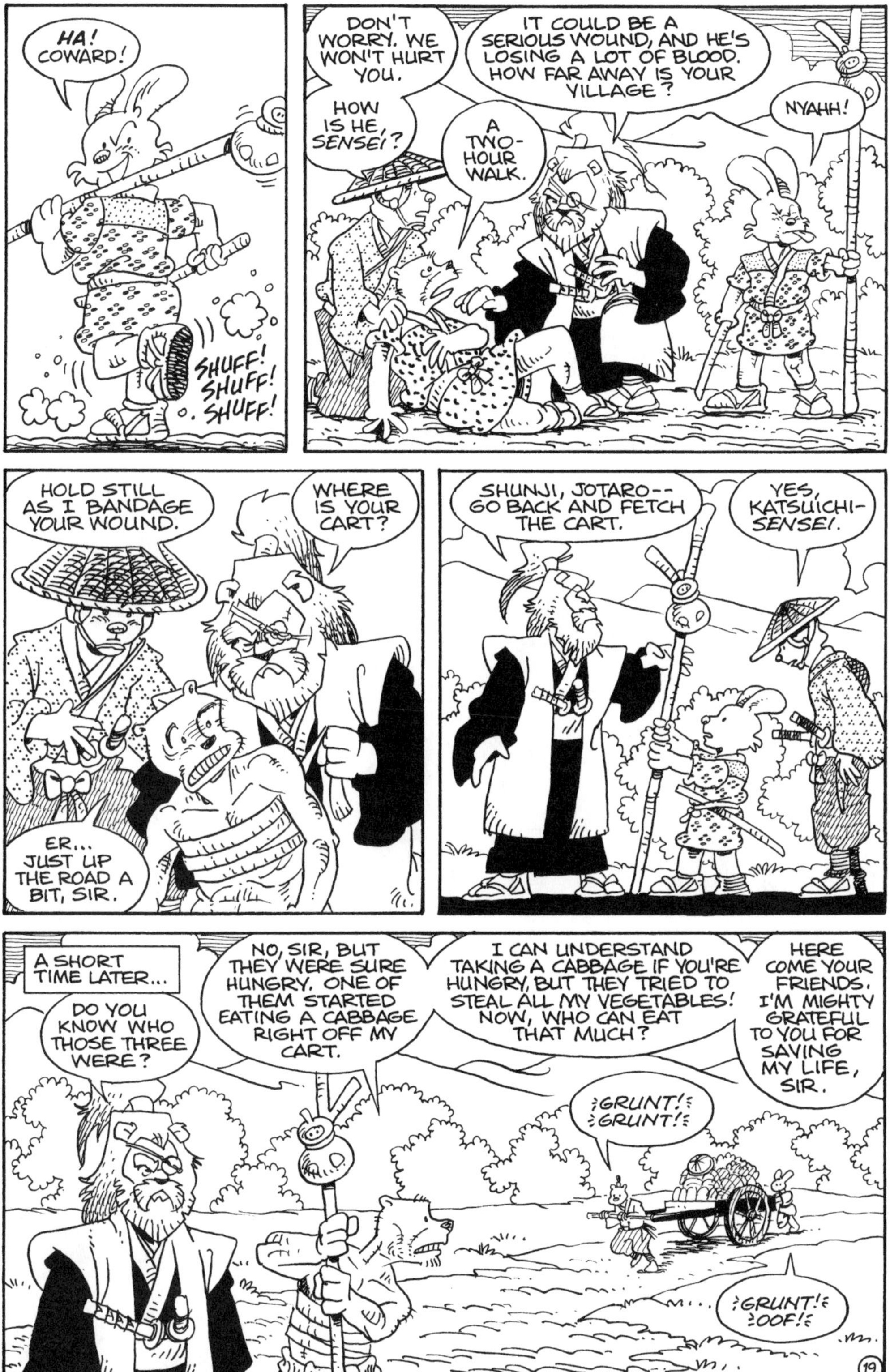
HA! COWARD!
SHUFF! SHUFF! SHUFF!
DON'T WORRY. WE WON'T HURT YOU.
HOW IS HE, SENSEI?
IT COULD BE A SERIOUS WOUND, AND HE'S LOSING A LOT OF BLOOD. HOW FAR AWAY IS YOUR VILLAGE?
A TWO-HOUR WALK.
NYAHH!
HOLD STILL AS I BANDAGE YOUR WOUND.
WHERE IS YOUR CART?
ER... JUST UP THE ROAD A BIT, SIR.
SHUNJI, JOTARO-- GO BACK AND FETCH THE CART.
YES, KATSUICHI-SENSEI.
A SHORT TIME LATER...
DO YOU KNOW WHO THOSE THREE WERE?
NO, SIR, BUT THEY WERE SURE HUNGRY. ONE OF THEM STARTED EATING A CABBAGE RIGHT OFF MY CART.
I CAN UNDERSTAND TAKING A CABBAGE IF YOU'RE HUNGRY, BUT THEY TRIED TO STEAL ALL MY VEGETABLES! NOW, WHO CAN EAT THAT MUCH?
HERE COME YOUR FRIENDS. I'M MIGHTY GRATEFUL TO YOU FOR SAVING MY LIFE, SIR.
GRUNT! GRUNT!
GRUNT! OOF!
19.

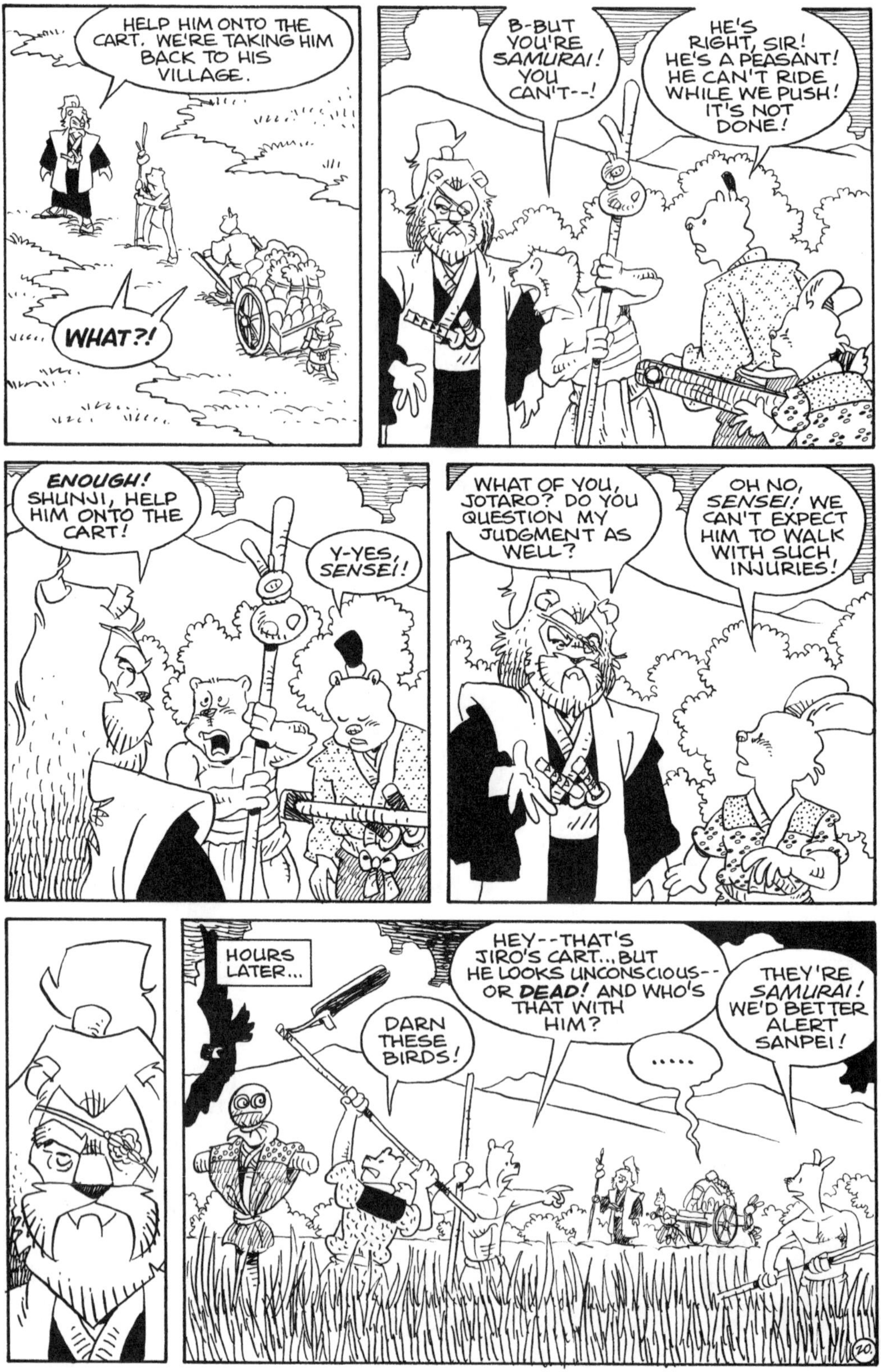
HELP HIM ONTO THE CART. WE'RE TAKING HIM BACK TO HIS VILLAGE.
WHAT?!
B-BUT YOU'RE SAMURAI! YOU CAN'T--!
HE'S RIGHT, SIR! HE'S A PEASANT! HE CAN'T RIDE WHILE WE PUSH! IT'S NOT DONE!
ENOUGH! SHUNJI, HELP HIM ONTO THE CART!
Y-YES, SENSEI!
WHAT OF YOU, JOTARO? DO YOU QUESTION MY JUDGMENT AS WELL?
OH NO, SENSEI! WE CAN'T EXPECT HIM TO WALK WITH SUCH INJURIES!
HOURS LATER...
DARN THESE BIRDS!
HEY--THAT'S JIRO'S CART... BUT HE LOOKS UNCONSCIOUS-- OR DEAD! AND WHO'S THAT WITH HIM?
.....
THEY'RE SAMURAI! WE'D BETTER ALERT SANPEI!
20.

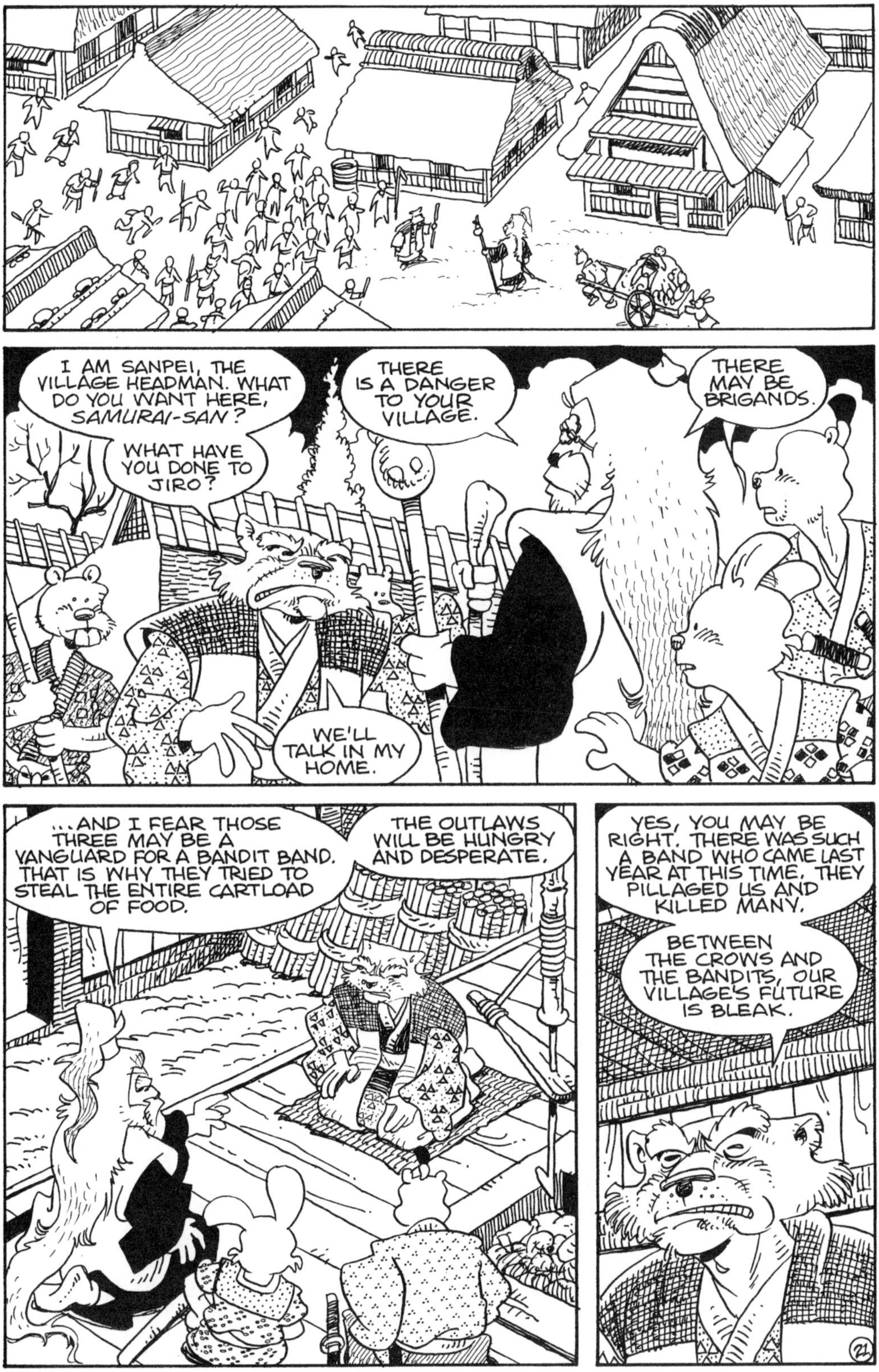
I AM SANPEI, THE VILLAGE HEADMAN. WHAT DO YOU WANT HERE, *SAMURAI-SAN*?
WHAT HAVE YOU DONE TO JIRO?
THERE IS A DANGER TO YOUR VILLAGE.
THERE MAY BE BRIGANDS.
WE'LL TALK IN MY HOME.
...AND I FEAR THOSE THREE MAY BE A VANGUARD FOR A BANDIT BAND. THAT IS WHY THEY TRIED TO STEAL THE ENTIRE CARTLOAD OF FOOD.
THE OUTLAWS WILL BE HUNGRY AND DESPERATE.
YES, YOU MAY BE RIGHT. THERE WAS SUCH A BAND WHO CAME LAST YEAR AT THIS TIME. THEY PILLAGED US AND KILLED MANY.
BETWEEN THE CROWS AND THE BANDITS, OUR VILLAGE'S FUTURE IS BLEAK.
21

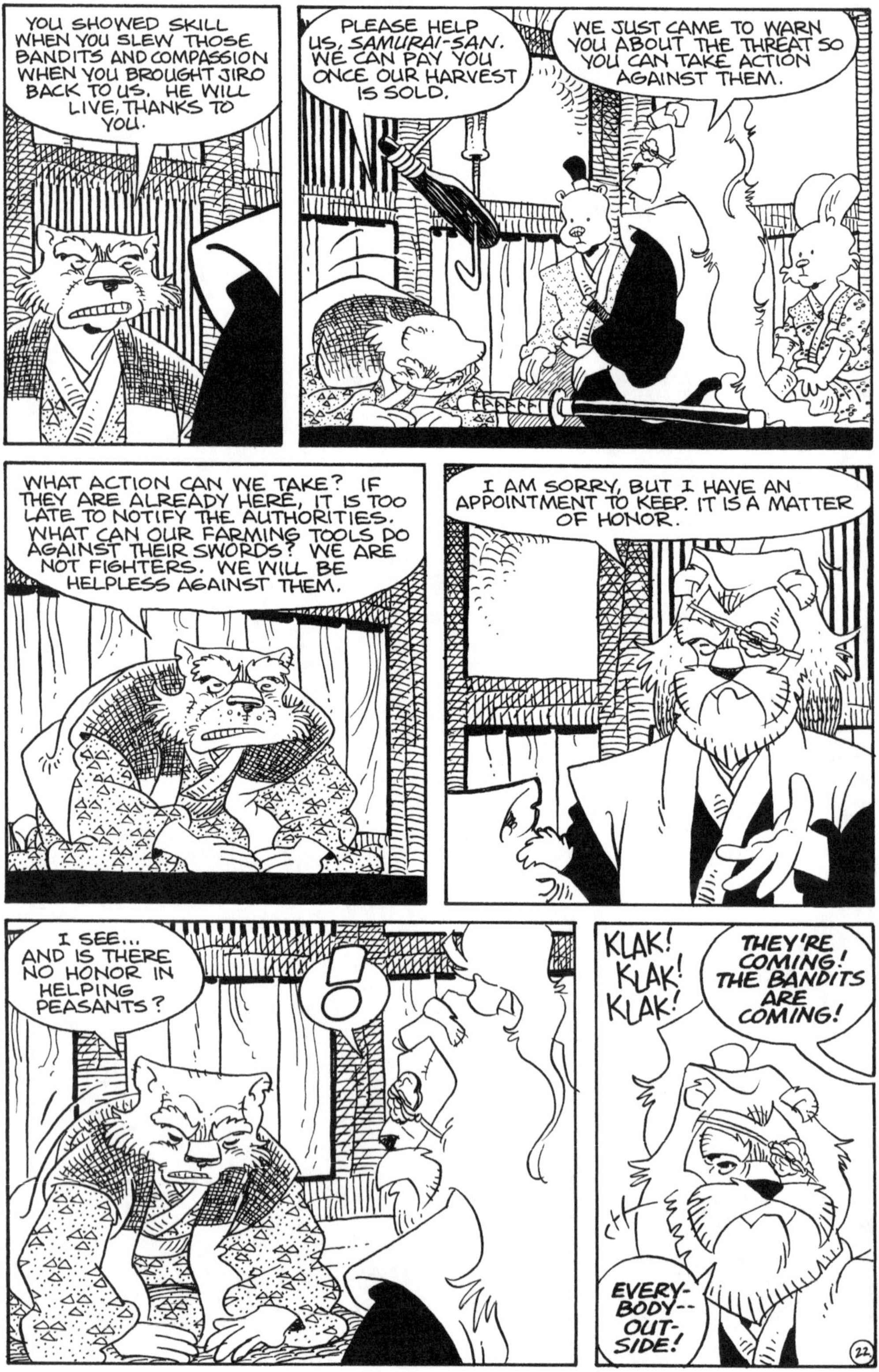
YOU SHOWED SKILL WHEN YOU SLEW THOSE BANDITS AND COMPASSION WHEN YOU BROUGHT JIRO BACK TO US. HE WILL LIVE, THANKS TO YOU.
PLEASE HELP US, SAMURAI-SAN. WE CAN PAY YOU ONCE OUR HARVEST IS SOLD.
WE JUST CAME TO WARN YOU ABOUT THE THREAT SO YOU CAN TAKE ACTION AGAINST THEM.
WHAT ACTION CAN WE TAKE? IF THEY ARE ALREADY HERE, IT IS TOO LATE TO NOTIFY THE AUTHORITIES. WHAT CAN OUR FARMING TOOLS DO AGAINST THEIR SWORDS? WE ARE NOT FIGHTERS. WE WILL BE HELPLESS AGAINST THEM.
I AM SORRY, BUT I HAVE AN APPOINTMENT TO KEEP. IT IS A MATTER OF HONOR.
I SEE... AND IS THERE NO HONOR IN HELPING PEASANTS?
!
KLAK! KLAK! KLAK!
THEY'RE COMING! THE BANDITS ARE COMING!
EVERY-BODY-- OUT-SIDE!
22

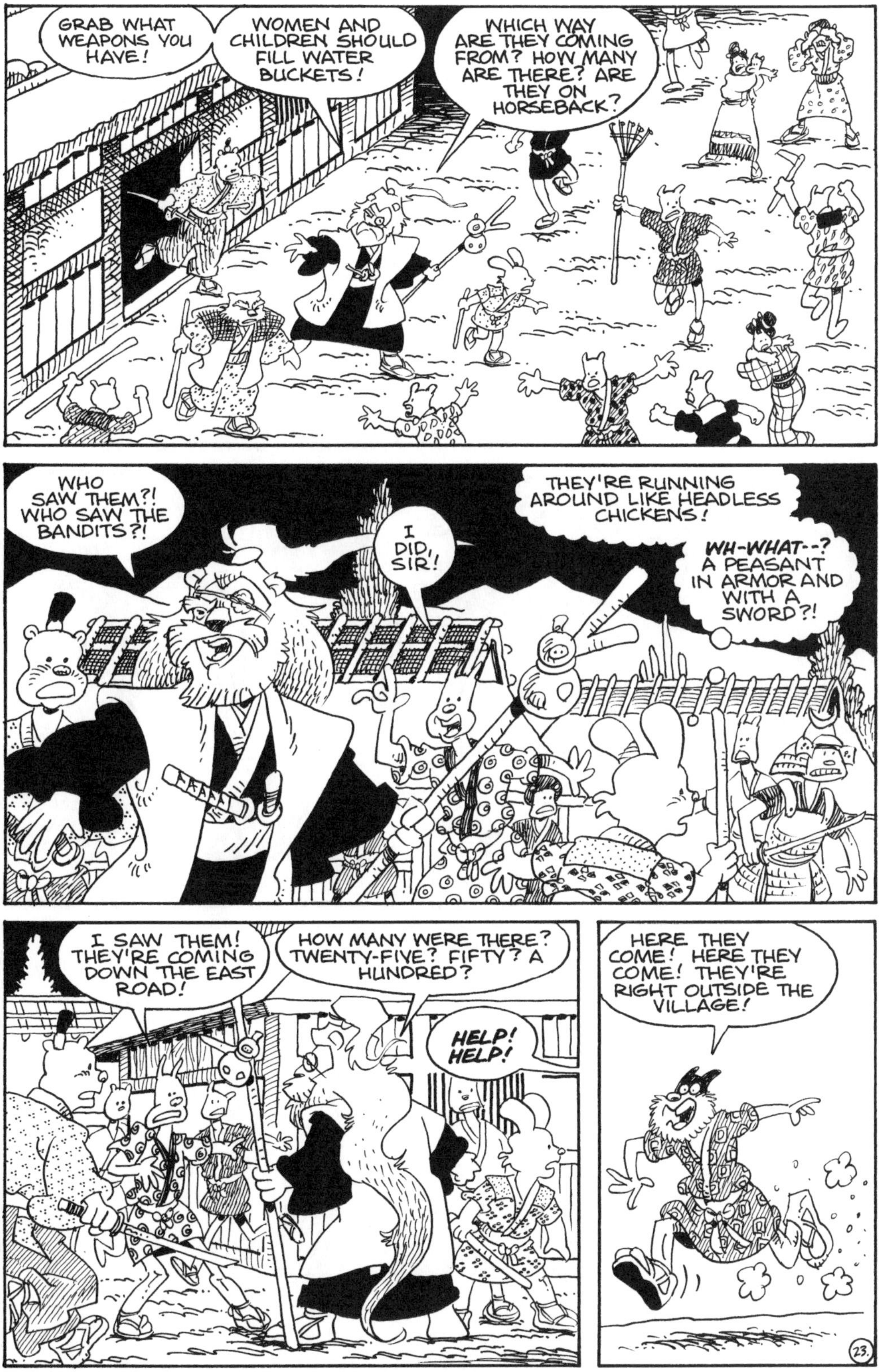
GRAB WHAT WEAPONS YOU HAVE!
WOMEN AND CHILDREN SHOULD FILL WATER BUCKETS!
WHICH WAY ARE THEY COMING FROM? HOW MANY ARE THERE? ARE THEY ON HORSEBACK?
WHO SAW THEM?! WHO SAW THE BANDITS?!
I DID, SIR!
THEY'RE RUNNING AROUND LIKE HEADLESS CHICKENS!
WH-WHAT--? A PEASANT IN ARMOR AND WITH A SWORD?!
I SAW THEM! THEY'RE COMING DOWN THE EAST ROAD!
HOW MANY WERE THERE? TWENTY-FIVE? FIFTY? A HUNDRED?
HELP! HELP!
HERE THEY COME! HERE THEY COME! THEY'RE RIGHT OUTSIDE THE VILLAGE!
23.

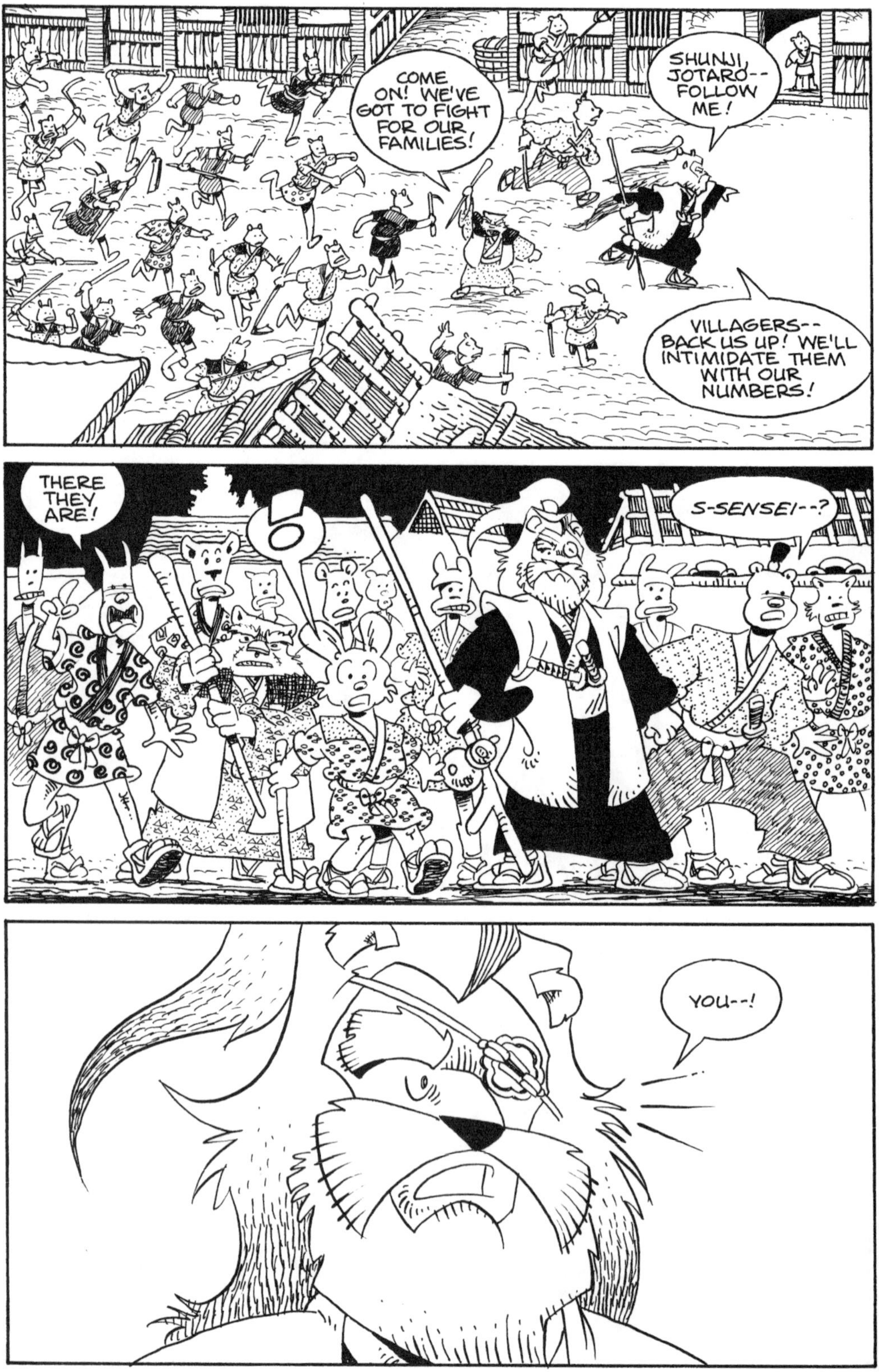
COME ON! WE'VE GOT TO FIGHT FOR OUR FAMILIES!
SHUNJI, JOTARO-- FOLLOW ME!
VILLAGERS-- BACK US UP! WE'LL INTIMIDATE THEM WITH OUR NUMBERS!
THERE THEY ARE!
S-SENSEI--?
YOU--!

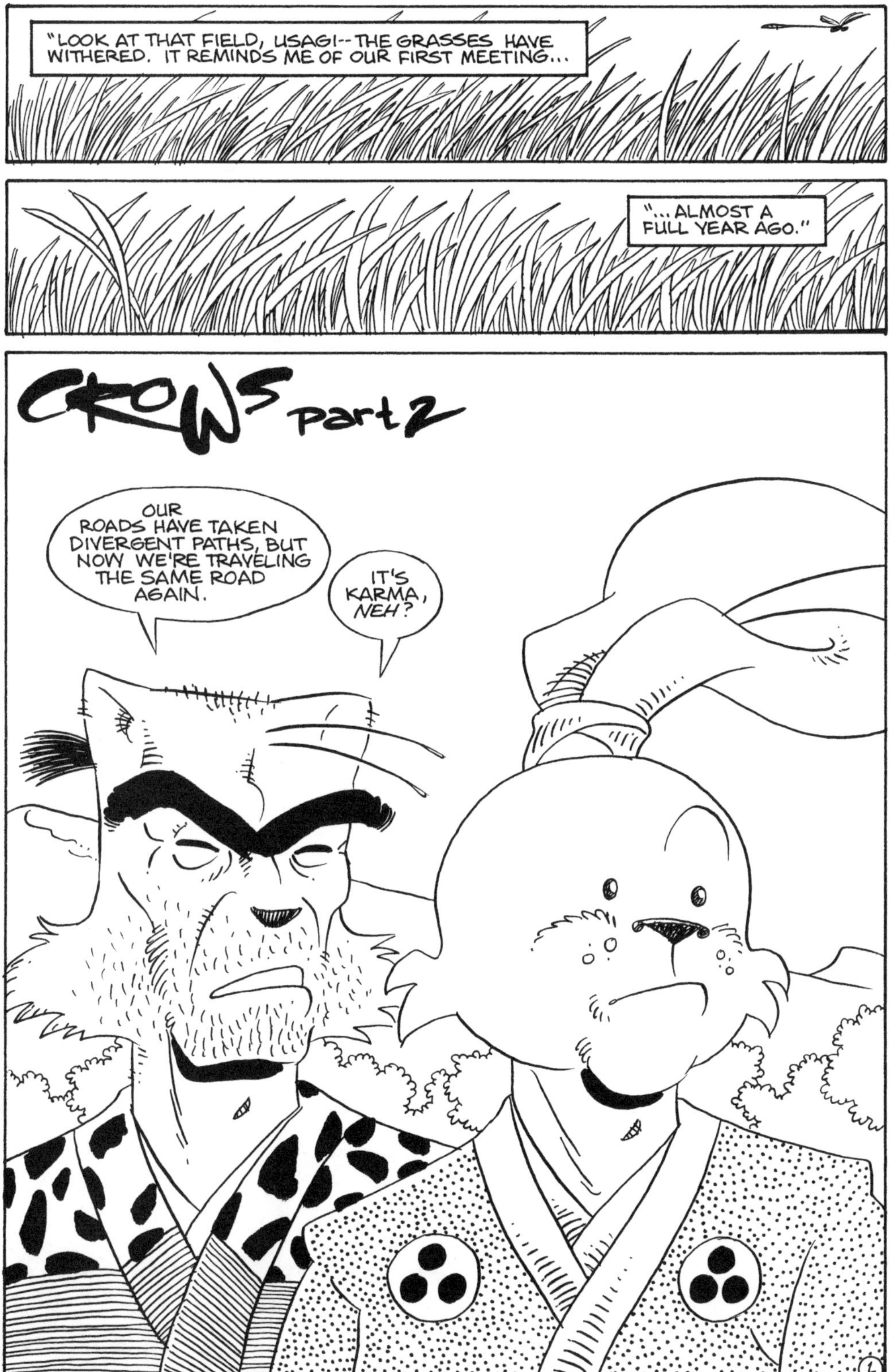
"LOOK AT THAT FIELD, USAGI--THE GRASSES HAVE WITHERED. IT REMINDS ME OF OUR FIRST MEETING...
"...ALMOST A FULL YEAR AGO."
CROWS part 2
OUR ROADS HAVE TAKEN DIVERGENT PATHS, BUT NOW WE'RE TRAVELING THE SAME ROAD AGAIN.
IT'S KARMA, *NEH*?
1

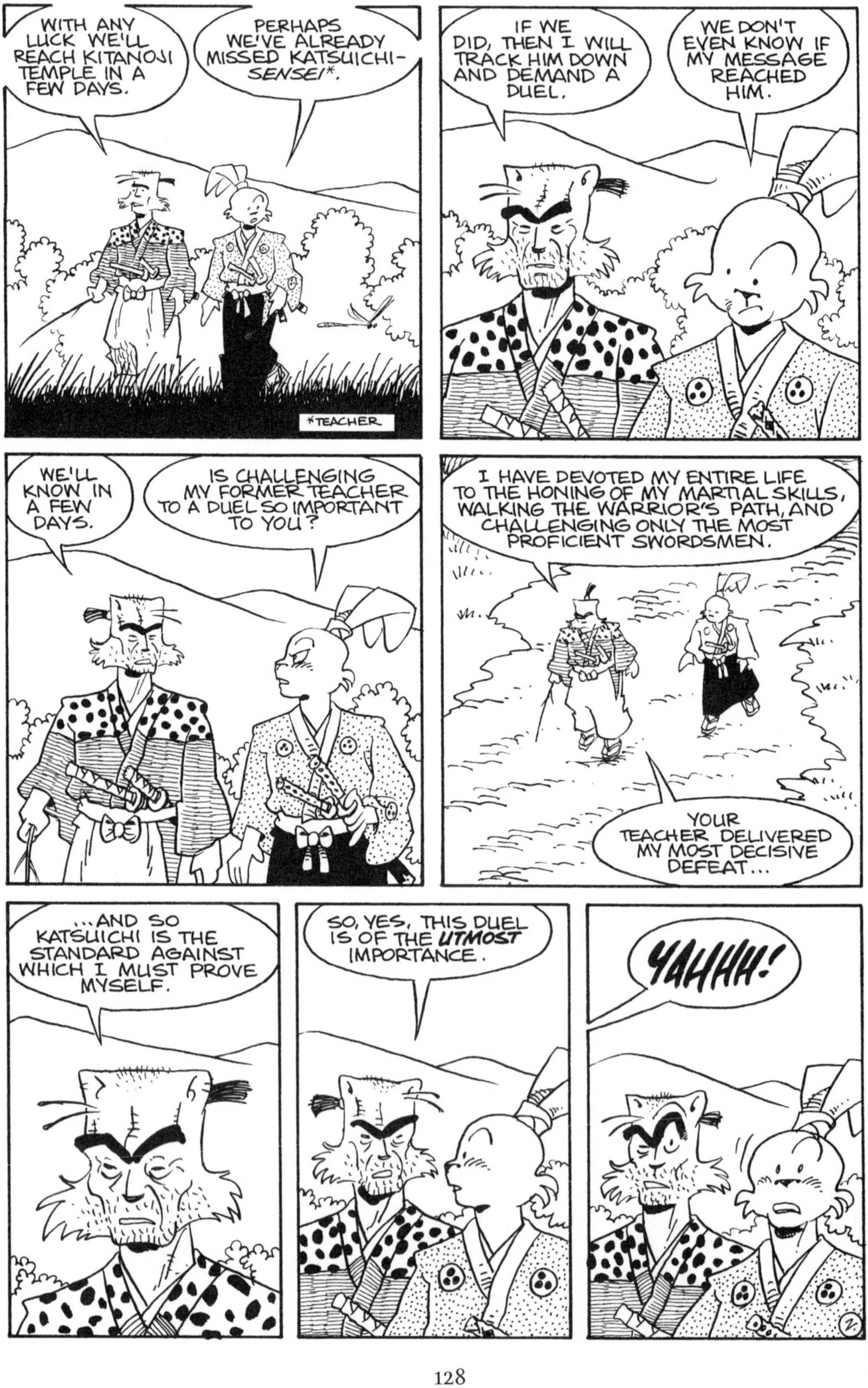
WITH ANY LUCK WE'LL REACH KITANOJI TEMPLE IN A FEW DAYS.
PERHAPS WE'VE ALREADY MISSED KATSUICHI-*SENSEI**.
*TEACHER
IF WE DID, THEN I WILL TRACK HIM DOWN AND DEMAND A DUEL.
WE DON'T EVEN KNOW IF MY MESSAGE REACHED HIM.
WE'LL KNOW IN A FEW DAYS.
IS CHALLENGING MY FORMER TEACHER TO A DUEL SO IMPORTANT TO YOU?
I HAVE DEVOTED MY ENTIRE LIFE TO THE HONING OF MY MARTIAL SKILLS, WALKING THE WARRIOR'S PATH, AND CHALLENGING ONLY THE MOST PROFICIENT SWORDSMEN.
YOUR TEACHER DELIVERED MY MOST DECISIVE DEFEAT...
...AND SO KATSUICHI IS THE STANDARD AGAINST WHICH I MUST PROVE MYSELF.
SO, YES, THIS DUEL IS OF THE ***UTMOST*** IMPORTANCE.
YAHHH!
2

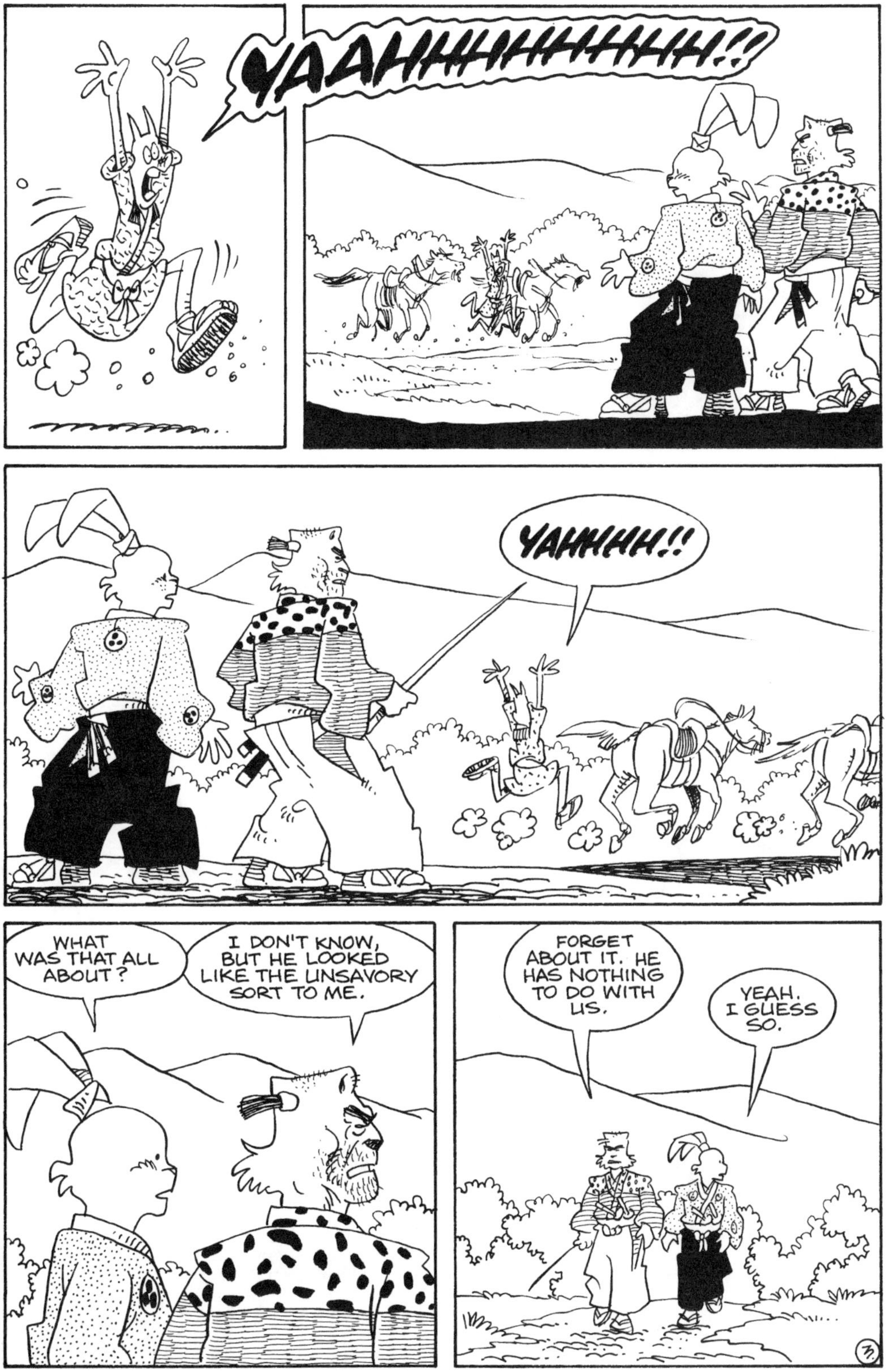
YAAHHHHHHHHH!!
YAHHHH!!
WHAT WAS THAT ALL ABOUT?
I DON'T KNOW, BUT HE LOOKED LIKE THE UNSAVORY SORT TO ME.
FORGET ABOUT IT. HE HAS NOTHING TO DO WITH US.
YEAH. I GUESS SO.
3.

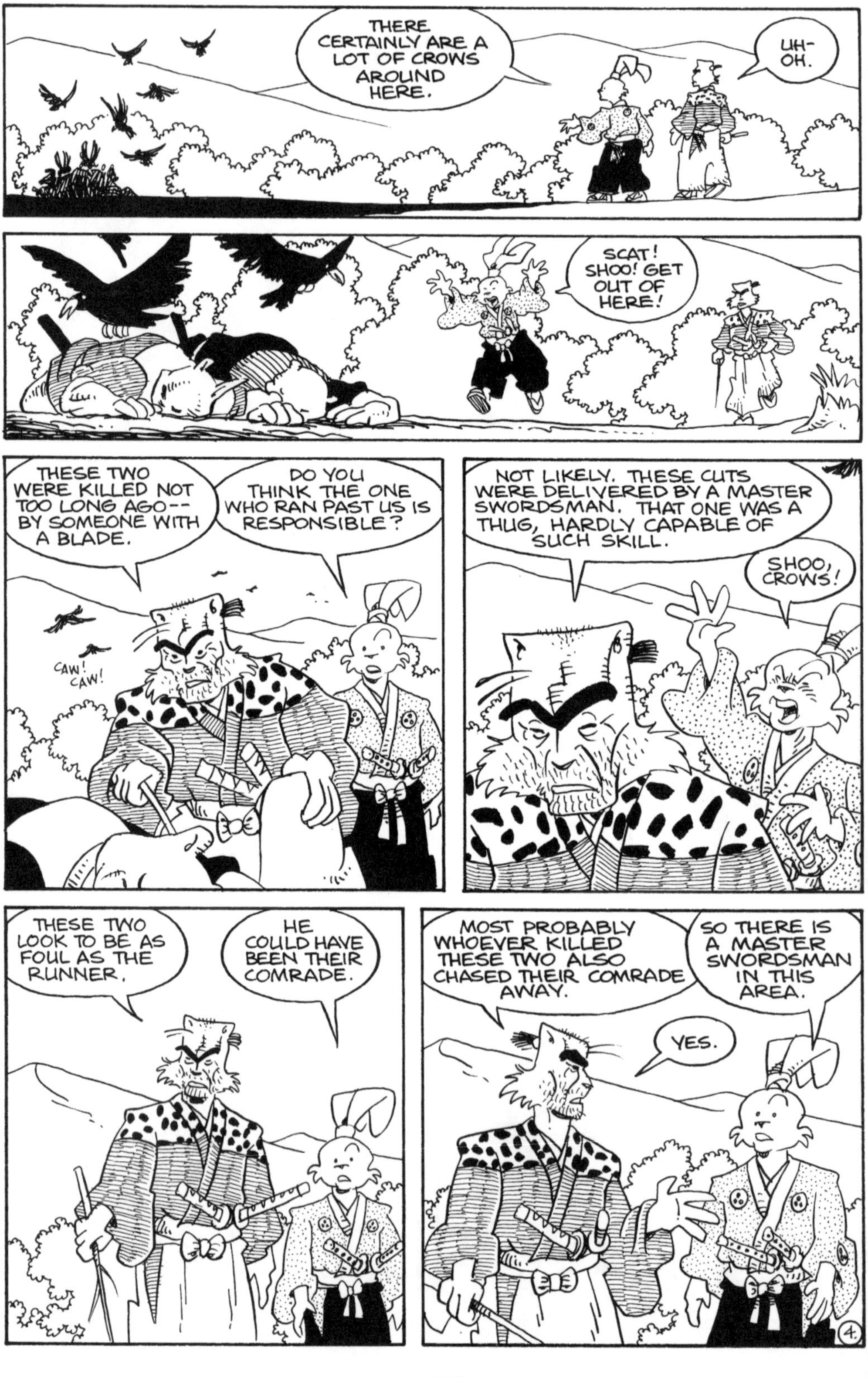
THERE CERTAINLY ARE A LOT OF CROWS AROUND HERE.
UH-OH.
SCAT! SHOO! GET OUT OF HERE!
THESE TWO WERE KILLED NOT TOO LONG AGO-- BY SOMEONE WITH A BLADE.
DO YOU THINK THE ONE WHO RAN PAST US IS RESPONSIBLE?
CAW! CAW!
NOT LIKELY. THESE CUTS WERE DELIVERED BY A MASTER SWORDSMAN. THAT ONE WAS A THUG, HARDLY CAPABLE OF SUCH SKILL.
SHOO, CROWS!
THESE TWO LOOK TO BE AS FOUL AS THE RUNNER.
HE COULD HAVE BEEN THEIR COMRADE.
MOST PROBABLY WHOEVER KILLED THESE TWO ALSO CHASED THEIR COMRADE AWAY.
SO THERE IS A MASTER SWORDSMAN IN THIS AREA.
YES.
4.

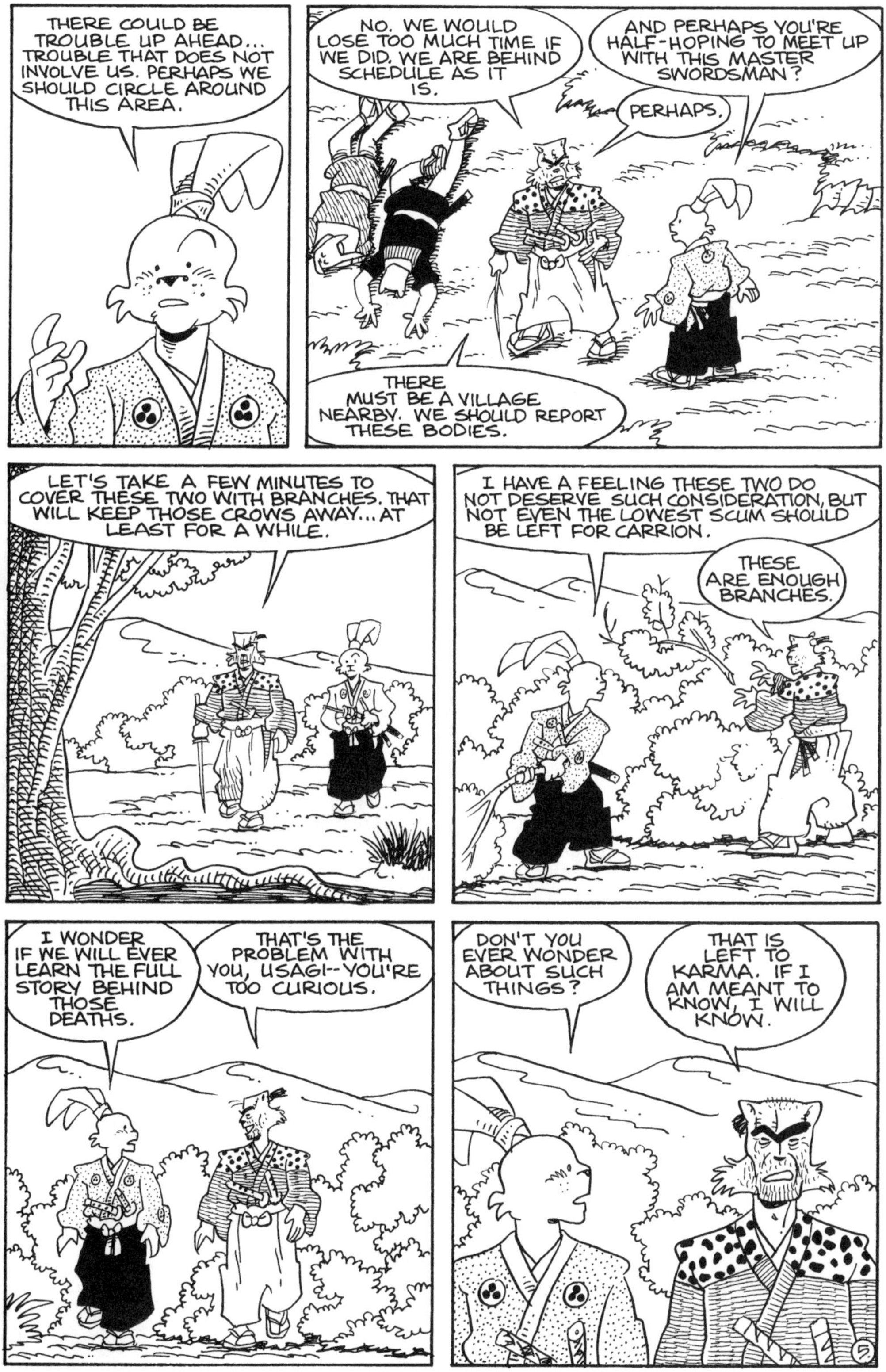
THERE COULD BE TROUBLE UP AHEAD... TROUBLE THAT DOES NOT INVOLVE US. PERHAPS WE SHOULD CIRCLE AROUND THIS AREA.
NO. WE WOULD LOSE TOO MUCH TIME IF WE DID. WE ARE BEHIND SCHEDULE AS IT IS.
AND PERHAPS YOU'RE HALF-HOPING TO MEET UP WITH THIS MASTER SWORDSMAN?
PERHAPS.
THERE MUST BE A VILLAGE NEARBY. WE SHOULD REPORT THESE BODIES.
LET'S TAKE A FEW MINUTES TO COVER THESE TWO WITH BRANCHES. THAT WILL KEEP THOSE CROWS AWAY... AT LEAST FOR A WHILE.
I HAVE A FEELING THESE TWO DO NOT DESERVE SUCH CONSIDERATION, BUT NOT EVEN THE LOWEST SCUM SHOULD BE LEFT FOR CARRION.
THESE ARE ENOUGH BRANCHES.
I WONDER IF WE WILL EVER LEARN THE FULL STORY BEHIND THOSE DEATHS.
THAT'S THE PROBLEM WITH YOU, USAGI--YOU'RE TOO CURIOUS.
DON'T YOU EVER WONDER ABOUT SUCH THINGS?
THAT IS LEFT TO KARMA. IF I AM MEANT TO KNOW, I WILL KNOW.
5

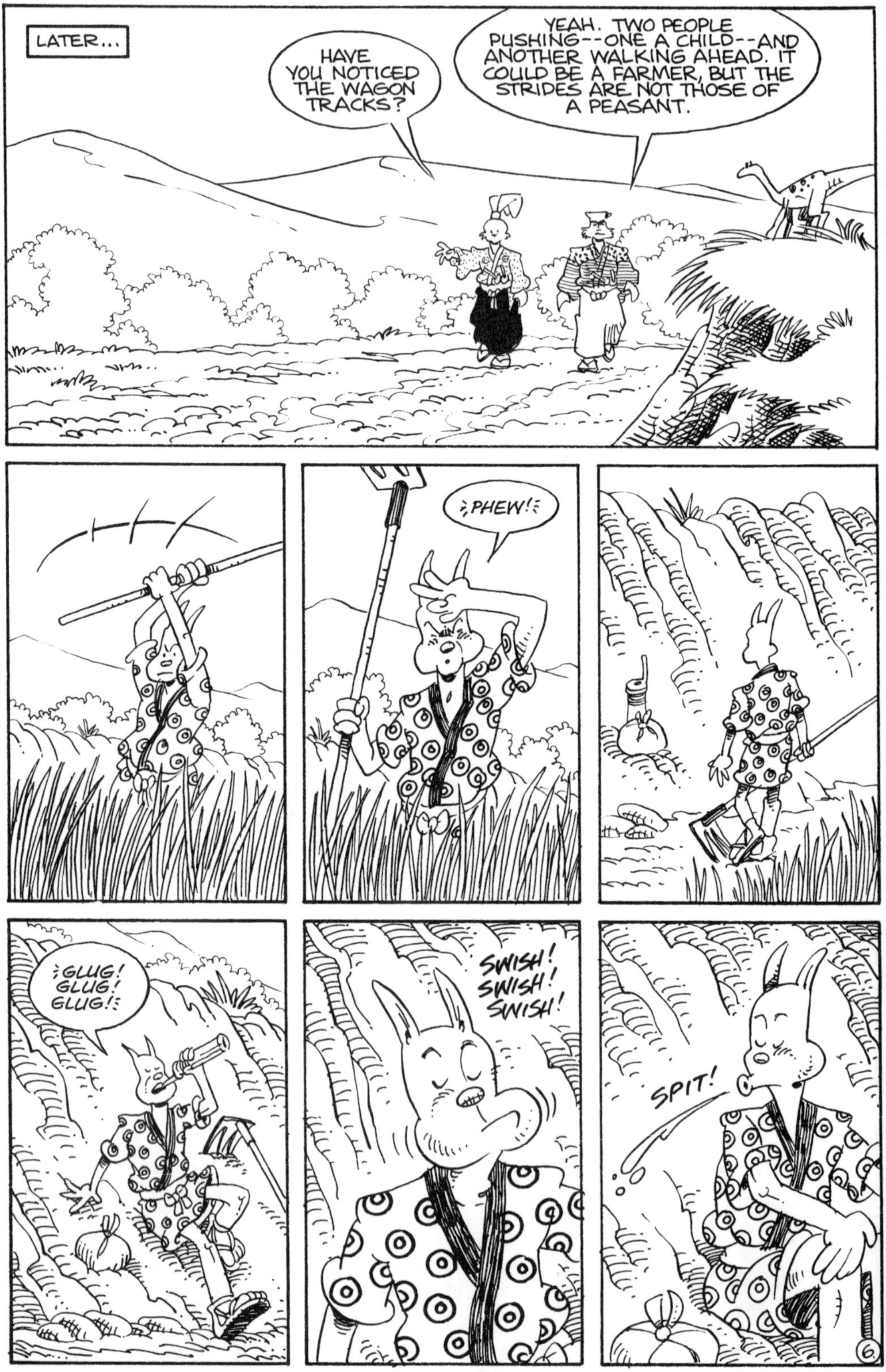
LATER...
HAVE YOU NOTICED THE WAGON TRACKS?
YEAH. TWO PEOPLE PUSHING--ONE A CHILD--AND ANOTHER WALKING AHEAD. IT COULD BE A FARMER, BUT THE STRIDES ARE NOT THOSE OF A PEASANT.
PHEW!
GLUG! GLUG! GLUG!
SWISH! SWISH! SWISH!
SPIT!
6

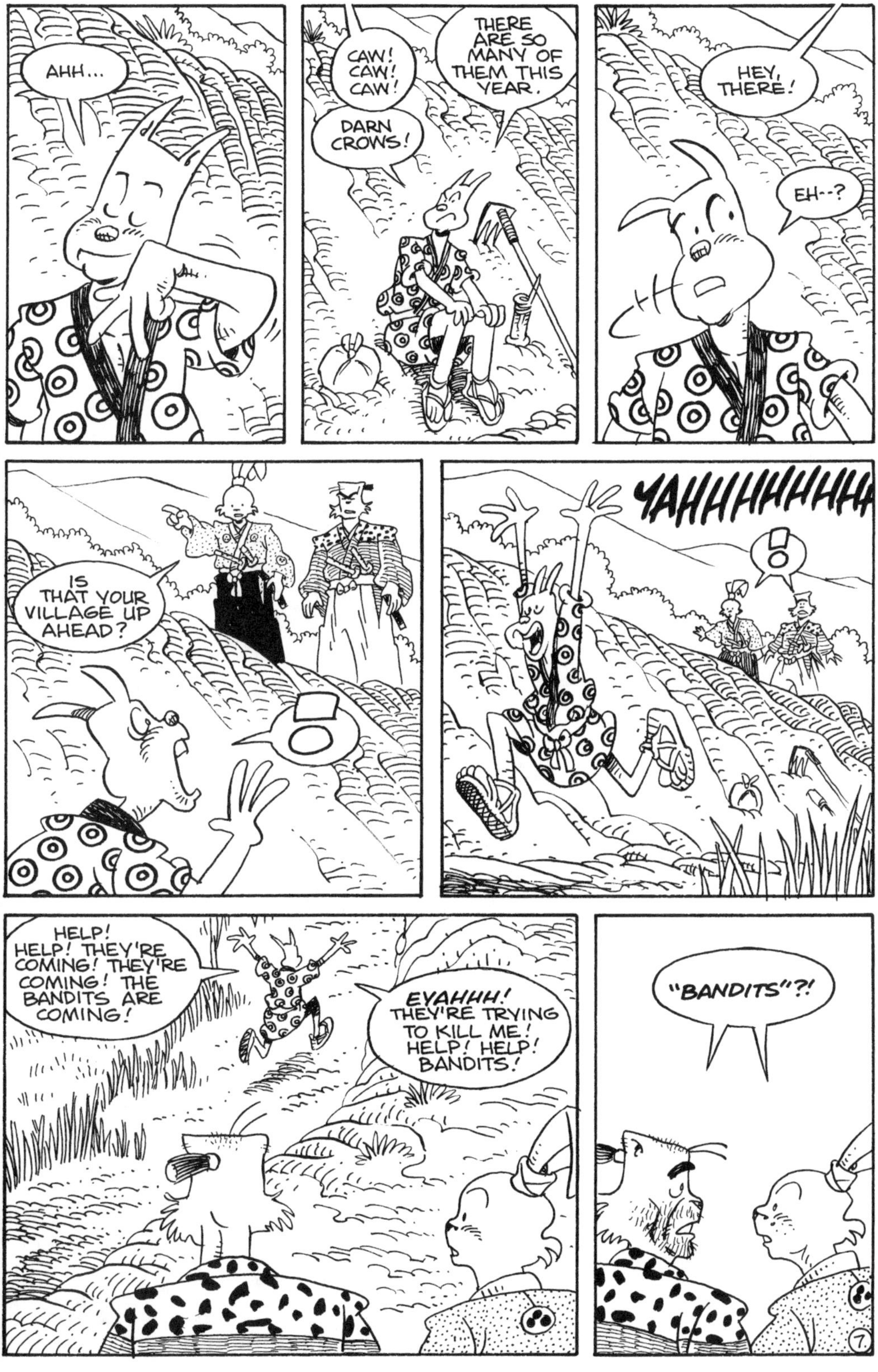
AHH...
CAW! CAW! CAW!
DARN CROWS!
THERE ARE SO MANY OF THEM THIS YEAR.
HEY, THERE!
EH--?
IS THAT YOUR VILLAGE UP AHEAD?
!
YAHHHHHHHH
!
HELP! HELP! THEY'RE COMING! THEY'RE COMING! THE BANDITS ARE COMING!
EYAHHH! THEY'RE TRYING TO KILL ME! HELP! HELP! BANDITS!
"BANDITS"?!
7

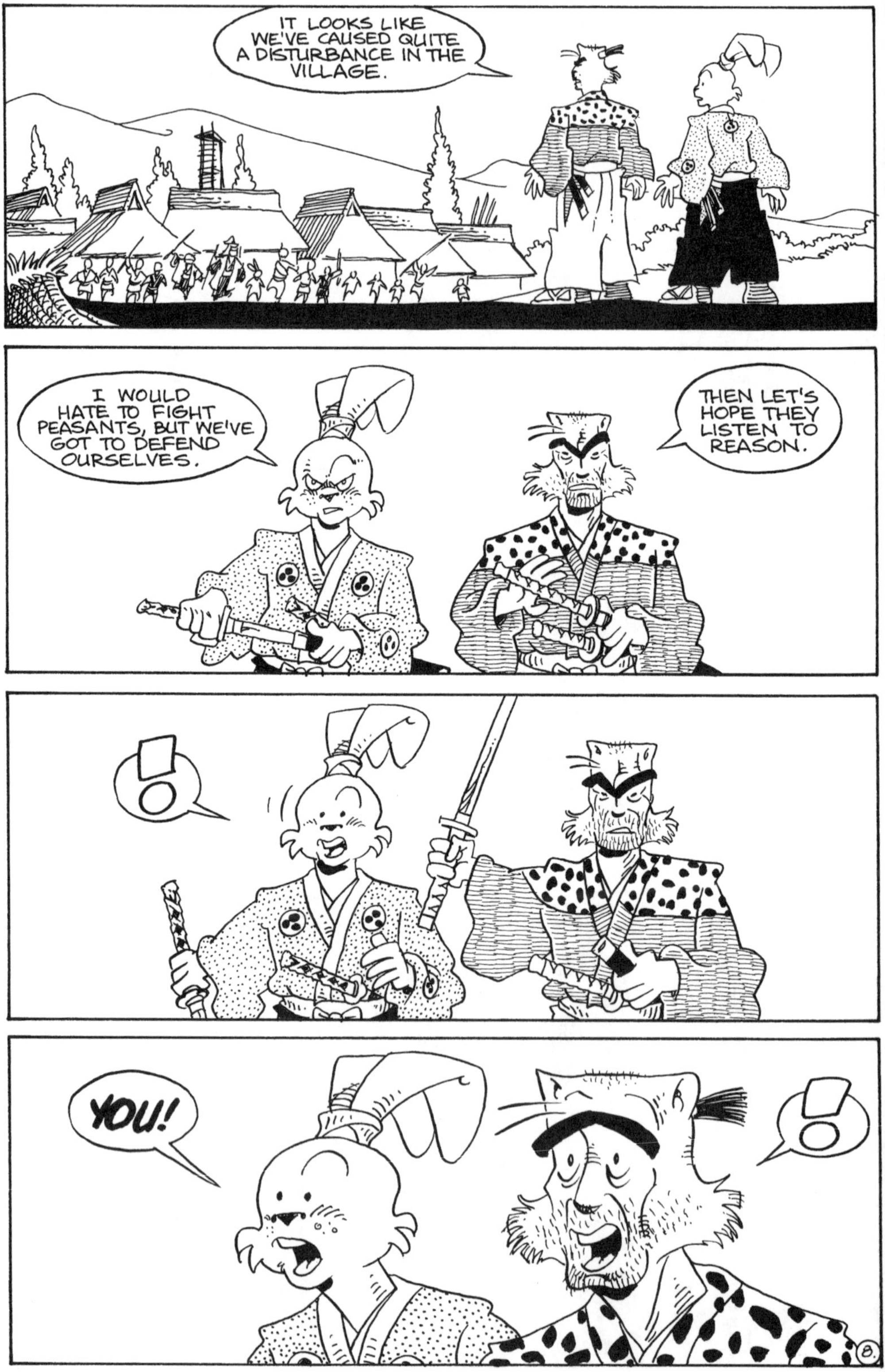
IT LOOKS LIKE WE'VE CAUSED QUITE A DISTURBANCE IN THE VILLAGE.
I WOULD HATE TO FIGHT PEASANTS, BUT WE'VE GOT TO DEFEND OURSELVES.
THEN LET'S HOPE THEY LISTEN TO REASON.
!
YOU!
!
8.

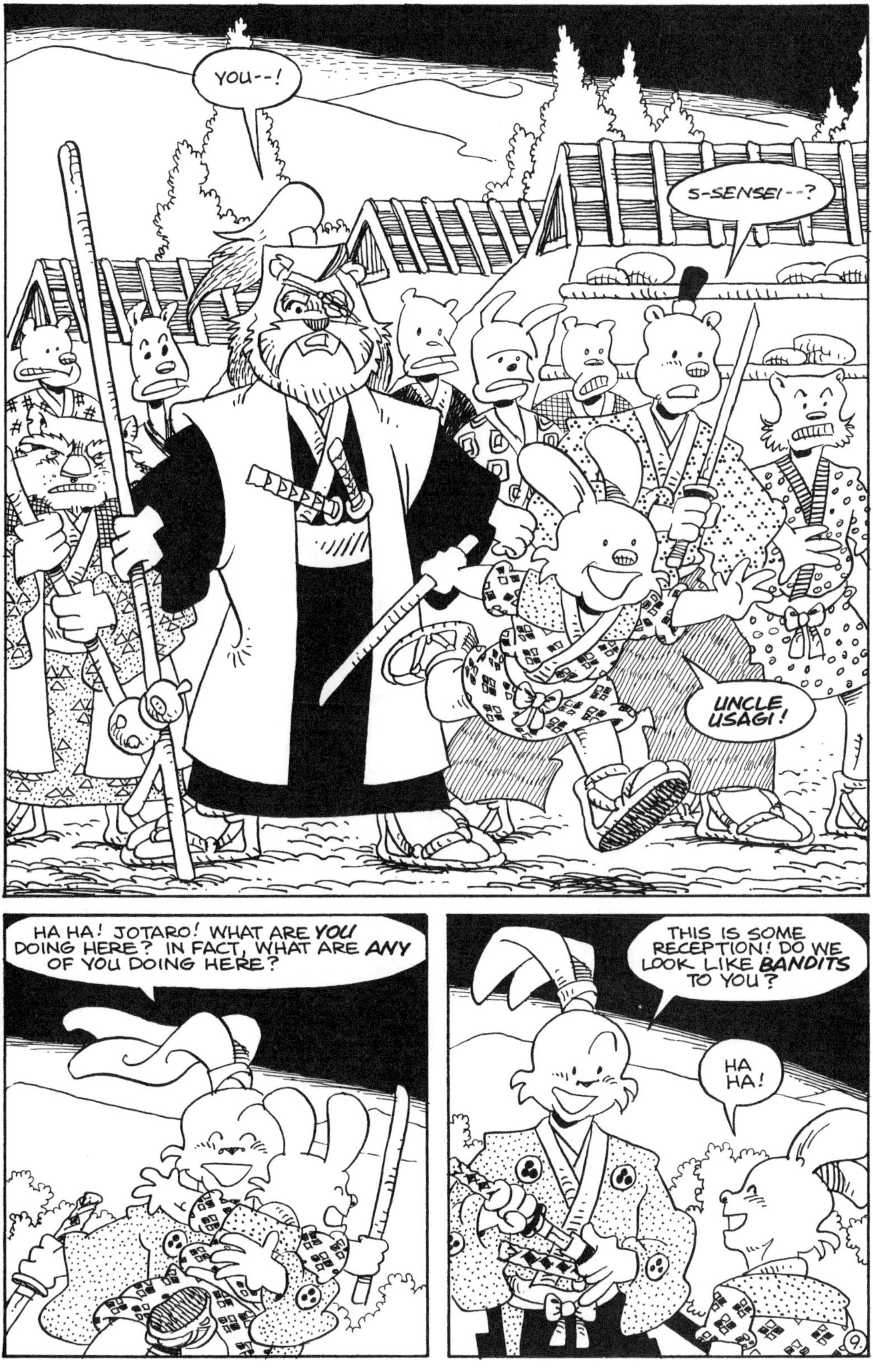
YOU--!
S-SENSEI--?
UNCLE USAGI!
HA HA! JOTARO! WHAT ARE YOU DOING HERE? IN FACT, WHAT ARE ANY OF YOU DOING HERE?
THIS IS SOME RECEPTION! DO WE LOOK LIKE BANDITS TO YOU?
HA HA!
9.

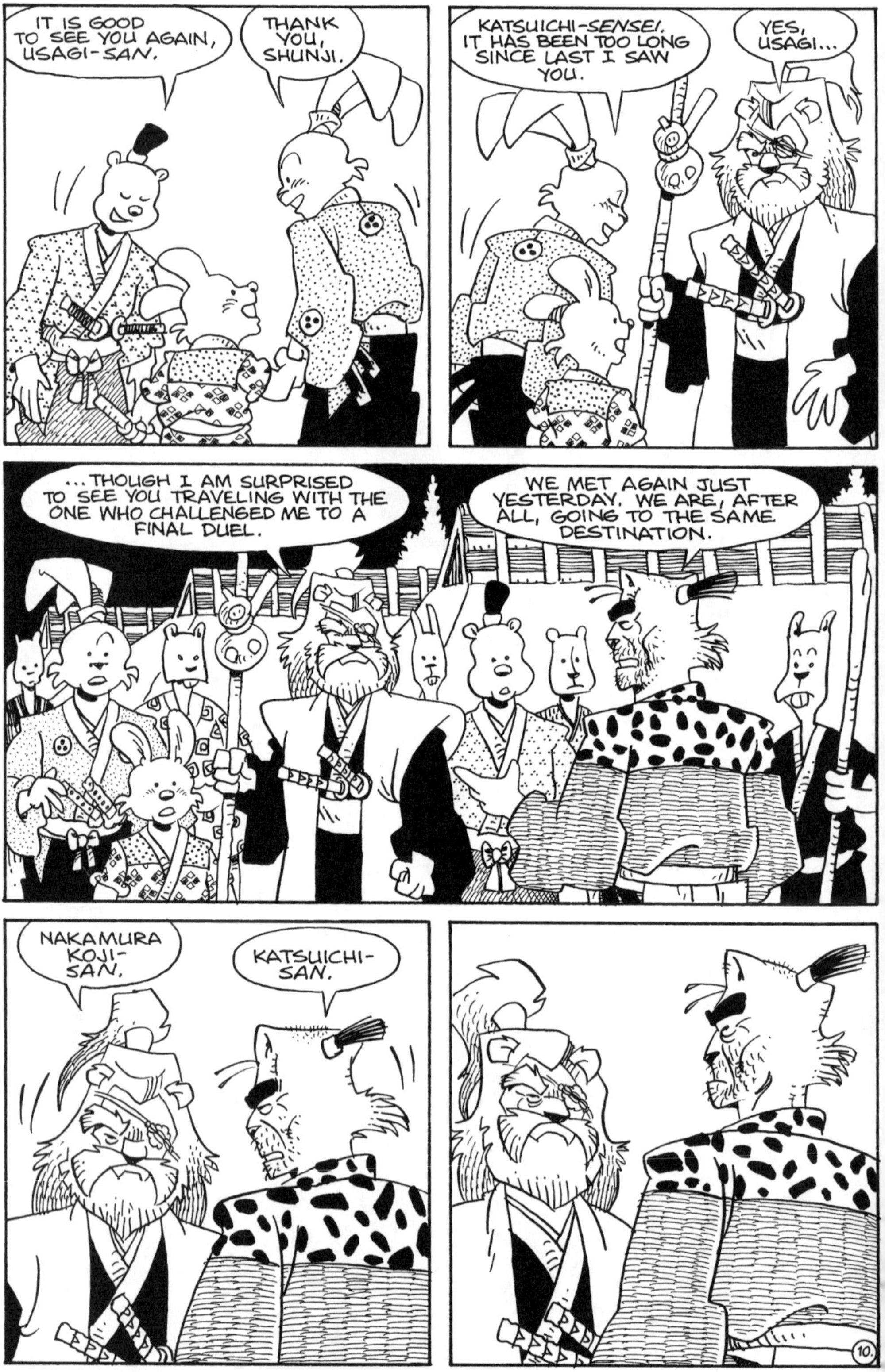
IT IS GOOD TO SEE YOU AGAIN, USAGI-SAN.
THANK YOU, SHUNJI.
KATSUICHI-SENSEI. IT HAS BEEN TOO LONG SINCE LAST I SAW YOU.
YES, USAGI...
...THOUGH I AM SURPRISED TO SEE YOU TRAVELING WITH THE ONE WHO CHALLENGED ME TO A FINAL DUEL.
WE MET AGAIN JUST YESTERDAY. WE ARE, AFTER ALL, GOING TO THE SAME DESTINATION.
NAKAMURA KOJI-SAN.
KATSUICHI-SAN.
10.

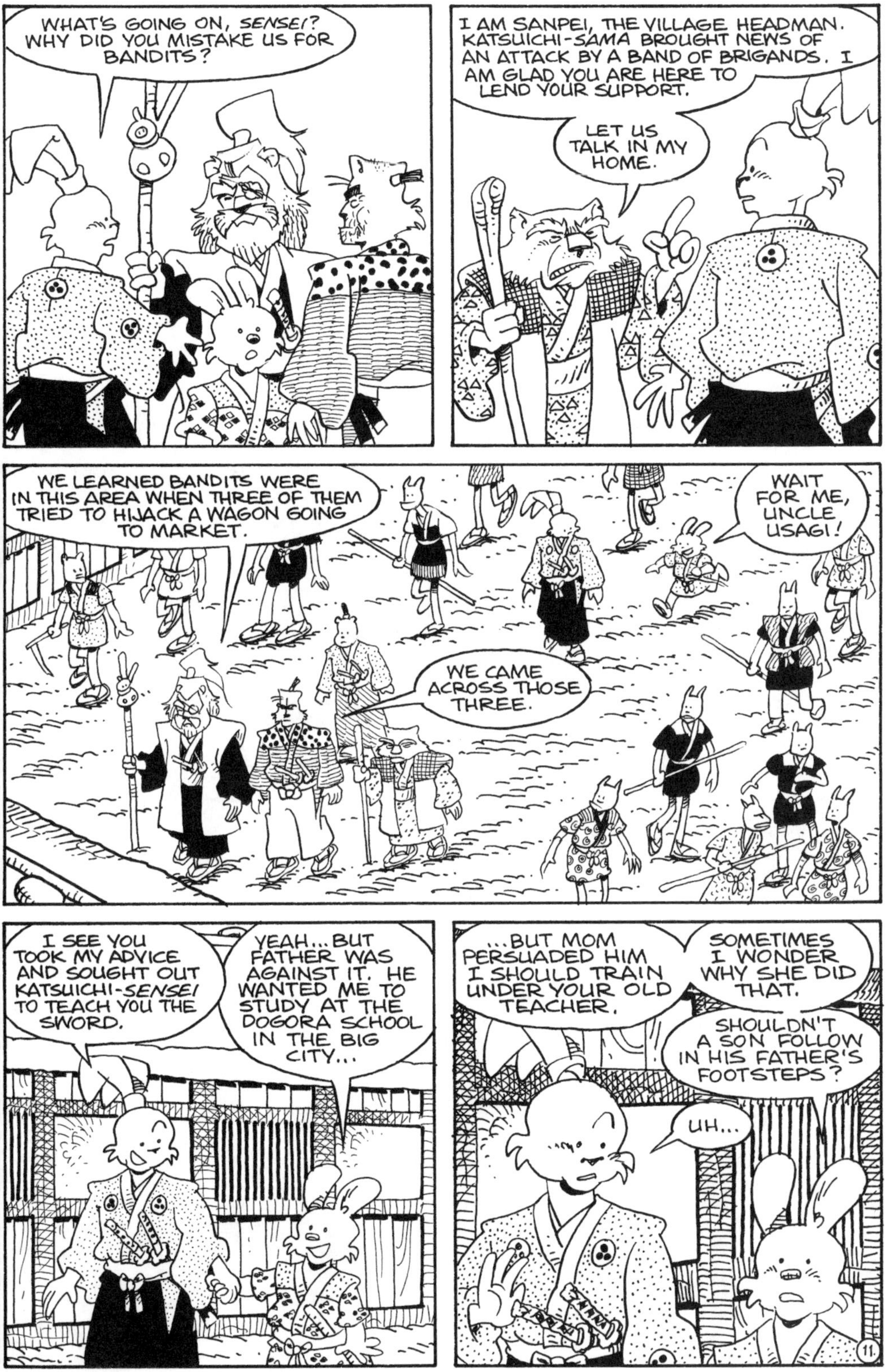
WHAT'S GOING ON, SENSEI? WHY DID YOU MISTAKE US FOR BANDITS?
I AM SANPEI, THE VILLAGE HEADMAN. KATSUICHI-SAMA BROUGHT NEWS OF AN ATTACK BY A BAND OF BRIGANDS. I AM GLAD YOU ARE HERE TO LEND YOUR SUPPORT.
LET US TALK IN MY HOME.
WE LEARNED BANDITS WERE IN THIS AREA WHEN THREE OF THEM TRIED TO HIJACK A WAGON GOING TO MARKET.
WE CAME ACROSS THOSE THREE.
WAIT FOR ME, UNCLE USAGI!
I SEE YOU TOOK MY ADVICE AND SOUGHT OUT KATSUICHI-SENSEI TO TEACH YOU THE SWORD.
YEAH... BUT FATHER WAS AGAINST IT. HE WANTED ME TO STUDY AT THE DOGORA SCHOOL IN THE BIG CITY...
...BUT MOM PERSUADED HIM I SHOULD TRAIN UNDER YOUR OLD TEACHER.
SOMETIMES I WONDER WHY SHE DID THAT.
SHOULDN'T A SON FOLLOW IN HIS FATHER'S FOOTSTEPS?
UH...
11.

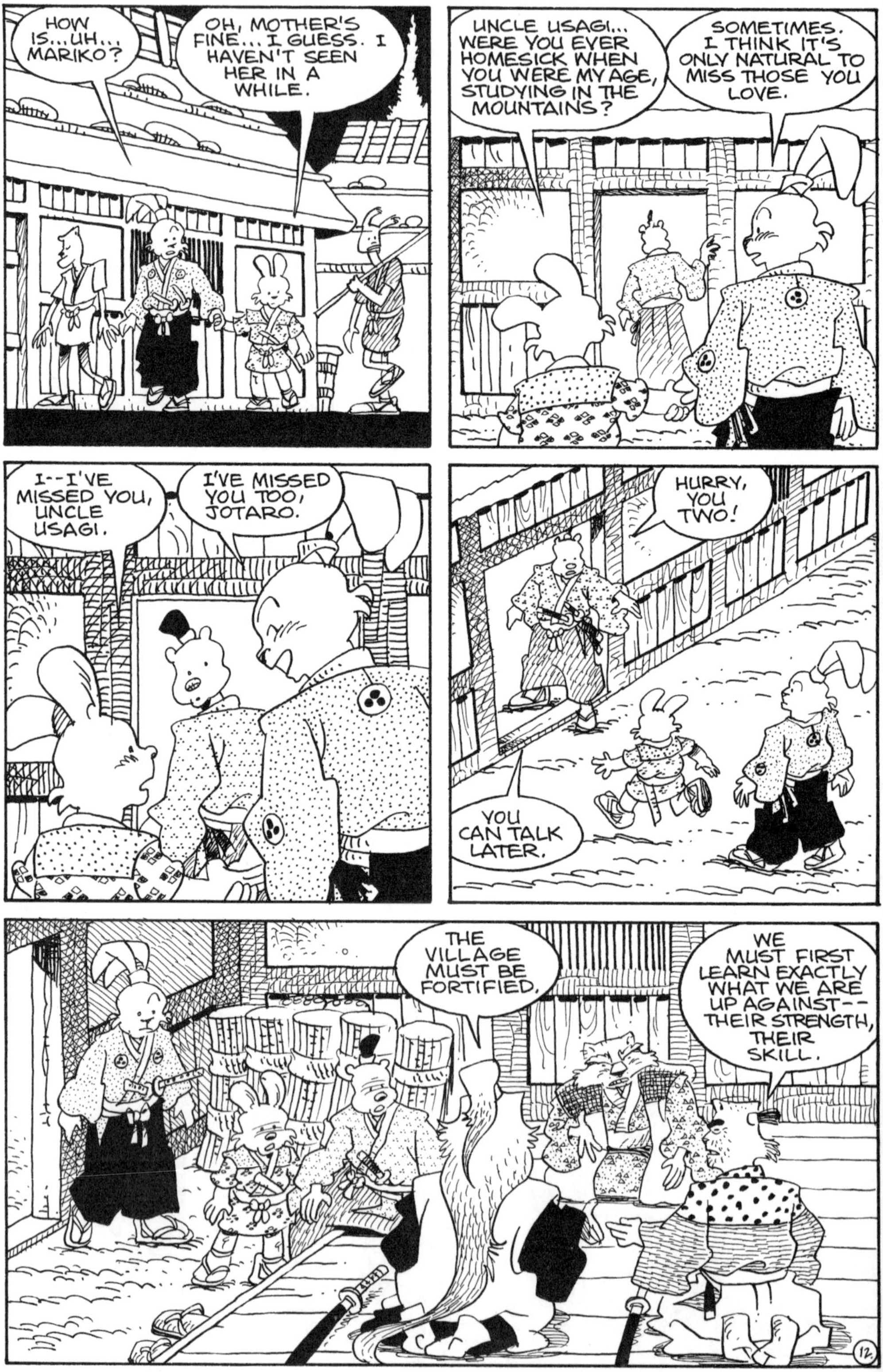
HOW IS...UH... MARIKO?
OH, MOTHER'S FINE... I GUESS. I HAVEN'T SEEN HER IN A WHILE.
UNCLE USAGI... WERE YOU EVER HOMESICK WHEN YOU WERE MY AGE, STUDYING IN THE MOUNTAINS?
SOMETIMES. I THINK IT'S ONLY NATURAL TO MISS THOSE YOU LOVE.
I--I'VE MISSED YOU, UNCLE USAGI.
I'VE MISSED YOU TOO, JOTARO.
HURRY, YOU TWO!
YOU CAN TALK LATER.
THE VILLAGE MUST BE FORTIFIED.
WE MUST FIRST LEARN EXACTLY WHAT WE ARE UP AGAINST-- THEIR STRENGTH, THEIR SKILL.
12

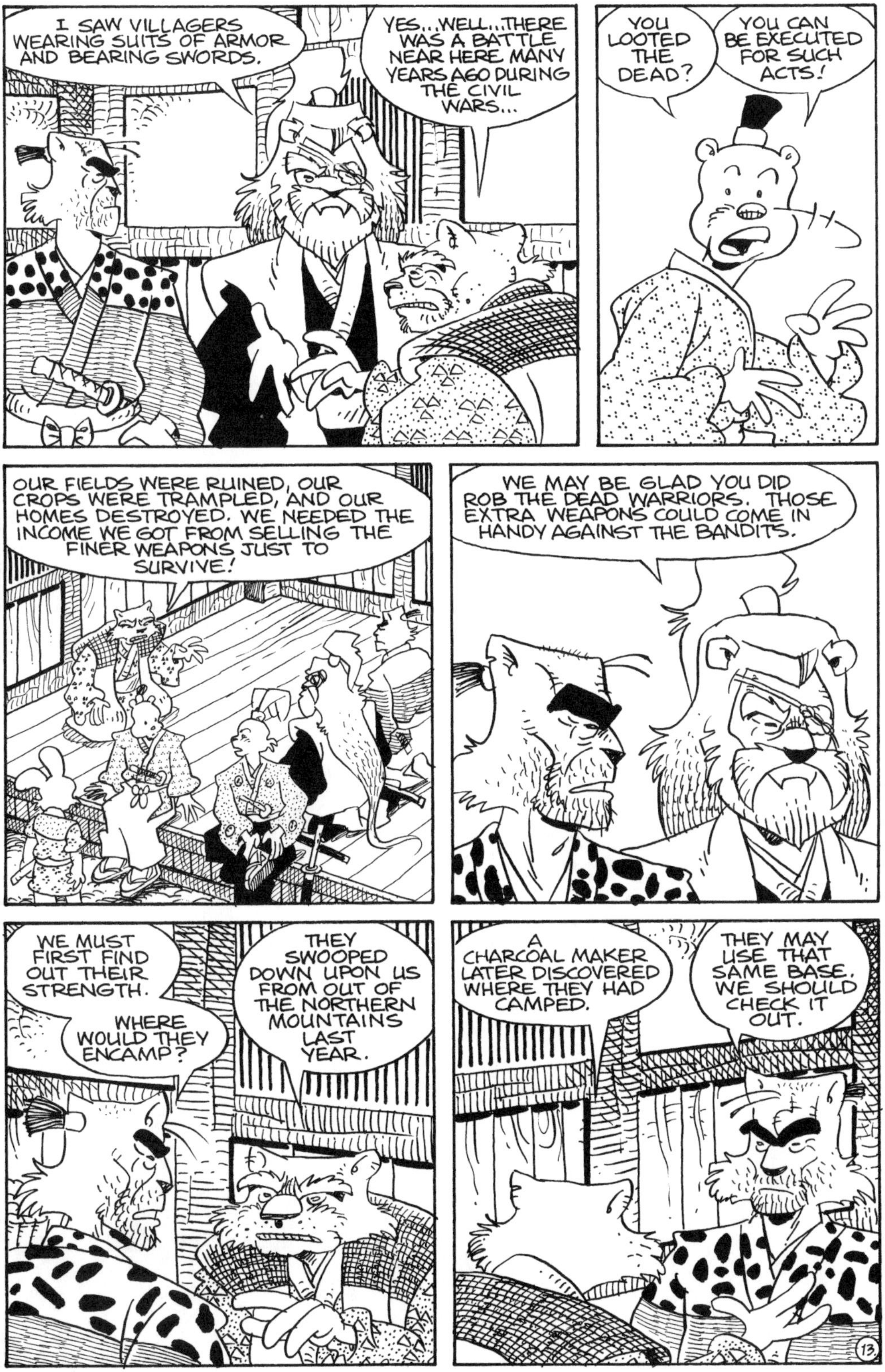
I SAW VILLAGERS WEARING SUITS OF ARMOR AND BEARING SWORDS.
YES...WELL...THERE WAS A BATTLE NEAR HERE MANY YEARS AGO DURING THE CIVIL WARS...
YOU LOOTED THE DEAD?
YOU CAN BE EXECUTED FOR SUCH ACTS!
OUR FIELDS WERE RUINED, OUR CROPS WERE TRAMPLED, AND OUR HOMES DESTROYED. WE NEEDED THE INCOME WE GOT FROM SELLING THE FINER WEAPONS JUST TO SURVIVE!
WE MAY BE GLAD YOU DID ROB THE DEAD WARRIORS. THOSE EXTRA WEAPONS COULD COME IN HANDY AGAINST THE BANDITS.
WE MUST FIRST FIND OUT THEIR STRENGTH.
WHERE WOULD THEY ENCAMP?
THEY SWOOPED DOWN UPON US FROM OUT OF THE NORTHERN MOUNTAINS LAST YEAR.
A CHARCOAL MAKER LATER DISCOVERED WHERE THEY HAD CAMPED.
THEY MAY USE THAT SAME BASE. WE SHOULD CHECK IT OUT.
13

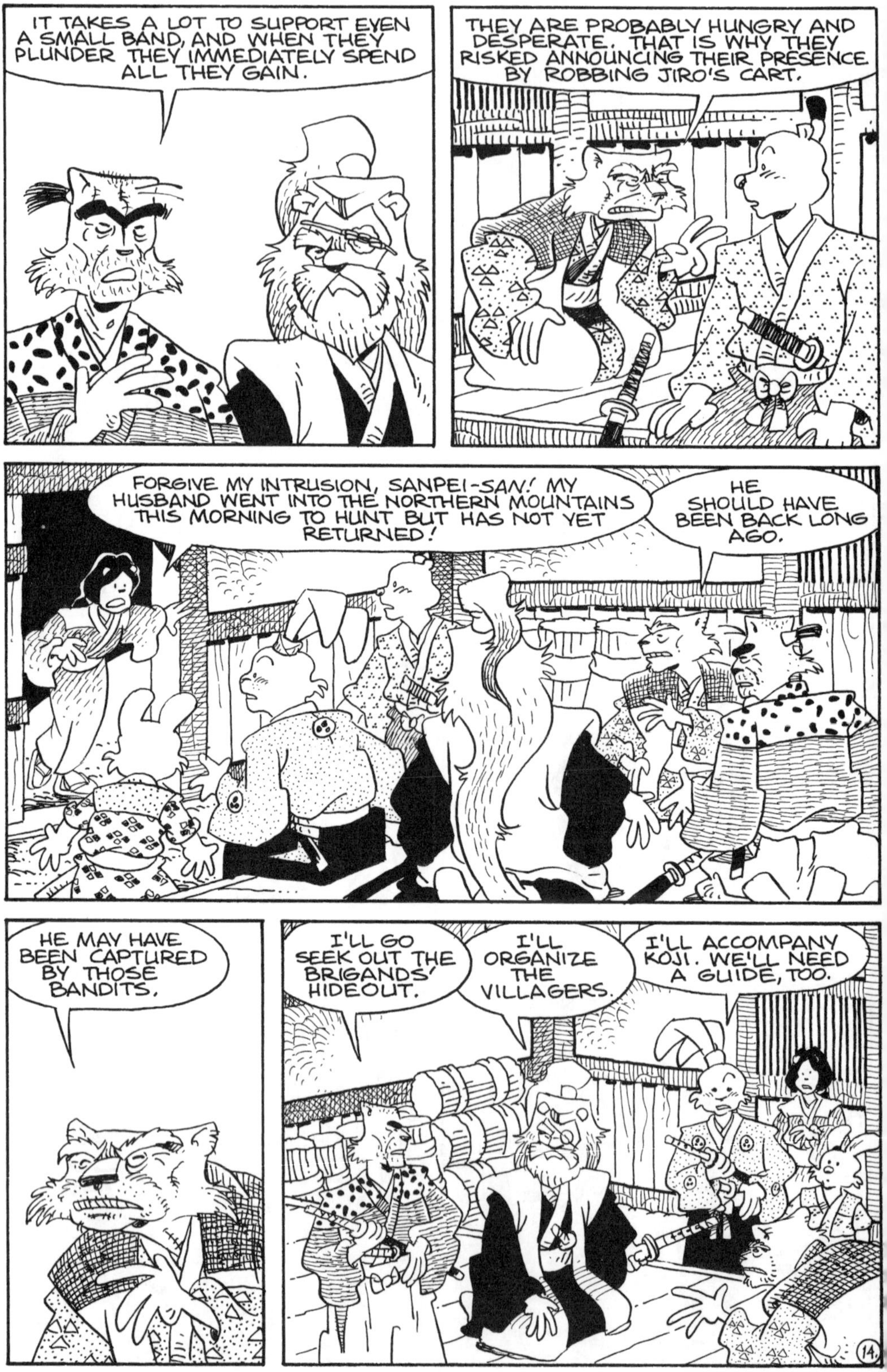
IT TAKES A LOT TO SUPPORT EVEN A SMALL BAND, AND WHEN THEY PLUNDER THEY IMMEDIATELY SPEND ALL THEY GAIN.
THEY ARE PROBABLY HUNGRY AND DESPERATE. THAT IS WHY THEY RISKED ANNOUNCING THEIR PRESENCE BY ROBBING JIRO'S CART.
FORGIVE MY INTRUSION, SANPEI-SAN! MY HUSBAND WENT INTO THE NORTHERN MOUNTAINS THIS MORNING TO HUNT BUT HAS NOT YET RETURNED!
HE SHOULD HAVE BEEN BACK LONG AGO.
HE MAY HAVE BEEN CAPTURED BY THOSE BANDITS.
I'LL GO SEEK OUT THE BRIGANDS' HIDEOUT.
I'LL ORGANIZE THE VILLAGERS.
I'LL ACCOMPANY KOJI. WE'LL NEED A GUIDE, TOO.
14.

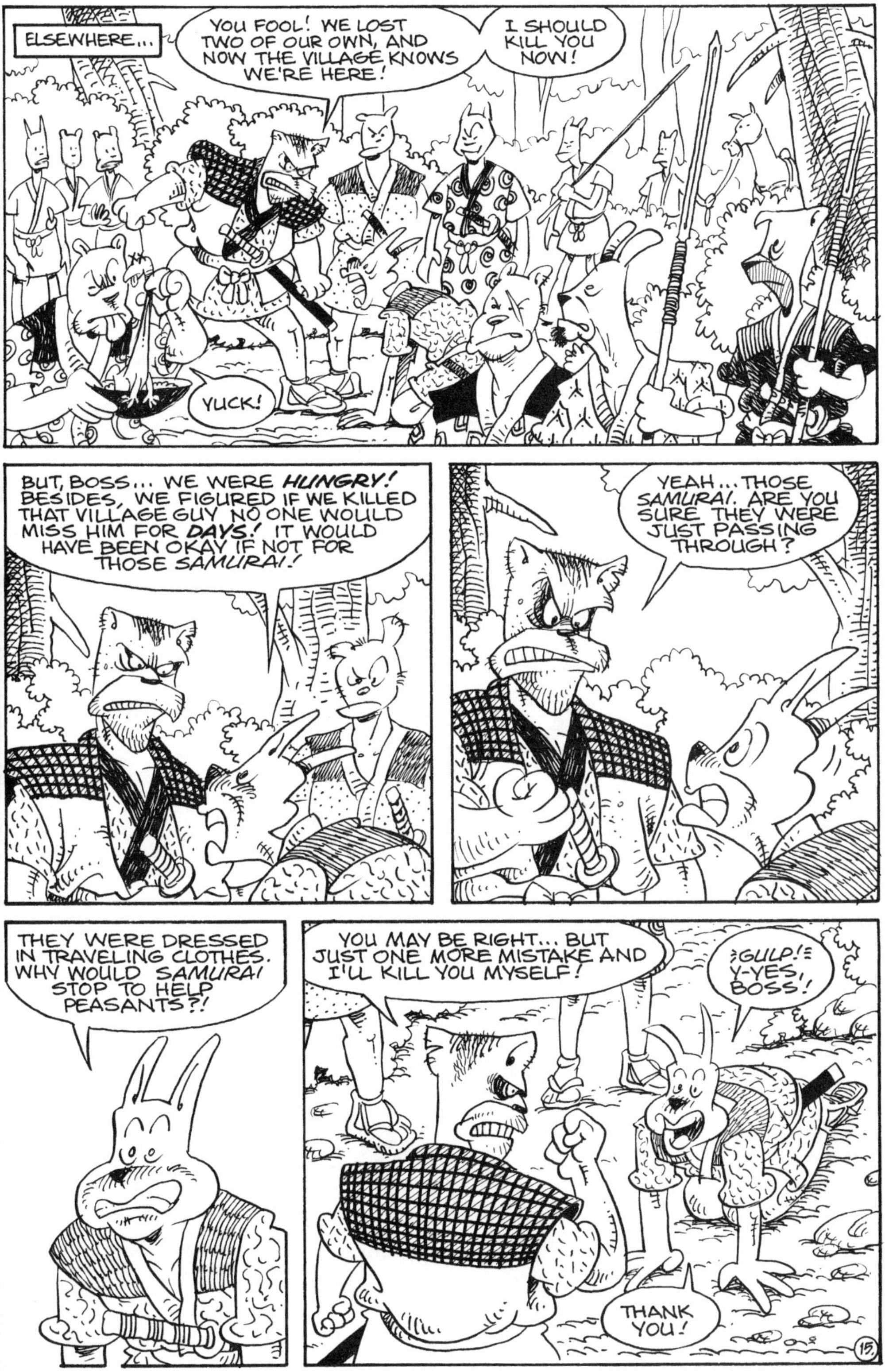
ELSEWHERE...
YOU FOOL! WE LOST TWO OF OUR OWN, AND NOW THE VILLAGE KNOWS WE'RE HERE!
I SHOULD KILL YOU NOW!
YUCK!
BUT, BOSS... WE WERE HUNGRY! BESIDES, WE FIGURED IF WE KILLED THAT VILLAGE GUY NO ONE WOULD MISS HIM FOR DAYS! IT WOULD HAVE BEEN OKAY IF NOT FOR THOSE SAMURAI!
YEAH... THOSE SAMURAI. ARE YOU SURE THEY WERE JUST PASSING THROUGH?
THEY WERE DRESSED IN TRAVELING CLOTHES. WHY WOULD SAMURAI STOP TO HELP PEASANTS?!
YOU MAY BE RIGHT... BUT JUST ONE MORE MISTAKE AND I'LL KILL YOU MYSELF!
GULP! Y-YES, BOSS!
THANK YOU!
15

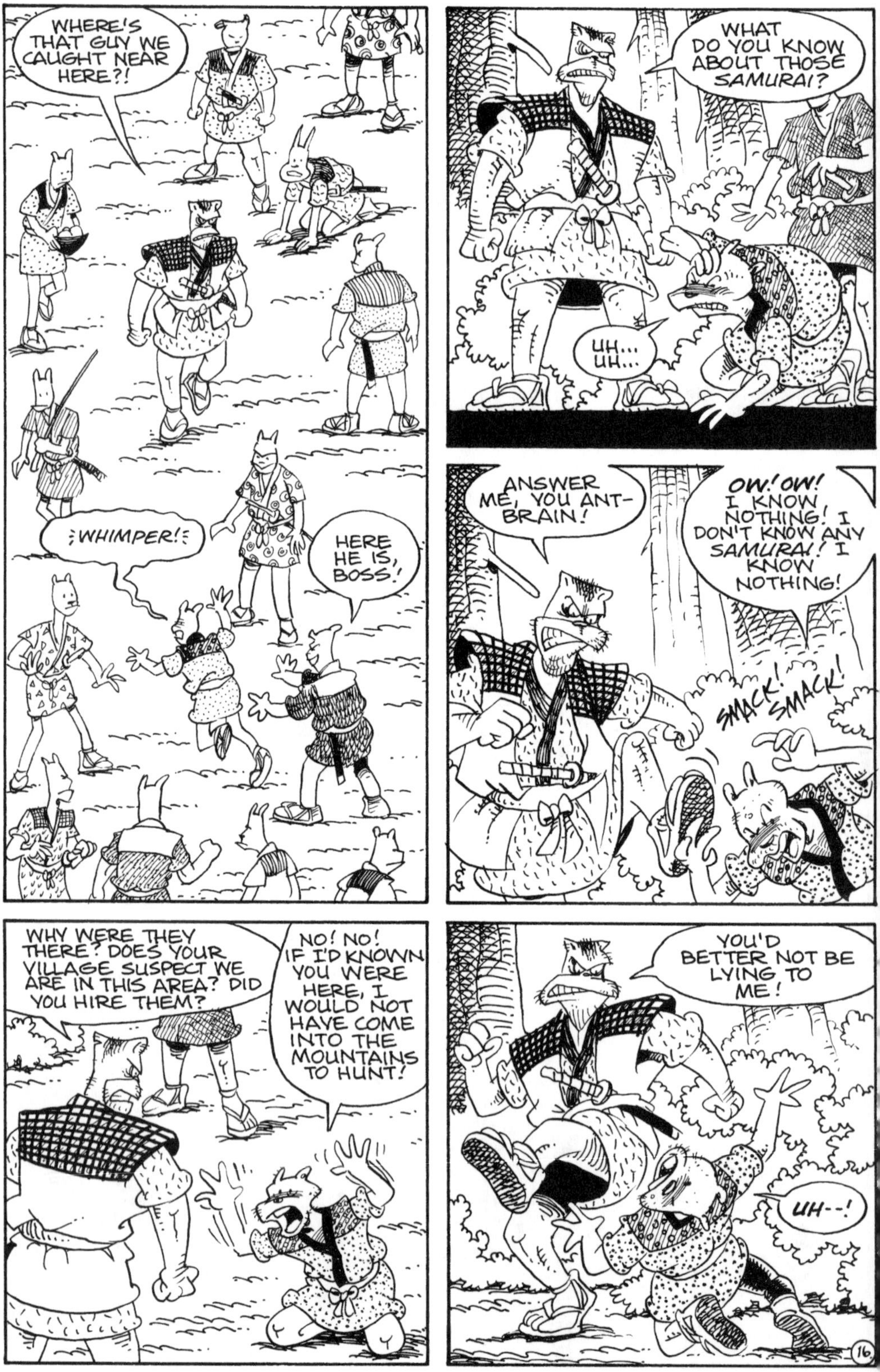
WHERE'S THAT GUY WE CAUGHT NEAR HERE?!
WHIMPER!
HERE HE IS, BOSS!
WHAT DO YOU KNOW ABOUT THOSE SAMURAI?
UH... UH...
ANSWER ME, YOU ANT-BRAIN!
OW! OW! I KNOW NOTHING! I DON'T KNOW ANY SAMURAI! I KNOW NOTHING!
SMACK! SMACK!
WHY WERE THEY THERE? DOES YOUR VILLAGE SUSPECT WE ARE IN THIS AREA? DID YOU HIRE THEM?
NO! NO! IF I'D KNOWN YOU WERE HERE, I WOULD NOT HAVE COME INTO THE MOUNTAINS TO HUNT!
YOU'D BETTER NOT BE LYING TO ME!
UH--!
16

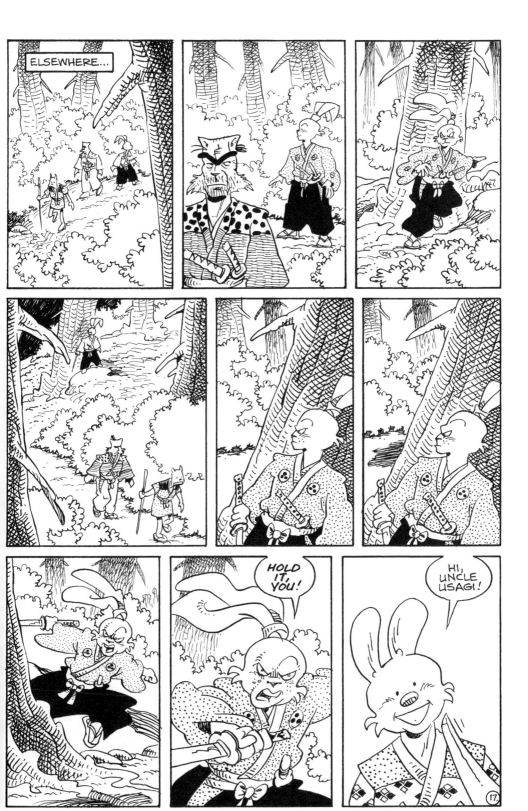

ELSEWHERE...

HOLD IT, YOU!

HI, UNCLE USAGI!

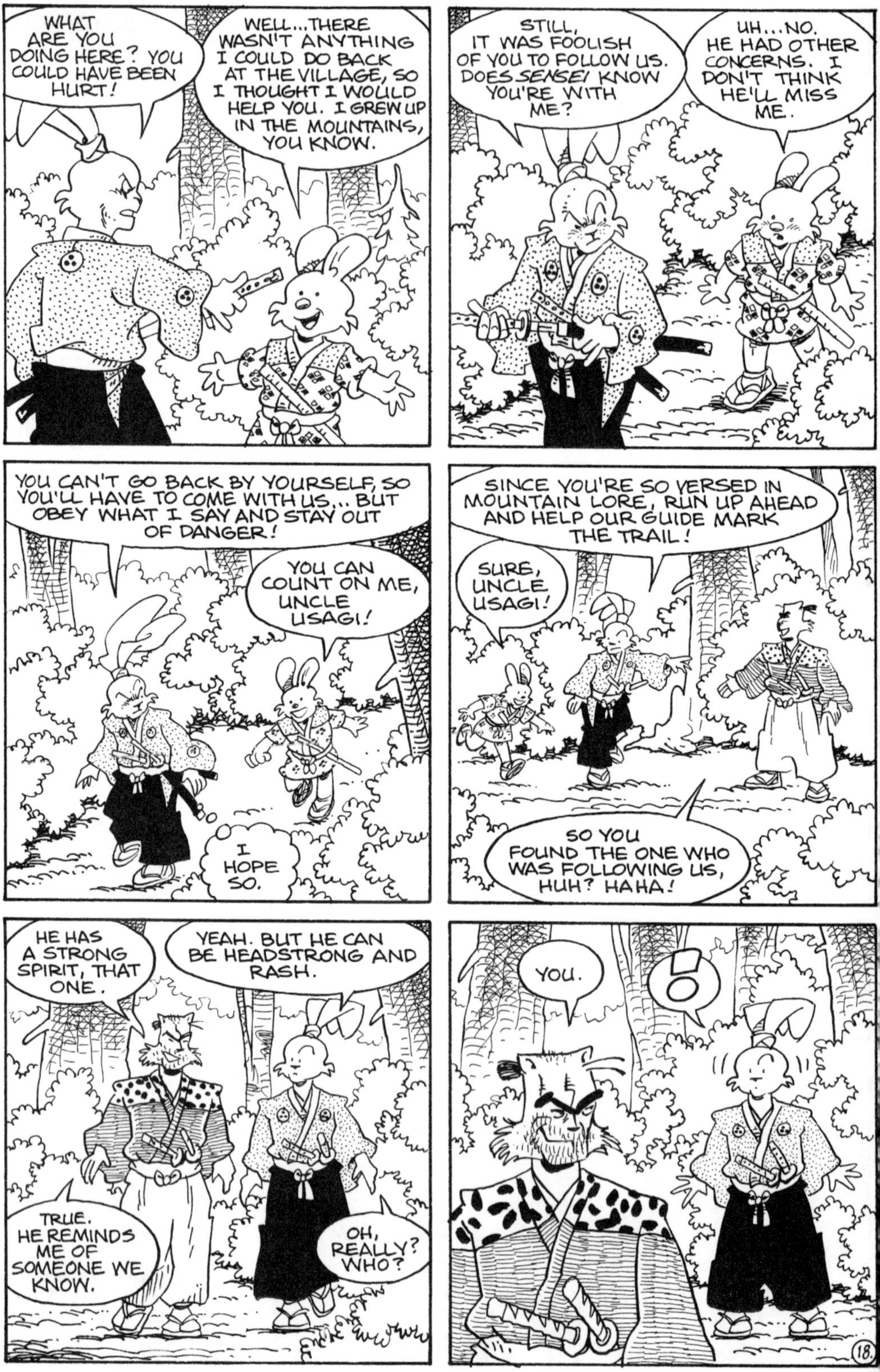
WHAT ARE YOU DOING HERE? YOU COULD HAVE BEEN HURT!
WELL...THERE WASN'T ANYTHING I COULD DO BACK AT THE VILLAGE, SO I THOUGHT I WOULD HELP YOU. I GREW UP IN THE MOUNTAINS, YOU KNOW.
STILL, IT WAS FOOLISH OF YOU TO FOLLOW US. DOES *SENSEI* KNOW YOU'RE WITH ME?
UH...NO. HE HAD OTHER CONCERNS. I DON'T THINK HE'LL MISS ME.
YOU CAN'T GO BACK BY YOURSELF, SO YOU'LL HAVE TO COME WITH US... BUT OBEY WHAT I SAY AND STAY OUT OF DANGER!
YOU CAN COUNT ON ME, UNCLE USAGI!
I HOPE SO.
SINCE YOU'RE SO VERSED IN MOUNTAIN LORE, RUN UP AHEAD AND HELP OUR GUIDE MARK THE TRAIL!
SURE, UNCLE USAGI!
SO YOU FOUND THE ONE WHO WAS FOLLOWING US, HUH? HAHA!
HE HAS A STRONG SPIRIT, THAT ONE.
YEAH. BUT HE CAN BE HEADSTRONG AND RASH.
TRUE. HE REMINDS ME OF SOMEONE WE KNOW.
OH, REALLY? WHO?
YOU.
!
18

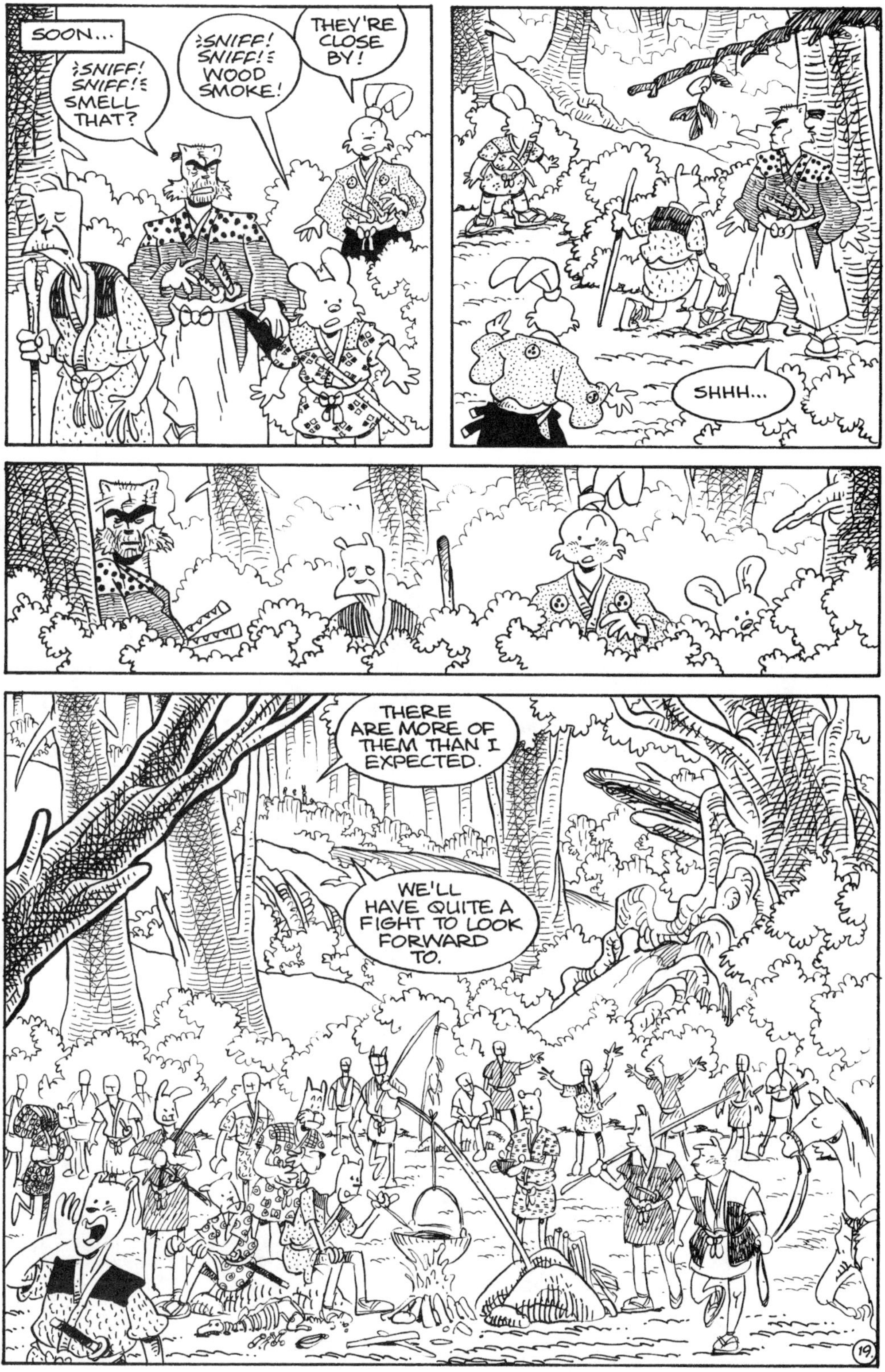
SOON...
SNIFF! SNIFF! SMELL THAT?
SNIFF! SNIFF! WOOD SMOKE!
THEY'RE CLOSE BY!
SHHH...
THERE ARE MORE OF THEM THAN I EXPECTED.
WE'LL HAVE QUITE A FIGHT TO LOOK FORWARD TO.
19

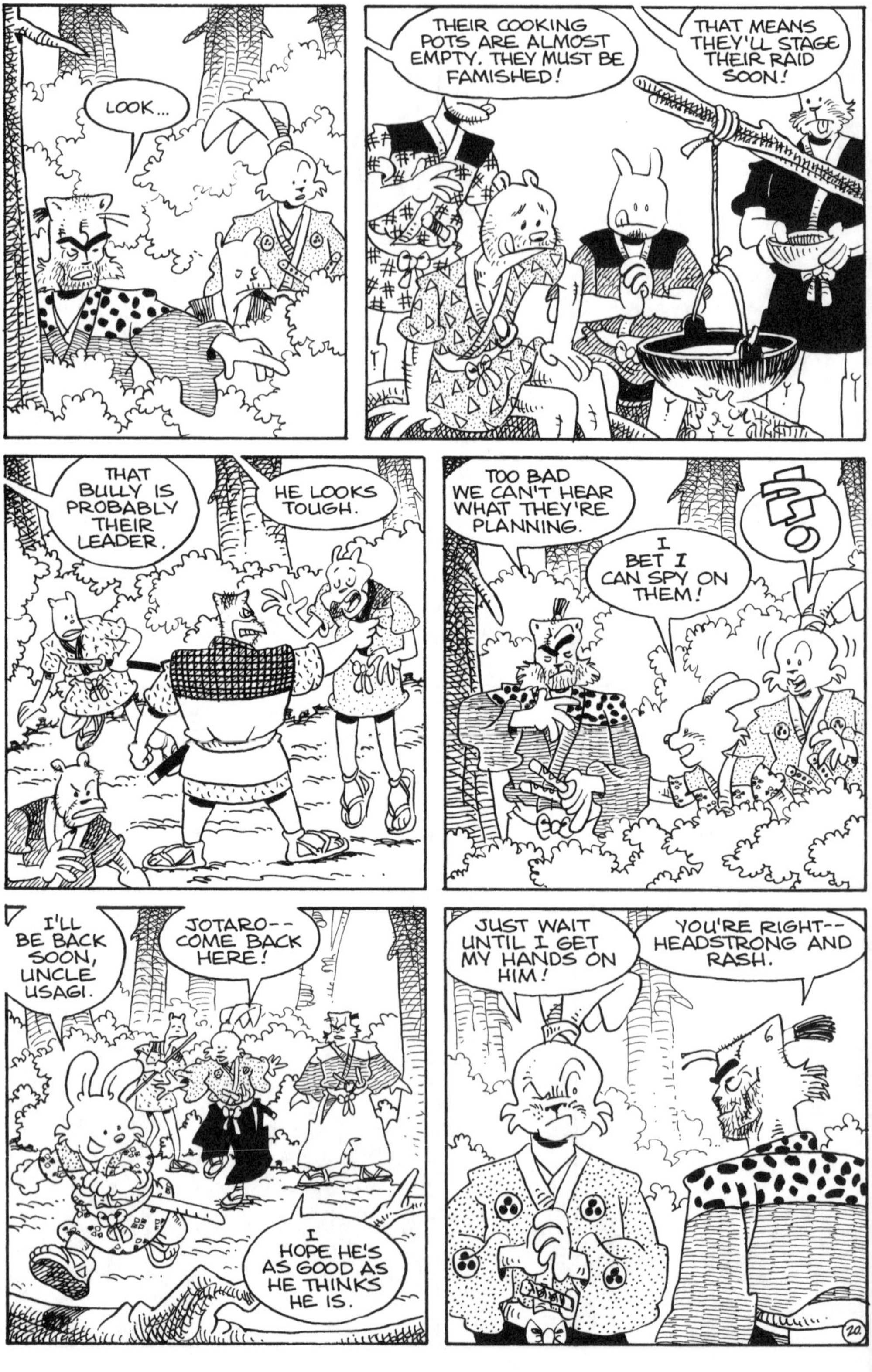

LOOK...
THEIR COOKING POTS ARE ALMOST EMPTY. THEY MUST BE FAMISHED!
THAT MEANS THEY'LL STAGE THEIR RAID SOON!
THAT BULLY IS PROBABLY THEIR LEADER.
HE LOOKS TOUGH.
TOO BAD WE CAN'T HEAR WHAT THEY'RE PLANNING.
I BET I CAN SPY ON THEM!
I'LL BE BACK SOON, UNCLE USAGI.
JOTARO-- COME BACK HERE!
I HOPE HE'S AS GOOD AS HE THINKS HE IS.
JUST WAIT UNTIL I GET MY HANDS ON HIM!
YOU'RE RIGHT-- HEADSTRONG AND RASH.
20.

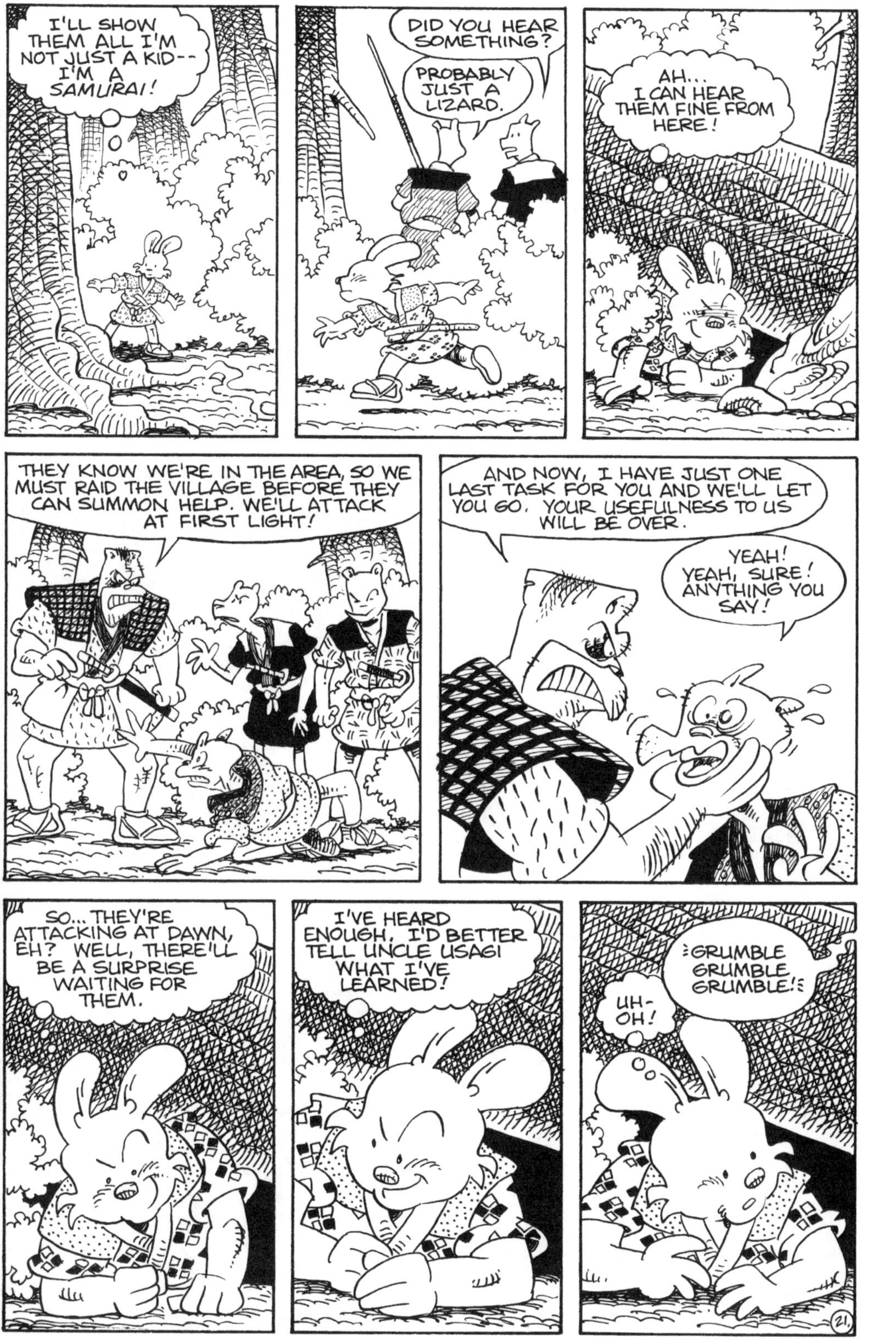
I'LL SHOW THEM ALL I'M NOT JUST A KID-- I'M A SAMURAI!
DID YOU HEAR SOMETHING?
PROBABLY JUST A LIZARD.
AH... I CAN HEAR THEM FINE FROM HERE!
THEY KNOW WE'RE IN THE AREA, SO WE MUST RAID THE VILLAGE BEFORE THEY CAN SUMMON HELP. WE'LL ATTACK AT FIRST LIGHT!
AND NOW, I HAVE JUST ONE LAST TASK FOR YOU AND WE'LL LET YOU GO. YOUR USEFULNESS TO US WILL BE OVER.
YEAH! YEAH, SURE! ANYTHING YOU SAY!
SO... THEY'RE ATTACKING AT DAWN, EH? WELL, THERE'LL BE A SURPRISE WAITING FOR THEM.
I'VE HEARD ENOUGH. I'D BETTER TELL UNCLE USAGI WHAT I'VE LEARNED!
GRUMBLE GRUMBLE GRUMBLE!
UH-OH!
21

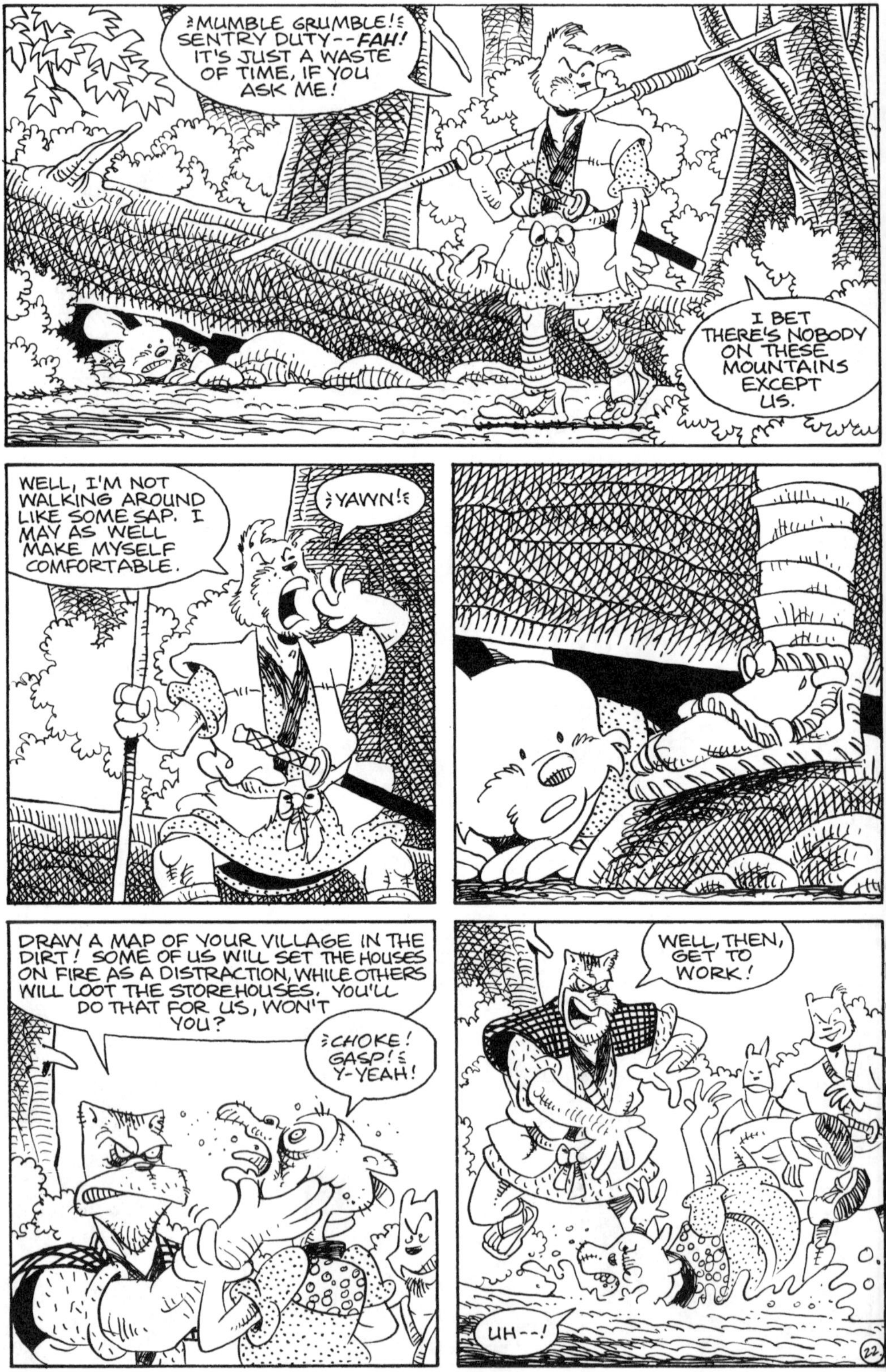
≷MUMBLE GRUMBLE!≶ SENTRY DUTY--FAH! IT'S JUST A WASTE OF TIME, IF YOU ASK ME!
I BET THERE'S NOBODY ON THESE MOUNTAINS EXCEPT US.
WELL, I'M NOT WALKING AROUND LIKE SOME SAP. I MAY AS WELL MAKE MYSELF COMFORTABLE.
≷YAWN!≶
DRAW A MAP OF YOUR VILLAGE IN THE DIRT! SOME OF US WILL SET THE HOUSES ON FIRE AS A DISTRACTION, WHILE OTHERS WILL LOOT THE STOREHOUSES. YOU'LL DO THAT FOR US, WON'T YOU?
≷CHOKE! GASP!≶ Y-YEAH!
WELL, THEN, GET TO WORK!
UH--!
22

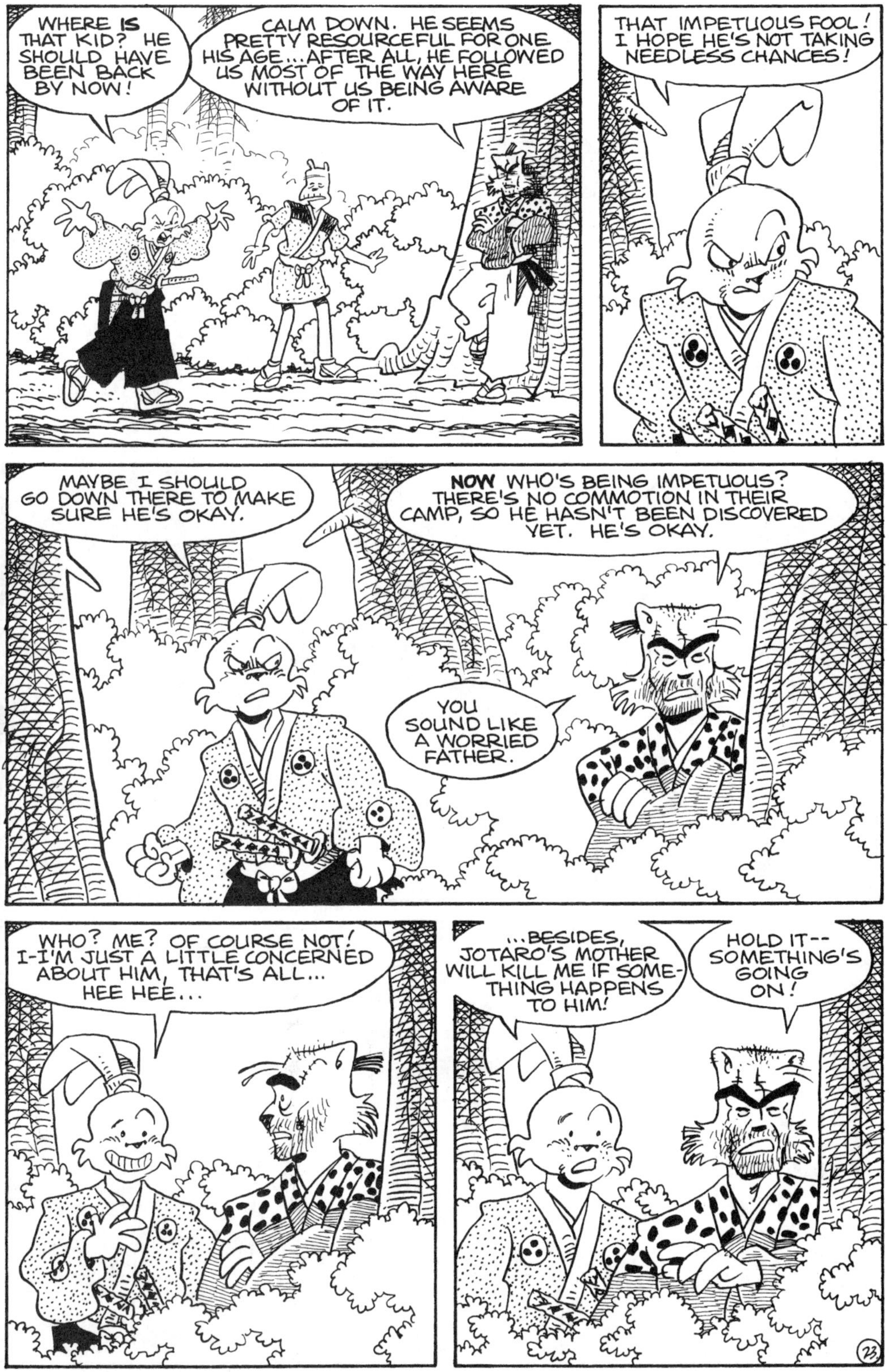
WHERE IS THAT KID? HE SHOULD HAVE BEEN BACK BY NOW!
CALM DOWN. HE SEEMS PRETTY RESOURCEFUL FOR ONE HIS AGE...AFTER ALL, HE FOLLOWED US MOST OF THE WAY HERE WITHOUT US BEING AWARE OF IT.
THAT IMPETUOUS FOOL! I HOPE HE'S NOT TAKING NEEDLESS CHANCES!
MAYBE I SHOULD GO DOWN THERE TO MAKE SURE HE'S OKAY.
NOW WHO'S BEING IMPETUOUS? THERE'S NO COMMOTION IN THEIR CAMP, SO HE HASN'T BEEN DISCOVERED YET. HE'S OKAY.
YOU SOUND LIKE A WORRIED FATHER.
WHO? ME? OF COURSE NOT! I-I'M JUST A LITTLE CONCERNED ABOUT HIM, THAT'S ALL... HEE HEE...
...BESIDES, JOTARO'S MOTHER WILL KILL ME IF SOMETHING HAPPENS TO HIM!
HOLD IT-- SOMETHING'S GOING ON!
23

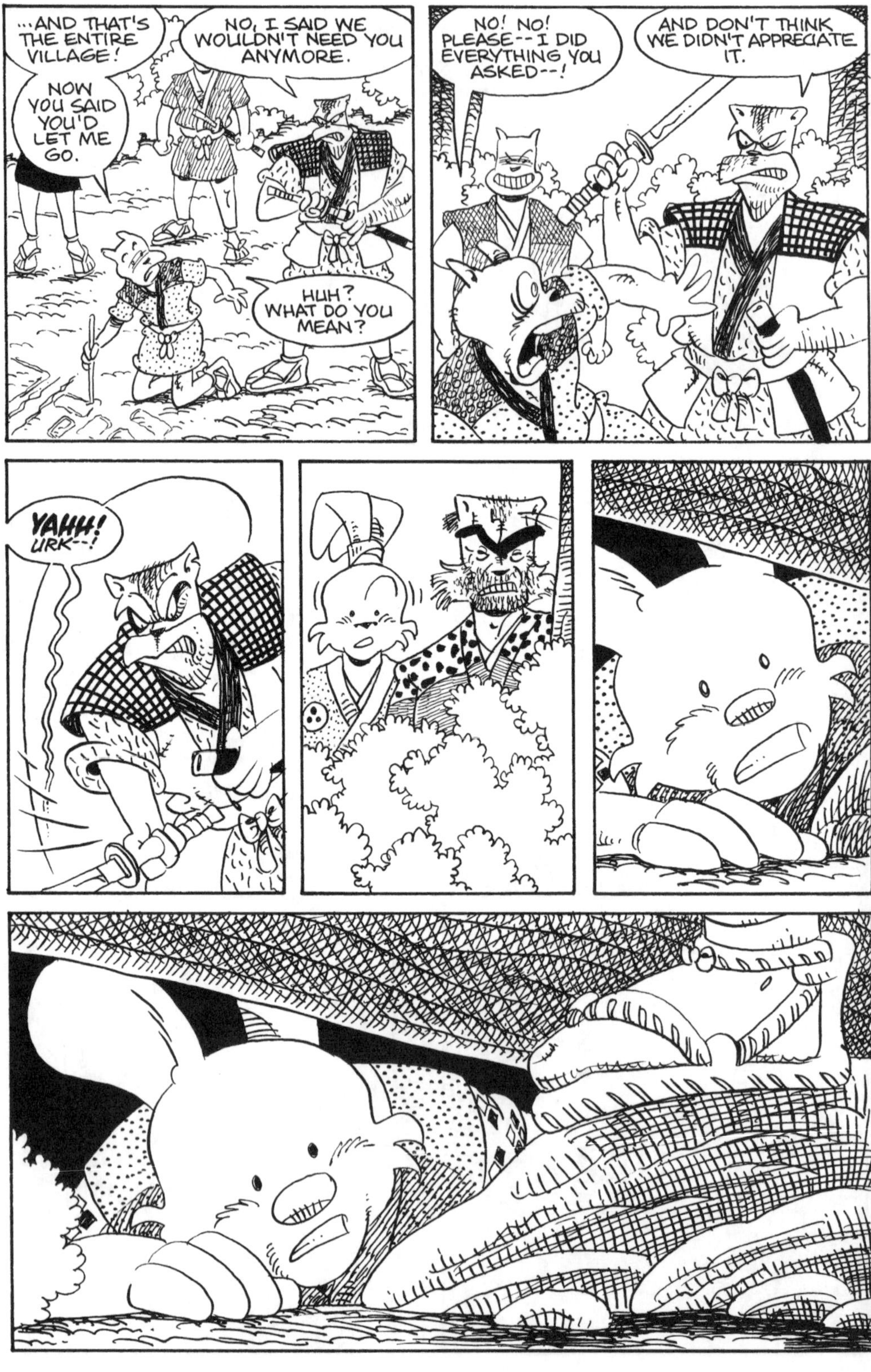

...AND THAT'S THE ENTIRE VILLAGE!
NOW YOU SAID YOU'D LET ME GO.
NO, I SAID WE WOULDN'T NEED YOU ANYMORE.
HUH? WHAT DO YOU MEAN?
NO! NO! PLEASE--I DID EVERYTHING YOU ASKED--!
AND DON'T THINK WE DIDN'T APPRECIATE IT.
YAHH! URK--!

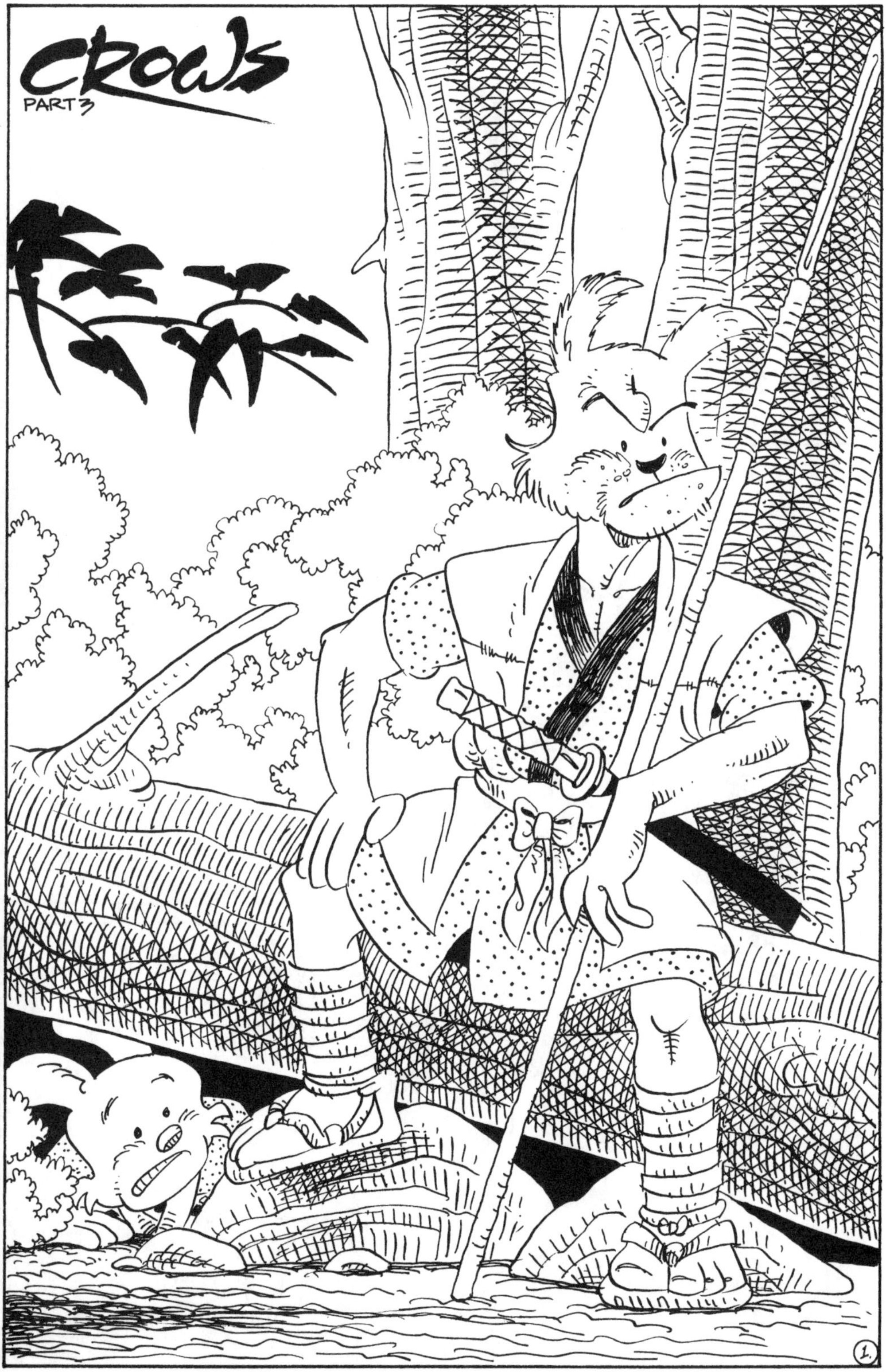
CROWS
PART 3
1.

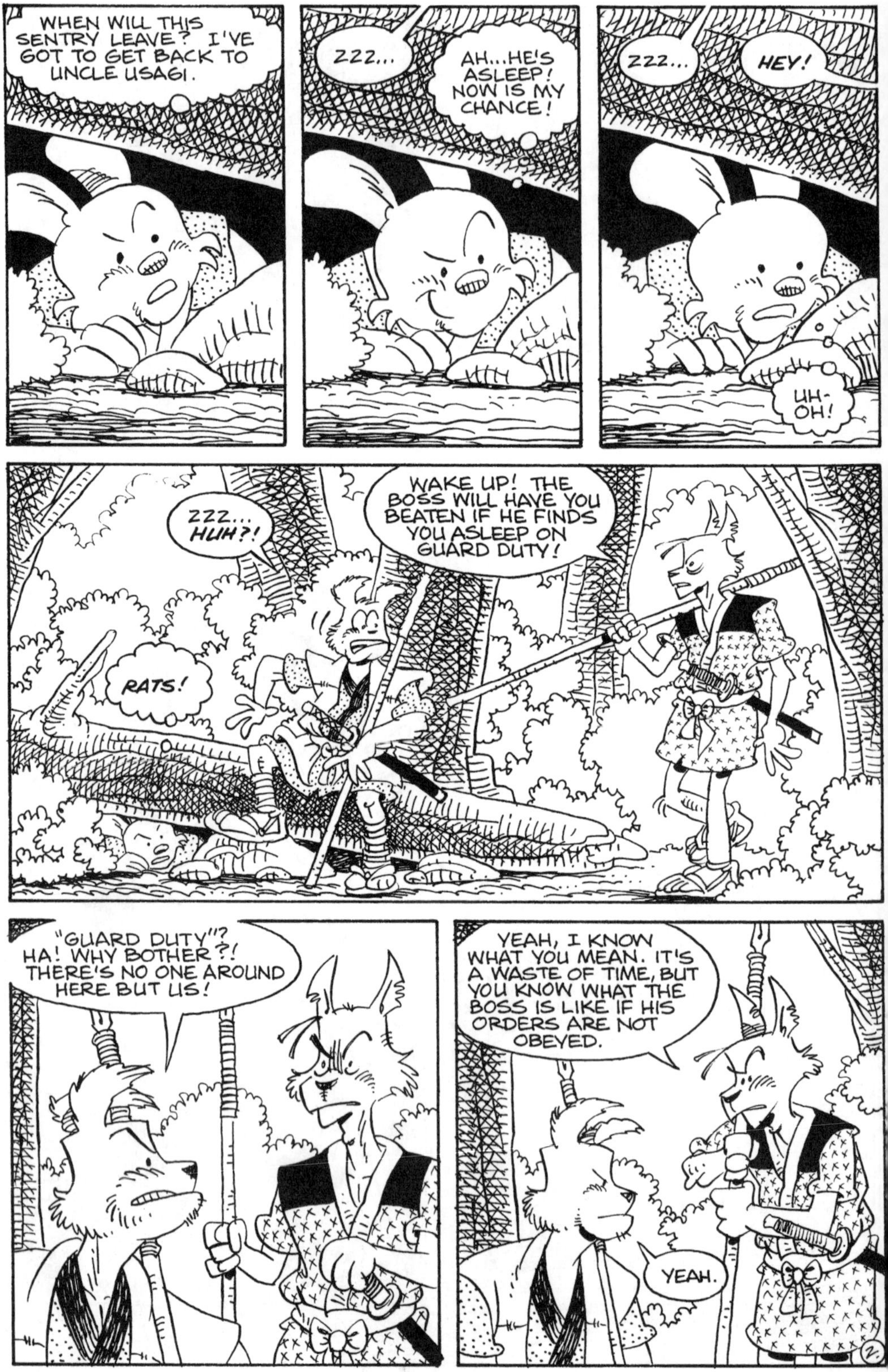
WHEN WILL THIS SENTRY LEAVE? I'VE GOT TO GET BACK TO UNCLE USAGI.
ZZZ...
AH...HE'S ASLEEP! NOW IS MY CHANCE!
ZZZ...
HEY!
UH-OH!
ZZZ... HUH?!
WAKE UP! THE BOSS WILL HAVE YOU BEATEN IF HE FINDS YOU ASLEEP ON GUARD DUTY!
RATS!
"GUARD DUTY"? HA! WHY BOTHER?! THERE'S NO ONE AROUND HERE BUT US!
YEAH, I KNOW WHAT YOU MEAN. IT'S A WASTE OF TIME, BUT YOU KNOW WHAT THE BOSS IS LIKE IF HIS ORDERS ARE NOT OBEYED.
YEAH.
2.

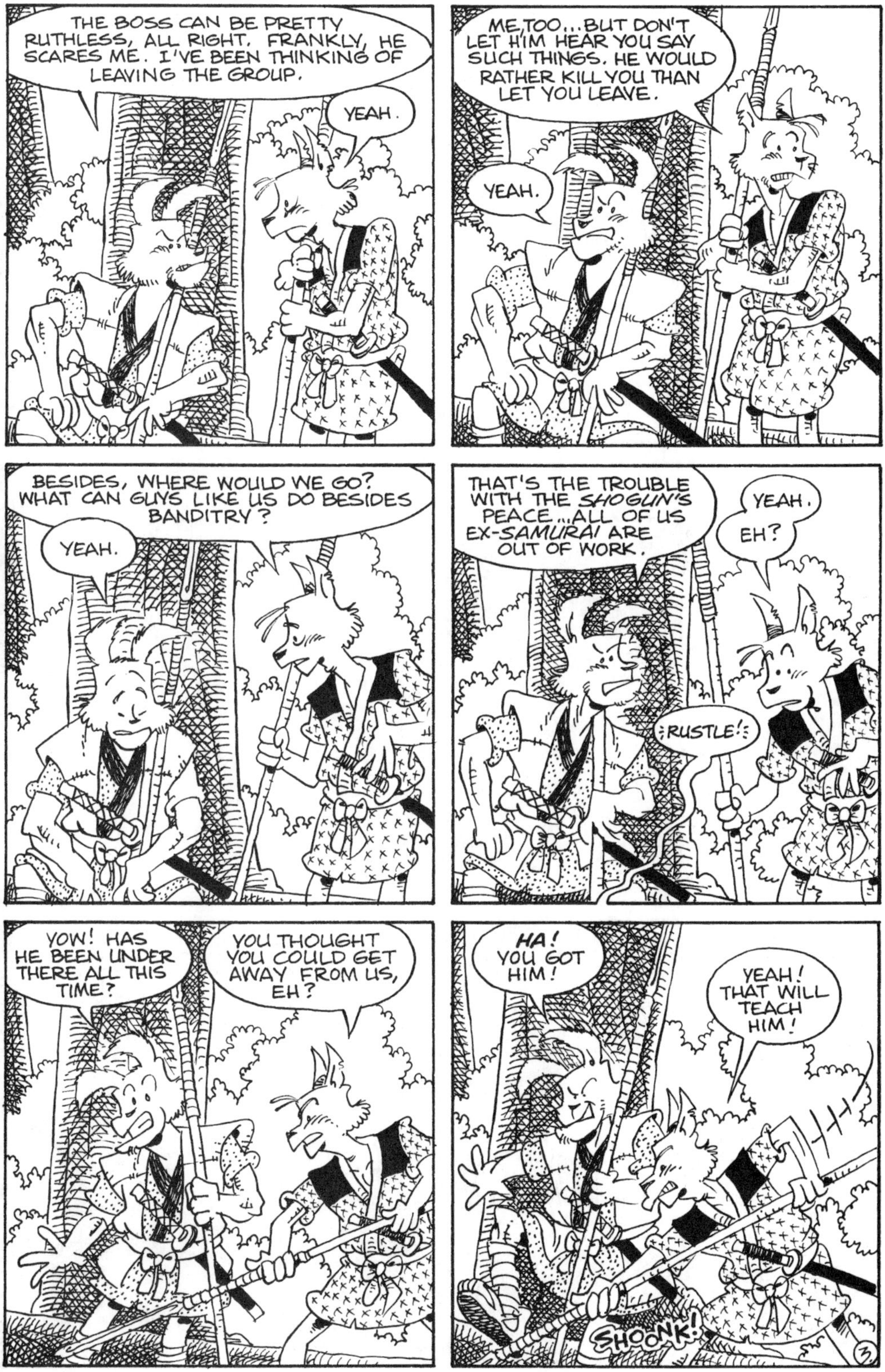
THE BOSS CAN BE PRETTY RUTHLESS, ALL RIGHT. FRANKLY, HE SCARES ME. I'VE BEEN THINKING OF LEAVING THE GROUP.
YEAH.
ME, TOO...BUT DON'T LET HIM HEAR YOU SAY SUCH THINGS. HE WOULD RATHER KILL YOU THAN LET YOU LEAVE.
YEAH.
BESIDES, WHERE WOULD WE GO? WHAT CAN GUYS LIKE US DO BESIDES BANDITRY?
YEAH.
THAT'S THE TROUBLE WITH THE *SHOGUN*'S PEACE...ALL OF US EX-*SAMURAI* ARE OUT OF WORK.
YEAH.
EH?
RUSTLE!
YOW! HAS HE BEEN UNDER THERE ALL THIS TIME?
YOU THOUGHT YOU COULD GET AWAY FROM US, EH?
HA! YOU GOT HIM!
YEAH! THAT WILL TEACH HIM!
SHOONK!
3.

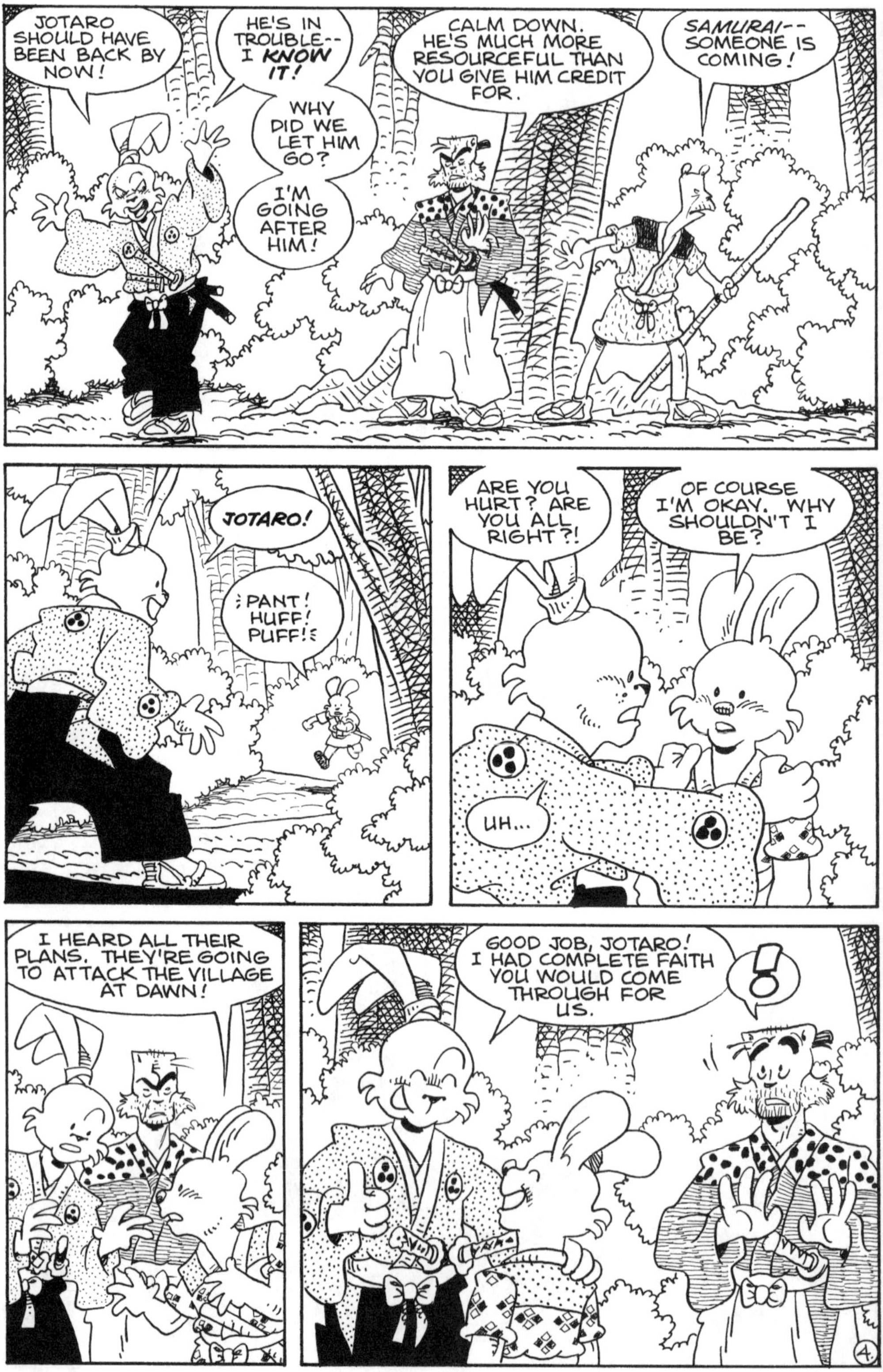
JOTARO SHOULD HAVE BEEN BACK BY NOW!
HE'S IN TROUBLE-- I **KNOW IT!**
WHY DID WE LET HIM GO?
I'M GOING AFTER HIM!
CALM DOWN. HE'S MUCH MORE RESOURCEFUL THAN YOU GIVE HIM CREDIT FOR.
SAMURAI-- SOMEONE IS COMING!
JOTARO!
PANT! HUFF! PUFF!
ARE YOU HURT? ARE YOU ALL RIGHT?!
OF COURSE I'M OKAY. WHY SHOULDN'T I BE?
UH...
I HEARD ALL THEIR PLANS. THEY'RE GOING TO ATTACK THE VILLAGE AT DAWN!
GOOD JOB, JOTARO! I HAD COMPLETE FAITH YOU WOULD COME THROUGH FOR US.
!
4.

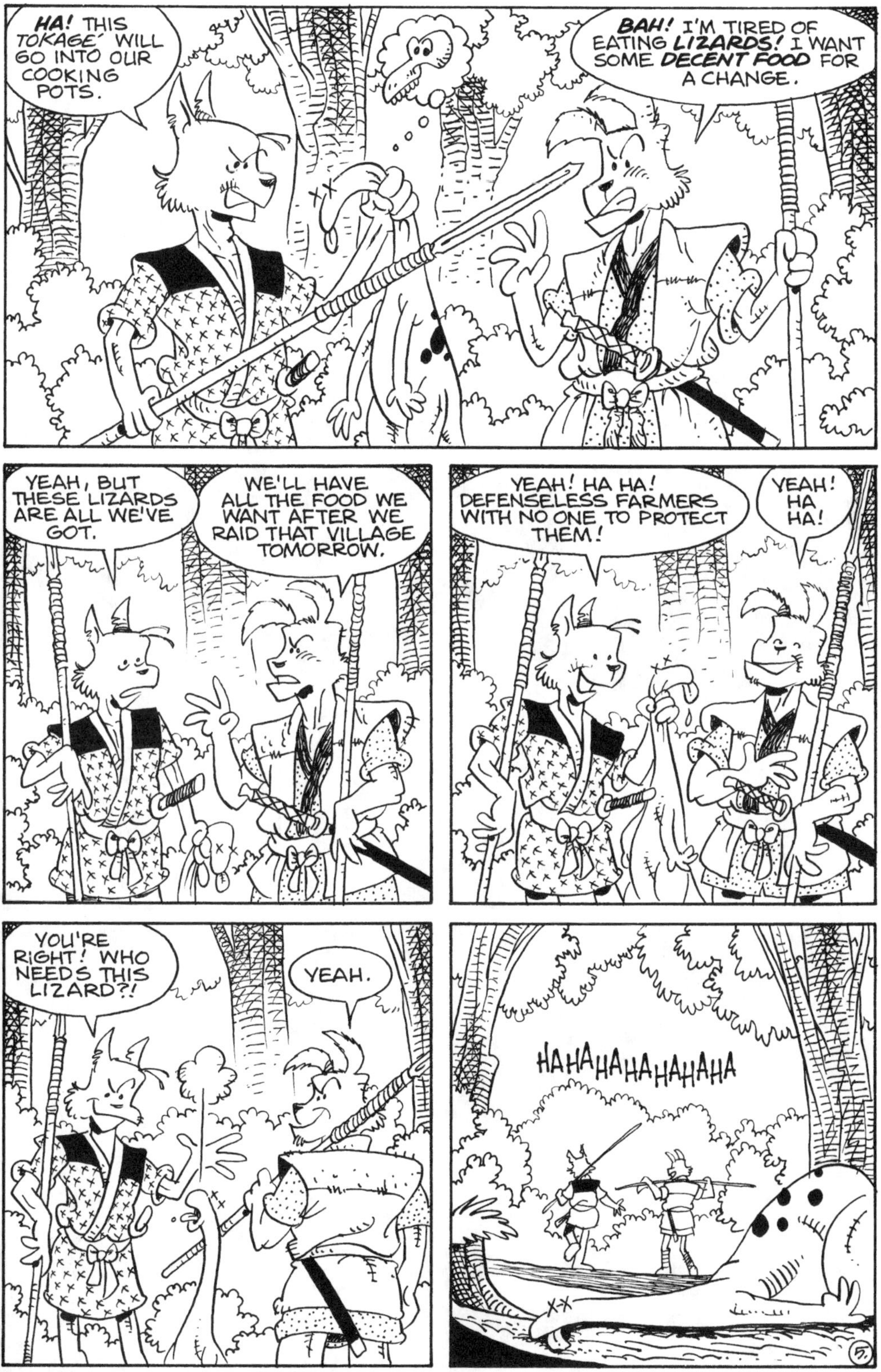
HA! THIS TOKAGE' WILL GO INTO OUR COOKING POTS.
BAH! I'M TIRED OF EATING LIZARDS! I WANT SOME DECENT FOOD FOR A CHANGE.
YEAH, BUT THESE LIZARDS ARE ALL WE'VE GOT.
WE'LL HAVE ALL THE FOOD WE WANT AFTER WE RAID THAT VILLAGE TOMORROW.
YEAH! HA HA! DEFENSELESS FARMERS WITH NO ONE TO PROTECT THEM!
YEAH! HA HA!
YOU'RE RIGHT! WHO NEEDS THIS LIZARD?!
YEAH.
HAHAHAHAHAHAHAHA

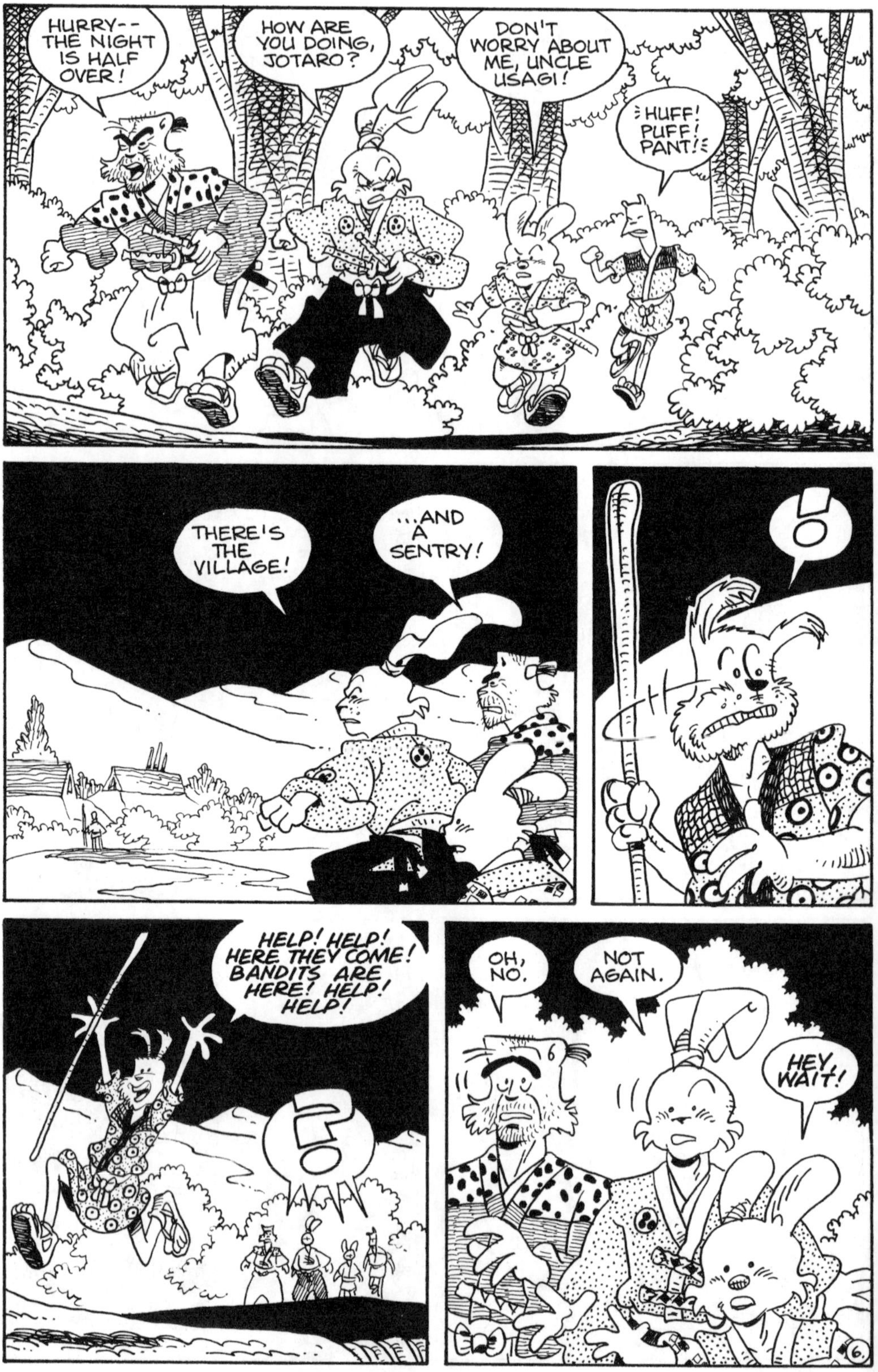
HURRY-- THE NIGHT IS HALF OVER!
HOW ARE YOU DOING, JOTARO?
DON'T WORRY ABOUT ME, UNCLE USAGI!
HUFF! PUFF! PANT!
THERE'S THE VILLAGE!
...AND A SENTRY!
HELP! HELP! HERE THEY COME! BANDITS ARE HERE! HELP! HELP!
OH, NO.
NOT AGAIN.
HEY, WAIT!

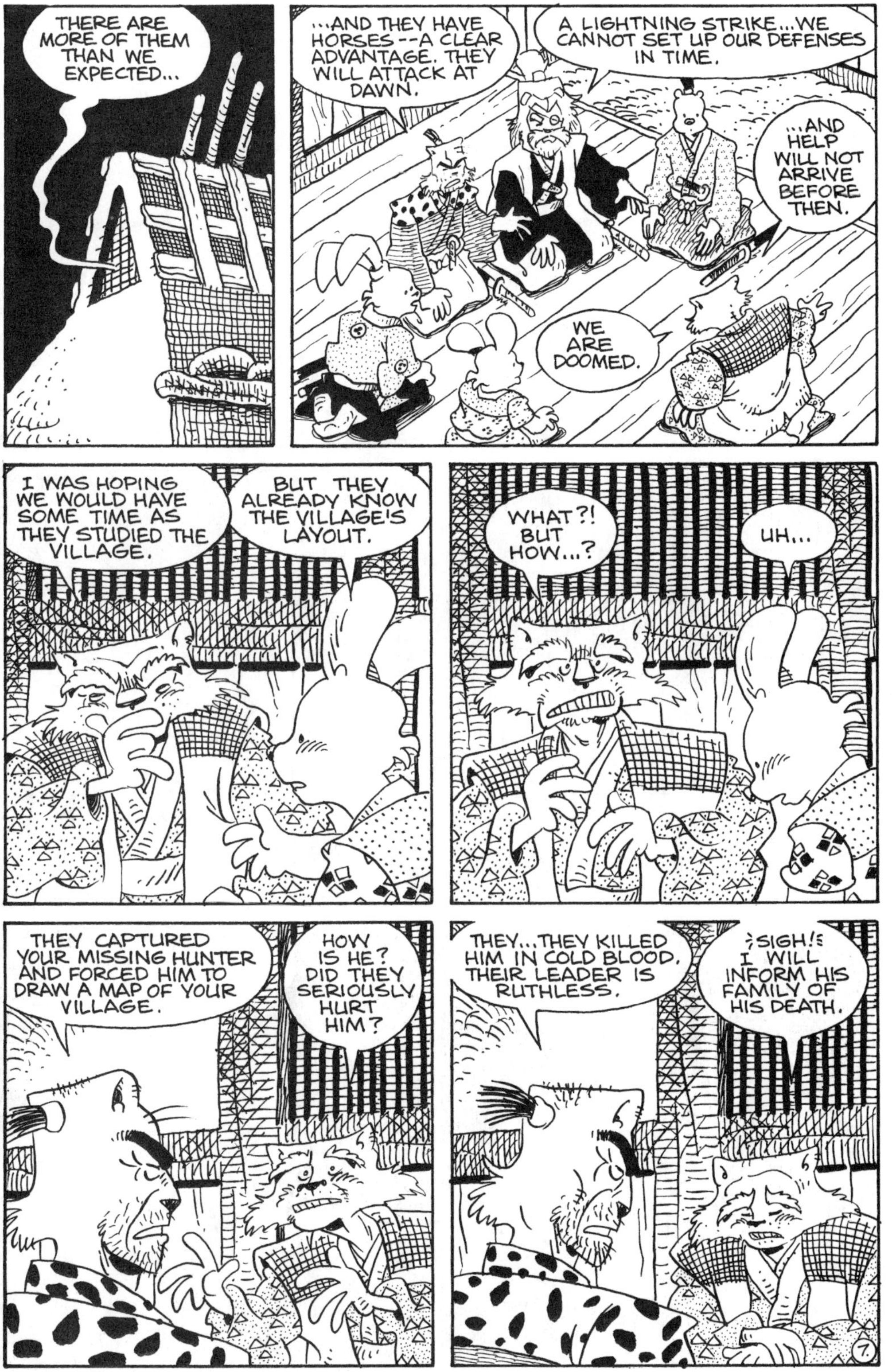

THERE ARE MORE OF THEM THAN WE EXPECTED...
...AND THEY HAVE HORSES--A CLEAR ADVANTAGE. THEY WILL ATTACK AT DAWN.
A LIGHTNING STRIKE...WE CANNOT SET UP OUR DEFENSES IN TIME.
...AND HELP WILL NOT ARRIVE BEFORE THEN.
WE ARE DOOMED.
I WAS HOPING WE WOULD HAVE SOME TIME AS THEY STUDIED THE VILLAGE.
BUT THEY ALREADY KNOW THE VILLAGE'S LAYOUT.
WHAT?! BUT HOW...?
UH...
THEY CAPTURED YOUR MISSING HUNTER AND FORCED HIM TO DRAW A MAP OF YOUR VILLAGE.
HOW IS HE? DID THEY SERIOUSLY HURT HIM?
THEY...THEY KILLED HIM IN COLD BLOOD. THEIR LEADER IS RUTHLESS.
SIGH! I WILL INFORM HIS FAMILY OF HIS DEATH.
7.

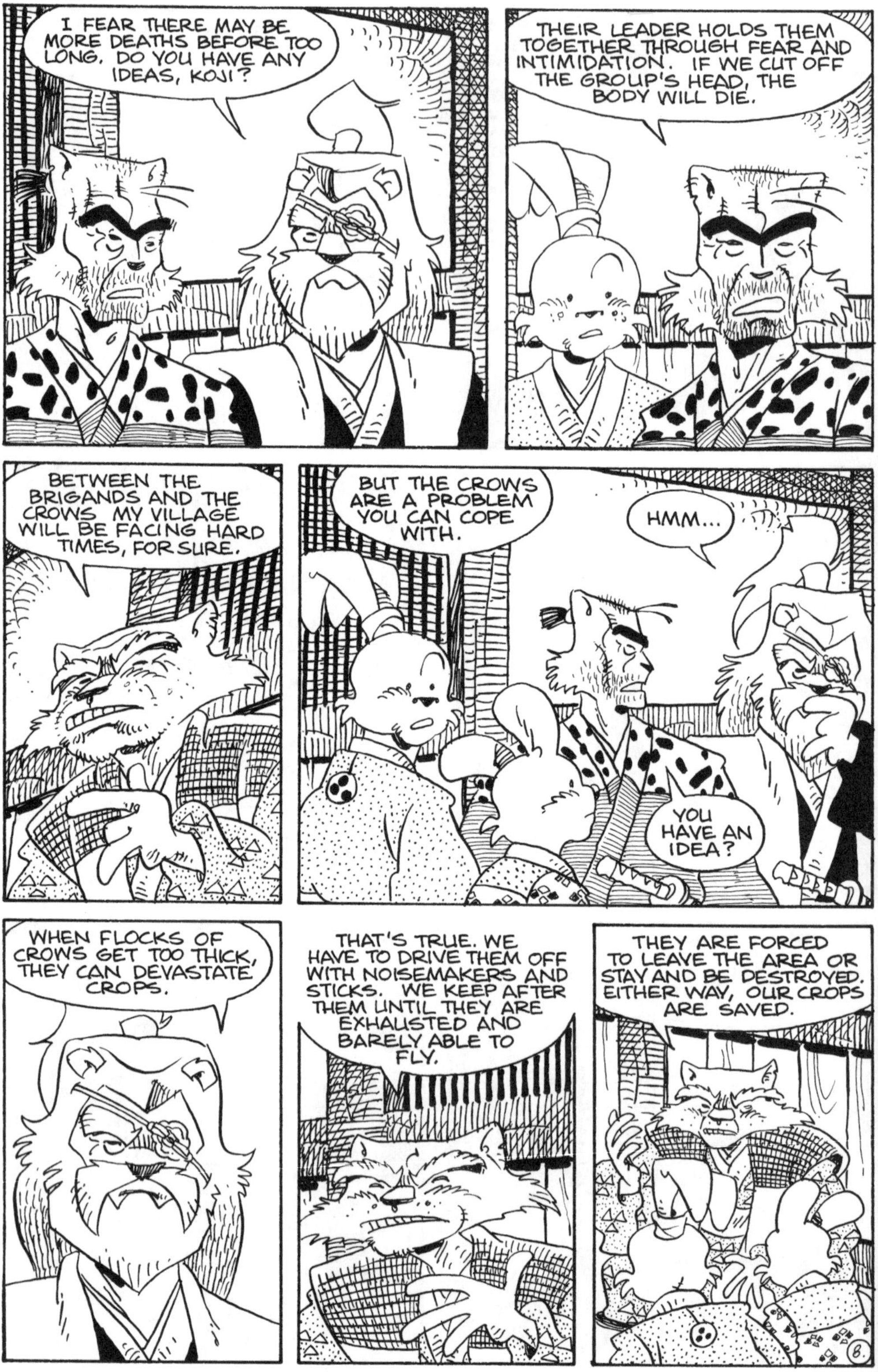
I FEAR THERE MAY BE MORE DEATHS BEFORE TOO LONG. DO YOU HAVE ANY IDEAS, KOJI?
THEIR LEADER HOLDS THEM TOGETHER THROUGH FEAR AND INTIMIDATION. IF WE CUT OFF THE GROUP'S HEAD, THE BODY WILL DIE.
BETWEEN THE BRIGANDS AND THE CROWS MY VILLAGE WILL BE FACING HARD TIMES, FOR SURE.
BUT THE CROWS ARE A PROBLEM YOU CAN COPE WITH.
HMM...
YOU HAVE AN IDEA?
WHEN FLOCKS OF CROWS GET TOO THICK, THEY CAN DEVASTATE CROPS.
THAT'S TRUE. WE HAVE TO DRIVE THEM OFF WITH NOISEMAKERS AND STICKS. WE KEEP AFTER THEM UNTIL THEY ARE EXHAUSTED AND BARELY ABLE TO FLY.
THEY ARE FORCED TO LEAVE THE AREA OR STAY AND BE DESTROYED. EITHER WAY, OUR CROPS ARE SAVED.
8.

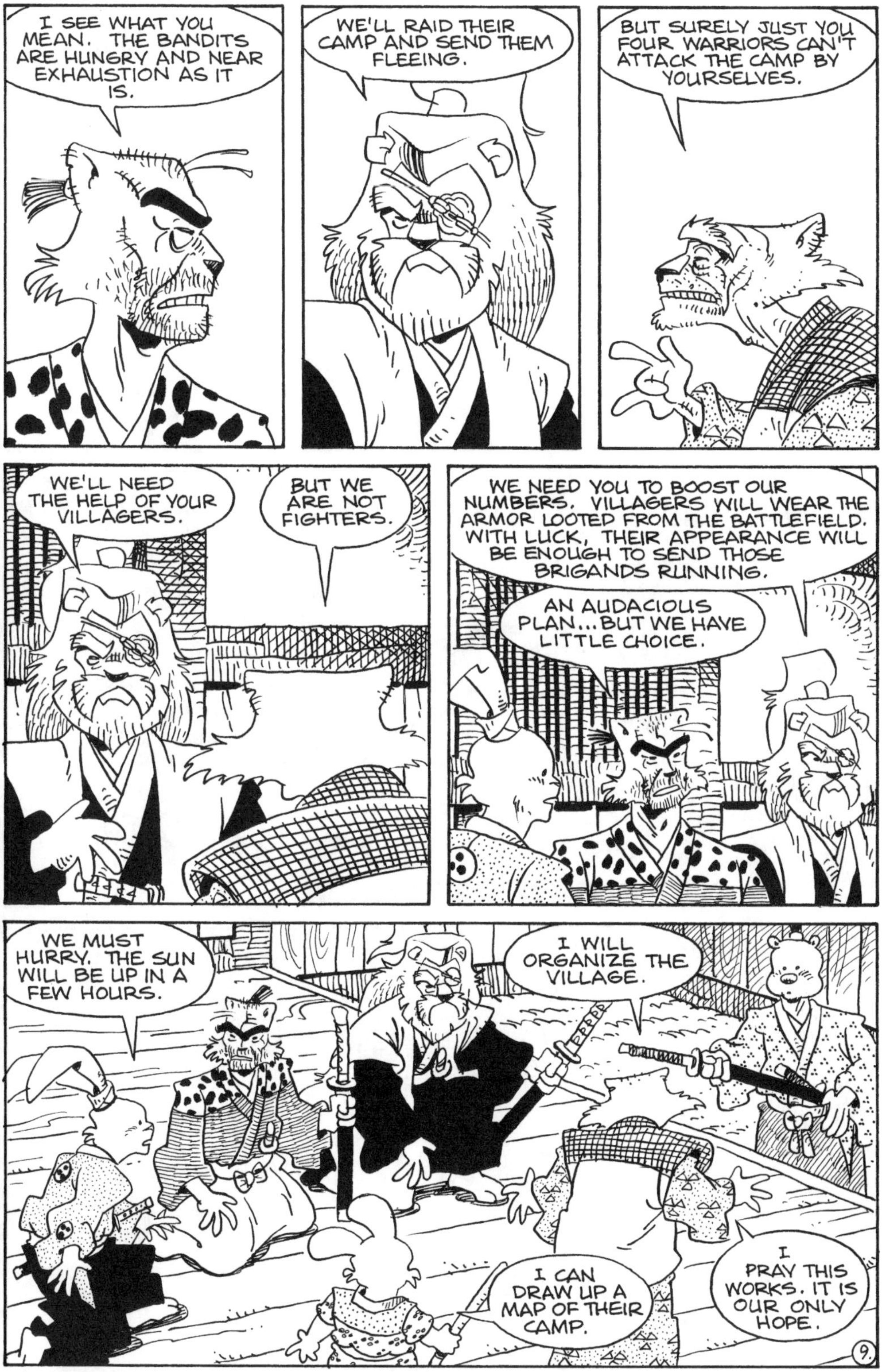
I SEE WHAT YOU MEAN. THE BANDITS ARE HUNGRY AND NEAR EXHAUSTION AS IT IS.
WE'LL RAID THEIR CAMP AND SEND THEM FLEEING.
BUT SURELY JUST YOU FOUR WARRIORS CAN'T ATTACK THE CAMP BY YOURSELVES.
WE'LL NEED THE HELP OF YOUR VILLAGERS.
BUT WE ARE NOT FIGHTERS.
WE NEED YOU TO BOOST OUR NUMBERS. VILLAGERS WILL WEAR THE ARMOR LOOTED FROM THE BATTLEFIELD. WITH LUCK, THEIR APPEARANCE WILL BE ENOUGH TO SEND THOSE BRIGANDS RUNNING.
AN AUDACIOUS PLAN... BUT WE HAVE LITTLE CHOICE.
WE MUST HURRY. THE SUN WILL BE UP IN A FEW HOURS.
I WILL ORGANIZE THE VILLAGE.
I CAN DRAW UP A MAP OF THEIR CAMP.
I PRAY THIS WORKS. IT IS OUR ONLY HOPE.
9.

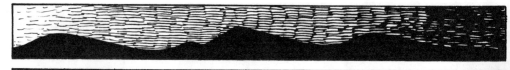

THE SUN'S ALMOST UP. I GUESS IT'S TIME TO WAKE UP THE BOSS.

BRR... IT'S COLD. AUTUMN IS ON US NOW, FOR SURE.

¡CLANK! KLANK! KLANG!

EH--? WHAT'S THAT?

HURRY, MEN-- SURROUND THEM!

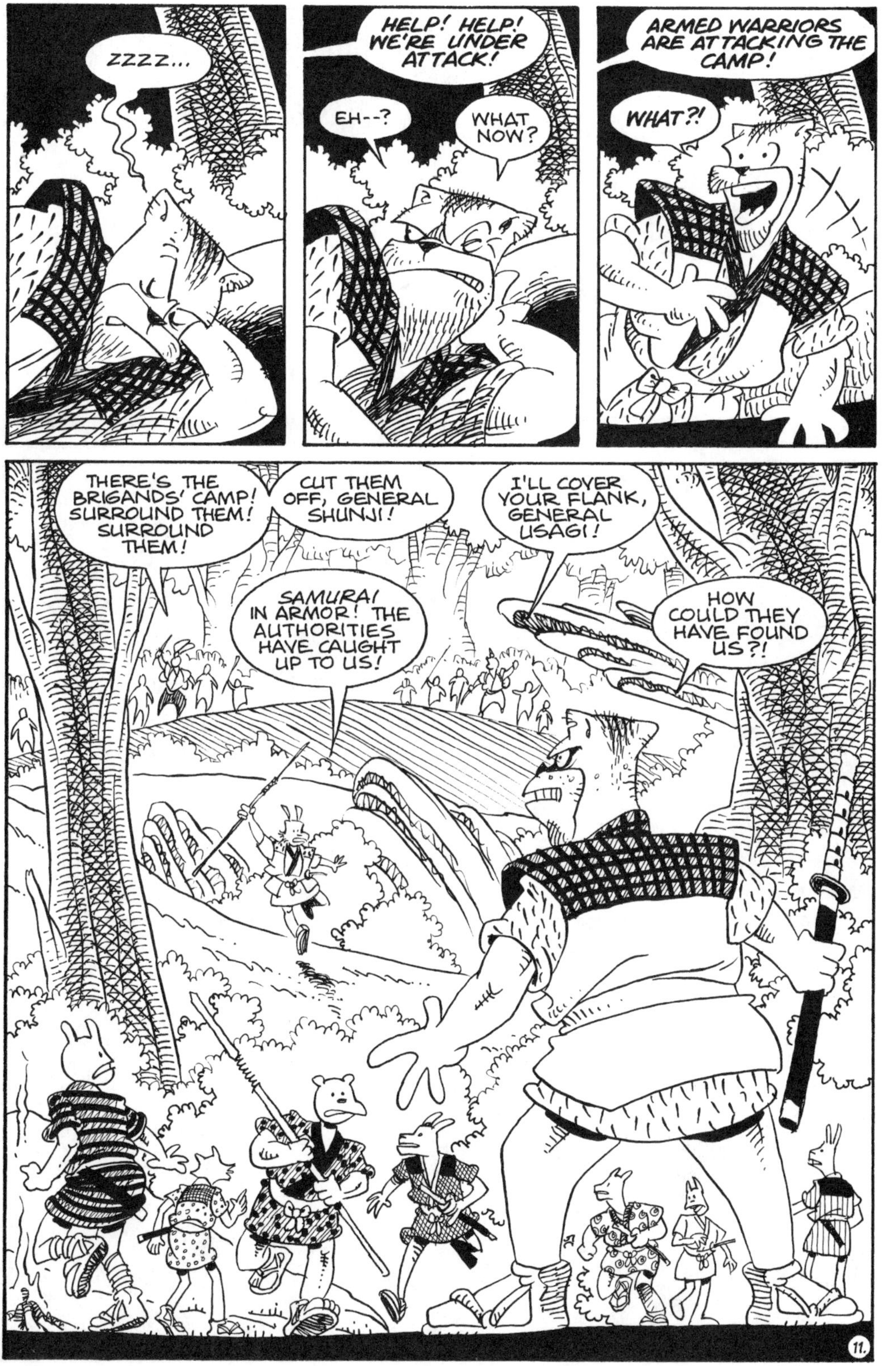
ZZZZ...
HELP! HELP! WE'RE UNDER ATTACK!
EH--?
WHAT NOW?
ARMED WARRIORS ARE ATTACKING THE CAMP!
WHAT?!
THERE'S THE BRIGANDS' CAMP! SURROUND THEM! SURROUND THEM!
CUT THEM OFF, GENERAL SHUNJI!
I'LL COVER YOUR FLANK, GENERAL USAGI!
SAMURAI IN ARMOR! THE AUTHORITIES HAVE CAUGHT UP TO US!
HOW COULD THEY HAVE FOUND US?!
11.

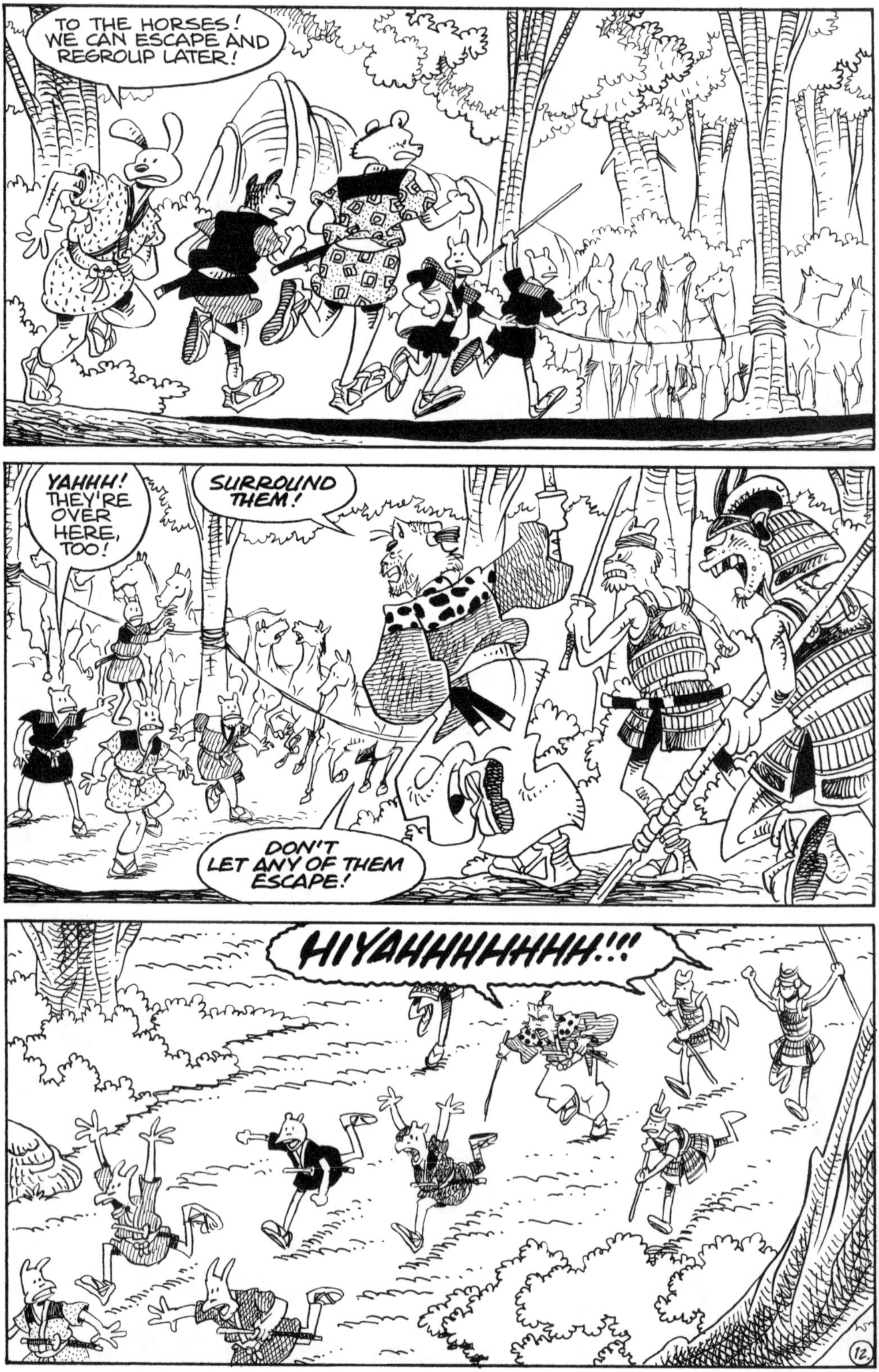

TO THE HORSES! WE CAN ESCAPE AND REGROUP LATER!
YAHHH! THEY'RE OVER HERE, TOO!
SURROUND THEM!
DON'T LET ANY OF THEM ESCAPE!
HIYAHHHHHHHH!!!
12.

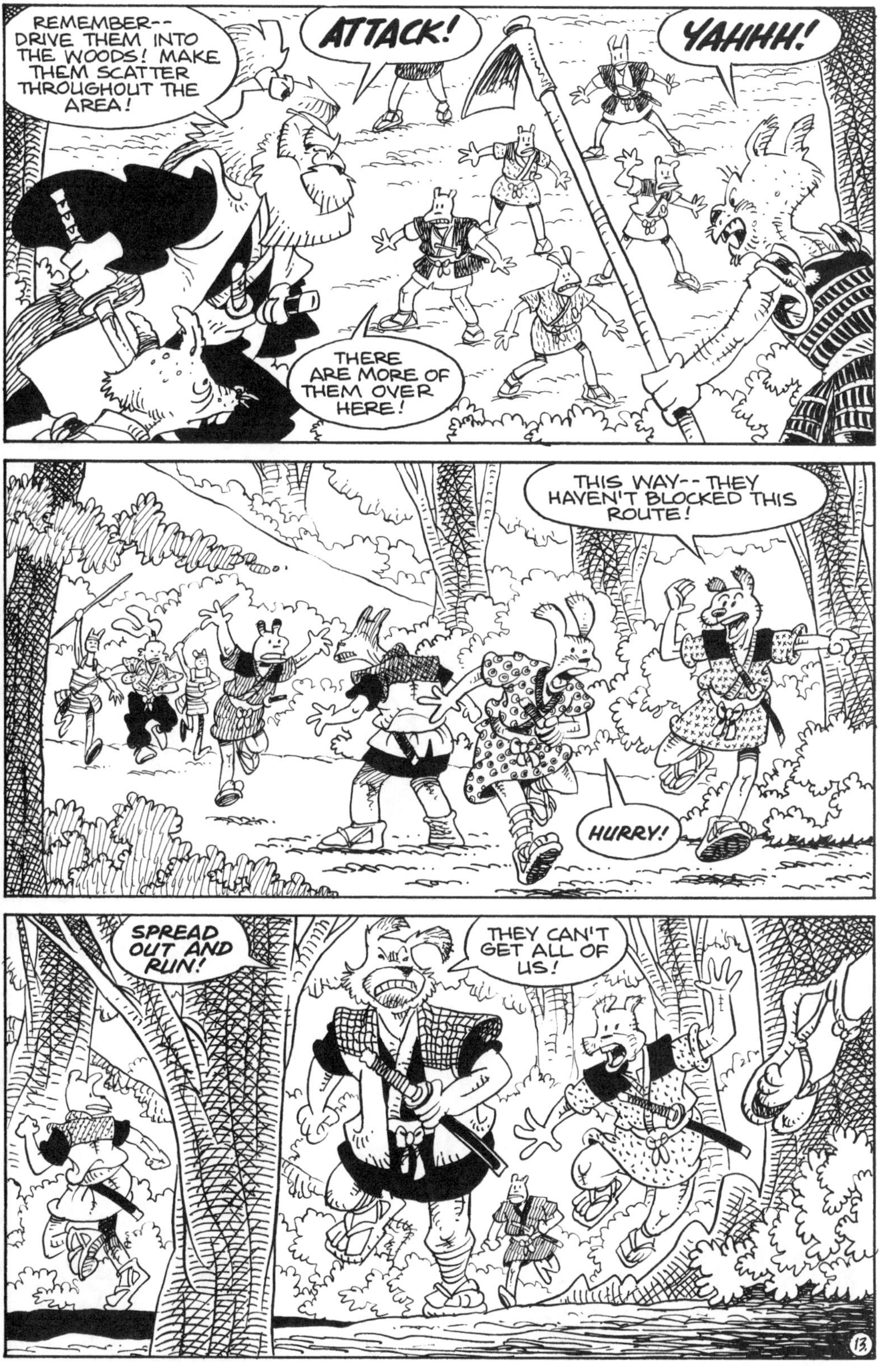
REMEMBER-- DRIVE THEM INTO THE WOODS! MAKE THEM SCATTER THROUGHOUT THE AREA!
ATTACK!
YAHHH!
THERE ARE MORE OF THEM OVER HERE!
THIS WAY-- THEY HAVEN'T BLOCKED THIS ROUTE!
HURRY!
SPREAD OUT AND RUN!
THEY CAN'T GET ALL OF US!
13.

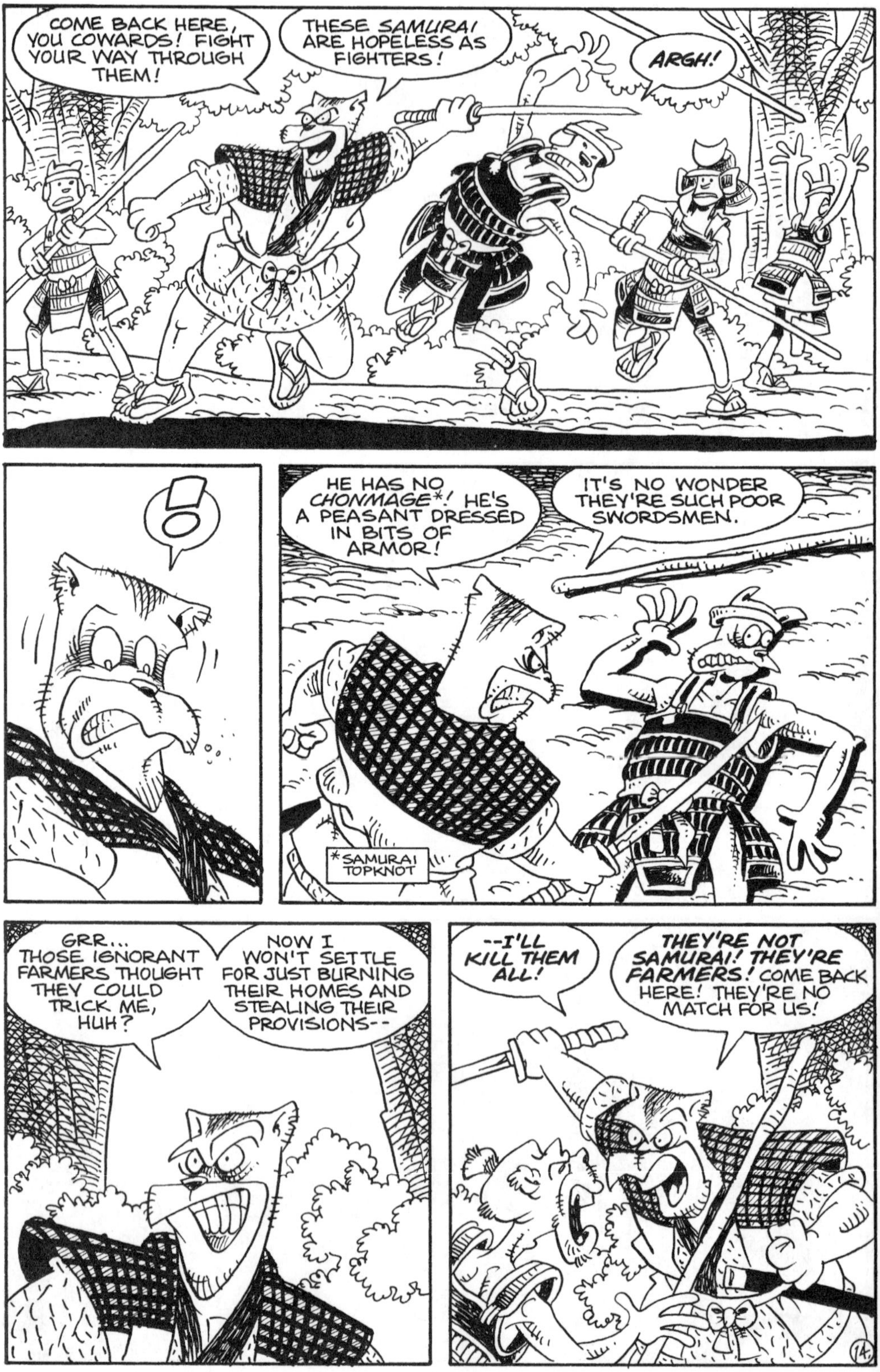
COME BACK HERE, YOU COWARDS! FIGHT YOUR WAY THROUGH THEM!
THESE SAMURAI ARE HOPELESS AS FIGHTERS!
ARGH!
!
HE HAS NO CHONMAGE*! HE'S A PEASANT DRESSED IN BITS OF ARMOR!
IT'S NO WONDER THEY'RE SUCH POOR SWORDSMEN.
*SAMURAI TOPKNOT
GRR... THOSE IGNORANT FARMERS THOUGHT THEY COULD TRICK ME, HUH?
NOW I WON'T SETTLE FOR JUST BURNING THEIR HOMES AND STEALING THEIR PROVISIONS--
--I'LL KILL THEM ALL!
THEY'RE NOT SAMURAI! THEY'RE FARMERS! COME BACK HERE! THEY'RE NO MATCH FOR US!
14.

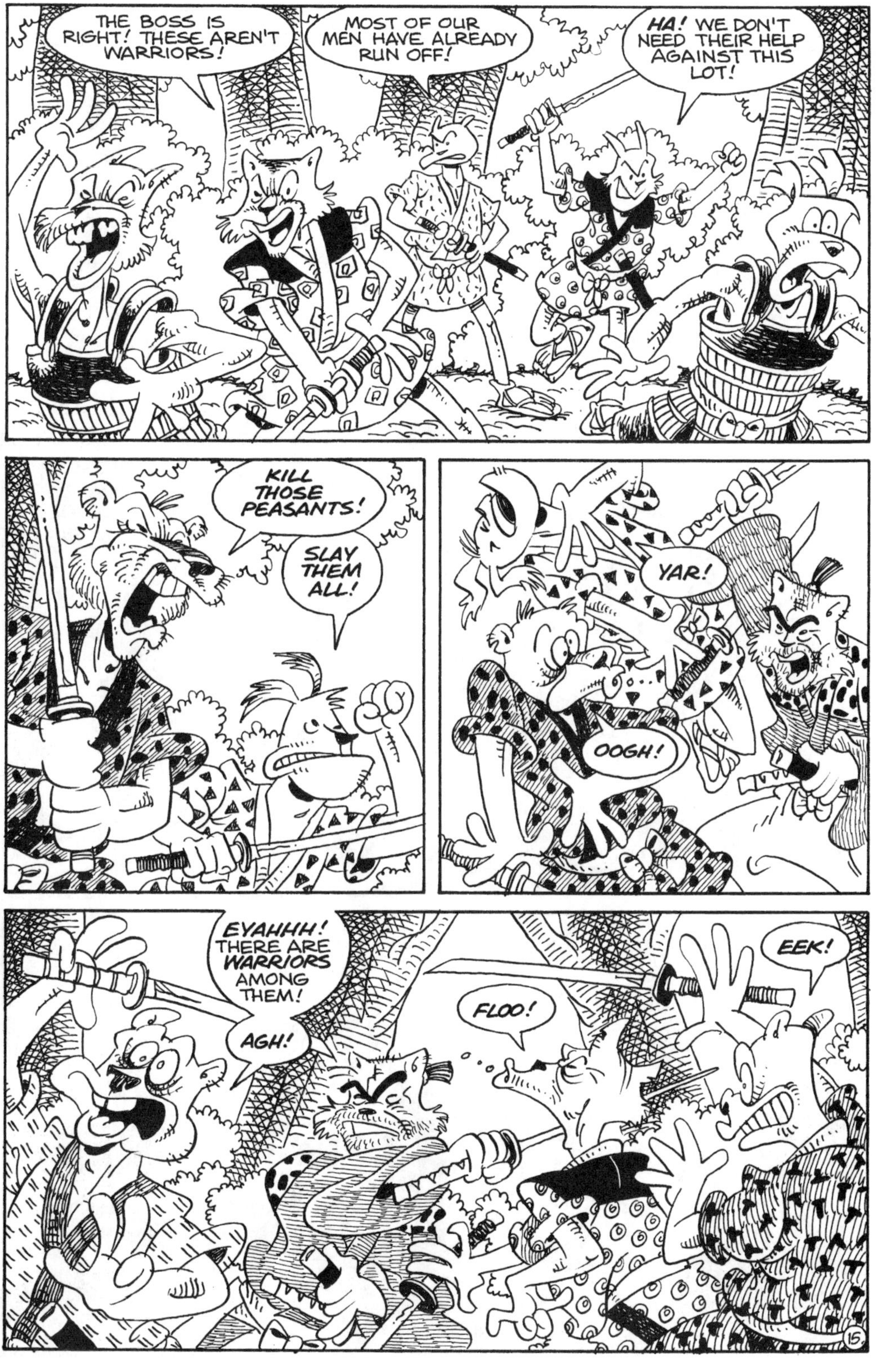
THE BOSS IS RIGHT! THESE AREN'T WARRIORS!
MOST OF OUR MEN HAVE ALREADY RUN OFF!
HA! WE DON'T NEED THEIR HELP AGAINST THIS LOT!
KILL THOSE PEASANTS!
SLAY THEM ALL!
YAR!
OOGH!
EYAHHH! THERE ARE WARRIORS AMONG THEM!
AGH!
FLOO!
EEK!
15

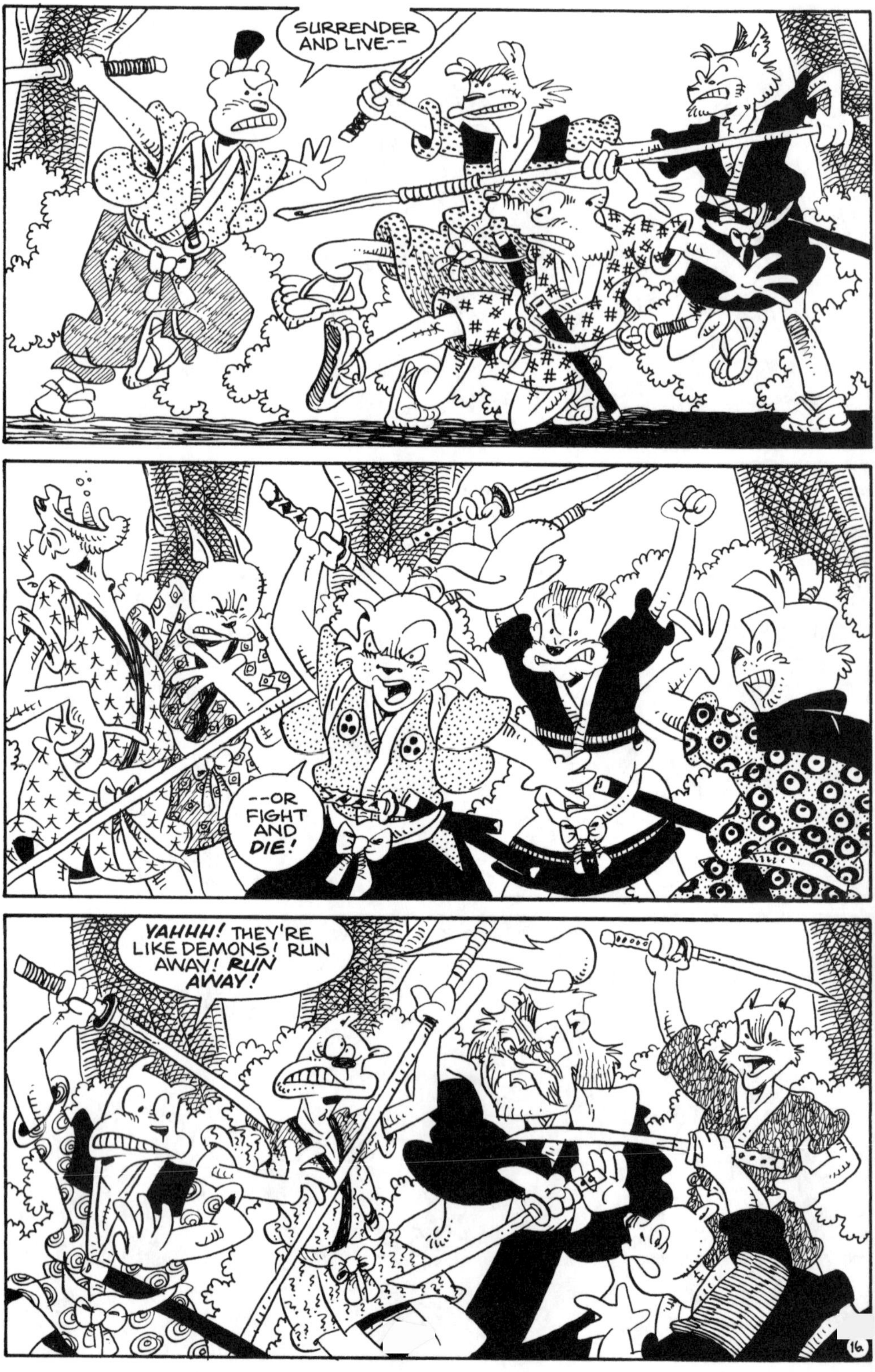
SURRENDER AND LIVE--
--OR FIGHT AND DIE!
YAHHH! THEY'RE LIKE DEMONS! RUN AWAY! RUN AWAY!
16.

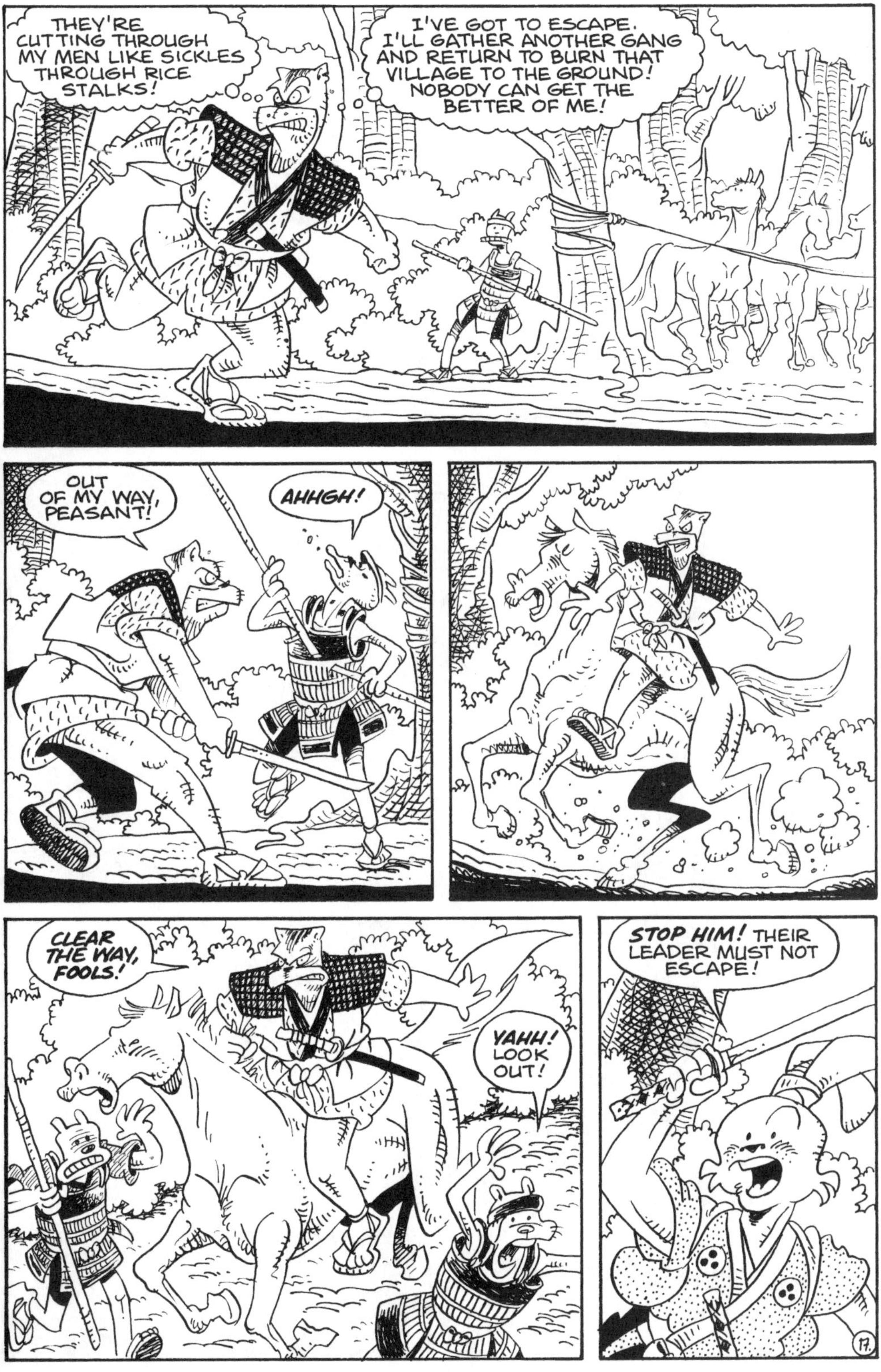
THEY'RE CUTTING THROUGH MY MEN LIKE SICKLES THROUGH RICE STALKS!
I'VE GOT TO ESCAPE. I'LL GATHER ANOTHER GANG AND RETURN TO BURN THAT VILLAGE TO THE GROUND! NOBODY CAN GET THE BETTER OF ME!
OUT OF MY WAY, PEASANT!
AHHGH!
CLEAR THE WAY, FOOLS!
YAHH! LOOK OUT!
STOP HIM! THEIR LEADER MUST NOT ESCAPE!
17.

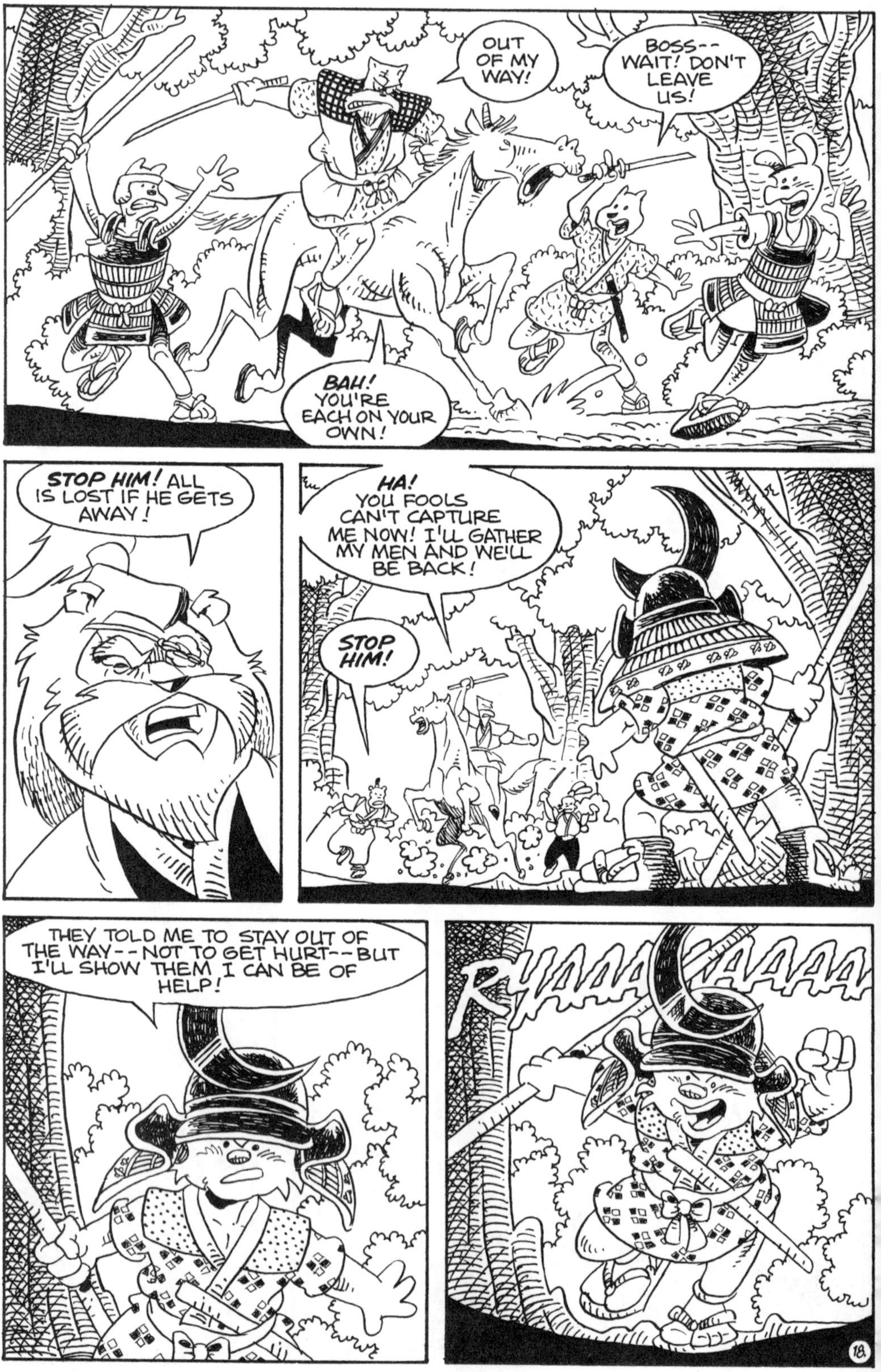
OUT OF MY WAY!
BOSS-- WAIT! DON'T LEAVE US!
BAH! YOU'RE EACH ON YOUR OWN!
STOP HIM! ALL IS LOST IF HE GETS AWAY!
HA! YOU FOOLS CAN'T CAPTURE ME NOW! I'LL GATHER MY MEN AND WE'LL BE BACK!
STOP HIM!
THEY TOLD ME TO STAY OUT OF THE WAY--NOT TO GET HURT--BUT I'LL SHOW THEM I CAN BE OF HELP!
RYAAAAAAAAA
18

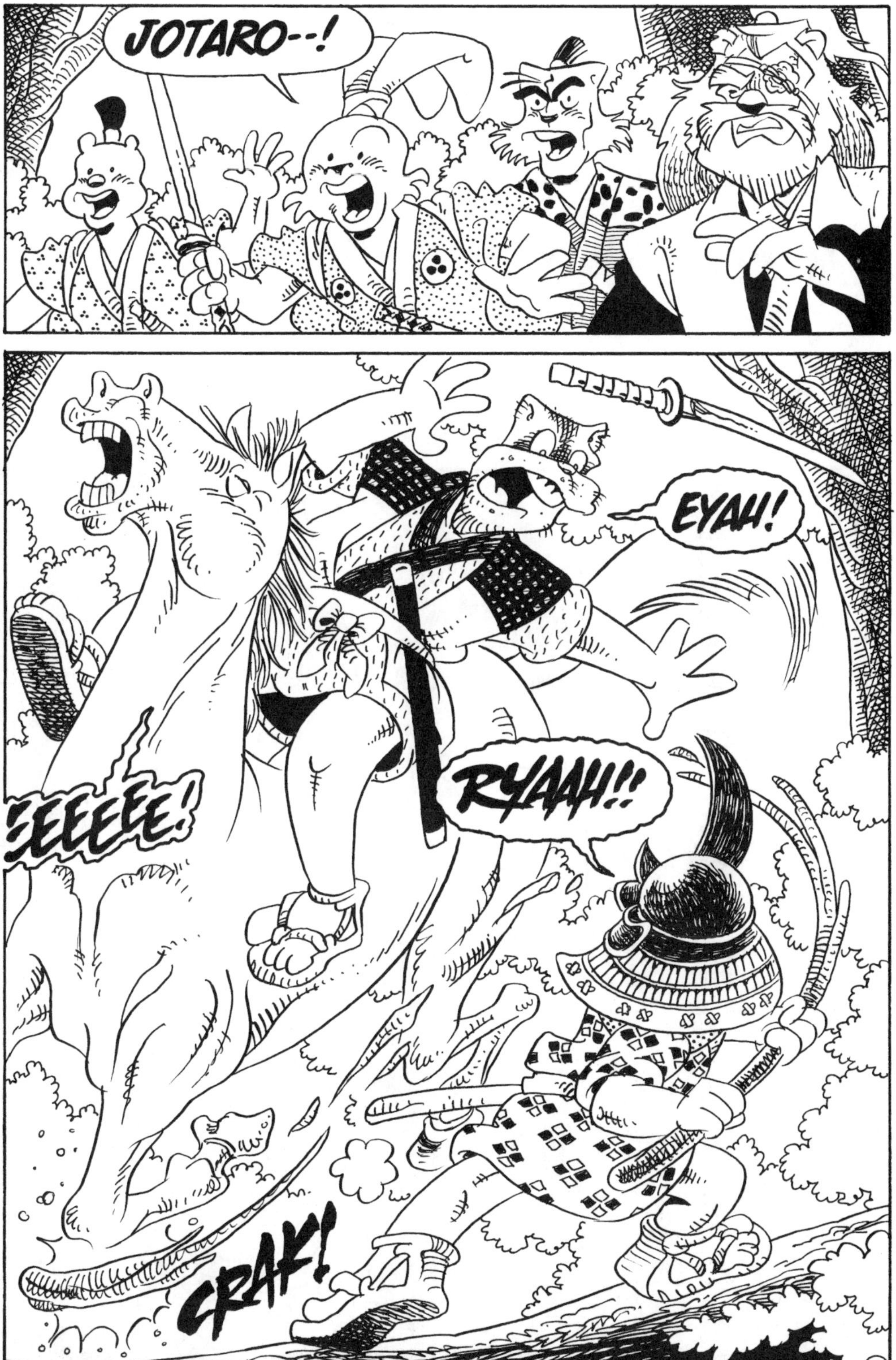
JOTARO--!
EYAH!
EEEEEE!
RYAAH!!
CRAK!
19.

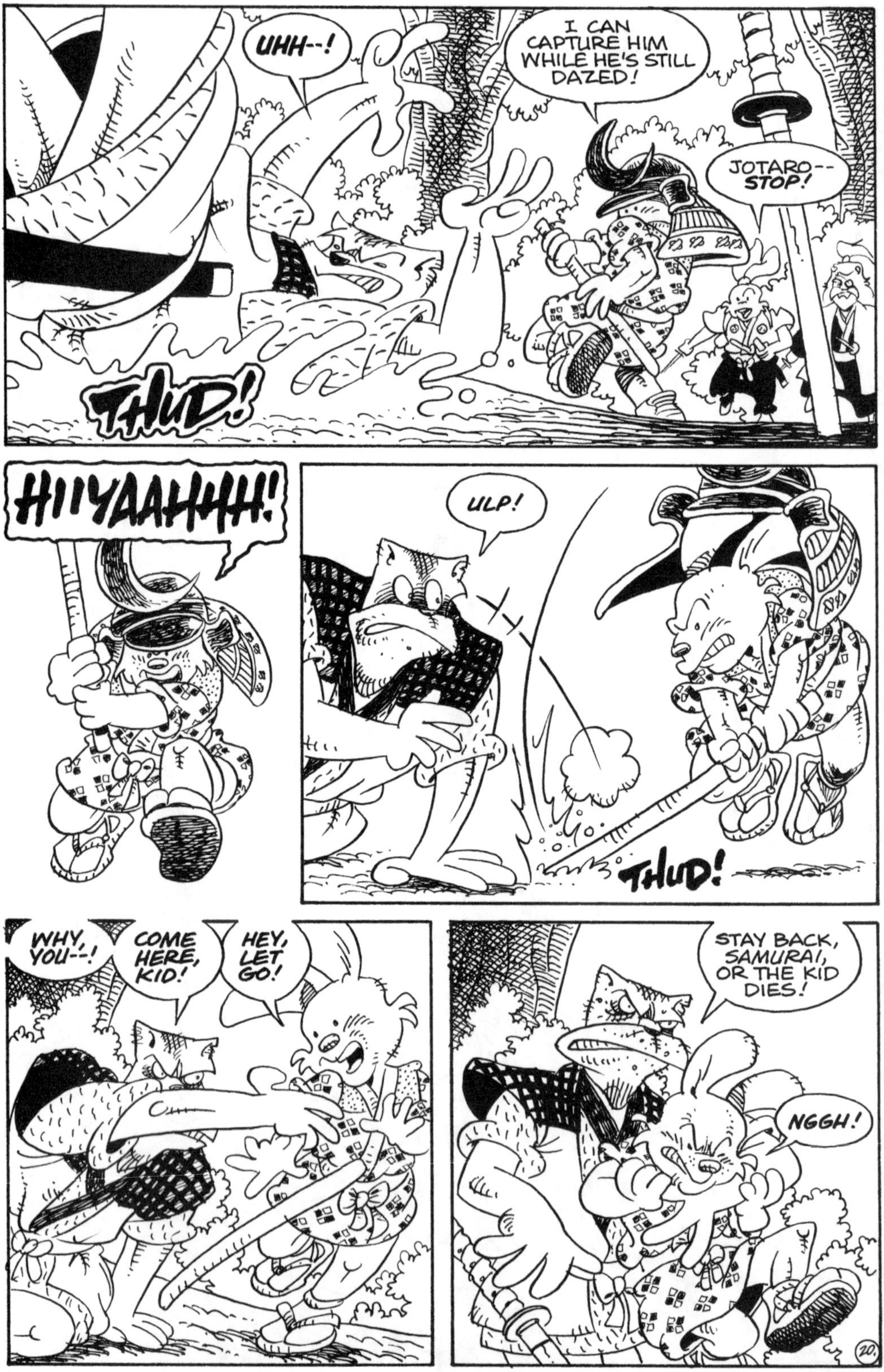
UHH--!
THUD!
I CAN CAPTURE HIM WHILE HE'S STILL DAZED!
JOTARO-- STOP!
HIIYAAHHH!
ULP!
THUD!
WHY, YOU--!
COME HERE, KID!
HEY, LET GO!
STAY BACK, SAMURAI, OR THE KID DIES!
NGGH!
20.

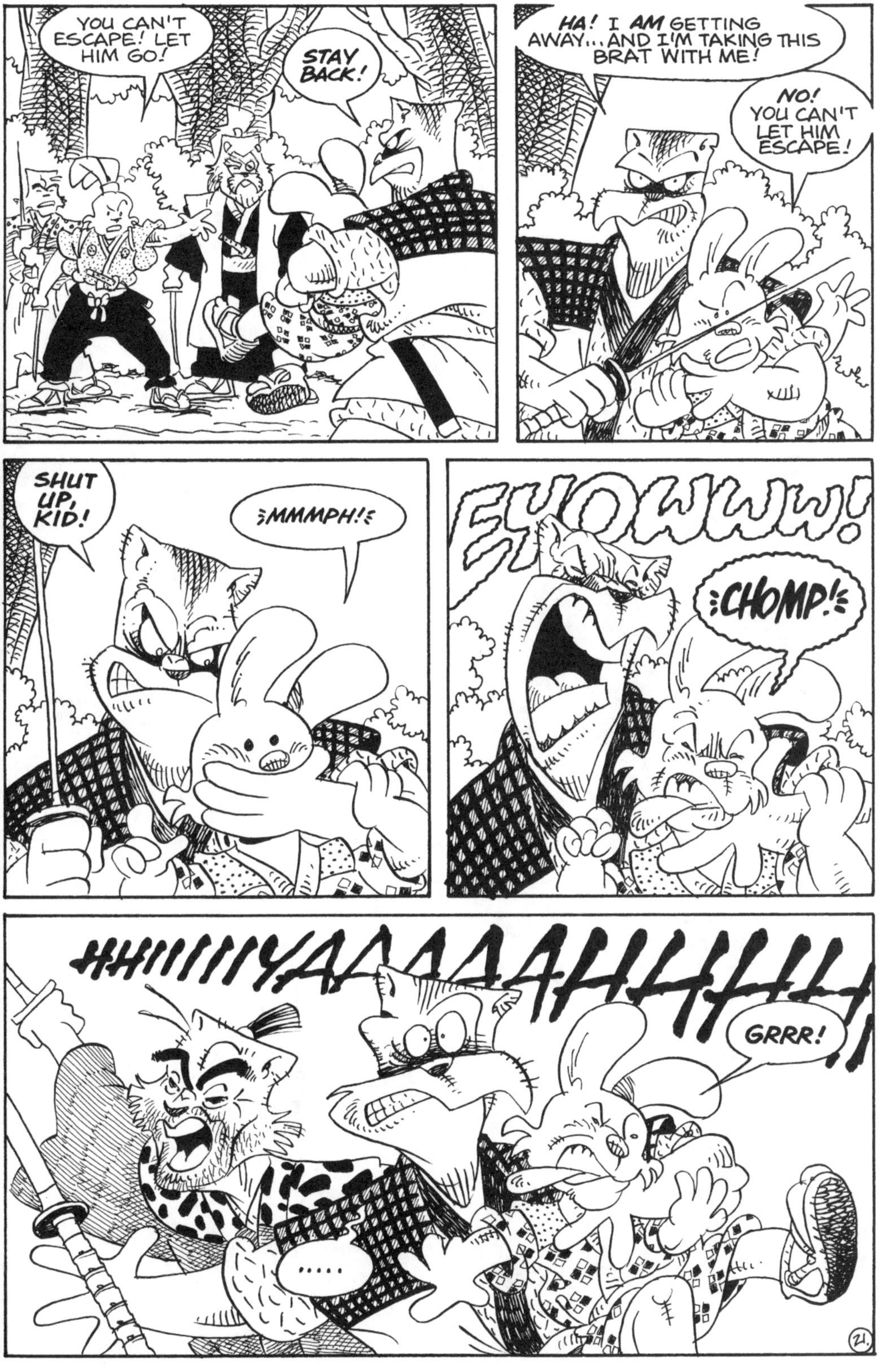
YOU CAN'T ESCAPE! LET HIM GO!
STAY BACK!
HA! I AM GETTING AWAY... AND I'M TAKING THIS BRAT WITH ME!
NO! YOU CAN'T LET HIM ESCAPE!
SHUT UP, KID!
MMMPH!
EYOWWW!
CHOMP!
HHIIIIIYAAAAAHHHH!
GRRR!
.....
21.

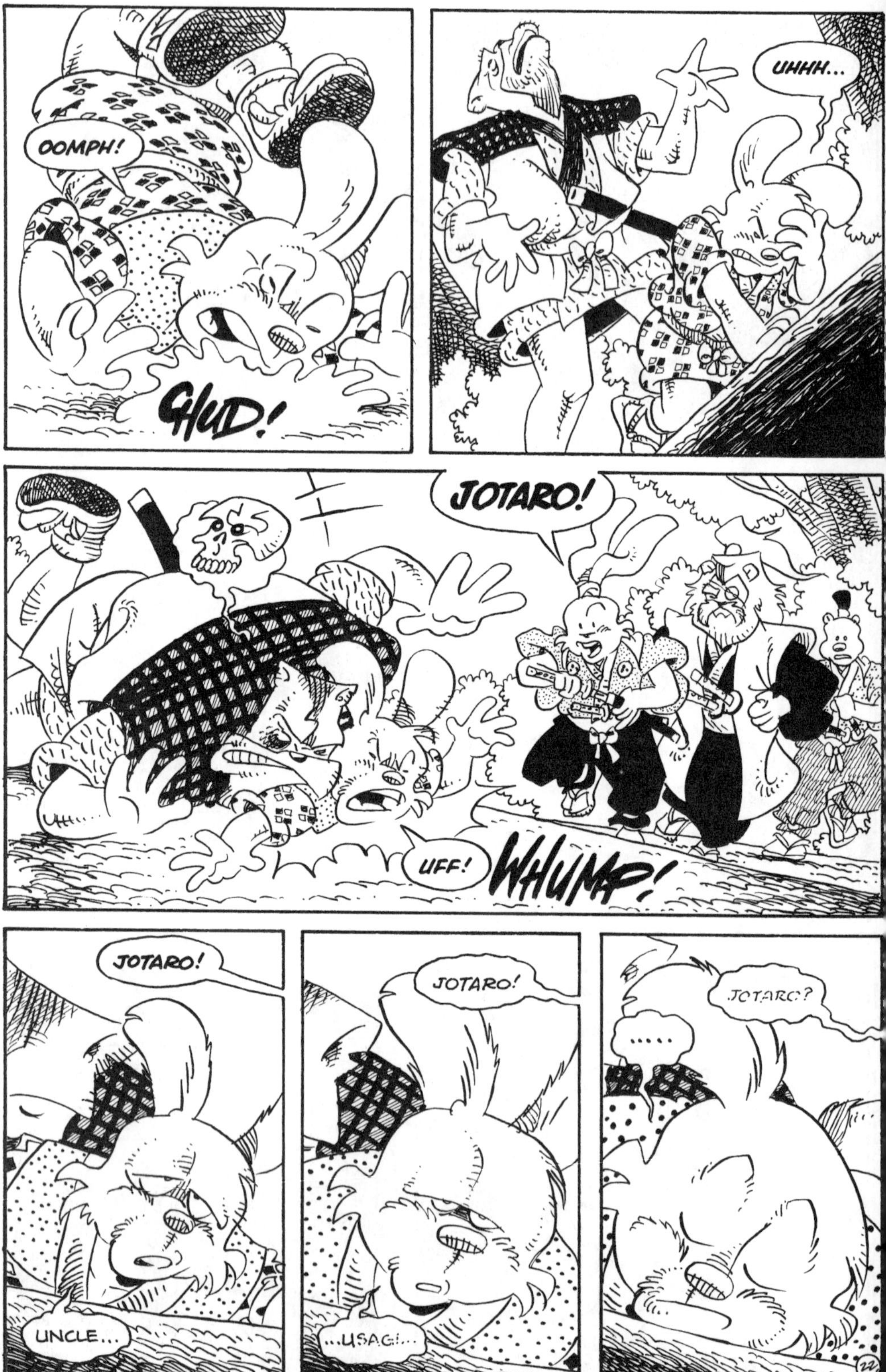
OOMPH!
CHUD!
UHHH...
JOTARO!
UFF!
WHUMP!
JOTARO!
UNCLE...
JOTARO!
...USAGI...
.....
JOTARO?
22

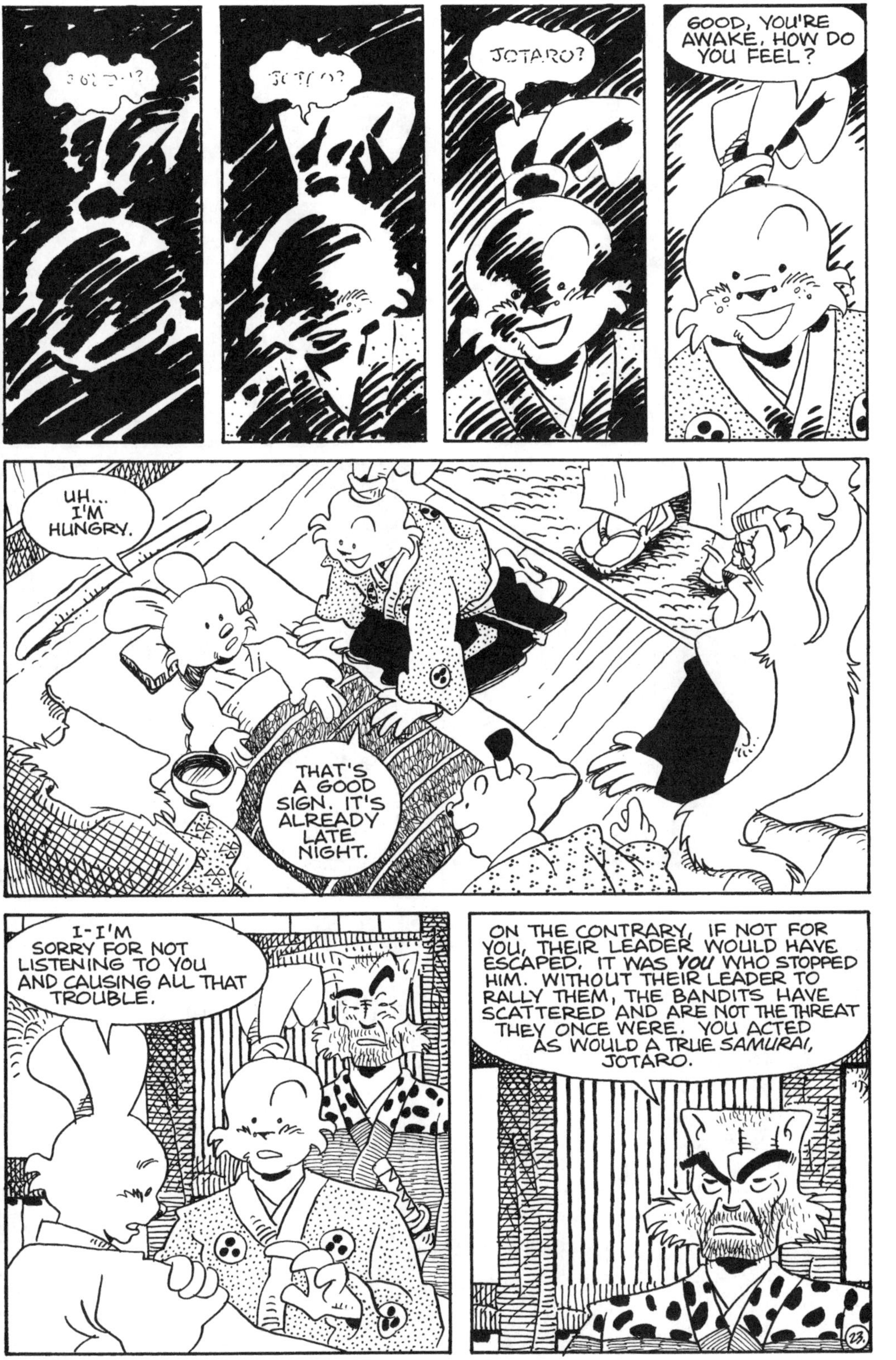
JOTARO?
GOOD, YOU'RE AWAKE. HOW DO YOU FEEL?
UH... I'M HUNGRY.
THAT'S A GOOD SIGN. IT'S ALREADY LATE NIGHT.
I-I'M SORRY FOR NOT LISTENING TO YOU AND CAUSING ALL THAT TROUBLE.
ON THE CONTRARY, IF NOT FOR YOU, THEIR LEADER WOULD HAVE ESCAPED. IT WAS *YOU* WHO STOPPED HIM. WITHOUT THEIR LEADER TO RALLY THEM, THE BANDITS HAVE SCATTERED AND ARE NOT THE THREAT THEY ONCE WERE. YOU ACTED AS WOULD A TRUE *SAMURAI*, JOTARO.
23.

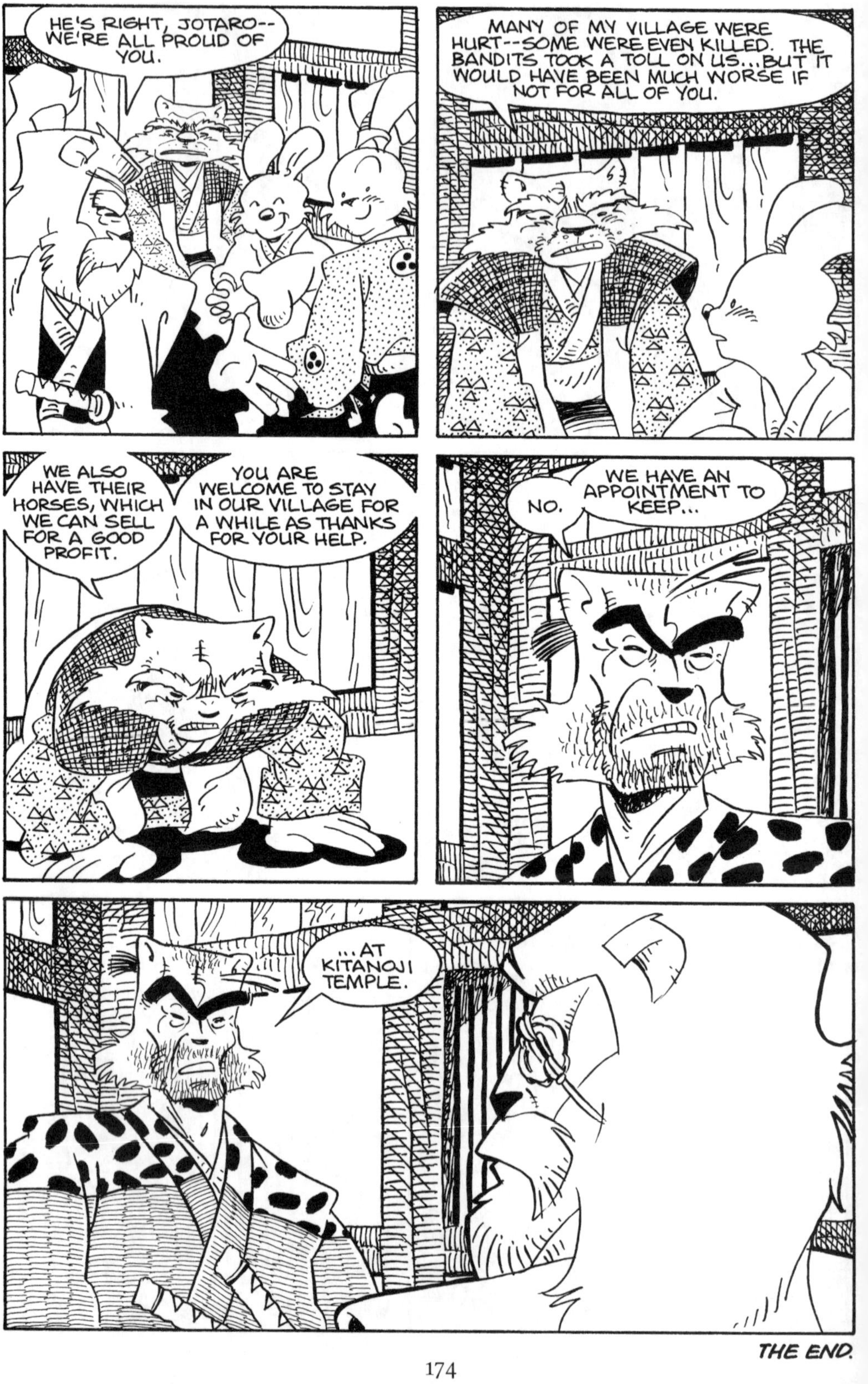
HE'S RIGHT, JOTARO-- WE'RE ALL PROUD OF YOU.
MANY OF MY VILLAGE WERE HURT--SOME WERE EVEN KILLED. THE BANDITS TOOK A TOLL ON US...BUT IT WOULD HAVE BEEN MUCH WORSE IF NOT FOR ALL OF YOU.
WE ALSO HAVE THEIR HORSES, WHICH WE CAN SELL FOR A GOOD PROFIT.
YOU ARE WELCOME TO STAY IN OUR VILLAGE FOR A WHILE AS THANKS FOR YOUR HELP.
NO.
WE HAVE AN APPOINTMENT TO KEEP...
...AT KITANOJI TEMPLE.

THE END.

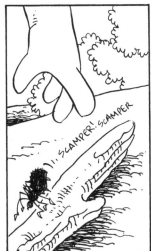

SCAMPER! SCAMPER!

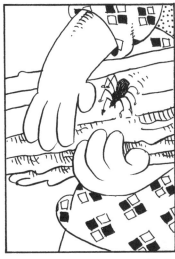

Duel at Kitanoji

WE'LL BE THERE EARLY TOMORROW MORNING, JOTARO.

WHEN WILL WE GET TO KITANOJI TEMPLE, UNCLE USAGI?

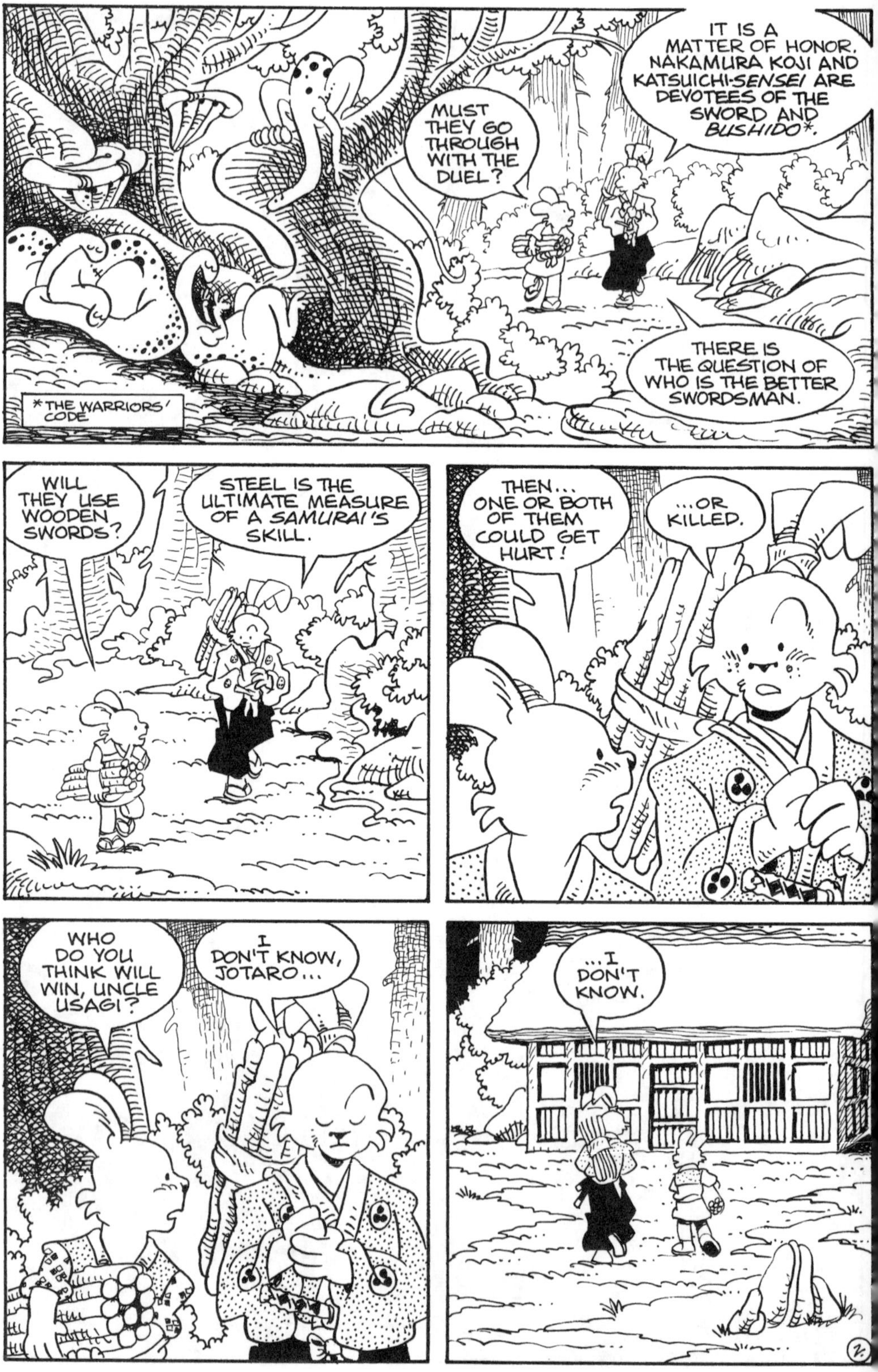
MUST THEY GO THROUGH WITH THE DUEL?
IT IS A MATTER OF HONOR. NAKAMURA KOJI AND KATSUICHI-*SENSEI* ARE DEVOTEES OF THE SWORD AND *BUSHIDO**.
THERE IS THE QUESTION OF WHO IS THE BETTER SWORDSMAN.
*THE WARRIORS' CODE
WILL THEY USE WOODEN SWORDS?
STEEL IS THE ULTIMATE MEASURE OF A *SAMURAI'S* SKILL.
THEN... ONE OR BOTH OF THEM COULD GET HURT!
...OR KILLED.
WHO DO YOU THINK WILL WIN, UNCLE USAGI?
I DON'T KNOW, JOTARO...
...I DON'T KNOW.
2.

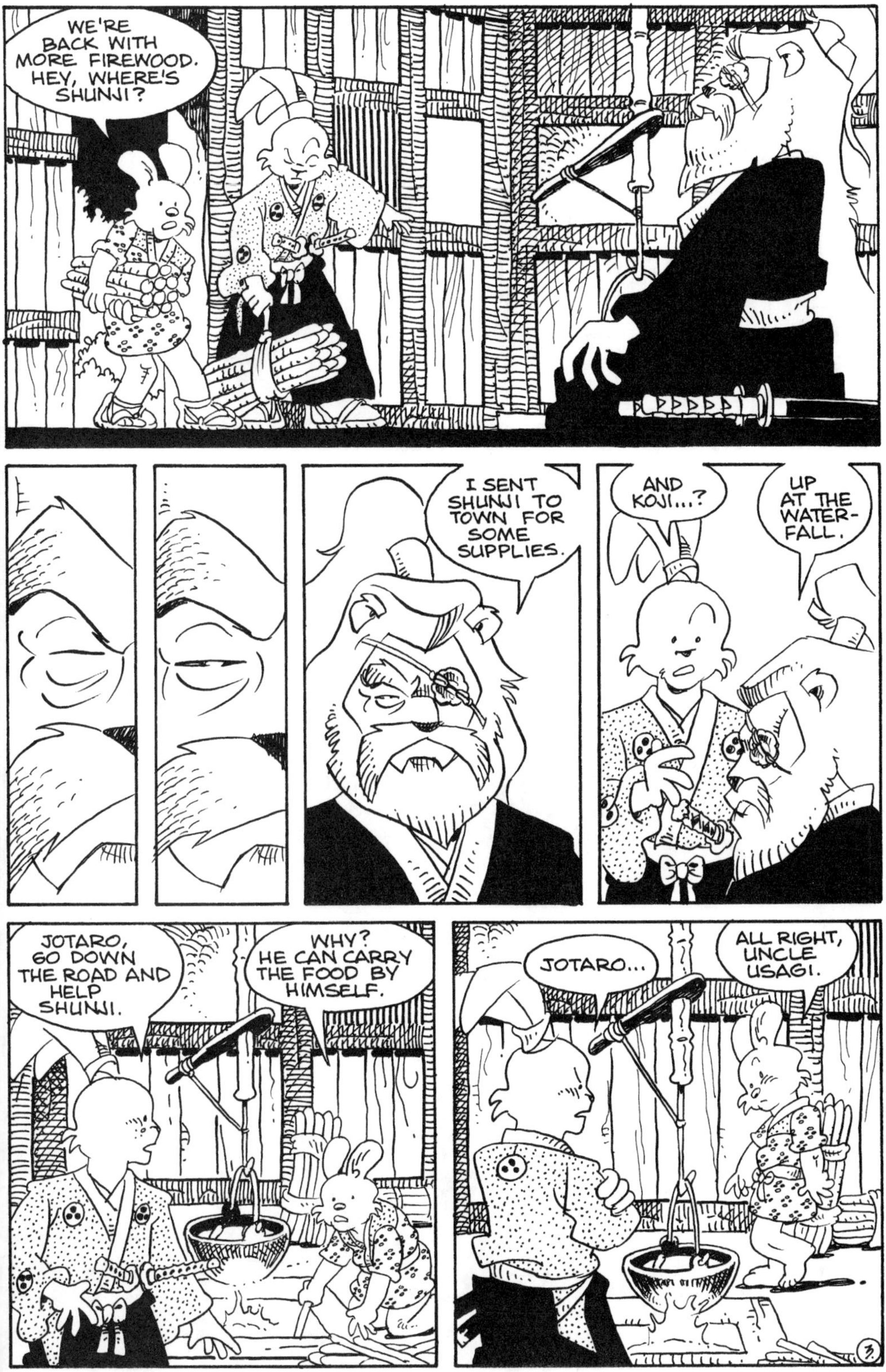
WE'RE BACK WITH MORE FIREWOOD. HEY, WHERE'S SHUNJI?
I SENT SHUNJI TO TOWN FOR SOME SUPPLIES.
AND KOJI...?
UP AT THE WATER-FALL.
JOTARO, GO DOWN THE ROAD AND HELP SHUNJI.
WHY? HE CAN CARRY THE FOOD BY HIMSELF.
JOTARO...
ALL RIGHT, UNCLE USAGI.
3.

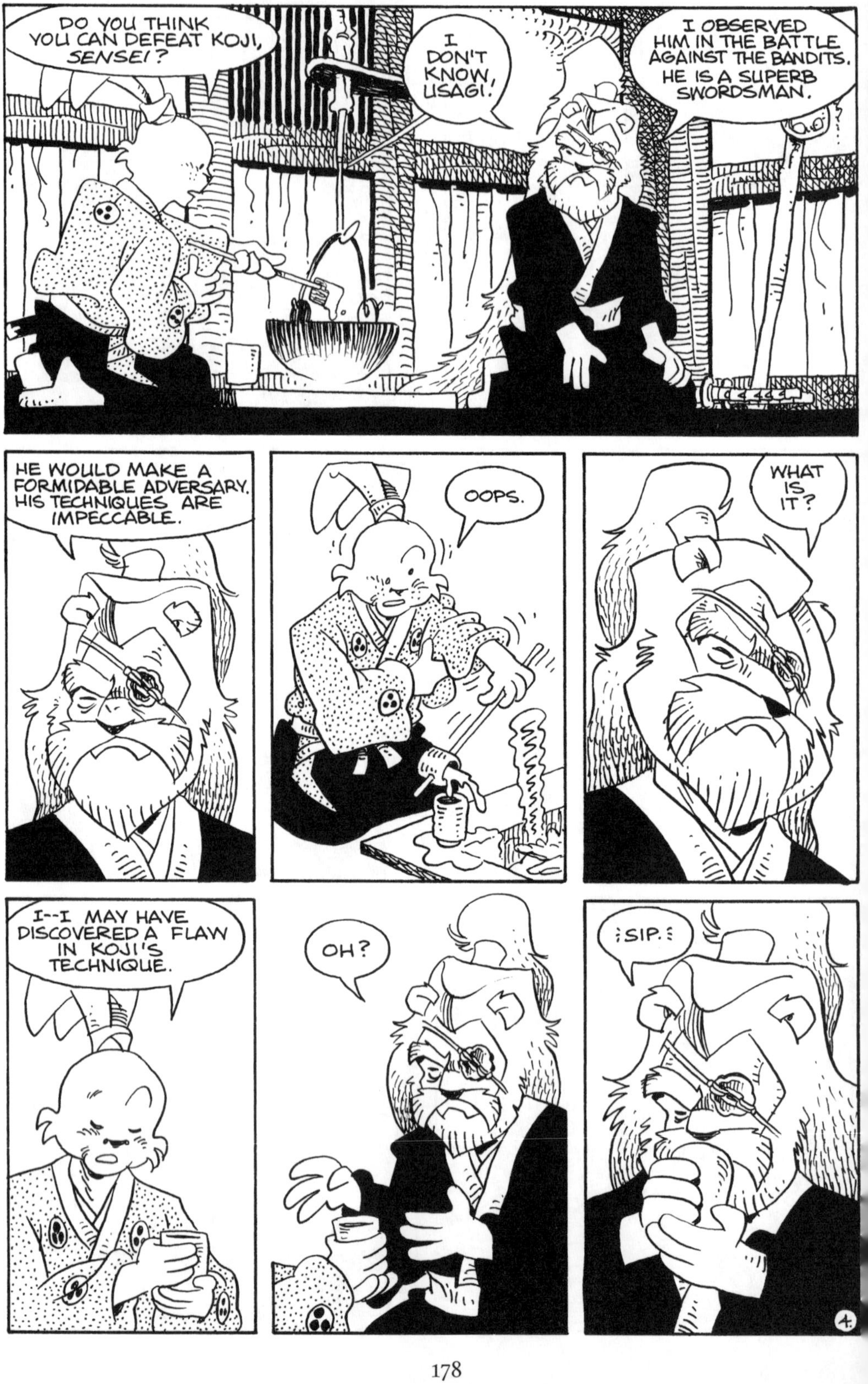

DO YOU THINK YOU CAN DEFEAT KOJI, SENSEI?
I DON'T KNOW, USAGI.
I OBSERVED HIM IN THE BATTLE AGAINST THE BANDITS. HE IS A SUPERB SWORDSMAN.
HE WOULD MAKE A FORMIDABLE ADVERSARY. HIS TECHNIQUES ARE IMPECCABLE.
OOPS.
WHAT IS IT?
I--I MAY HAVE DISCOVERED A FLAW IN KOJI'S TECHNIQUE.
OH?
SIP.
4.

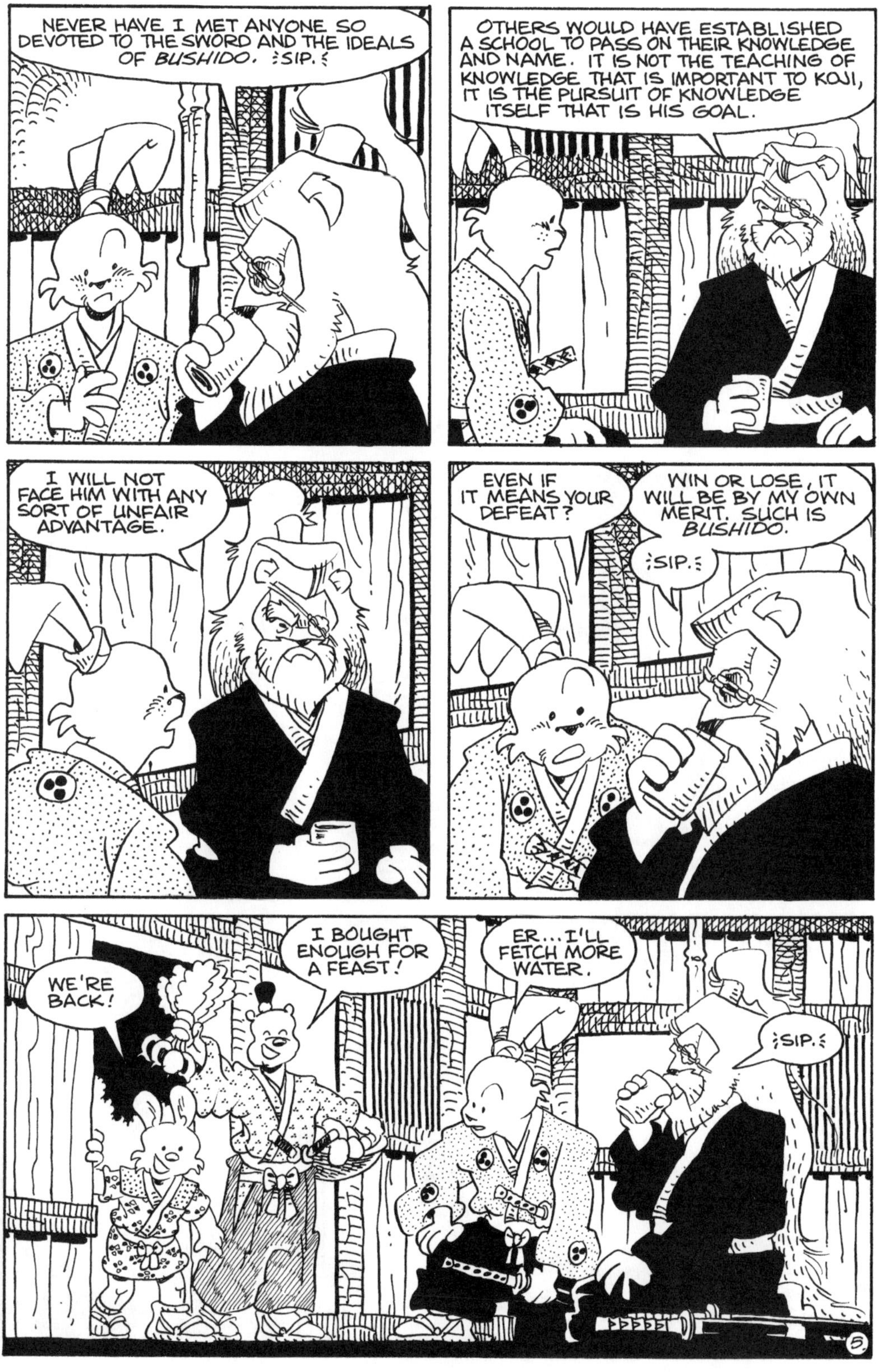
NEVER HAVE I MET ANYONE SO DEVOTED TO THE SWORD AND THE IDEALS OF *BUSHIDO*. SIP.
OTHERS WOULD HAVE ESTABLISHED A SCHOOL TO PASS ON THEIR KNOWLEDGE AND NAME. IT IS NOT THE TEACHING OF KNOWLEDGE THAT IS IMPORTANT TO KOJI, IT IS THE PURSUIT OF KNOWLEDGE ITSELF THAT IS HIS GOAL.
I WILL NOT FACE HIM WITH ANY SORT OF UNFAIR ADVANTAGE.
EVEN IF IT MEANS YOUR DEFEAT?
WIN OR LOSE, IT WILL BE BY MY OWN MERIT. SUCH IS *BUSHIDO*.
SIP.
WE'RE BACK!
I BOUGHT ENOUGH FOR A FEAST!
ER... I'LL FETCH MORE WATER.
SIP.
5.

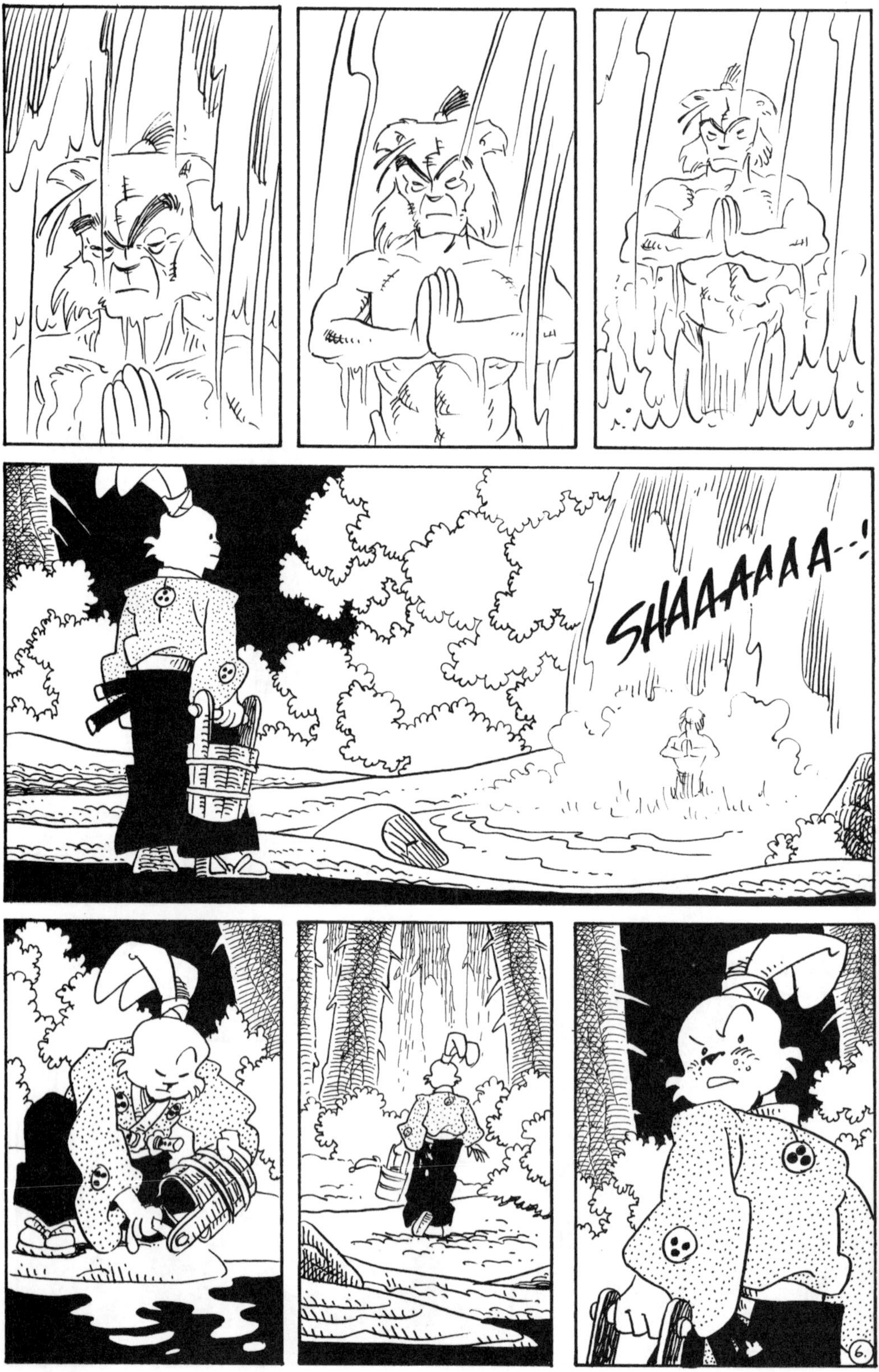
SHAAAAAA--!
6.

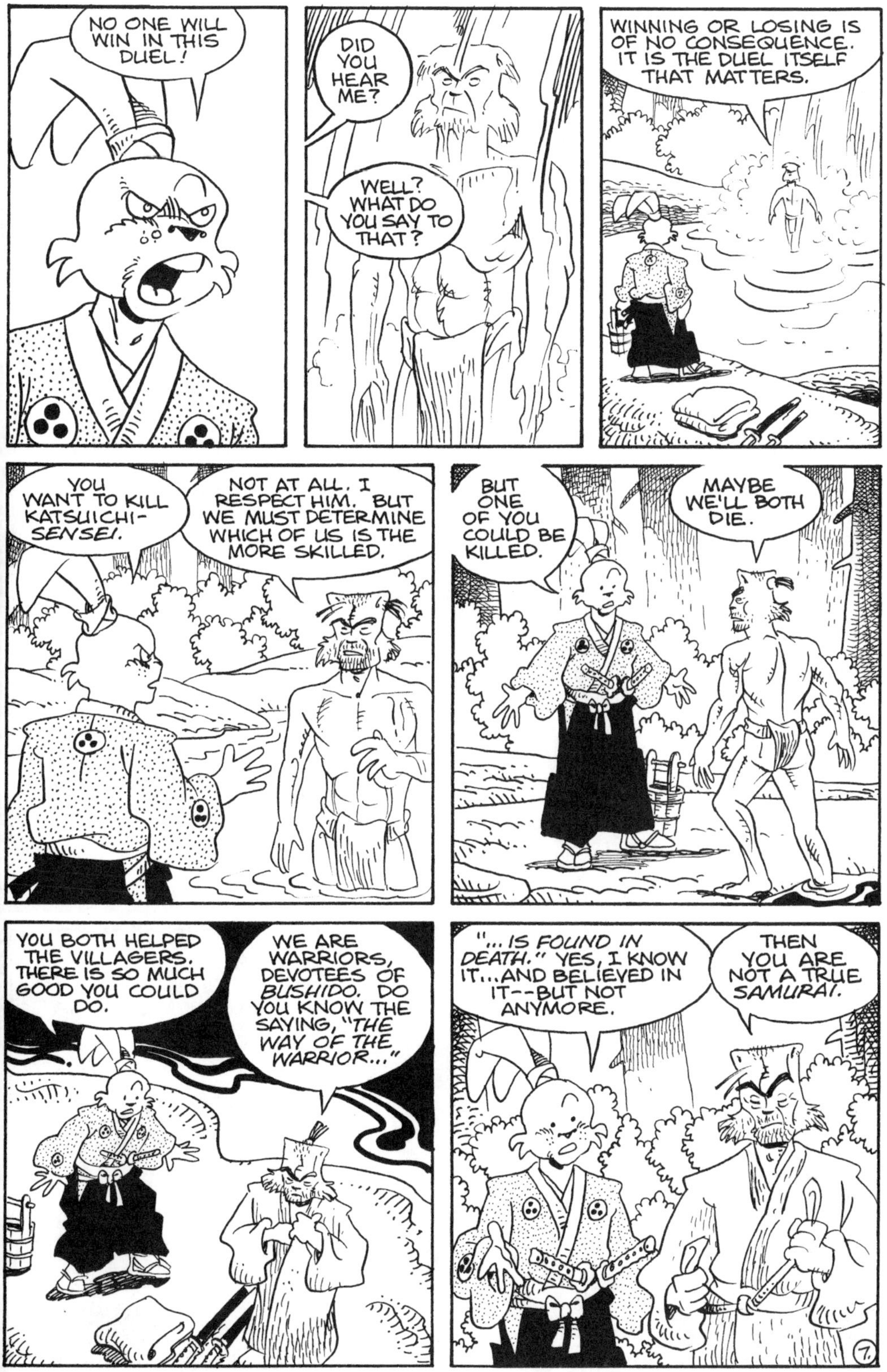
NO ONE WILL WIN IN THIS DUEL!
DID YOU HEAR ME?
WELL? WHAT DO YOU SAY TO THAT?
WINNING OR LOSING IS OF NO CONSEQUENCE. IT IS THE DUEL ITSELF THAT MATTERS.
YOU WANT TO KILL KATSUICHI-*SENSEI*.
NOT AT ALL. I RESPECT HIM. BUT WE MUST DETERMINE WHICH OF US IS THE MORE SKILLED.
BUT ONE OF YOU COULD BE KILLED.
MAYBE WE'LL BOTH DIE.
YOU BOTH HELPED THE VILLAGERS. THERE IS SO MUCH GOOD YOU COULD DO.
WE ARE WARRIORS, DEVOTEES OF *BUSHIDO*. DO YOU KNOW THE SAYING, "*THE WAY OF THE WARRIOR...*"
"...*IS FOUND IN DEATH*." YES, I KNOW IT...AND BELIEVED IN IT--BUT NOT ANYMORE.
THEN YOU ARE NOT A TRUE *SAMURAI*.
7.

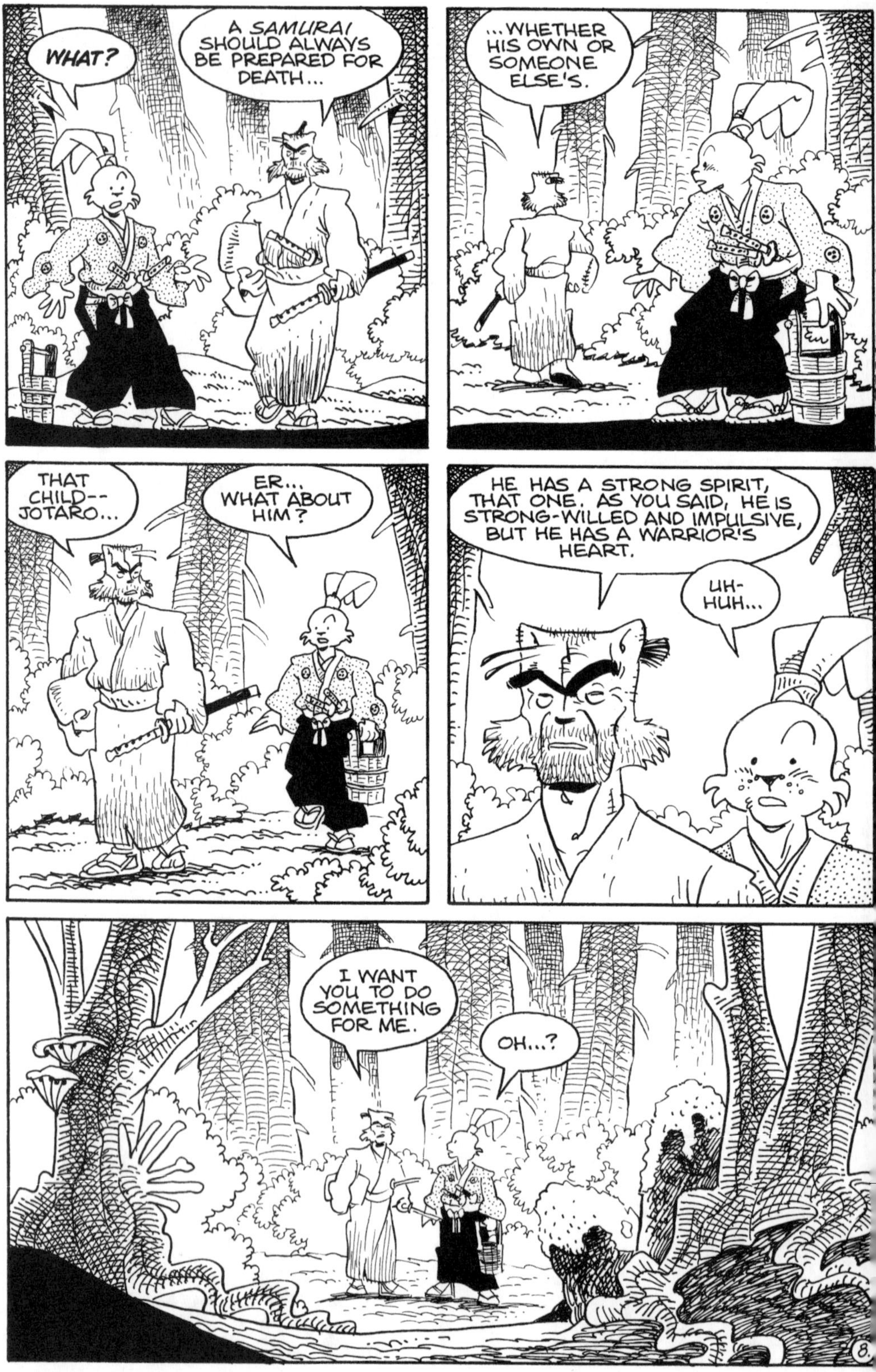
WHAT?
A SAMURAI SHOULD ALWAYS BE PREPARED FOR DEATH...
...WHETHER HIS OWN OR SOMEONE ELSE'S.
THAT CHILD-- JOTARO...
ER... WHAT ABOUT HIM?
HE HAS A STRONG SPIRIT, THAT ONE. AS YOU SAID, HE IS STRONG-WILLED AND IMPULSIVE, BUT HE HAS A WARRIOR'S HEART.
UH-HUH...
I WANT YOU TO DO SOMETHING FOR ME.
OH...?
8

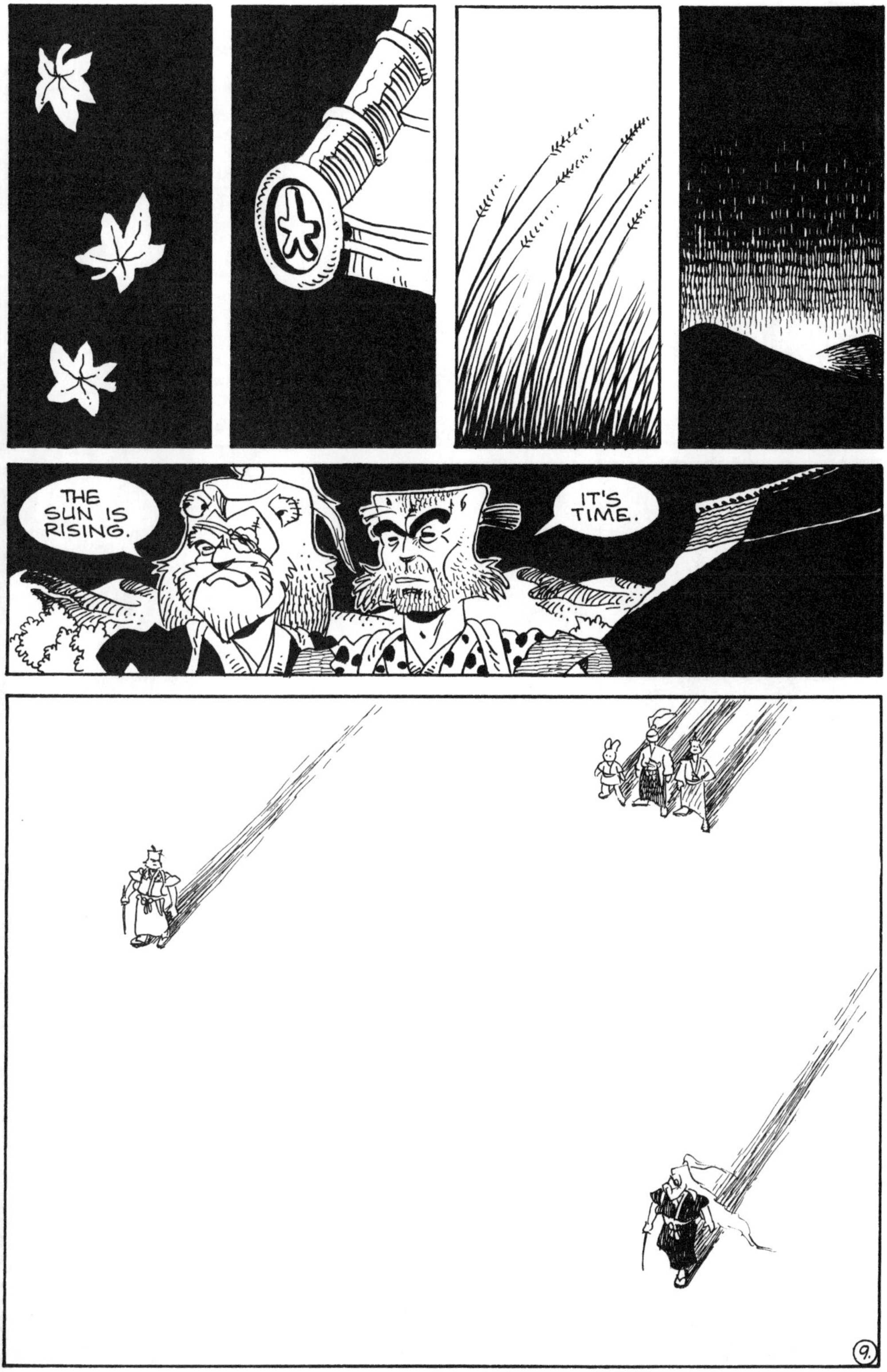
THE SUN IS RISING.
IT'S TIME.
9.

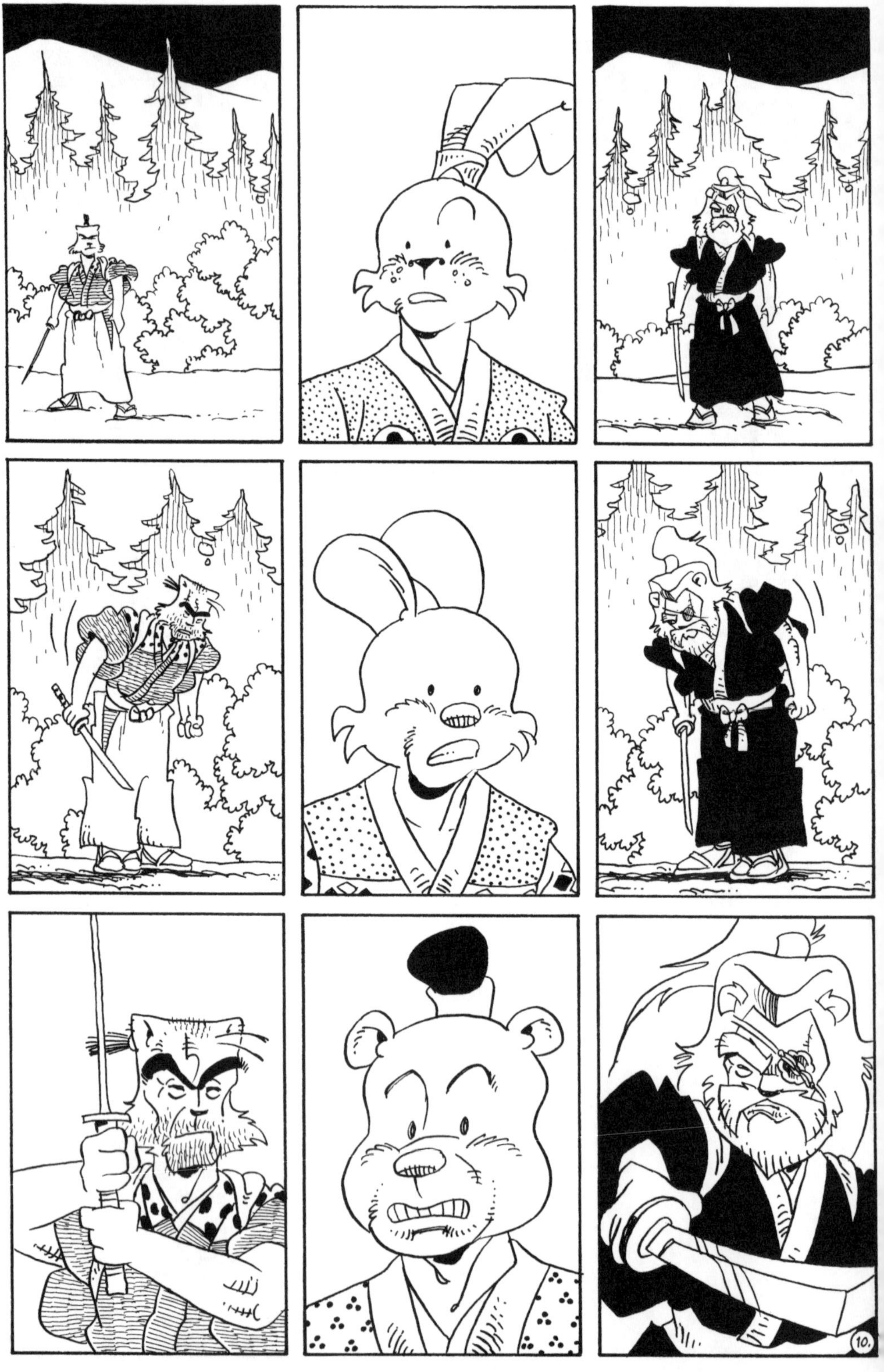
10.

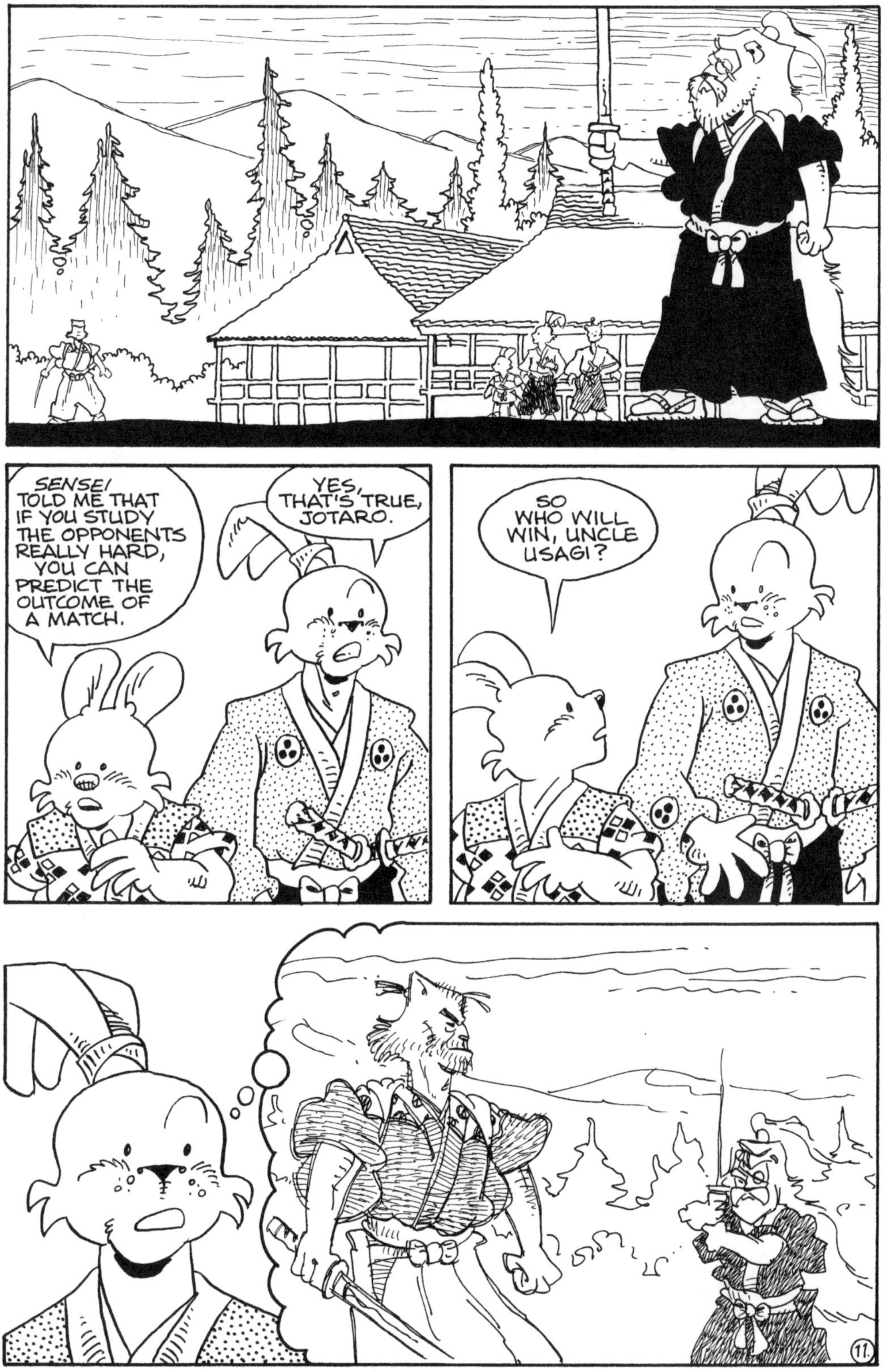
SENSEI TOLD ME THAT IF YOU STUDY THE OPPONENTS REALLY HARD, YOU CAN PREDICT THE OUTCOME OF A MATCH.
YES, THAT'S TRUE, JOTARO.
SO WHO WILL WIN, UNCLE USAGI?
11.

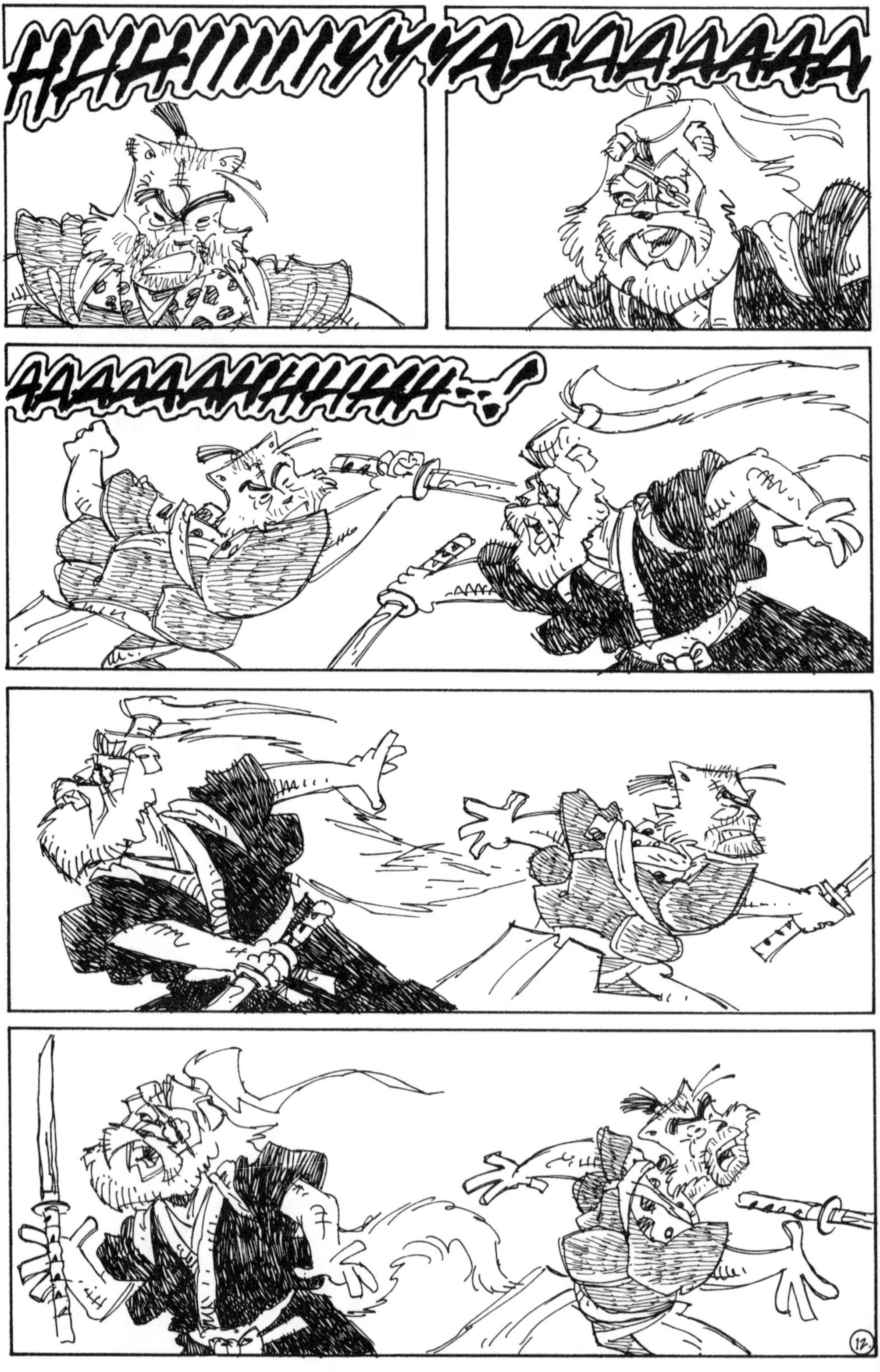
HHHIIIIIYYYAAAAAAAA
AAAAAAHHHHHH--!
12

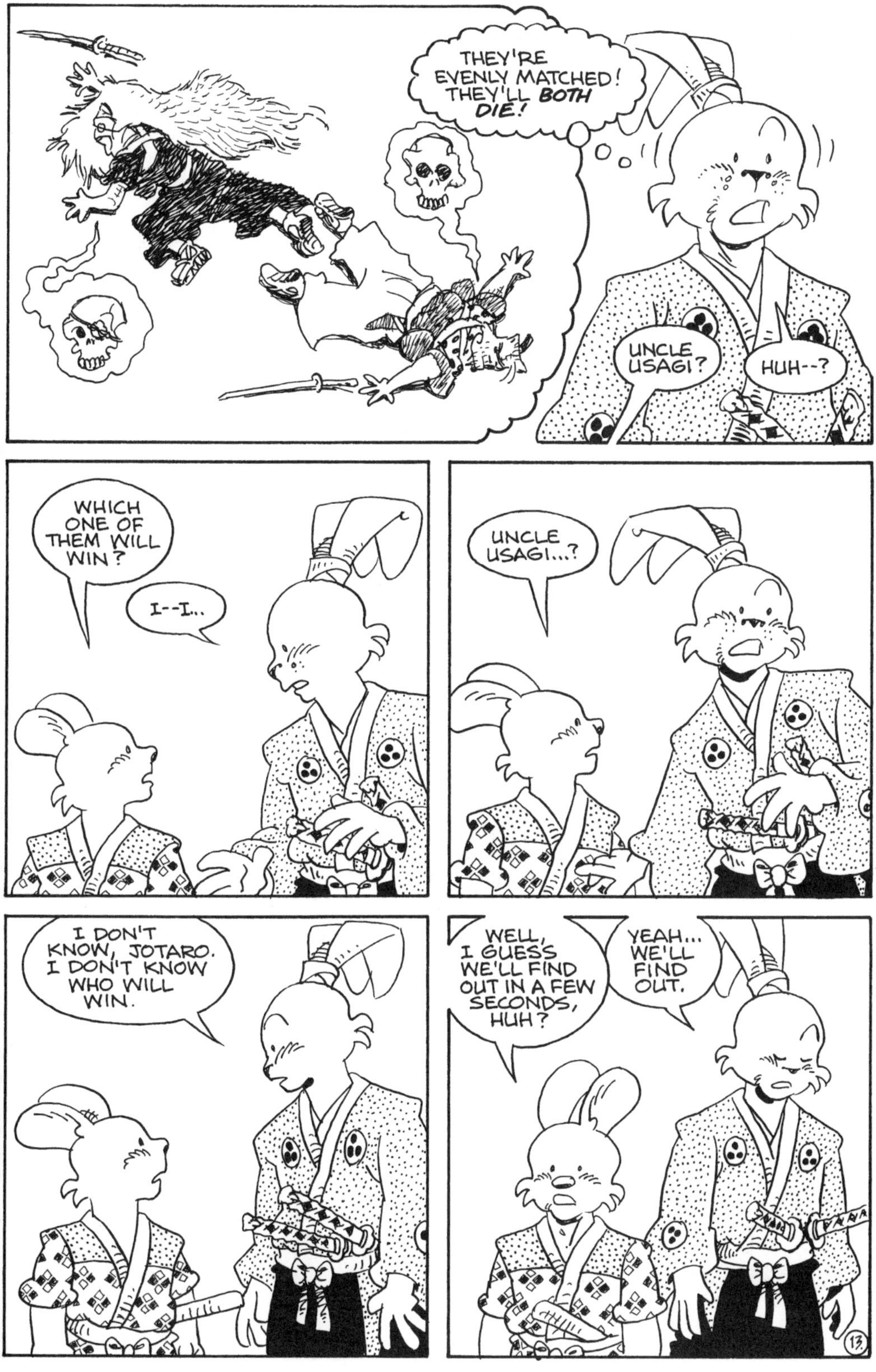
THEY'RE EVENLY MATCHED! THEY'LL BOTH DIE!
UNCLE USAGI?
HUH--?
WHICH ONE OF THEM WILL WIN?
I--I...
UNCLE USAGI...?
I DON'T KNOW, JOTARO. I DON'T KNOW WHO WILL WIN.
WELL, I GUESS WE'LL FIND OUT IN A FEW SECONDS, HUH?
YEAH... WE'LL FIND OUT.
13

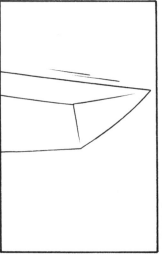

THERE-- THAT SLIGHT DIP OF KOJI'S BLADE! HE'S GOING TO STRIKE!

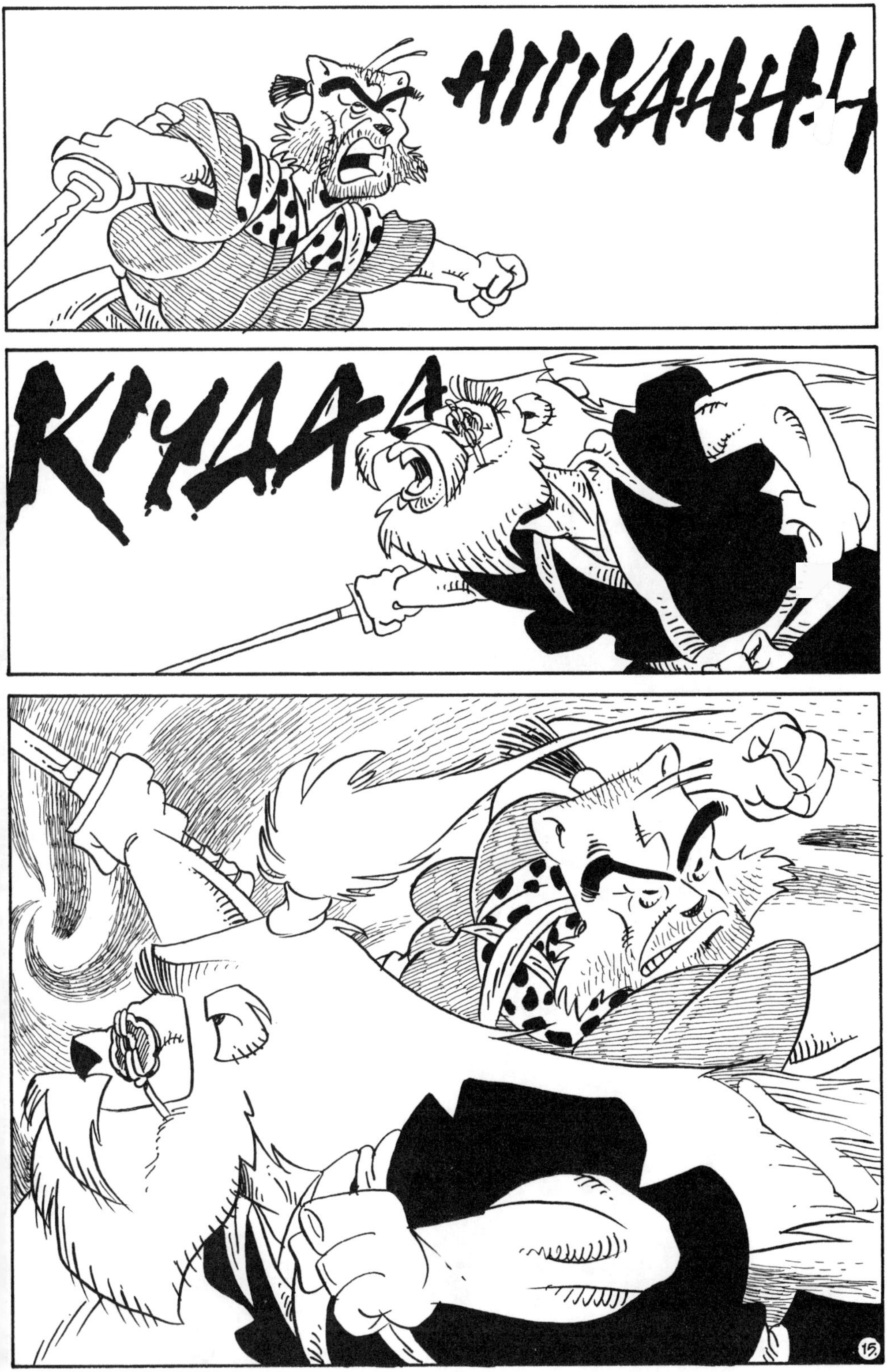
HIIIYAHHHH
KIYAAA
15.

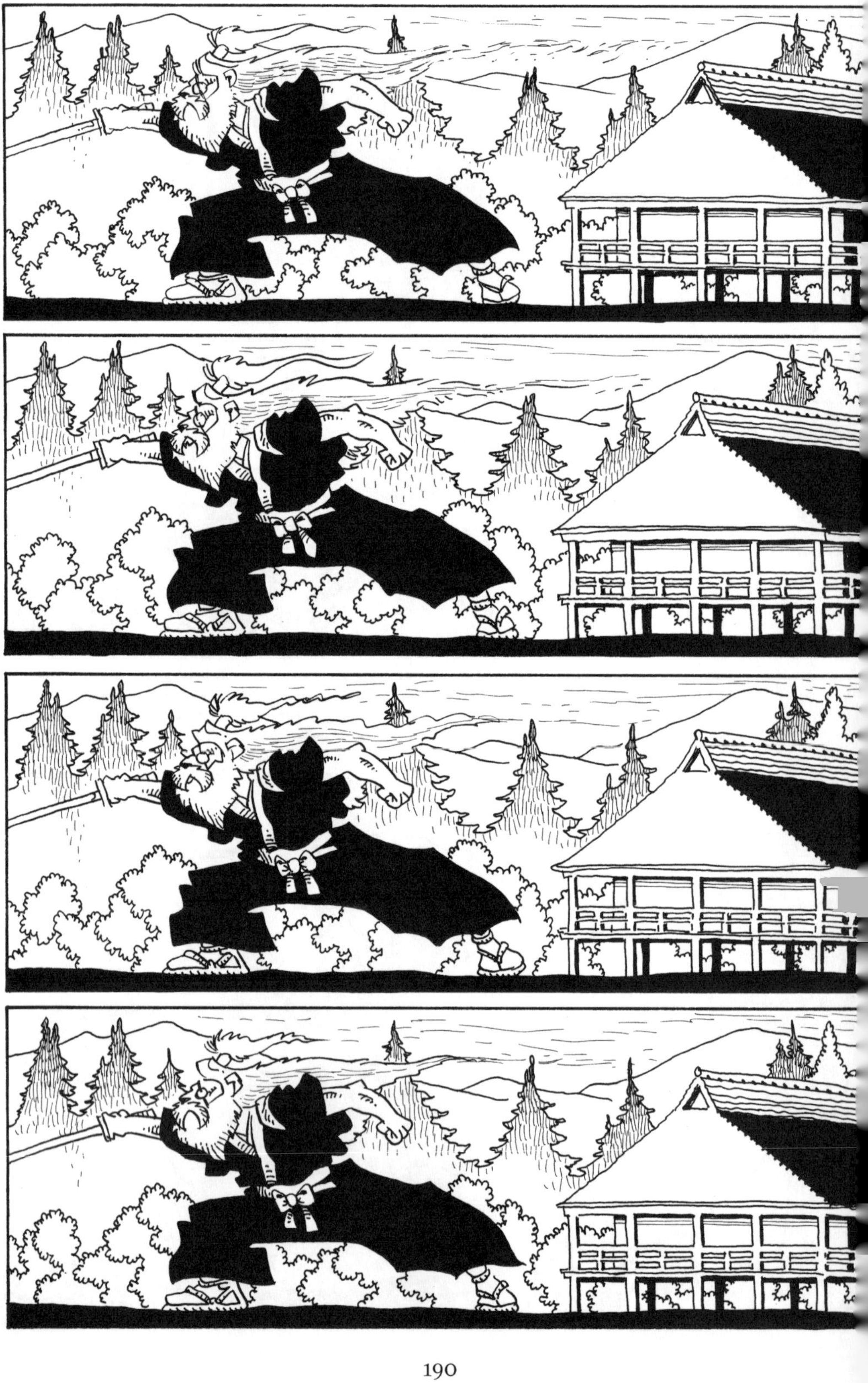

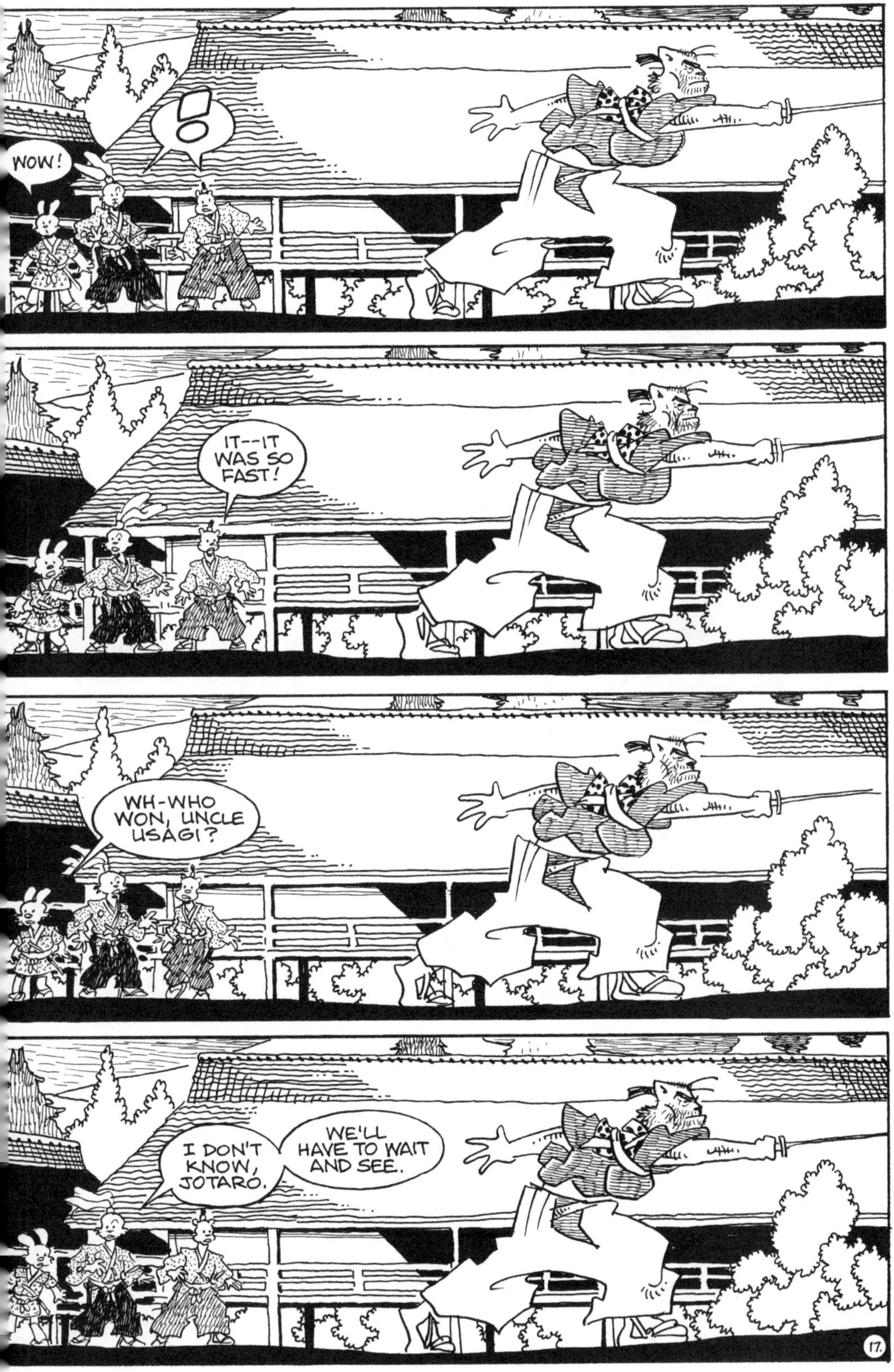
!
WOW!
IT--IT WAS SO FAST!
WH-WHO WON, UNCLE USAGI?
I DON'T KNOW, JOTARO.
WE'LL HAVE TO WAIT AND SEE.
17.

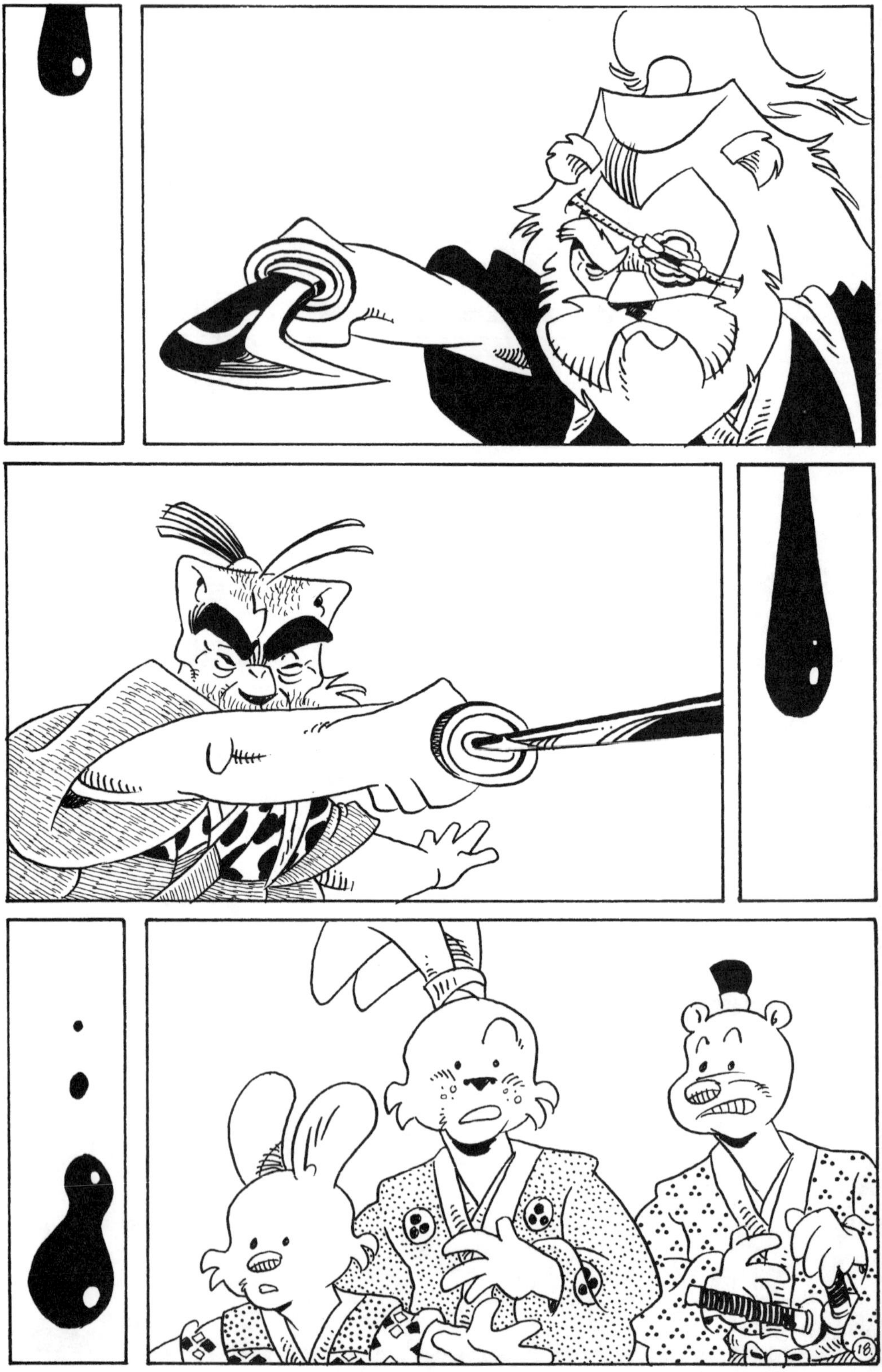
18.

PLIP!

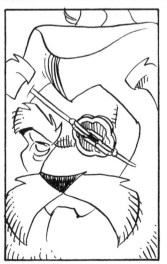

PLIP!
PLIP!

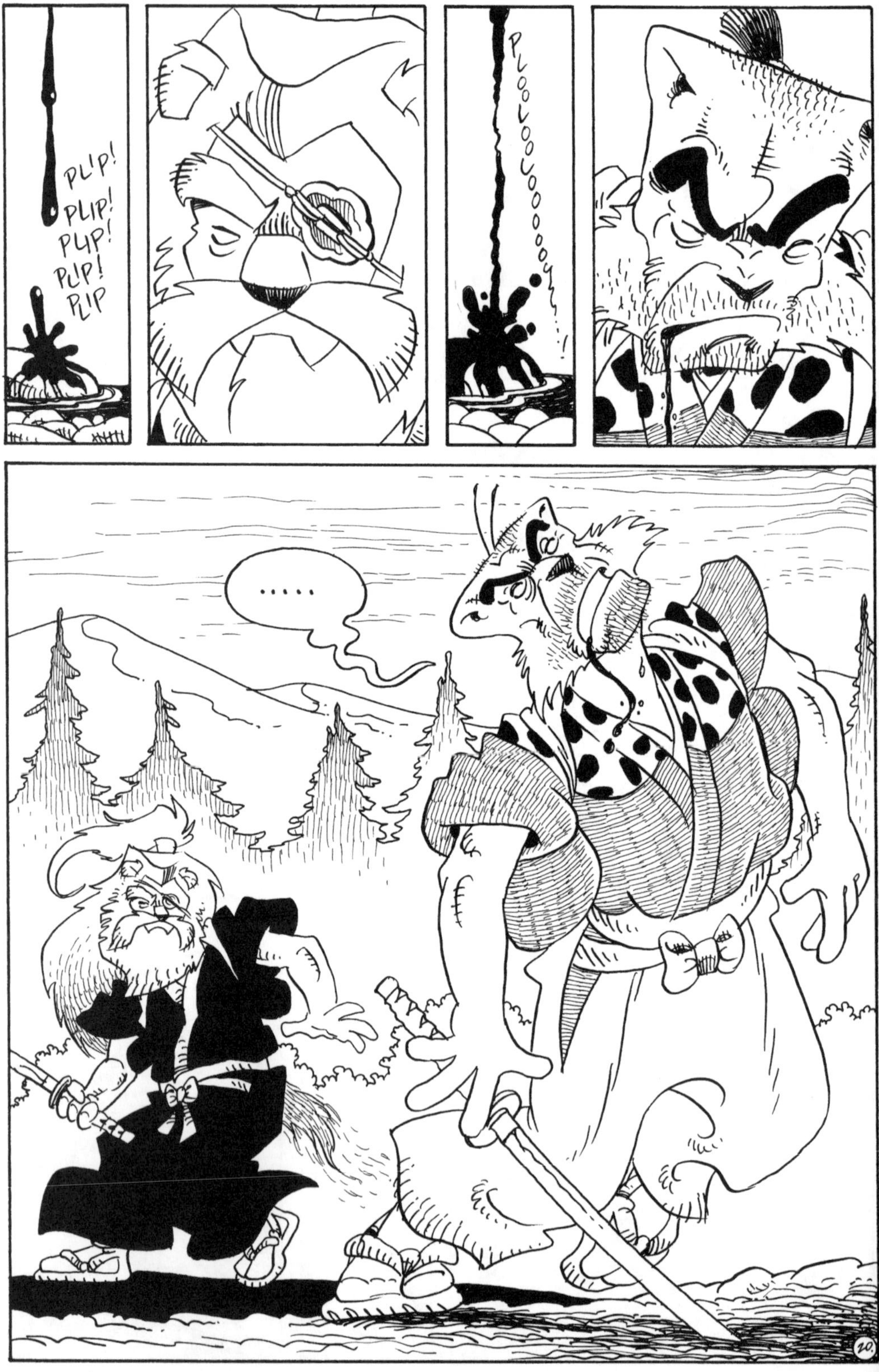
PLIP!
PLIP!
PLIP!
PLIP!
PLIP
PLOOOOOOOOOOOOOOO...!
.....
20.

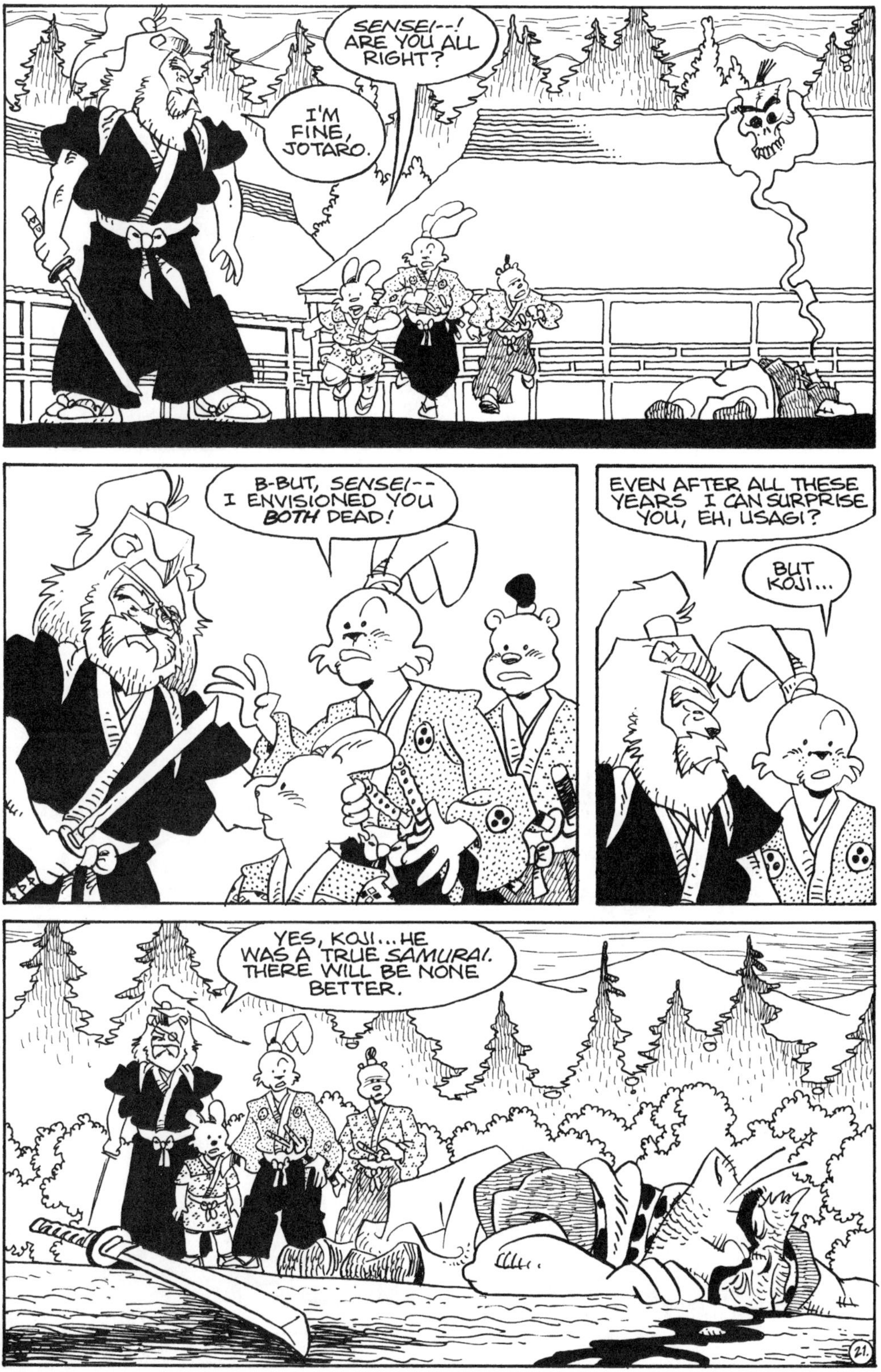

SENSEI--! ARE YOU ALL RIGHT?
I'M FINE, JOTARO.
B-BUT, SENSEI-- I ENVISIONED YOU BOTH DEAD!
EVEN AFTER ALL THESE YEARS I CAN SURPRISE YOU, EH, USAGI?
BUT KOJI...
YES, KOJI... HE WAS A TRUE SAMURAI. THERE WILL BE NONE BETTER.
21.

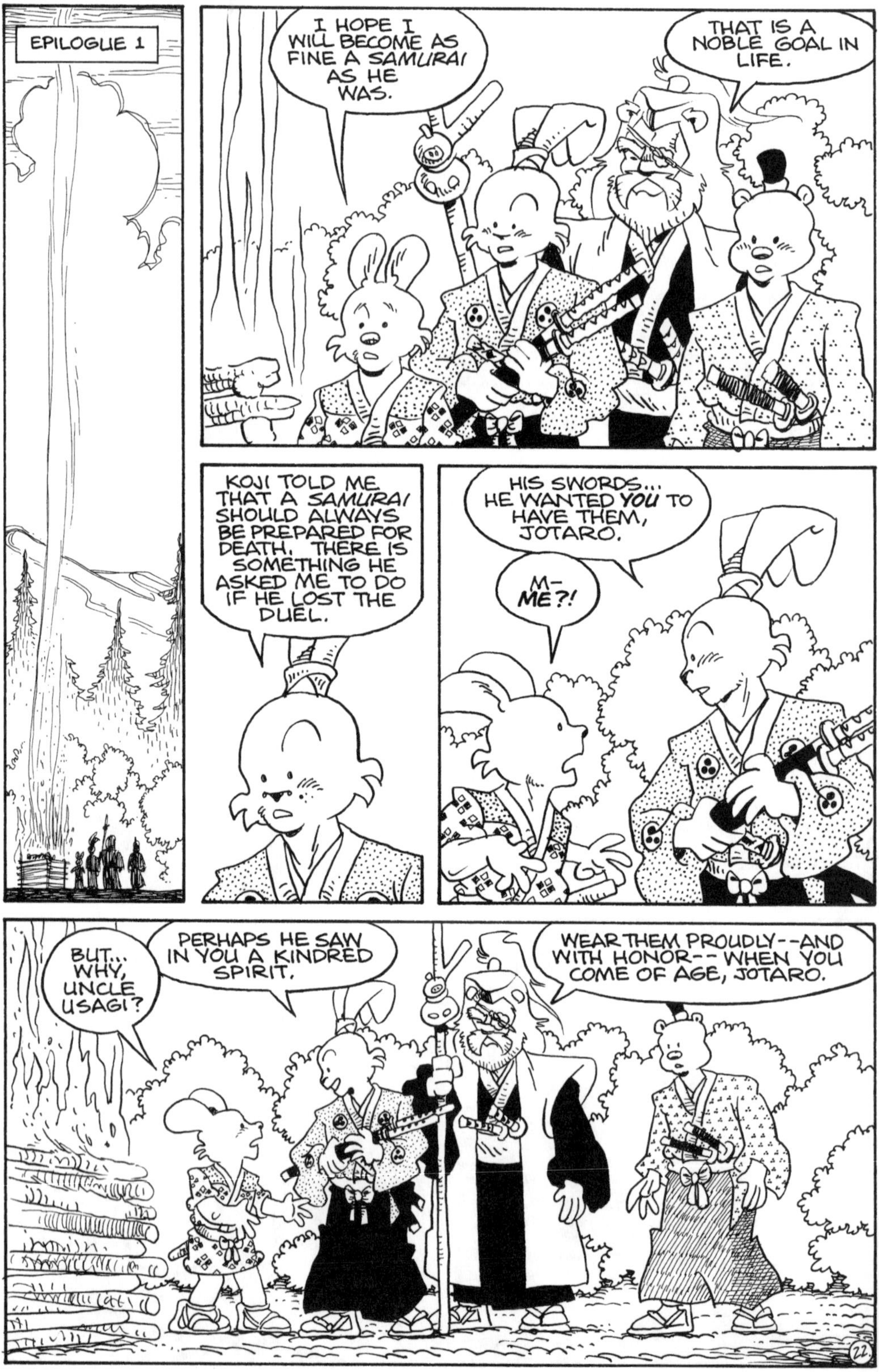
EPILOGUE 1
I HOPE I WILL BECOME AS FINE A SAMURAI AS HE WAS.
THAT IS A NOBLE GOAL IN LIFE.
KOJI TOLD ME THAT A SAMURAI SHOULD ALWAYS BE PREPARED FOR DEATH. THERE IS SOMETHING HE ASKED ME TO DO IF HE LOST THE DUEL.
HIS SWORDS... HE WANTED YOU TO HAVE THEM, JOTARO.
M-ME?!
BUT... WHY, UNCLE USAGI?
PERHAPS HE SAW IN YOU A KINDRED SPIRIT.
WEAR THEM PROUDLY--AND WITH HONOR-- WHEN YOU COME OF AGE, JOTARO.
22

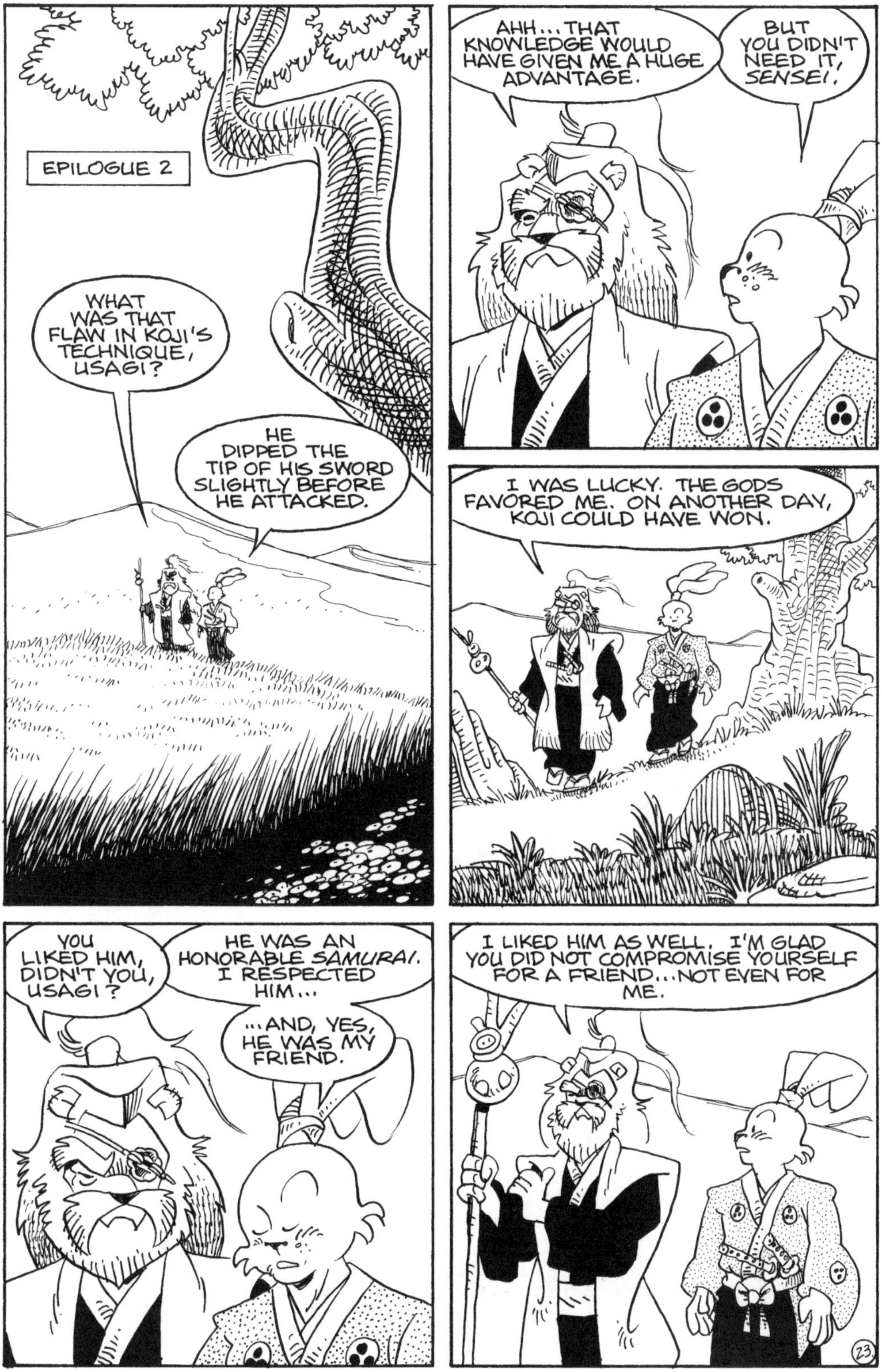
EPILOGUE 2
WHAT WAS THAT FLAW IN KOJI'S TECHNIQUE, USAGI?
HE DIPPED THE TIP OF HIS SWORD SLIGHTLY BEFORE HE ATTACKED.
AHH... THAT KNOWLEDGE WOULD HAVE GIVEN ME A HUGE ADVANTAGE.
BUT YOU DIDN'T NEED IT, *SENSEI*.
I WAS LUCKY. THE GODS FAVORED ME. ON ANOTHER DAY, KOJI COULD HAVE WON.
YOU LIKED HIM, DIDN'T YOU, USAGI?
HE WAS AN HONORABLE *SAMURAI*. I RESPECTED HIM...
...AND, YES, HE WAS MY FRIEND.
I LIKED HIM AS WELL. I'M GLAD YOU DID NOT COMPROMISE YOURSELF FOR A FRIEND... NOT EVEN FOR ME.
23

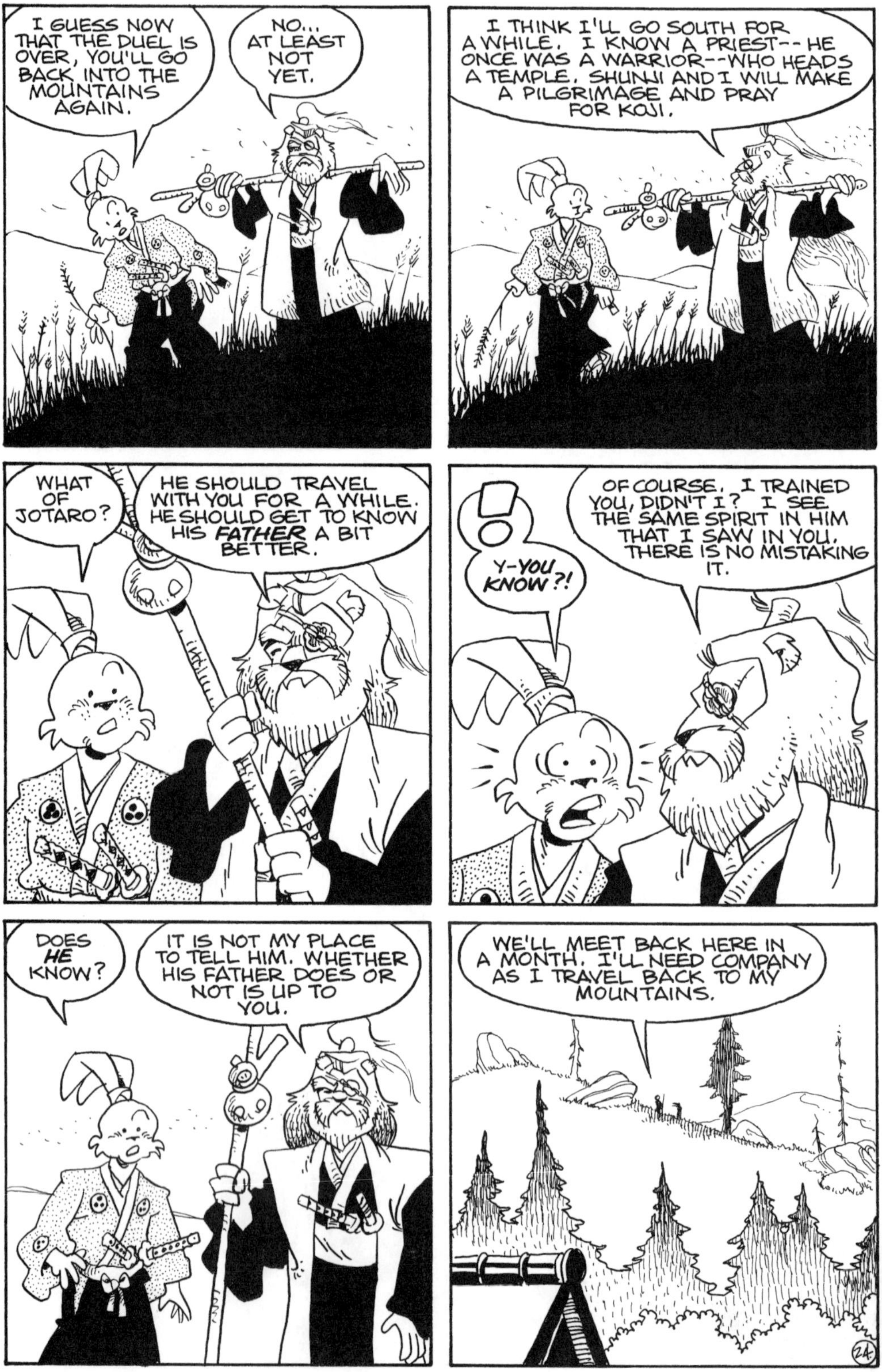
I GUESS NOW THAT THE DUEL IS OVER, YOU'LL GO BACK INTO THE MOUNTAINS AGAIN.
NO... AT LEAST NOT YET.
I THINK I'LL GO SOUTH FOR A WHILE. I KNOW A PRIEST-- HE ONCE WAS A WARRIOR--WHO HEADS A TEMPLE. SHUNJI AND I WILL MAKE A PILGRIMAGE AND PRAY FOR KOJI.
WHAT OF JOTARO?
HE SHOULD TRAVEL WITH YOU FOR A WHILE. HE SHOULD GET TO KNOW HIS FATHER A BIT BETTER.
!
Y-YOU KNOW?!
OF COURSE. I TRAINED YOU, DIDN'T I? I SEE THE SAME SPIRIT IN HIM THAT I SAW IN YOU. THERE IS NO MISTAKING IT.
DOES HE KNOW?
IT IS NOT MY PLACE TO TELL HIM. WHETHER HIS FATHER DOES OR NOT IS UP TO YOU.
WE'LL MEET BACK HERE IN A MONTH. I'LL NEED COMPANY AS I TRAVEL BACK TO MY MOUNTAINS.
24.

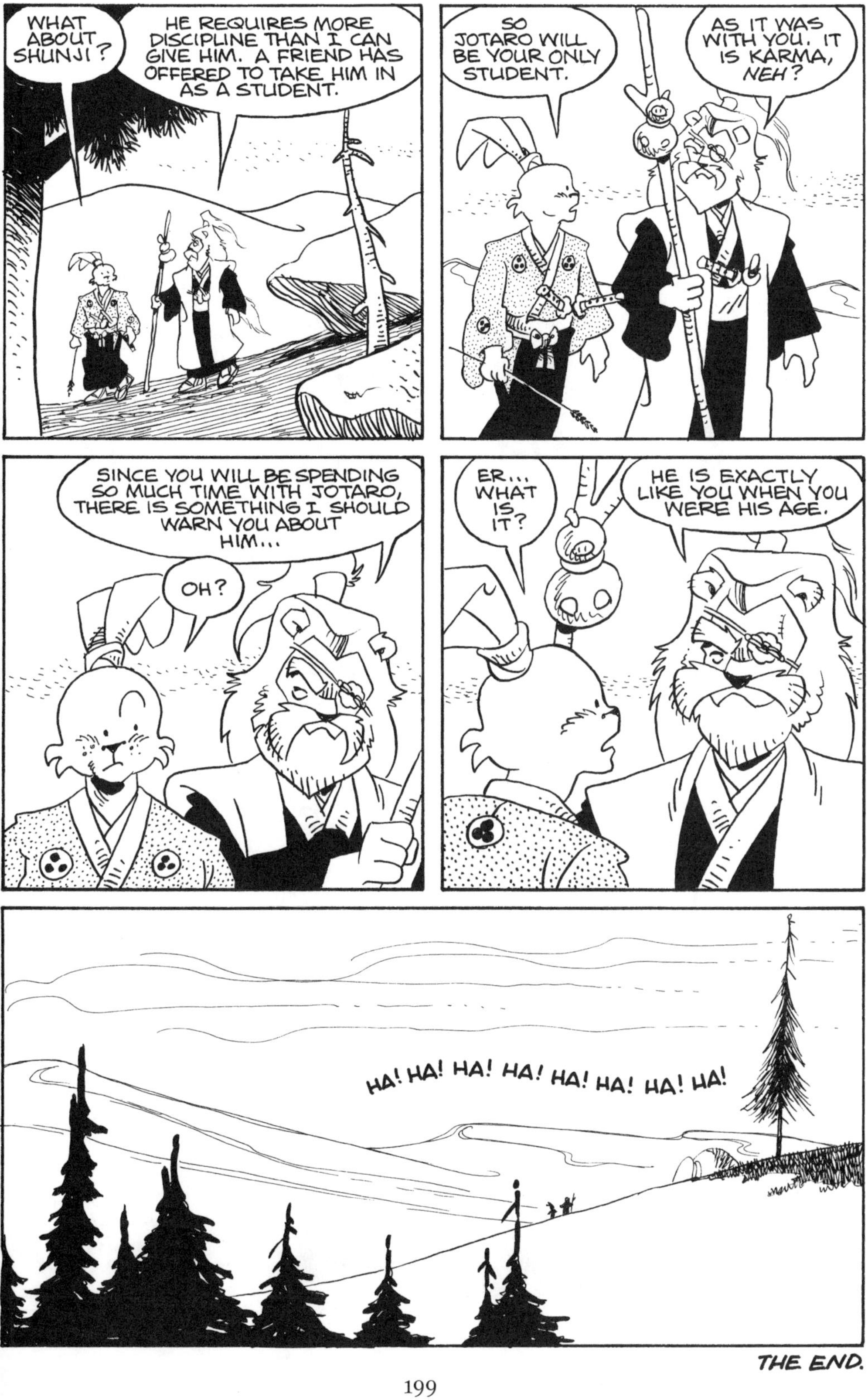
WHAT ABOUT SHUNJI?
HE REQUIRES MORE DISCIPLINE THAN I CAN GIVE HIM. A FRIEND HAS OFFERED TO TAKE HIM IN AS A STUDENT.
SO JOTARO WILL BE YOUR ONLY STUDENT.
AS IT WAS WITH YOU. IT IS KARMA, *NEH*?
SINCE YOU WILL BE SPENDING SO MUCH TIME WITH JOTARO, THERE IS SOMETHING I SHOULD WARN YOU ABOUT HIM...
OH?
ER... WHAT IS IT?
HE IS EXACTLY LIKE YOU WHEN YOU WERE HIS AGE.
HA! HA! HA! HA! HA! HA! HA! HA!

THE END.

兎用心棒

A LESSON IN COURTESY

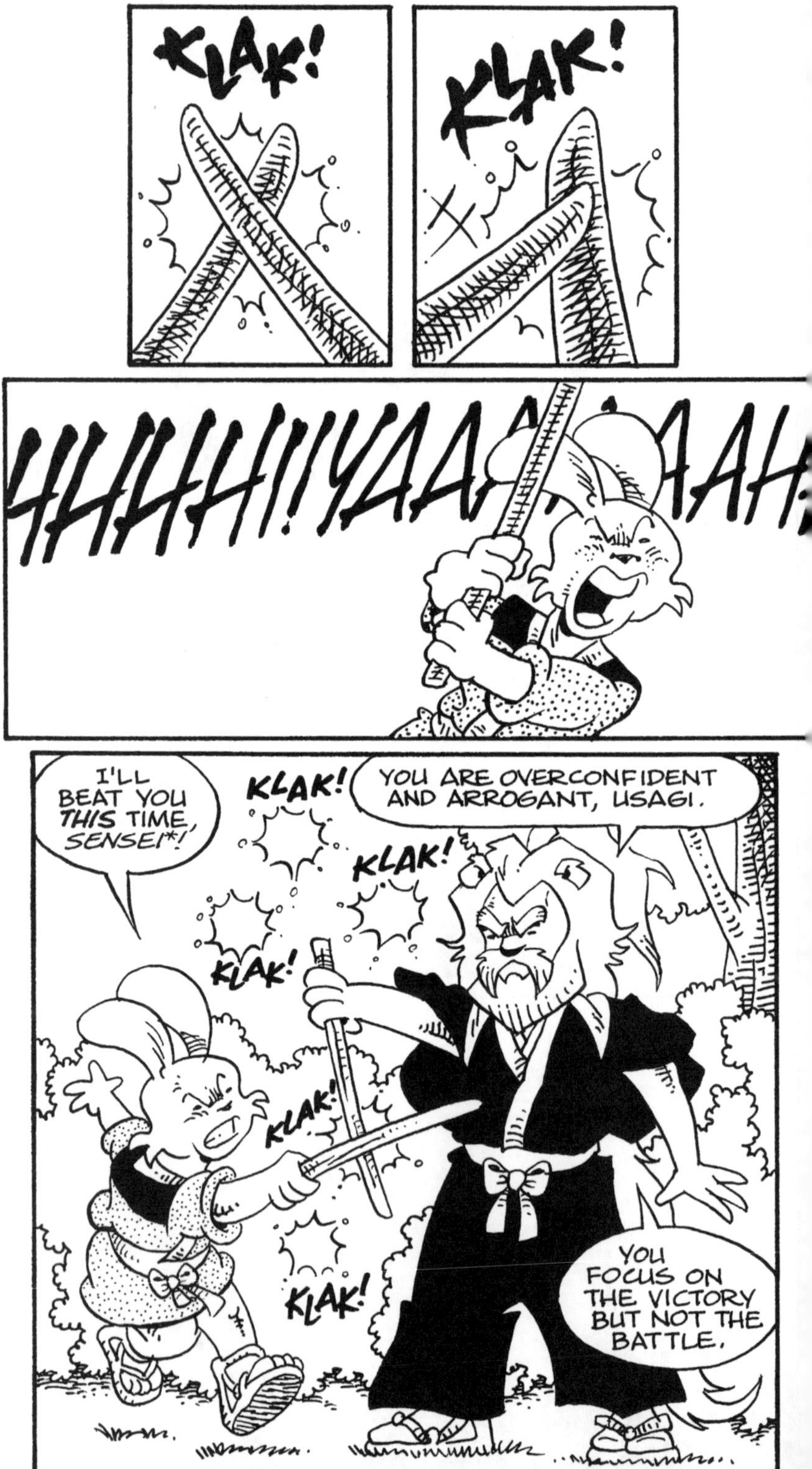

KLAK!
KLAK!
HHHHH!IYAAA AAAH
I'LL BEAT YOU *THIS* TIME, SENSEI*!
KLAK!
YOU ARE OVERCONFIDENT AND ARROGANT, USAGI.
KLAK!
KLAK!
KLAK!
KLAK!
YOU FOCUS ON THE VICTORY BUT NOT THE BATTLE.

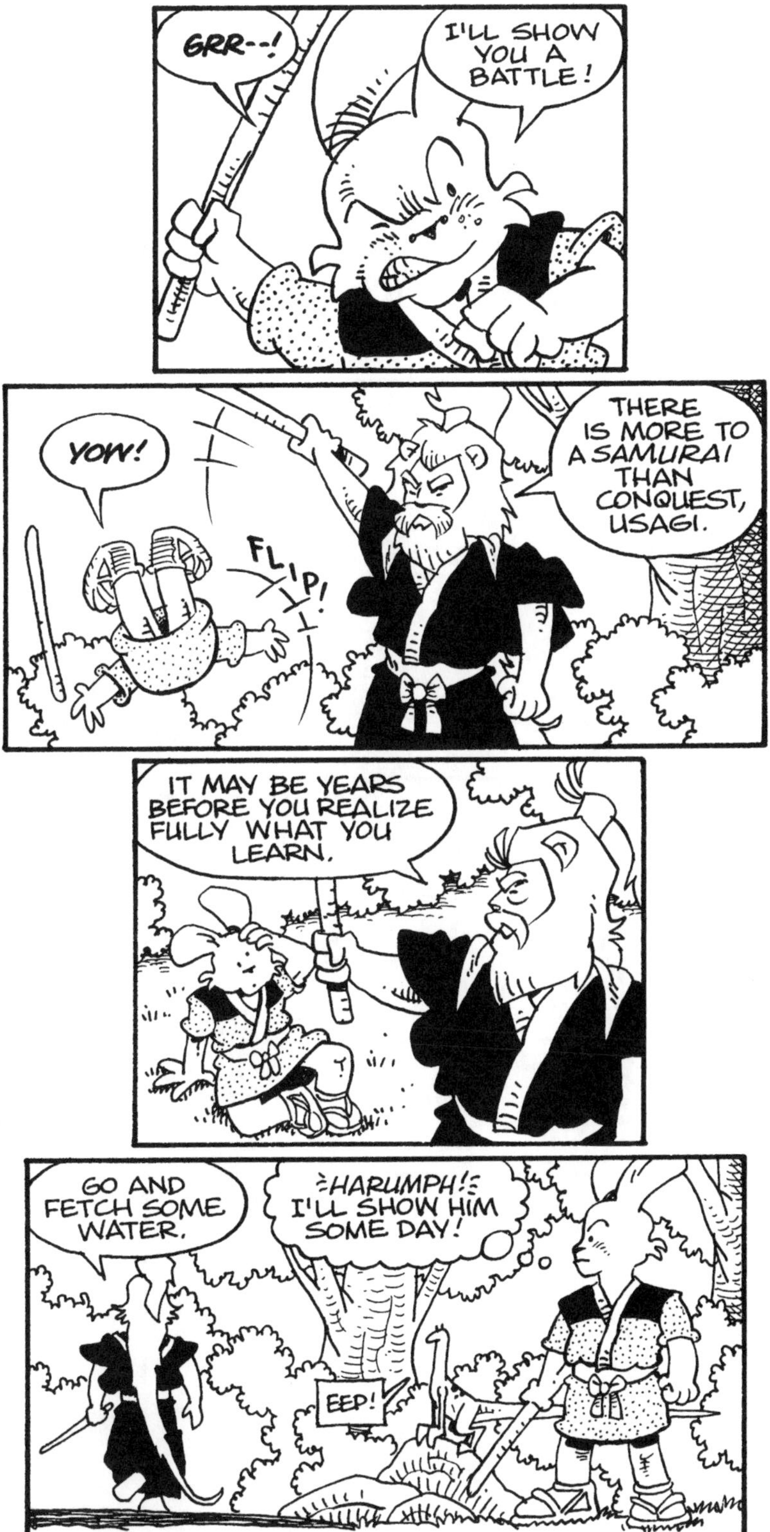

GRR--!
I'LL SHOW YOU A BATTLE!
YOW!
FLIP!
THERE IS MORE TO A SAMURAI THAN CONQUEST, USAGI.
IT MAY BE YEARS BEFORE YOU REALIZE FULLY WHAT YOU LEARN.
GO AND FETCH SOME WATER.
HARUMPH! I'LL SHOW HIM SOME DAY!
EEP!

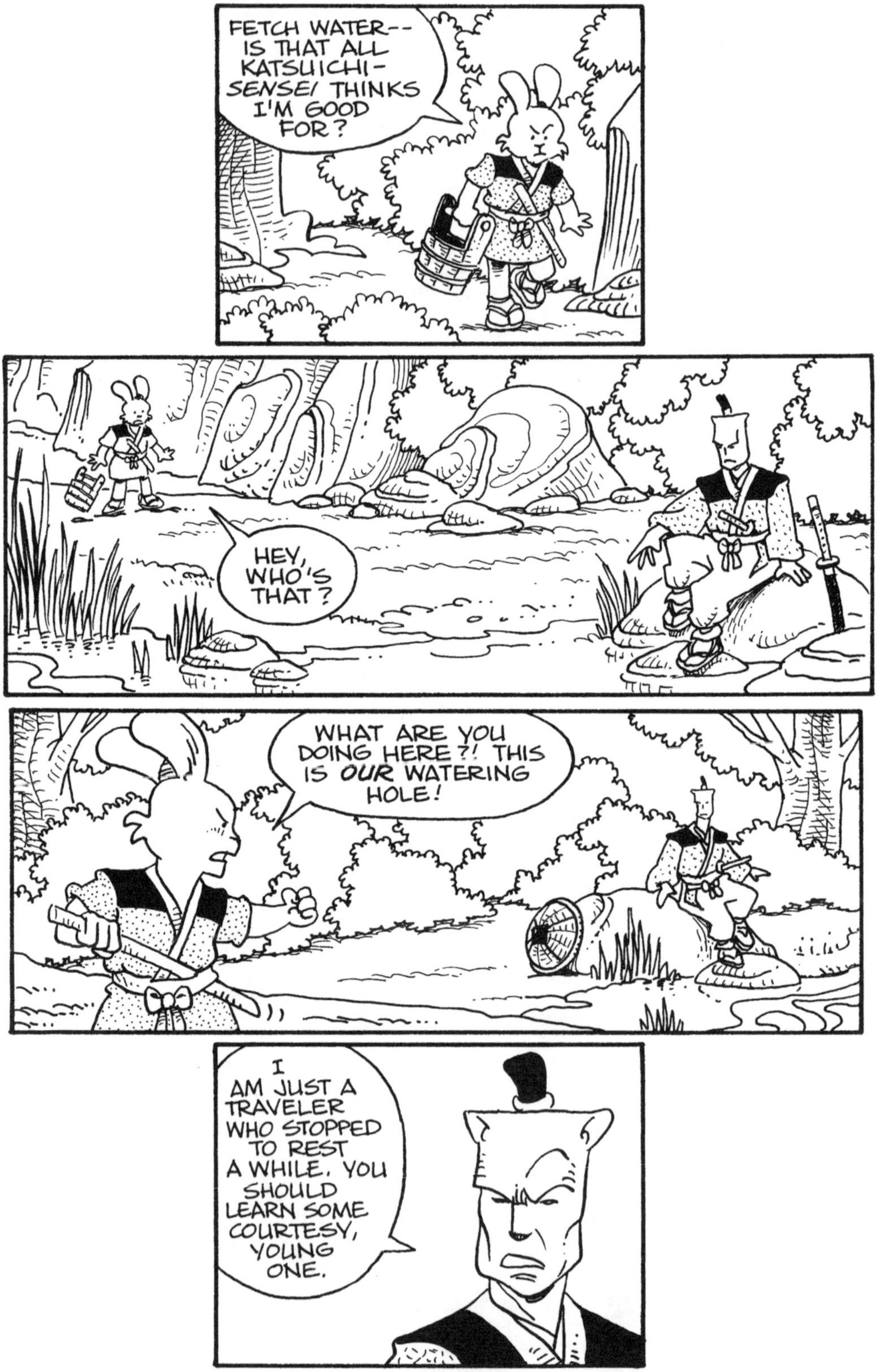
FETCH WATER-- IS THAT ALL KATSUICHI-SENSEI THINKS I'M GOOD FOR?
HEY, WHO'S THAT?
WHAT ARE YOU DOING HERE?! THIS IS OUR WATERING HOLE!
I AM JUST A TRAVELER WHO STOPPED TO REST A WHILE. YOU SHOULD LEARN SOME COURTESY, YOUNG ONE.

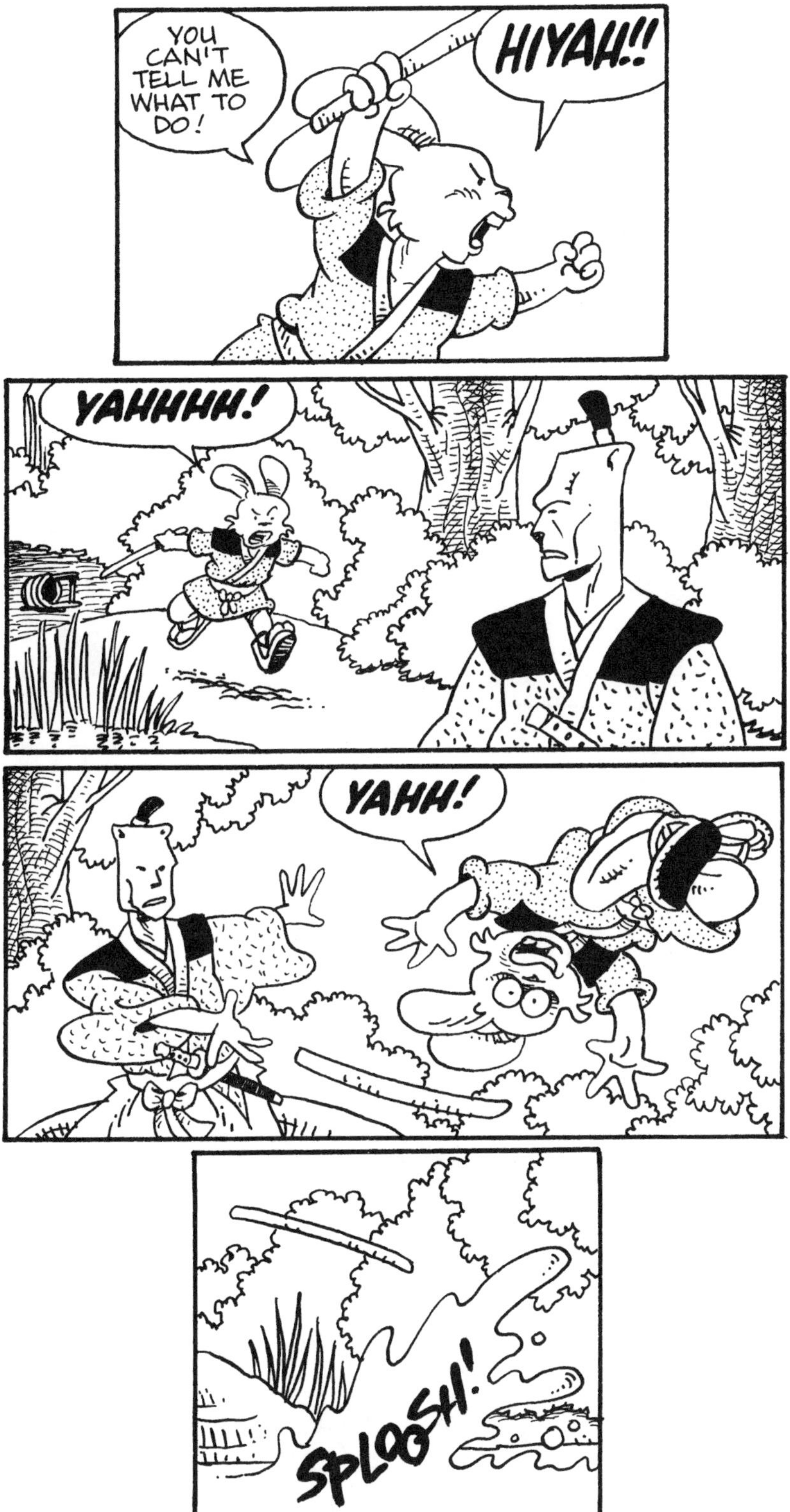
YOU CAN'T TELL ME WHAT TO DO!
HIYAH!!
YAHHHH!
YAHH!
SPLOOSH!

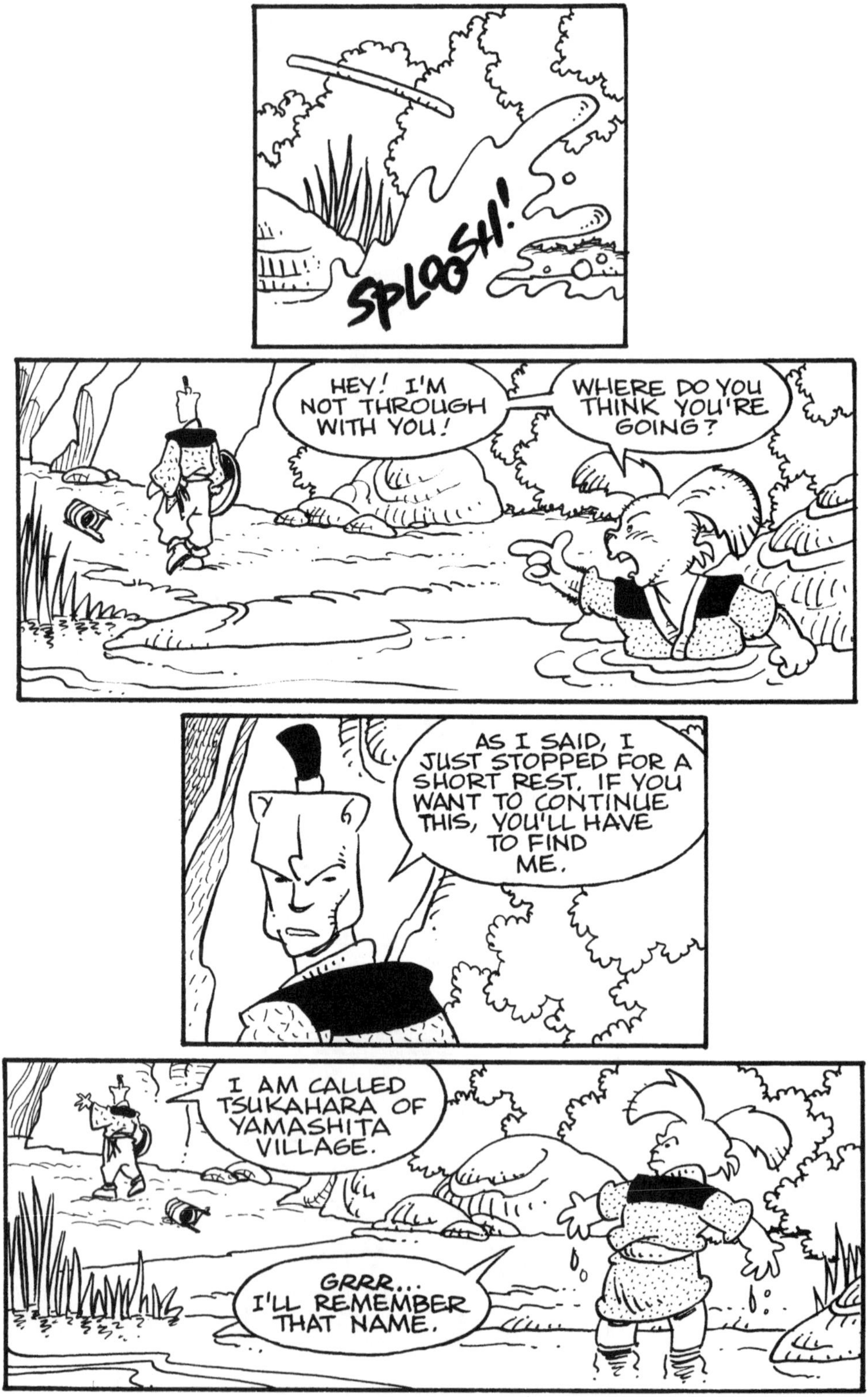
SPLOOSH!
HEY! I'M NOT THROUGH WITH YOU!
WHERE DO YOU THINK YOU'RE GOING?
AS I SAID, I JUST STOPPED FOR A SHORT REST. IF YOU WANT TO CONTINUE THIS, YOU'LL HAVE TO FIND ME.
I AM CALLED TSUKAHARA OF YAMASHITA VILLAGE.
GRRR... I'LL REMEMBER THAT NAME.

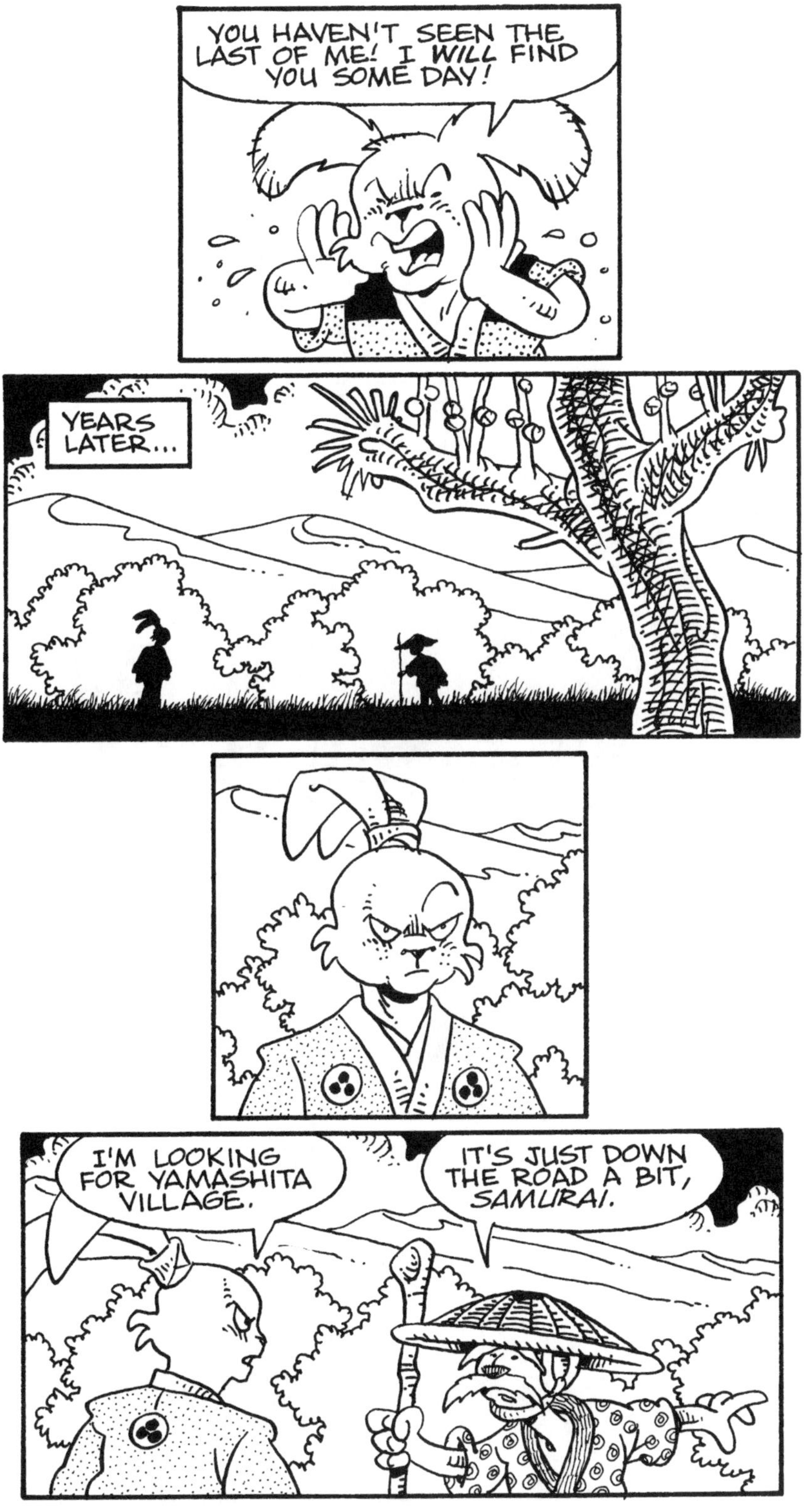
YOU HAVEN'T SEEN THE LAST OF ME! I WILL FIND YOU SOME DAY!
YEARS LATER...
I'M LOOKING FOR YAMASHITA VILLAGE.
IT'S JUST DOWN THE ROAD A BIT, SAMURAI.

IS THIS THE HOME OF TSUKAHARA?

YES IT IS, SAMURAI.

THIS WAY. THE MASTER IS IN THE GARDEN.

TSUKAHARA-SAN, A VISITOR...

WHO IS HE?

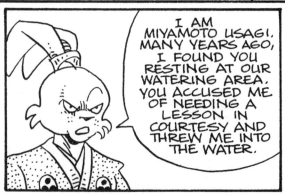

I AM MIYAMOTO USAGI. MANY YEARS AGO, I FOUND YOU RESTING AT OUR WATERING AREA. YOU ACCUSED ME OF NEEDING A LESSON IN COURTESY AND THREW ME INTO THE WATER.

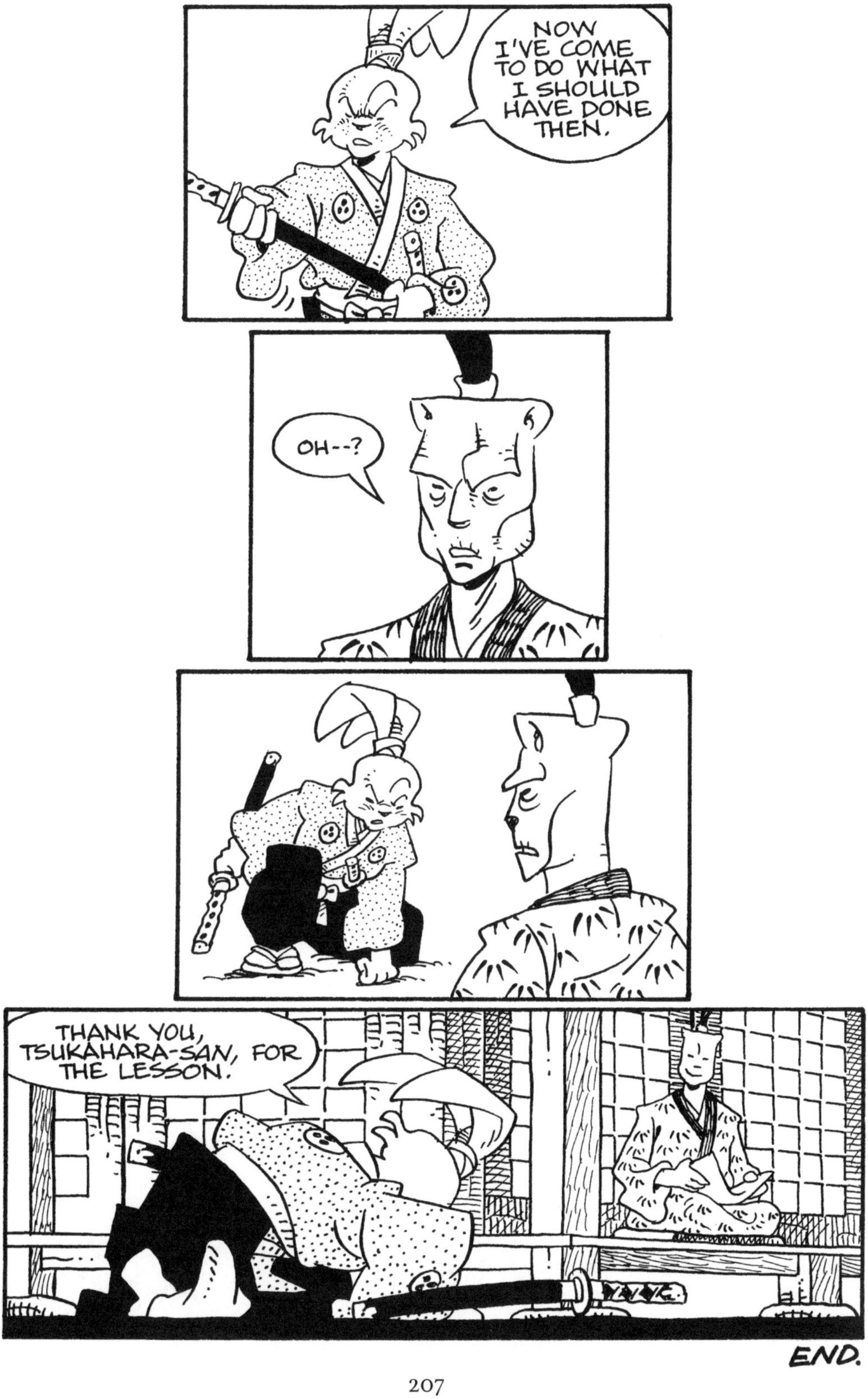
NOW I'VE COME TO DO WHAT I SHOULD HAVE DONE THEN.
OH--?
THANK YOU, TSUKAHARA-SAN, FOR THE LESSON.
END.

USAGI YOJIMBO

Story Notes

VENDETTA

"No man can live under the same sky as the murderer of his father." So goes the ancient Confucian precept. The Japanese extended it to "the murderer of his master," who, as the lord, was the father of the clan. The *samurai* who sought revenge was regarded as a man of honor, but he who let the killer go free was looked upon as weak and was despised by his companions.

Laws were passed that encouraged vendettas, or *kataki-uchi*, though they had to be registered with the proper authorities and carried out without delay. Vengeance was completed when the head of the killer was placed on the master's tomb.

The most famous vendetta in Japanese history is the incident of the forty-seven *samurai*. In 1701, Lord Asano of Ako in Harima Province drew his sword in the presence of Shogun Tokugawa Tsunayoshi, wounding Kira Kozukenosuke, the Grand Master of Ceremonies who had continuously insulted him. Asano was ordered to commit *seppuku*, or ritualized suicide. Also, his lands were confiscated and his more than 200 *samurai* retainers were declared masterless, or *ronin*. Oishi Kuranosuke, one of Asano's chief retainers, devised a plan where they would meet in a year to exact their vengeance.

In the meantime, Oishi, watched by Kira's agents, led a life of drunkenness and debauchery. Forty-six of the *ronin* met with Oishi at the prearranged time, and they attacked Kira's mansion, killing their enemy. They paraded the head through town and laid it at the gravesite of their master. They were ordered by the *shogun* to commit *seppuku*.

You can visit the graves of the loyal *samurai* in Tokyo. On December 14, the day they avenged their master, Sengakuji Temple is crowded with people paying homage to the heroes.

CROWS

My good friend Sergio Aragonés and I were walking in downtown Columbus, Ohio, one November many years ago when a sudden noise startled flocks of blackbirds in the barren trees. They flew around for a while, blackening out the sky, then returned to their branches. Sergio whistled, startling them again, and they took off, circling us before flying back to the trees. As we continued on our way, he told me the story of a province in China that was plagued by an abundance of birds one year. The villagers in the area got together and devised a plan to harass the pests with noisemakers. They chased them unrelentingly day and night until the birds flew off or were too exhausted to fly. Months later, I saw on the news that a county in the midwestern portion of the U.S. had an infestation of blackbirds. The local police used sirens and other noisemakers, pursuing the birds until they finally left the area. I thought I had a story there somewhere. It was years before I finally got around to it.

STAN

Gallery

The following pages feature Stan Sakai's cover art from issues fifty-three through sixty of Dark Horse's Usagi Yojimbo Volume Three *series.*

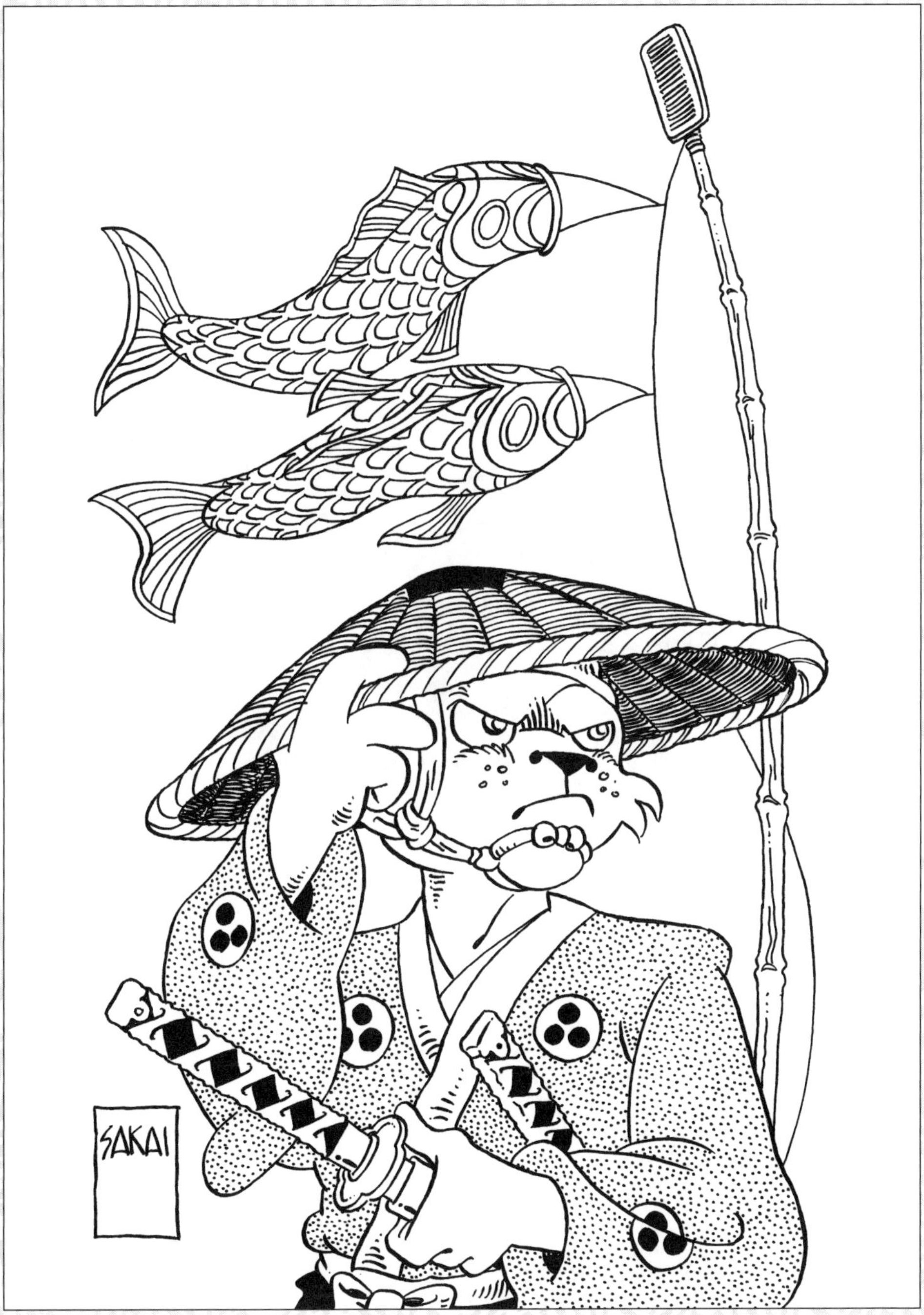
SAKAI

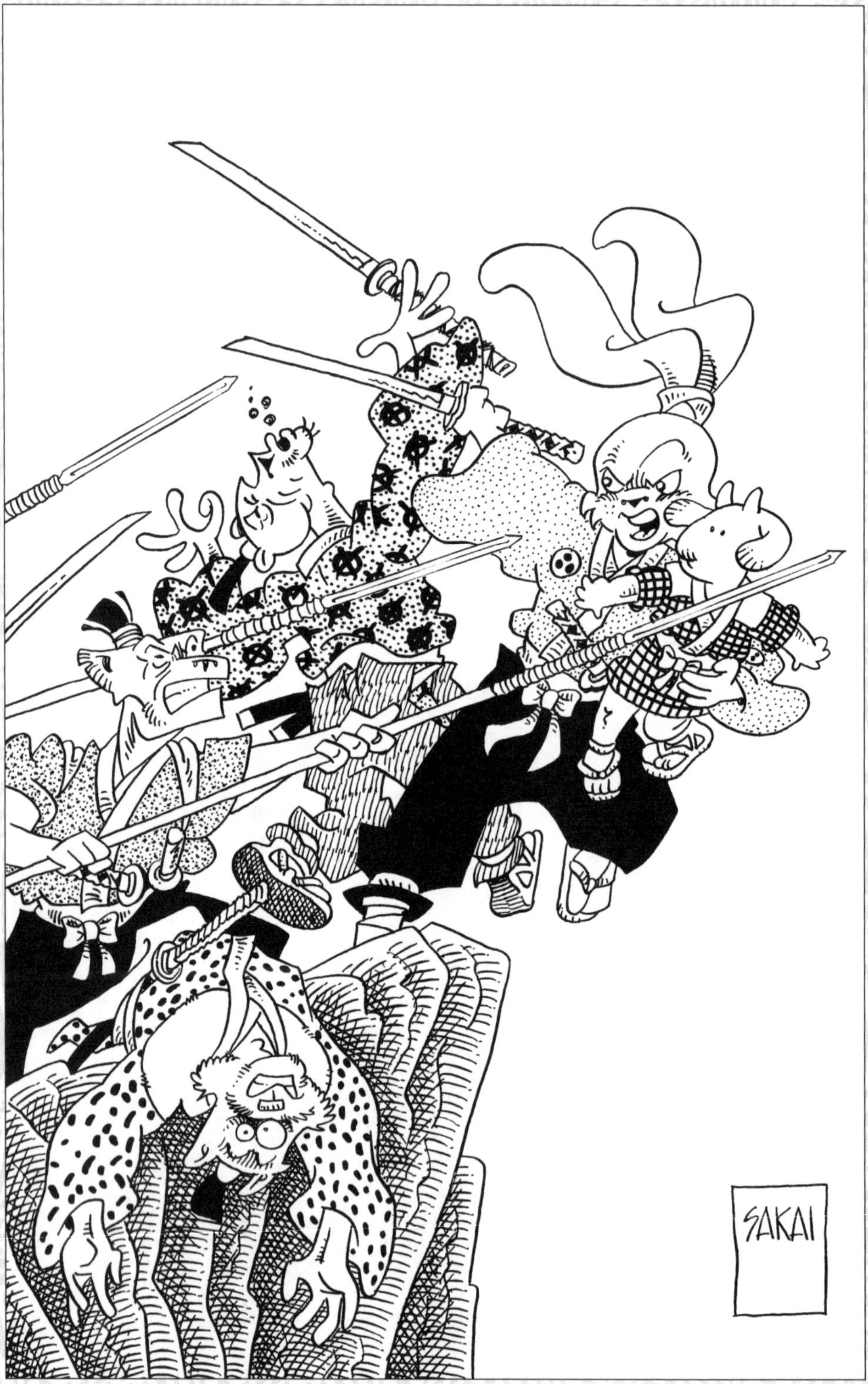
SAKAI

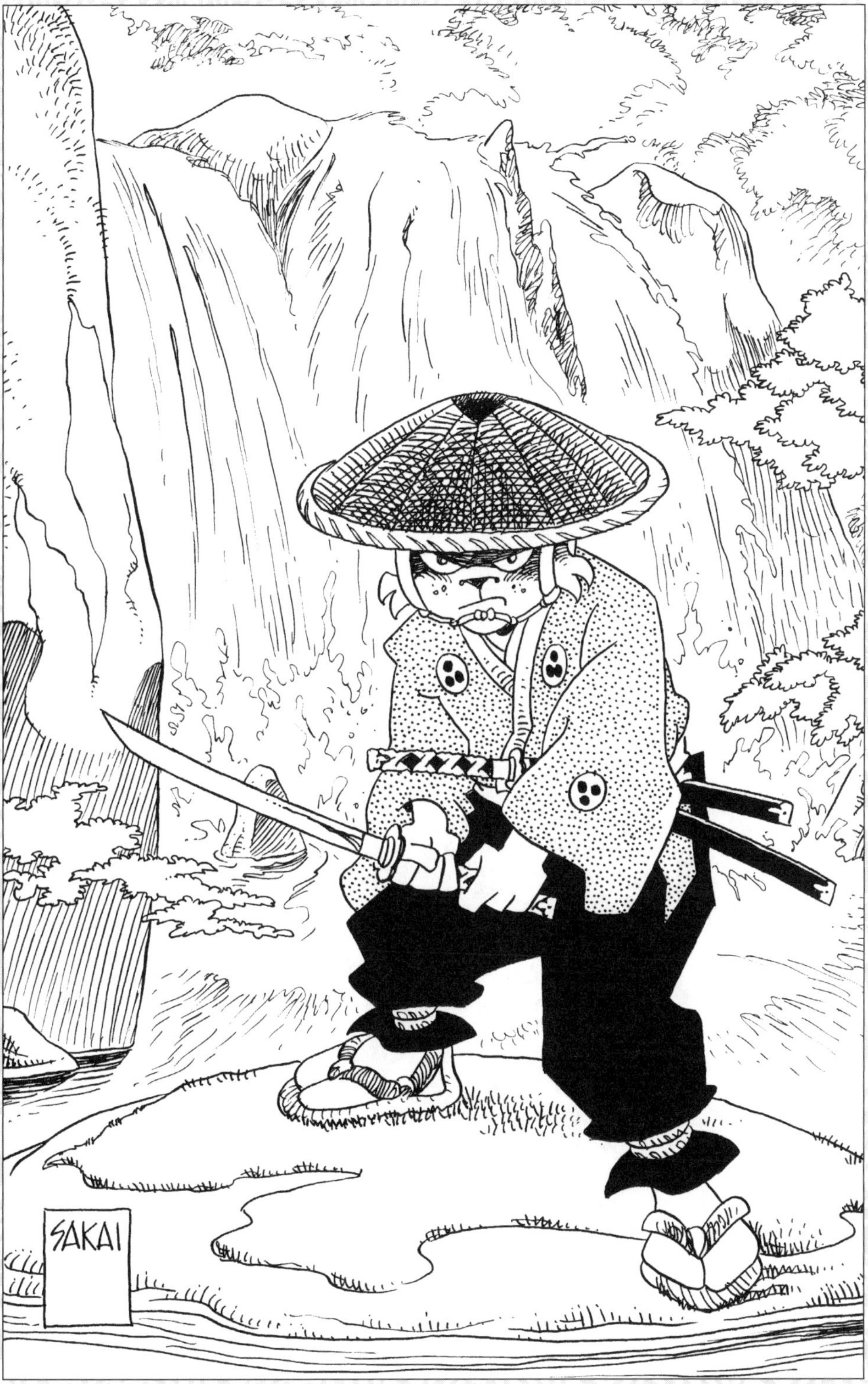
SAKAI

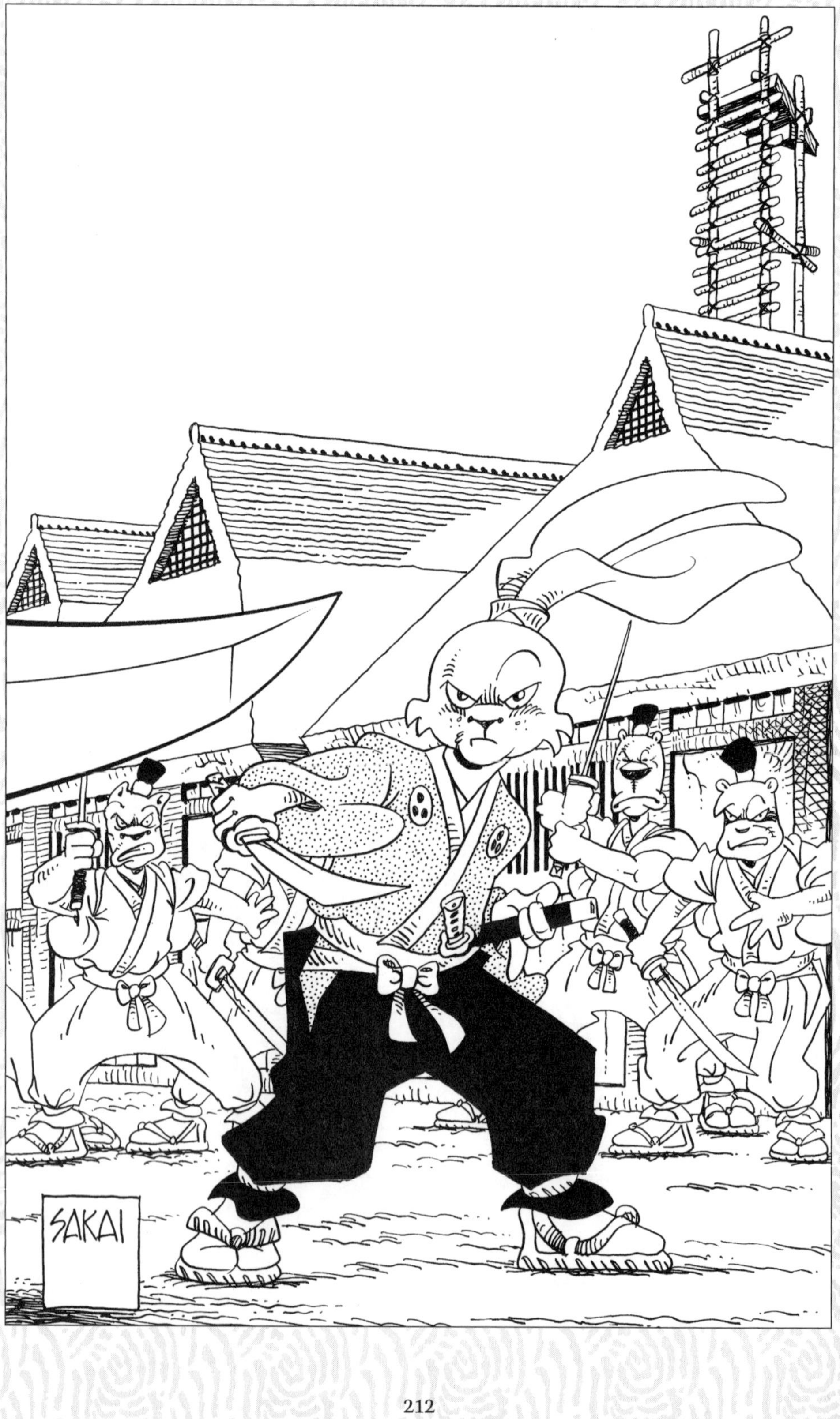
SAKAI

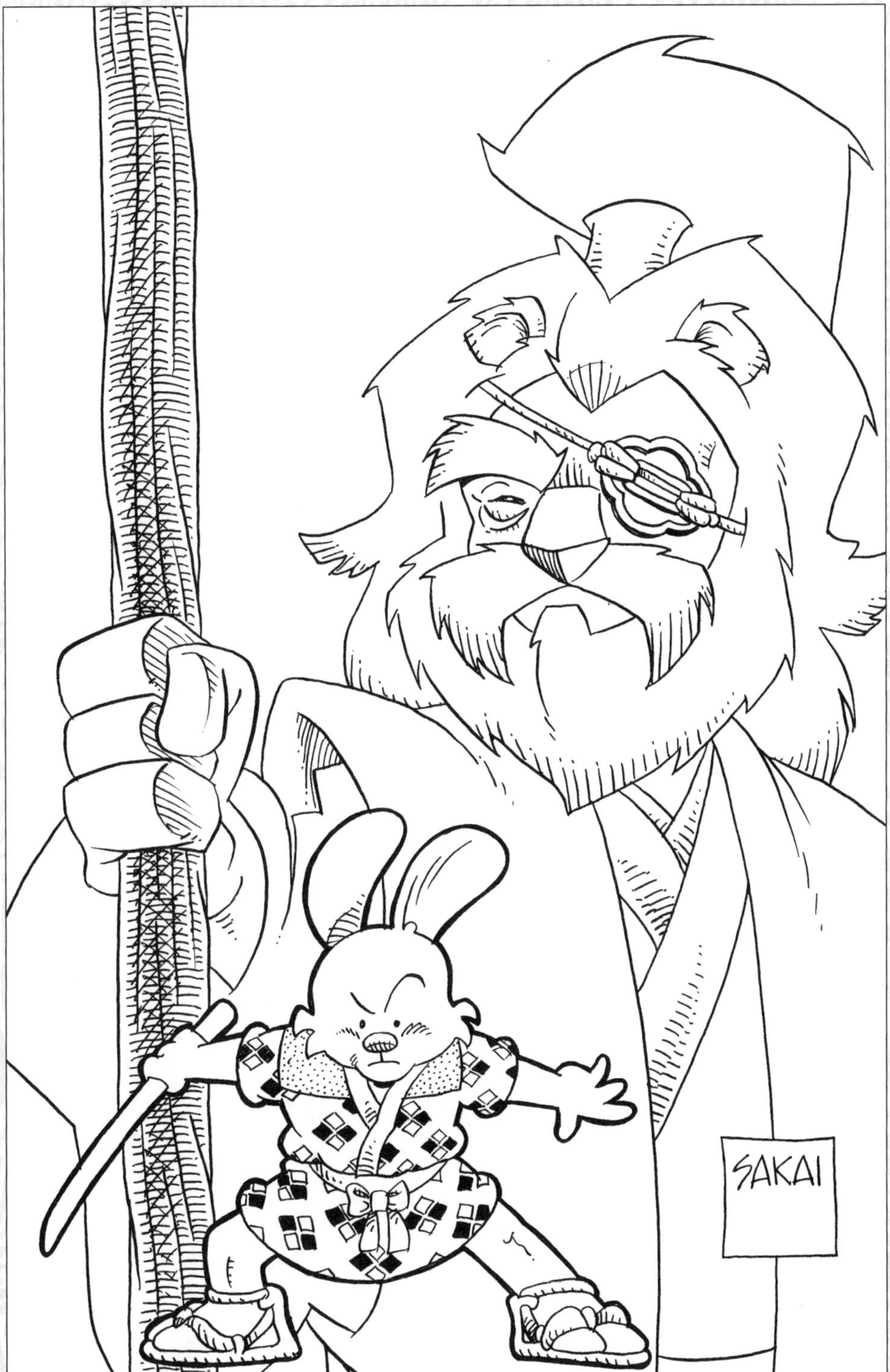
SAKAI

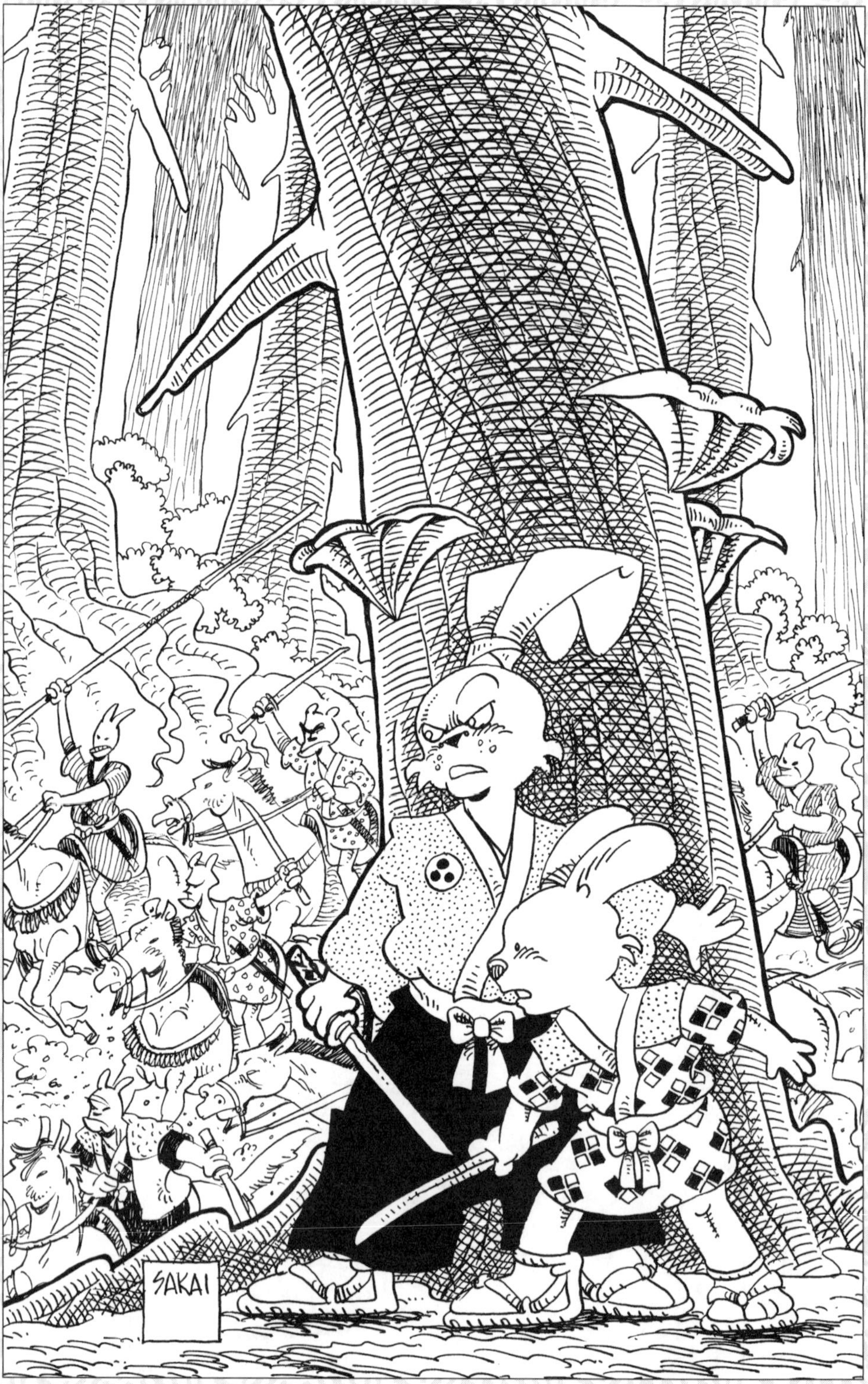
SAKAI

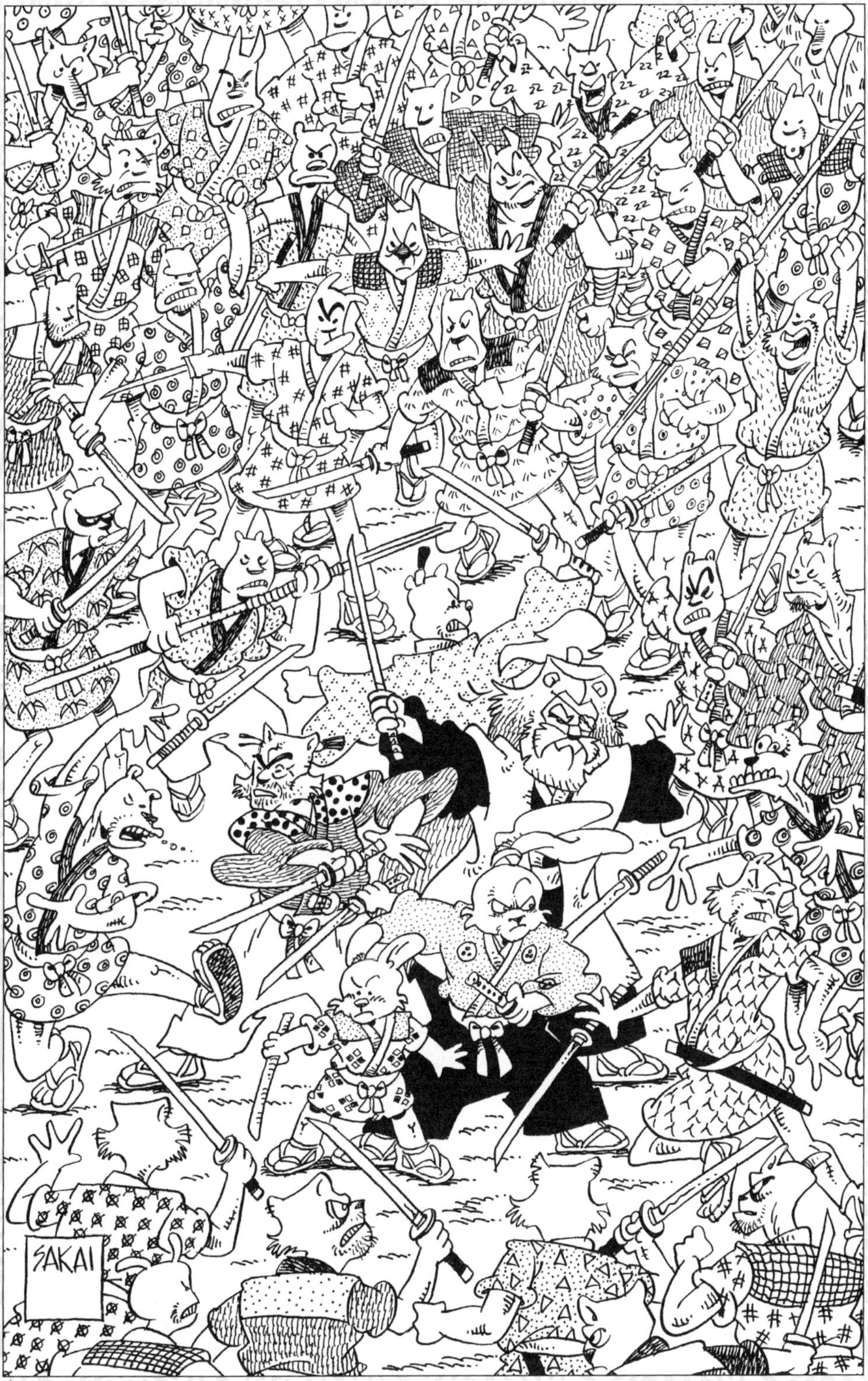
SAKAI

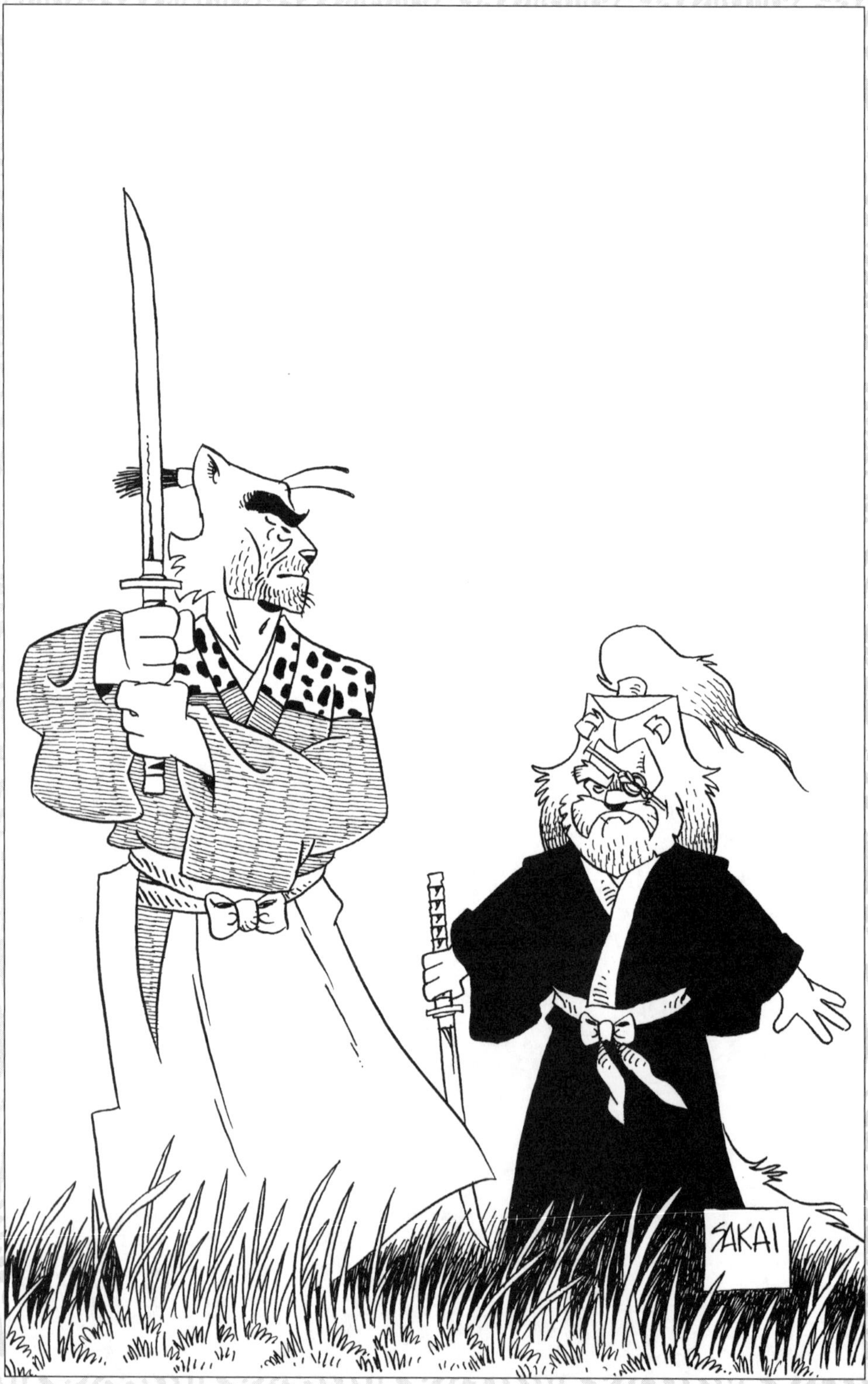
SAKAI

SKETCHBOOK

The following pages feature the evolution of this volume's cover art, from Stan Sakai's preliminary design ideas to final black-and-white illustration prior to the artist's actual cover painting.

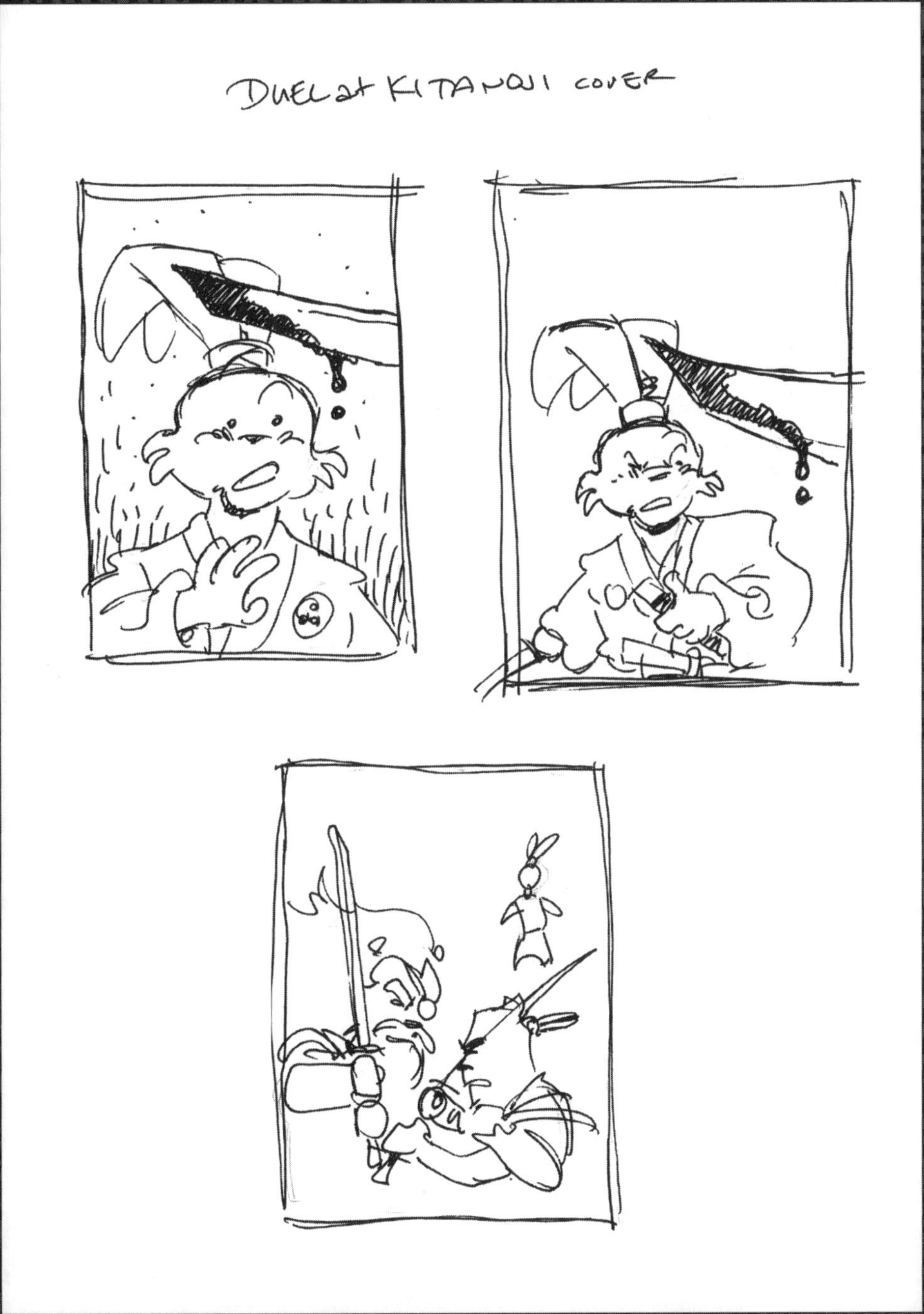
DUEL at KITANOJI COVER

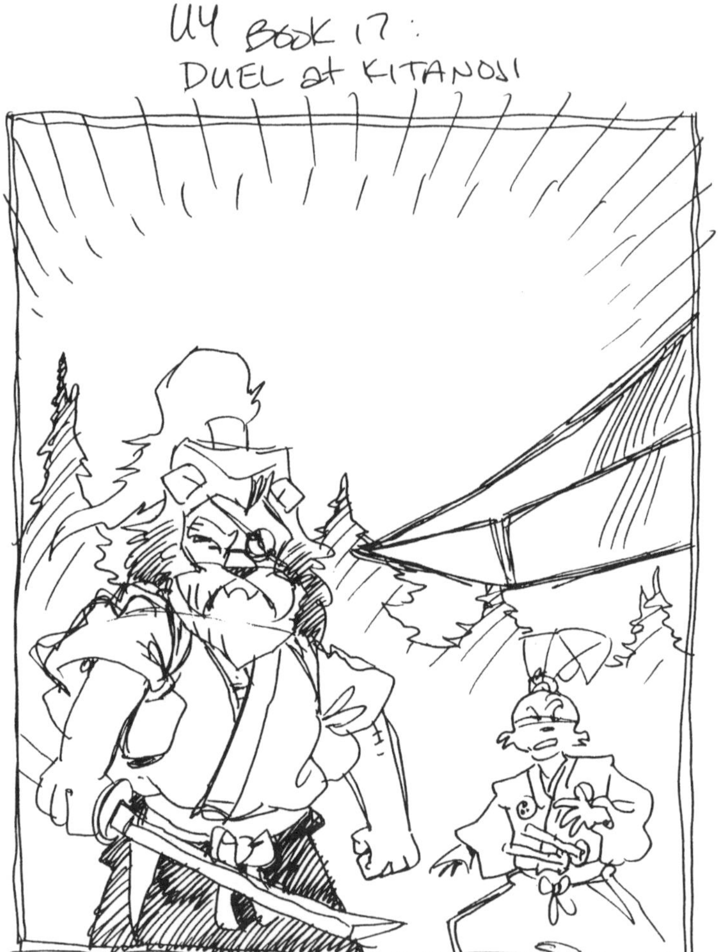
UY BOOK 17:
DUEL at KITANOJI
LOWER TREES

USAGI YOJIMBO BK 17: DUEL at KITANOJI COVER

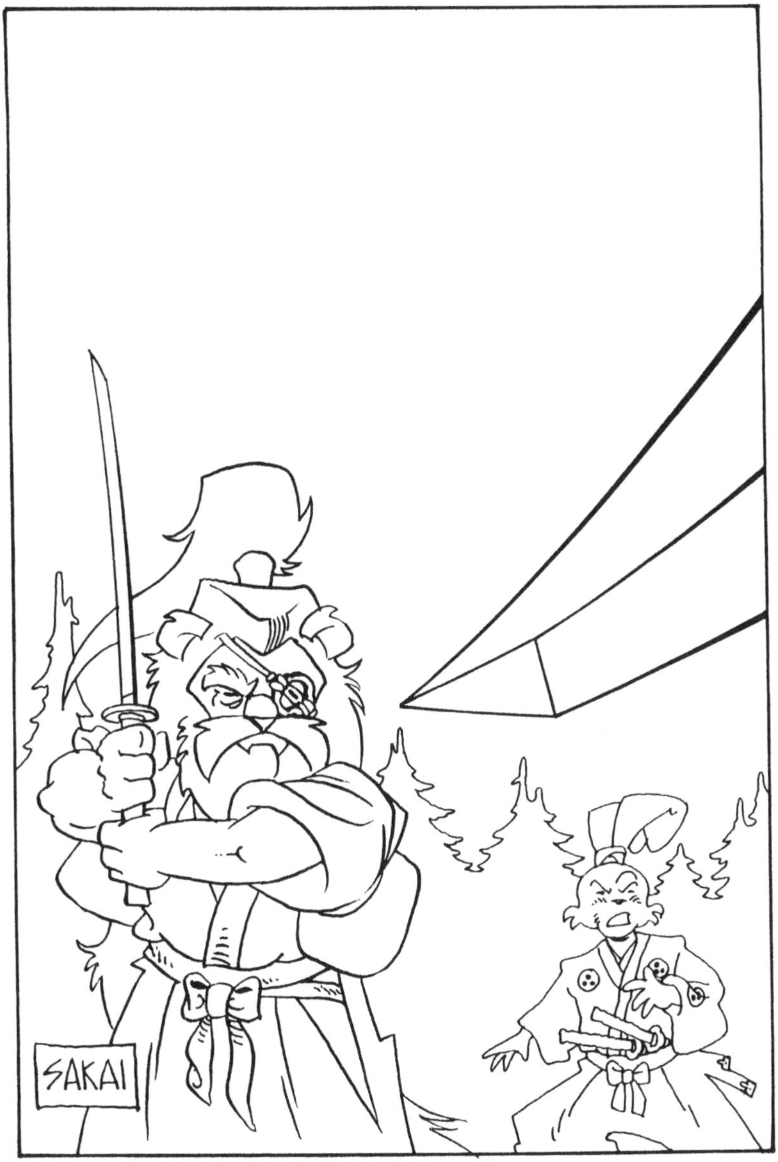
SAKAI

Biography

Stan Sakai

Stan Sakai and the legendary Jack Davis celebrate Stan's National Cartoonists Society comic book division award. *Photo by Sharon Sakai*

STAN SAKAI was born in Kyoto, Japan, grew up in Hawaii, and now lives in California with his wife, Sharon, and children, Hannah and Matthew. He received a Fine Arts degree from the University of Hawaii and furthered his studies at Art Center College of Design in Pasadena, California.

His creation, Usagi Yojimbo, first appeared in comics in 1984. Since then, Usagi has been on television as a guest of the Teenage Mutant Ninja Turtles and has been made into toys, seen on clothing, and featured in a series of trade-paperback collections.

In 1991, Stan created *Space Usagi*, a series about the adventures of a descendant of the original Usagi that dealt with samurai in a futuristic setting.

Stan is also an award-winning letterer for his work on Sergio Aragonés' *Groo*, the "Spider-Man" Sunday newspaper strips, and *Usagi Yojimbo*.

Stan is a recipient of a Parents' Choice Award, an Inkpot Award, an American Library Association Award, two Spanish Haxtur Awards, three Eisner Awards, and the National Cartoonists Society Comic Book Division Award.

Usagi Yojimbo

Other books by Stan Sakai

From Dark Horse Comics
<www.darkhorse.com>

Book 8: Shades of Death
Book 9: Daisho
Book 10: The Brink of Life and Death
Book 11: Seasons
Book 12: Grasscutter
Book 13: Grey Shadows
Book 14: Demon Mask
Book 15: Grasscutter II — Journey to Atsuta Shrine
Book 16: The Shrouded Moon
Space Usagi

From Fantagraphics Books
<www.fantagraphics.com>

Book 1: The Ronin
Book 2: Samurai
Book 3: The Wanderer's Road
Book 4: The Dragon Bellow Conspiracy
Book 5: Lone Goat and Kid
Book 6: Circles
Book 7: Gen's Story